T0373349

MURTY CLASSICAL
LIBRARY OF INDIA

Sheldon Pollock, General Editor

SVAYAMBHUDEVA
THE LIFE OF PADMA
VOLUME 2

MCLI 35

SVAYAMBHUDEVA

स्वयम्भूदेव

THE LIFE
OF PADMA

VOLUME 2

Edited and Translated by
EVA DE CLERCQ

MURTY CLASSICAL LIBRARY OF INDIA

HARVARD UNIVERSITY PRESS

Cambridge, Massachusetts

London, England

2023

SERIES DESIGN BY M9DESIGN

Library of Congress Cataloging-in-Publication Data

Names: Svayambhū, author. |
De Clercq, Eva, editor, translator. |
Container of (expression): Svayambhū. Paumacariyu. |
Container of (expression): Svayambhū. Paumacariyu. English.
Title: The life of Padma / Svayambhudeva ;
edited and translated by Eva De Clercq.
Other titles: Murty classical library of India ; 35.
Description: Cambridge, Massachusetts :
Harvard University Press, 2023.
Series: Murty classical library of India ; 35 |
English and Hindi; Devanagari alphabet. |
Includes bibliographical references and index.
Contents: Volume 2: Book of Ayodhya.
Identifiers: LCCN 2017016437
ISBN 978-0-674-66036-6 (cloth: alk. paper) (vol. 1)
ISBN 978-0-674-27123-4 (cloth: alk. paper) (vol. 2)
Subjects: LCSH: Rāma (Hindu deity)—Poetry.
Classification: LCC PK1428.9.S83 L54 2018 | DDC 891.3—dc23
LC record available at https://lccn.loc.gov/2017016437

CONTENTS

INTRODUCTION

Svayambhudeva and His Work

The *Paümacariu* (The Life of Padma) adapts the famous epic story of Rama from the distinct perspective of the Jains, or followers of Jainism, an ancient Indic religion centering on nonviolence and the ideal of asceticism. It was written in Apabhramsha, a Middle Indic literary language, by Svayambhudeva, a successful professional poet who flourished in the second half of the ninth to the first half of the tenth century.[1] He is mentioned among great authors, such as Bhasa, Vyasa, and Kalidasa, whom Pushpadanta, author of *Mahāpurāṇu,* looked up to.[2] Reference to the royal house of the Seunas, as well as some other evidence, suggests that Svayambhudeva and his patron, Dhananjaya, lived in peninsular India. They may well have been connected to the court of either the Seunas themselves, or to the Rashtrakutas, of whom the Seunas were feudatories. As is typical of a classical Indian poet, Svayambhudeva says very little about himself or his patron in his work. As far as religious affiliation is concerned, he is thought to have belonged to the Yapaniyas—a now-extinct branch of Jainism intermediate to the two main sects, the Shvetambaras and the Digambaras—although the doctrinal positions he adopts in his works align more closely to Digambara works.[3]

In addition to *Life of Padma,* we have two other extant works by Svayambhudeva. The *Riṭṭhaṇemicariu* (Life of Arishtanemi), his most voluminous work, tells the story of

the twenty-second Jina (also, Tirthankara), or prophet of
Jainism, called Arishtanemi, and includes the well-known
Hindu deities Krishna and Balarama transformed into two
cousins of Arishtanemi. It also includes Jain versions of
the classical Indian epic Mahabharata and the *Bṛhatkathā*
(Great Story), a narrative cycle of amorous conquests, here
experienced by Krishna's father, Vasudeva.[4] In this work,
Svayambhudeva is the first Jain author to focus squarely on
the Mahabharata narrative. His third work, *Svayambhūc-
chandas,* is a manual in eight chapters dealing with Prakrit
meters and Apabhramsha meters. Several of the anony-
mously quoted verses in the *Svayambhūcchandas* are found
in the *Paümacariu.*[5] In addition to these three known works,
later sources attribute several compositions to Svayambhu-
deva that are no longer extant.

The Life of Padma: A Jain Ramayana

The Life of Padma relates, from a distinctly Jain angle, the
famous story of Rama, the hero of the classical Sanskrit
epic *Rāmāyaṇa*. In the title, Rama is referred to as Padma,
"Lotus," though throughout the poem he is generally named
Rama or given one of his common epithets, and only very
rarely called Padma.[6] The poem consists of 1,269 sections,
divided over ninety chapters and five books. Volume 1 of the
Murty Classical Library's *The Life of Padma* includes the
first of these five books, and Volume 2 includes the second.

The classical Sanskrit epic *Rāmāyaṇa*, ascribed to the
poet Valmiki and composed for the most part some centu-
ries before the Common Era, tells the story of Rama, prince

and heir to the throne of Ayodhya. Through the intrigues of his stepmother, he is exiled to live in the forest, together with his younger half-brother Lakshmana and his beloved wife, Sita. During their exile, Sita is abducted by Ravana, king of the Rakshasa demons who inhabit Lanka. With the help of the Vanaras, the monkey people, led by King Sugriva and his chief minister Hanuman, Rama defeats Ravana, recovers his wife, and eventually becomes the rightful king of Ayodhya. In the first centuries of the Common Era the hero Rama came to be identified with the Brahmanical god Vishnu as an avatar. It is in this Hindu context that Rama and his story are nowadays best known. Nevertheless, different retellings by different authors from diverse backgrounds abound in and beyond South Asia.[7]

The Jains incorporated this popular story into their universal history, their narrative of the history of all humanity in the different parts of the world as they perceived it. In practice, the Jain universal history consists of the biographies of the great men (*śalākāpuruṣa* or *mahāpuruṣa*) in texts called Deeds or Biographies (*carita*) or Ancient Treatises (*purāṇa*), which were composed in the literary languages of Sanskrit, Prakrit, or Apabhramsha, as well as vernaculars such as Kannada, Gujarati, and Hindi. Normative lists enumerate sixty-three such great men in every time period: twenty-four Jinas/Tirthankaras; twelve universal emperors (*cakravartin*); and nine triads of a Baladeva, Vasudeva, and Prativasudeva—respectively, a righteous Jain hero, his younger, fiercer half-brother, and their enemy, all three living simultaneously. The main characters of the Rama story, Rama, his half-brother Lakshmana, and their enemy Ravana, are

understood to be the eighth Baladeva, Vasudeva, and Prati-
vasudeva of the current cosmic era, living simultaneously to
the twentieth Tirthankara, Muni Suvrata.

Although there are some differences between individual
Jain texts narrating this Rama story, most agree on its core,
which resembles that of Valmiki's Sanskrit epic but trans-
formed in significant ways.[8] A major difference from Valmi-
ki's version is that in the Jain narrative it is Lakshmana and
not Rama who in the end kills Ravana. As Ravana is catego-
rized as the Prativasudeva, it is his fate that he be killed by the
Vasudeva—that is, Lakshmana, the more active and violent
brother, compared to the more benign Baladeva. Another
significant difference concerns the characterization of the
Vanaras, the monkey people, and the Rakshasas, the demons.
In Valmiki's *Rāmāyaṇa*, King Sugriva and Hanuman are
animals, though possessing distinctly human traits such as
the ability to speak and a sense of morality; in the Jain texts
they become humans, a branch of the larger Vidyadhara
dynasty, all of whose members possess one or more "genies"
(*vidyās*) that grant them all kinds of superhuman powers,
including the power of flight.[9] In the Jain texts, Sugriva and
Hanuman are still called monkeys (*vānara*) because their
dynasty has a monkey as the emblem of its flag. Moreover,
the ancestral homeland of this Vanara dynasty is Vanara
island, profusely inhabited by monkeys. Similarly, Ravana
and his kin are not demons but members of the Rakshasa
dynasty, another branch of the larger Vidyadhara dynasty.
These Rakshasas are named thus because they possess an
ancestral protective *vidyā* called Rakshasi, and one of their
early kings is called Rakshas.

According to the traditional Jain account, the story of Rama was first told by Mahavira, the last Jina, and was transmitted through his disciples, and then passed on to Jain authors. The importance of the authority of the Jina as the source of the story is underlined by the narrative setting that encases the story: Shrenika, the king of Rajagriha, attends the holy assembly (*samavasarana*) of Mahavira, expresses his doubts about so-called false versions of the Rama story, and requests to hear the "true" account. Svayambhudeva names Ravishena as his direct source. Ravishena was well known as a Digambara author who composed a *Padma-purāṇa* (Ancient Treatise on Padma)—also called *Padmacar-ita* (Life of Padma)—a Sanskrit account of the Jain Rama story in c. 18,000 verses and 123 cantos.[10] A comparison of *The Life of Padma* with Ravishena's work reveals that Svayambhudeva followed its content more or less faithfully, though it is far from a translation of Ravishena's Sanskrit text into late Middle Indic Apabhramsha. *The Life of Padma* is an original rendering of the narrative in the more lyrical, poetic style of Apabhramsha, to which Svayambhudeva has added his own accents. The *Padmapurāṇa* is itself an extended reproduction—often even including language almost identical to the oldest known Jain Ramayana, the *Paümacari-yam,* which consists of c. 10,000 verses in 118 cantos and was composed in the Middle Indic language Maharashtri Prakrit by Vimalasuri, who was probably a Shvetambara and lived in or before the fifth century.[11]

Form and Language

The language in which the *Paümacariu* is composed is a late Middle Indic literary language called Apabhramsha. Like Sanskrit and most modern north Indian vernaculars, it belongs to the Indo-European language family, and linguistically it represents the stage between the Middle Indic Prakrit languages and early vernacular languages of north India, possibly dating from as early as the fourth century.[12] Like Sanskrit and Maharashtri Prakrit, the other classical literary languages of the subcontinent, Apabhramsha was not limited to a particular region or creed; however, almost all extant Apabhramsha literary works were composed by Jains, in particular Digambaras. Later authors name Svayambhudeva as one of the three greatest Apabhramsha litterateurs.

The Life of Padma is, moreover, composed in a form peculiar for the Apabhramsha language, namely, the "bound in chapters" (*sandhibandha*) style, and it was meant to be sung before an audience.[13] It is divided into five books (*kāṇḍa*), totaling ninety chapters (*sandhi*), each consisting on average of fifteen sections (*kaḍavakas*). These sections are themselves made up of a body of rhyming couplets (*yamaka*) followed by a stanza (*ghattā*) of two, four, or six quarter-verses with a complex rhyming scheme. Each of the different structural units of a section, i.e., the main body of couplets and its closing stanza, has its own set of meters.[14] Each chapter opens with a stanza usually in the same meter as the closing stanzas of the sections of that chapter. Sometimes the sections commence with a longer stanza of two or four quarter-verses before the body of rhyming couplets.[15] The final long stanza of the last section of each chapter contains an echo of the name of its composer (*nāmamudrā*) integrated into the verse, as, for instance, in the syllables *saïṃ bhu* in the final stanza from the thirtieth chapter, translated as the words "himself" (*saïṃ*) and the first syllable of the word for "arm" (*bhuva*) (30.11.9).

Apabhramsha *sandhibandhas* fall under the genre of *kāvya*, refined literature, and poets writing in this form avail themselves of the same array of literary embellishments and figures of speech used by prominent classical Sanskrit poets. Used with particular abundance in *The Life of Padma* are similes (*upamā*) and metaphors (*rūpaka*), enhancing the composition's poetic expressivity. These are mostly drawn from a collection of stock comparisons. A beautiful woman's face, for instance, is compared to the full moon; her hair to peacock feathers; her eyes to lotus petals; her breasts to the frontal lobes of an elephant; her gait to that of a goose; and her voice to that of a cuckoo. Fighting warriors are compared to elephants or lions; their arms to branches, clubs, or elephants' trunks; their chest to the firmament. Sometimes Jain doctrinal elements are the object of comparison, such as in the description of the nine treasures of a universal emperor.[16] Some comparisons are more idiosyncratic and original, such as the description of Lakshmana being embraced by the city as if it were an overly assertive merchant with arm-like ramparts, and, as he enters, passing a mountain of bones from the suitors of princess Jitapadma, who were all executed by her father.[17] Particularly striking here is the image of the merchant who menacingly embraces the unwary customer. In his descriptions, Svayambhudeva frequently uses "similes in garland" (*mālopamā*), cluster-ing similes for the same subject of comparison. An example is the description of a mass of clouds advancing in the sky at the advent of the monsoon at the beginning of chapter 28; another is the description of Chandranakhi as she returns from her encounter with Rama and Lakshmana in chapter 37.[18] These "garlands" result in an emphasis on the subject of the comparison and interrupt the narrative flow.

Another literary device popular among classical Indian poets and employed occasionally by Svayambhudeva, often combined with a simile, is the pun (*śleṣa*), where a word has a double (or sometimes even triple) meaning. These puns are often expanded on in the Notes to the Translation.

A typical example from chapter 24 is the following:

24.14.3   *vaṇaṃ jiṇālayaṃ jahā sacandaṇaṃ; jiṇindasāsaṇaṃ
jahā sasāvayaṃ.*

> The forest was as full of sandalwood trees as a Jina
> temple with sandalwood paste; with beasts of
> prey like the Jain order with laymen.

In the first half verse, the word *sacandaṇaṃ* is translated twice: first qualifying the forest of "sandalwood trees," and second as a characteristic of a temple where "sandalwood paste" is used to perform rituals venerating icons. In the second half verse, the word *sasāvayaṃ* is also translated twice, and here has two different etymologies: first as "with beasts of prey" for the forest description, and second as "with laymen" for the simile of the Jain order.

In support of the lyrical quality of the poem, Svayam-
bhudeva frequently makes use of repetition and anaphora,
at times beginning (almost) every line of a section with the
same word or word group.[19] In the "similes in garland" at the
beginning of chapter 28, for instance, each line commences
with *pasaraï jema,* "it advanced like." Another example is
the first section of chapter 34, where Rama asks some sages
to explain the benefits of taking up certain vows. Here every
one of the seven couplets commences with *kāiṃ phalu,*
"what is the fruit," except for one instance which inverts
the word order, reading *phalu kāī* (with the same meaning),
in order to break the monotony.

Other sound-embellishments are also found, the most
significant being the end-rhyme in all verses: from the simple
AB rhyme in the couplets (*yamaka* is also the name of the
figure of speech including rhyme), to more complex schemes
in the closing stanzas. An example of more complex play
with sounds and words is found in the poet's benediction of
the Jina Muni Suvrata:

40.1.1   *taṃ santaṃ gayāgasaṃ dhīsaṃ saṃtāvapāvasaṃtāsaṃ
cārurucāṇaeṇa vaṃde devaṃ saṃsāraghorasāsaṃ*

> With prudence and brilliant splendor I salute that
> gentle lord, whose sins have vanished, master of
> his mind, frightening away anguish and evil, who
> holds back the horrors of samsara

Across the boundaries of the individual words these two lines consist of a chain of palindromic groups of syllables, except for rhyming *saṃtāvapāva* in the first line.

The Life of Padma at times almost seems like a concatenation of such literary devices, placing itself firmly within the century-old tradition of classical Indian literature known and loved by the audience. The genius of the poet Svayambhudeva lies therein—he manages to strike just the right balance, exploiting literary devices to their full potential without becoming too ornate, transforming the Jain Ramayana narrative into a stirring, impressionist poem.

Book of Ayodhya

After a lengthy introduction of the main antagonist, the Prativasudeva Ravana, in the first book, "Book of the Vidyadharas," from the second book onward we learn the story of Rama proper. Svayambhudeva's "Book of Ayodhya" spans, in one book of twenty-two chapters, the events of the first three books of the Sanskrit Ramayana. At its core, the storyline follows Valmiki's version, though there are some interesting departures. Some of these reframe the story within a typical Jain context. As in the Sanskrit Ramayana, Rama, as the eldest son of Dasharatha, the king of Ayodhya, is destined to ascend the throne. In due course Dasharatha decides the time is right to abdicate, as he wishes to renounce the material world and become a Jain ascetic. His young son Bharata, Rama's half-brother, wants to join him to also become an ascetic. Desperate to prevent her son from leaving home, Bharata's mother Kaikeyi asks Dasharatha to give the crown to Bharata instead of Rama, as a boon promised to her by the king long ago. To avoid conflict over the kingship, Rama voluntarily goes into exile, together with his favorite half-brother Lakshmana and his wife Sita.

EN ROUTE TO THE FOREST

The three set out on a journey to build a new life in the forest somewhere in the south. Svayambhudeva's account of the journey, the places they visit, and the people they encounter is very different from the Sanskrit Ramayana. There Rama, Lakshmana, and Sita leave Ayodhya to travel from ashram to ashram, visiting sages, avoiding contact with the "civilized" world of kings, cities, and householders, and in the end settle in their own ashram in Panchavati in the vast Dandaka forest. In Svayambhudeva's text, Rama, Lakshmana, and Sita do eventually come to reside in the Dandaka forest. Their journey toward it is not filled with visits to sages, however, but with a long series of adventures and encounters in and around cities. In the first two cities, Rama and Lakshmana come to the aid of a ruler and restore peace; in two other instances Lakshmana's marriage to a princess is the central theme; and in one instance a city is built especially for Rama. Throughout, Ayodhya and its king, Bharata, are present in the background: at the end of nearly every encounter, the kings agree to forge an alliance with Bharata and Ayodhya. One visit revolves around a king who threatens to attack Ayodhya to force Bharata into submission. In a comical scene, Rama and a small band of warriors manage to thwart this king's plan by entering the palace disguised as a troupe of cross-dressing performers. The king thereupon renounces the material world and becomes a Jain ascetic, after marrying his daughters to Bharata and Lakshmana. By contrast, in the version of Valmiki, there is a far greater sense of distance between Rama and his life in Ayodhya, with Rama occasionally suffering episodes of sadness and melancholy during his journey.

These innovative adventures and encounters and the centrality of Ayodhya in *The Life of Padma* support the positioning of the Rama story within the Jain universal history, in which Ayodhya is a sacred city, associated with the first Jina, Rishabha, and the capital of the first universal emperor, Rishabha's son Bharata, as narrated in the first volume. Rama, Lakshmana, and their enemy Ravana are the eighth Baladeva, Vasudeva, and Prativasudeva of the current time period, and as such, the three are all "half-universal emperors" (*ardhacakravartin*), ruling over half the known world (i.e., South Asia). These city adventures and encounters, in particular the alliances struck with kings, underscore the overall supremacy of the imperial city of Ayodhya and Rama's and Lakshmana's efforts to enlarge its dominion as its future rulers.[20]

The Jain categories of Baladeva, Vasudeva, and Prativasudeva are modeled after the Brahmanical deity Krishna, who is also known as Vasudeva, and his elder half-brother Balarama, or Baladeva; along with their enemy Jarasandha as the Prativasudeva, they form the ninth such triad of this time period. Despite the fact that in the Hindu version Krishna is the parallel of Rama, as both are avatars of Vishnu, in the Jain account the parallel is inverted: as the older brother,

Rama is the parallel of Balarama; Lakshmana, the parallel of Krishna, the younger brother. As a result, the physical description and attributes of Rama do not match those of Krishna, as they do in the Hindu accounts, but those of Balarama: the Jain Rama is fair-skinned (hence the alternative name Padma ("white-pinkish lotus") and has a plow for a weapon (in addition to his bow), while the Jain Lakshmana is dark-skinned and has a discus as his weapon. The parallel is especially clear in the epithets used by Svayambhudeva for the two characters: Rama is referred to as the Baladeva, and as the one armed with or holding the plow-weapon. Lakshmana is frequently referred to by one of the many epithets of the Hindu Krishna, such as the "youth" or "prince," Hari, "bearer of the bow Sharnga," "destroyer of the demon Madhu," Narayana, and others.[21]

In addition to using such terms for the Baladeva, Svayambhudeva occasionally refers to Rama as the "Rama-moon" (*rāmacandra*), a designation for the Hindu Rama that is very common in the modern devotional setting, but that nevertheless does not appear in Valmiki's text, and is said to only have made its entrance around the eighth century, coming into more common use with the development of Rama theology in the tenth or eleventh century. Svayambhudeva's fairly regular use of the name (I counted forty-six variants of *rāmacandra* and *rāghavacandra*), in addition to King Shrenika's rejection of certain elements linked to Rama theology from the "popular" Rama story in the first book, indicates that Svayambhudeva was confronted with an environment in which Rama theology had become prominent, in the late ninth to early tenth century.[22]

MEETING JATAYIN

When Rama, Sita, and Lakshmana enter the Dandaka forest they have two encounters with sages, allowing for some Jain didactic interludes in the form of stories of the sages' previous births, as well as straightforward advocacy for Jain doctrine. During the second of these encounters the bird Jatayin, Jatayu of Valmiki's Ramayana story, enters the narrative. Contrary to Valmiki's vulture-king Jatayu, Svayambhudeva's Jatayin is a simple bird without the ability to speak, whom Sita embraces as if he were her son.[23] The way in which the Jain authors exploit this occasion is a fine example of how they sought to transform wide-ranging, sometimes disparate epic narrative material into a more polished and overall more coherent and convincing Jain account. The sages explain that the bird Jatayin in a previous existence had been King Dandaka, after whom the Dandaka forest was named.[24] One day, this Buddhist king tried to chase a Jain sage away from his royal park by tying a dead snake around his neck, a motif that for South Asian audiences must have clearly echoed the similar story of King Parikshit and the sage Shamika in the first book of the Mahabharata. When Dandaka later returns to find the sage has not moved, the two engage in a conversation in which the superiority of the Jain philosophy to that of the Buddhists is established, and Dandaka becomes a Jain and protector of Jain sages. However, as the result of an elaborate scheme set up by his queen to discredit the sages, Dandaka becomes blind with rage and orders all the sages under his protection to be killed. Dandaka's city and all of its inhabitants, including the king and queen, are later scorched by the yogic powers of an angry sage who had managed to escape. The annihilated city was in time overgrown and turned into the Dandaka forest, and the king eventually became a bird in this forest. Thus Svayambhu-deva not only provides a typically Jain framing for Jatayin's entry, he links it in a coherent way to the background story of the legendary Dandaka forest. Moreover, the account is deeply infused with Jain doctrine through the presence of the Jain sages and supernatural effects, and it is interspersed with sermons and previous birth stories explaining Jain karma theory. More importantly, the story, the sermons on the doctrine that precede and follow it, and Rama and Sita's formal acceptance of the Jain lay vows put the audience in a Jain mindset before a major turning point in the narrative, namely, the death of Ravana's nephew, which indirectly will lead to the abduction of Sita.[25]

CHANDRANAKHI AND SHAMBUKA

Notorious in the story of Rama are the so-called stress points, defined as episodes that have "proven troubling to audiences and have generated much questioning and debate."[26] After the meeting with Jatayin, the Jain authors recreated an episode combining—and, in their way, solving—two such stress points, namely, the death of Shambuka and the treatment of Shurpanakha.

In Valmiki's *Rāmāyaṇa,* the character of Shambuka appears in the final book after Rama's return to Ayodhya and ascent to the throne.[27] One day a Brahman visits Rama's court in Ayodhya carrying the body of his young son. He blames the boy's death on Rama's incompetent rule.

According to one of King Rama's advisers, the premature death of the boy was caused by a low-caste man, a Sudra, engaging in penance, a practice that was only allowed for the upper classes. Rama goes in search of this man, and eventually finds him, Shambuka, performing penance while hanging upside-down from a tree. Rama unhesitatingly cuts off his head with a sword and the Brahman boy revives. This story, which scholars consider a later addition to the epic, seems to have fit into a Brahmanical redaction emphasizing that asceticism and mendicancy are off-limits to the lower classes, and that the violation of such restrictions leads to cosmic disorder and is therefore punishable by death. Later authors, Brahmanical and others, have dealt with this episode in different ways: some altogether deleting it from the epic, others transforming it, for instance, by emphasizing malevolent motives for Shambuka's penance or redirecting the focus to the salvific consequence of Shambuka's death at the hand of Rama.

The second stress point involves the treatment of Ravana's sister, Shurpanakha: in Valmiki's account, when Rama, Sita, and Lakshmana have settled at Panchavati, one day the demoness Shurpanakha happens to pass by. Seeing Rama, she becomes infatuated with him and addresses him, inquiring about his identity, earnestly professing her love for him, and offering to kill Lakshmana and Sita. Instead of straightforwardly rejecting her advances, Rama ridicules the naïve Shurpanakha, lying that his brother Lakshmana is unmarried and looking for a wife, after which the fickle demoness turns her attention toward Lakshmana. Lakshmana provokes her further, directing her again at Rama and mentioning that

Rama will soon get rid of Sita. Thinking that Sita is the only hindrance to her potential marital happiness with Rama, she charges toward her. On Rama's orders, Lakshmana then draws his sword and cuts off Shurpanakha's ears and nose. She flees the scene to her brother Khara, who seeks to avenge her by attacking Rama and Lakshmana. After Khara and his troops are defeated, Shurpanakha approaches Ravana in Lanka, announcing the destruction of her brother and describing Sita's beauty at length, and how she would fit well in Ravana's harem. Ravana then comes up with a plan to abduct Sita, which will ultimately lead to his demise. For Jain authors, it would have been impossible to include the mendicant Shambuka's death at the hands of Rama in the story. But instead of simply omitting the episode, Svayambhudeva chose to transform its valence, bringing him forward and making his death the central catalyst to the narrative. After accepting the Jain vows from the sages, Rama, Lakshmana, and Sita head farther into the Dandaka forest and eventually set up a shelter near the river Krauncha. One autumn day, during a walk in the forest, Lakshmana sees a magical sword hovering in the air. He grabs the sword and takes a swing at a nearby bamboo shrub, accidentally cutting off the head of a young man, Shambuka, the son of Ravana's sister Chandranakhi, who had been performing penance for twelve years to obtain that sword. When Chandranakhi arrives to find her son dead, she is initially overcome with sorrow and swears to avenge her son's death. When she sees Rama and Lakshmana in the distance, though, she realizes that Lakshmana is responsible for Shambuka's death and is suddenly flooded with feelings of lust and desire for them. Taking on the appearance of a young woman, she approaches them and asks first Rama and then Lakshmana to marry her. When they straightforwardly reject her, she takes on a demonic form and attacks. Lakshmana draws his sword and chases her away without physically harming her.[28] Chandranakhi wounds herself with her nails and goes to Khara, here her husband, claiming to have been molested by two young men, one of whom, moreover, killed their son Shambuka. After sending a messenger to Ravana informing him of Shambuka's death and their intent to avenge it, Khara, his brother Dushana, and their Rakshasa army set out. While Rama stays with Sita, Lakshmana confronts the army. When Ravana hears about the death of his nephew and alleged molestation of his sister, he sets out toward the Dandaka forest. It is only when he arrives there and his eyes fall on Sita that he is overcome with desire; then and there he decides that he must have her. He uses one of his *vidyās* to lure Rama away from her and pulls her into his chariot, killing Jatayin.

In the concluding section of this book, when Rama returns from the battlefield and finds Sita abducted and Jatayin slain, he faints, only to be comforted by the words of two passing sages on the foulness of women and the body. He soon forgets these insights and is again overcome with grief. Lakshmana, joined by Viradhita, whose father was killed by Khara and Dushana, wins the battle and returns to find Sita missing. Viradhita sends out his army to search for her, taking the two brothers to his recaptured city of Patalalanka. Meanwhile, in Lanka, Sita resists all of Ravana's attempts to seduce her. When Ravana's courtiers and relatives find out about Sita's abduction, they prepare for a possible war.

Through interventions at the "stress points" described above, Jain authors not only absolve the hero Rama of any grave sins, such as lying, ordering the mutilation of a woman, or killing a mendicant, they also give more nuance to Ravana's character. His trip to the Dandaka forest and even the subsequent war between Rama and the Rakshasas is motivated not (solely) by his lust for a stranger's wife, but also by his goal of avenging the unlawful death of Prince Shambuka, a beloved family member, as is stressed time and again by Svayambhudeva. Shambuka himself is transformed from a marginal character into a central, albeit still passive, one.

This motif of Lakshmana killing Shurpanakha's son proved to be popular also in later non-Jain retellings of the story, especially in South India. However, the identification of Shurpanakha's son with the mendicant Shambuka appears to have faded, since he was identified with various different names as these stories developed.[29] As a result, some Rama stories appear to have doubled the character: the *Ānandarāmāyaṇa,* a devotional Ramayana from the fifteenth century, for instance, includes the episode of Shurpanakha's son Shambukumara being killed by Lakshmana, and, at the end of the composition, also includes the episode where Rama beheads the Sudra Shambuka.

Acknowledgments

I thank the Murty Classical Library of India and Harvard University Press for this opportunity to publish my English translation of the *Paümacariu*, and I am especially grateful to Whitney Cox for his time and effort in vetting the translation, to Sheldon Pollock for his coordination and guidance, and to Heather Hughes and Melissa Rodman for their meticulous care in producing this volume. I also express my gratitude to the Bharatiya Vidya Bhavan in Mumbai for granting me the permission to use the critical edition of the text prepared by H. C. Bhayani and published in their Singhi Jain Series. I am further grateful to the Bhandarkar Oriental Institute in Pune and the Apabhramsha Sahitya Akademi in Jaipur for allowing me to make a copy of their *Paümacariu* manuscripts. Over the years many scholars have helped me as I worked on this text by offering expert advice and guidance, including Frank Van Den Bossche, Eddy Moerloose, M. D. Vasantharaj, Hampa Nagarajaiah, V. M. Kulkarni, Siddharth Wakankar, Harivallabh C. Bhayani, Kamal Chand Sogani, John and Mary Brockington, Erik Seldeslachts, Christophe Vielle, Nalini Balbir, and Vit Bubenik. My sincere thanks to all!

NOTES

1   The lower limit of this date is inferred from mention of the land of the Seunas, a royal house named after its king Seunachandra, who lived in the latter part of the ninth century. The upper limit was established from references to the poet Svayambhudeva in Pushpadanta's *Mahāpurāṇu*, the composition of which began in 959. Murthy 1971: 9–10 and 22; Bhayani 1953–1960: vol. 3, Introduction, 41. For a discussion on Pushpadanta's date, see Alsdorf 1936: 2–3.

2   *Mahāpurāṇu* 1.9.5. In *Mahāpurāṇu* 69.1.7, Pushpadanta refers to Svayambhu as the author of a Ramayana.

3   Premi 1942: 374. Yapaniya monks were outwardly Digambara, i.e., nude, in contrast to the Shvetambara monks, who wore white robes. On some doctrinal disputes between the Digambaras and Shvetambaras, however, particularly whether an enlightened being still takes food and whether women can attain enlightenment, the Yapaniyas sided with the Shvetambaras. Both Digambara and Shvetambara authors denounce them. The Yapaniya branch is often seen as representing an ecumenical Jainism, and a high degree of tolerance, whether or not it is correct, has been ascribed to them. See Upadhye 1983 and Jaini 1991: 41–48. See De Clercq (forthcoming) for an overview.

4   For more on the Jain stories of Krishna and Mahabharata, see De Clercq 2008.

5   The two works may have been written simultaneously, or perhaps verses from the metrical work were later added to the poem. The *Svayambhūcchandas* was edited and thoroughly analyzed by Velankar (in Svayambhudeva 1962).

6   In two instances: 88.6.1 and 89.4.6. Vimalasuri, the author of another Jain Rama narrative, explains in his *Paümacariyaṃ* that Rama was named "Lotus" because his face resembled a blooming lotus and his eyes were like lotus petals (25.7–8).

7   For discussions on the plurality of Rama stories, see Richman 1991 and 2000. Bulcke 1950 examines and compares a great number of Rama stories from India and beyond.

8   Different accounts of the Jain Rama story have been compared in V. M. Kulkarni 1990.

9   Vidyadharas are a category of beings common to the folklore and mythologies of all religious traditions that arose in South Asia, the Hindu traditions, Buddhism, and Jainism. Their characterization varies over time and in different sources. They have been thor-oughly examined from the earliest sources in Grafe 2001.

10 Edited by Pannalal Jain with a Hindi translation (Ravishena 1958–1959).

11 Edited by Hermann Jacobi and Muni Punyavijayaji (Vimalasuri, 1962–1968), with a Hindi translation. The *Paümacariyaṃ* was analyzed in K. R. Chandra 1970.

12 Tagare 1948: 1.

13 Marginal comments in the manuscripts for chapters 48, 49, and 81

describe cadence and musical notes, indicating the text's musical connections.

14 These meters are described by Bhayani in his introductions to each volume of the *Paümacariu* edition.

15 The Introduction to *The Life of Padma, Volume 1* gives an example from Svayambhudeva's celebrated description of Sahasrakirana's water play.

16 See *The Life of Padma, Volume 1*, 4.6.6.

17 See 31.7.1.

18 See 28.1 and 37.3.

19 Note that in the translation these repetitions were often left out.

20 I discuss these episodes at length in De Clercq 2022.

21 For a discussion on the development of these characters, see Jaini 1993, especially pp. 211–213.

22 See Brockington 1997 for an overview of this epithet in Sanskrit sources.

23 Note that in Valmiki's *Rāmāyaṇa*, as well as the Jain versions of Vimalasuri and Ravishena, this bird is explicitly described as a vulture. Svayambhudeva leaves out this specification.

24 In Valmiki's *Rāmāyaṇa*, the background story of the Dandaka forest is narrated in the final book, *Uttarakāṇḍa*.

25 I elaborate on this in De Clercq 2010.

26 Lutgendorf 2004: 151.

27 *Uttarakāṇḍa*, chs. 64–67.

28 The accounts of Vimalasuri and Ravishena are devoid of any violence in this episode: when Chandranakhi approaches Rama and Lakshmana, she is simply met with silence. Taking this as a rejection, she runs away toward her husband. Svayambhudeva's choice to include a violent outburst on the part of Chandranakhi and Lakshmana may be evidence that elements of violence were particularly popular among general audiences, even including Jains.

29 See, for instance, the edited volume by Mary and John Brockington (2016), several chapters of which deal with Shurpanakha and her ascetic son.

NOTE ON THE TEXT
AND TRANSLATION

The edition presented here is the critical edition (CE) of
Harivallabh C. Bhayani, published in the Singhi Jain Series
by Bharatiya Vidya Bhavan in Bombay (Mumbai), who have
graciously given permission for the text to be reprinted.
Bhayani's edition is based on three manuscripts:

A. Copied in V.S. 1541 (1484–5). From the Amer Shastra
Bhandar in Jaipur, run by the Shri Digambar Atishay Kshetra
Shri Mahavirji Prabandh-Karini Committee. Currently this
manuscript is held at the Apabhramsha Sahitya Academy, of
the same trust, under the directorship of Dr. K. C. Sogani.
Bhayani considered this manuscript superior and took it as
the basis of his edition.
P (PC). Copied in V.S. 1521 (1464–5) in Gwalior Fort. From
the Bhandarkar Oriental Research Institute in Pune, no.
1120 of the collection of 1887. This manuscript also contains
a commentary (PC) in the form of a marginal gloss in corrupt
Sanskrit.
S. Copied before V.S. 1775 (1718–9), when it was presented
to the manuscript library of the Godika temple in Sanganer
near Jaipur.
JC. Bhayani later found an undated commentary, no. 942 in
the manuscript collection of the Terahpantha Digambar Jain
Bada Mandir in Jaipur, which contains another commentary
(JC). This commentary partially overlaps with PC.

None of the manuscripts was copied near where the original text was thought to have been composed, namely, in a Kannada-speaking area, modern Karnataka or Maharashtra.

Bhayani remarks that Apabhramsha manuscripts are particularly prone to irregular and defective orthography. For his critical edition, he attempted to make the spelling as uniform as possible. Thus, for example, the instrumental-locative plural endings, given variably in the manuscripts as *-ehiṃ, -ihiṃ, -ehi,* or *-ihi* depending on metrical requirements, were regularized to *-ehiṃ, -ĕhiṃ, -ehī,* or *-ĕhī,* even when none of the manuscripts read *e* for *i*.

During my doctoral research I managed to obtain digital copies of manuscripts A and P. In the present translation I have silently corrected what I consider to have been typographical errors by the editor in the critical edition, after verifying with the manuscripts, or metrically incorrect forms (e.g., metrically short *ĕ, ŏ, ĭ, ŭ,* against long *e, o, iṃ, uṃ*). I sometimes divide words differently from the critical edition (e.g., as individual nouns as opposed to compounded). I only make this explicit in a note when my emendation has a substantial bearing on the meaning, not for an obvious typographical error. Words and syllables in square brackets represent metrically redundant syllables, which are considered spurious. Restorations required by the meter are enclosed in angle brackets.

In my translation I often abandon a literal and grammatically correct rendering of the original Apabhramsha text in favor of a more readable translation and a better understanding of its content. The Apabhramsha chapter headings, absent from the manuscripts themselves, were provided by the editor of the critical edition, and I have kept them. Contrary to common practice, *The Life of Padma* does not consistently place a colophon at the end of each chapter. In this volume there is just one occurrence, namely, at the end of the book.

For terms and names peculiar to (Digambara) Jainism and its doctrine, I adopt the English translations suggested in P. S. Jaini (1998). If the term is not described there or otherwise not current, I explain in an endnote.

BOOK OF AYODHYA

Leaving Ayodhya

एक्कवीसमो संधि

सायरवुद्धि विहीसणेण
परिपुच्छिउ जयसिरिमाणणहों ।
कहें केत्तडउ कालु अचलु
जउ जीविउ रज्जु दसाणणहों ॥

१

पभणइ सायरवुद्धि भडारउ ।
कुसुमाउहसरपसरणिवारउ ॥
सुणु अक्खमि रहुवंसु पहाणउ ।
दसरहु अत्थि अउज्झहें राणउ ॥
तासु पुत्त होसन्ति धुरन्धर ।
वासुएववलएव धणुद्धर ॥
तेहिँ हणेवउ रक्खु महारणें ।
जणयणराहिवतणयहें कारणें ॥
तो सहसत्ति पलित्तु विहीसणु ।
णं घयघडएँहिँ सित्तु हुआसणु ॥
जाम ण लङ्काावल्लरि सुक्कइ ।
जाम ण मरणु दसासणें ढुक्कइ ॥
तोडमि ताम ताहुँ भयभीसइँ ।
दसरहजणयणराहिवसीसइँ ॥
तो तं वयणु सुणेेवि कलियारउ ।

4

Chapter 21

Vibhishana asked Sagarabuddhi, "Tell me, how long will the triumph, life, and reign of Ravana, the ten-faced, who glories in victory, endure?"[1]

1

Noble Sagarabuddhi, who checked the onslaught of
Kama's arrows, said, "Listen, I will tell you about the
famous dynasty of Raghu: Dasharatha is the king
of Ayodhya. He will have sons, archers laden with
qualities, a Vasudeva and a Baladeva. They will kill the
Rakshasa in a great battle for Janaka's daughter." At
this Vibhishana at once became incensed, like a fire
sprinkled with pots of ghee: "Before the creeper of
Lanka withers and Ravana's death draws near, I will
cut off the heads of those dreadful kings Dasharatha
and Janaka." When the troublemaker Narada heard
this, he set out to inform Dasharatha and Janaka:

वड्ढावणहँ पधाइउ णारउ ॥
अज्जु विहीसणु उप्परि एसइ ।
तुम्हहँ विहि मि सिरइँ तोडेसइ ॥
दसरहजणय विणीसरिय
लेप्पमउ थवेप्पिणु अप्पणउ ।
णियइँ सिरइँ विज्जाहरेंहिँ
परियणहों करेप्पिणु चप्पणउ ॥

२

दसरहजणय वे वि गय तेत्तहें ।
पुरवरु कउतुकमङ्गलु जेत्तहें ॥
जेम्मइ जेत्थु अमग्गियलद्धउ ।
सूरकन्तमणिहुयवहरद्धउ ॥
जहिँ जलु चन्दकन्तिणिज्झरणेंहिँ ।
सुप्पइ पडियपुप्फपत्थरणेंहिँ ॥
जहिँ णेउरझङ्कारियचलणेंहिँ ।
रम्मइ अङ्गणपुप्फक्खलणेंहिँ ॥
जहिँ पासायसिहरें णिहसिज्जइ ।
तेण मियङ्कु वङ्कु किसु किज्जइ ॥
तहिँ सुहमइणामेण पहाणउ ।
णं सुरपुरहों पुरन्दरु राणउ ॥
पिहुसिरि तहों महएवि मणोहर ।
सुरकरिकर कुम्भयलपओहर ॥
णन्दणु ताहें दोणु उप्पज्जइ ।

6

"Today Vibhishana will attack. He will cut off both your heads."

Dasharatha and Janaka installed a clay replica of themselves and fled. The Vidyadharas crushed their retinue and took the heads away with them.[2]

2

The two, Dasharatha and Janaka, went to the great city of Kautukamangala. There, people ate food they received without ever asking and cooked on fires of sunstones. There was water aplenty from cascading moonstones.[3] People slept on beds of fallen blossoms. As women's feet tripped over flowers strewn in worship, their anklets jingled, giving delight. The palace spire was so high that it scraped against the moon, rendering it curved and thin. The king there was named Sukhamati, like Indra of the city of the gods. His breathtaking chief queen was Prithushri, her sinuous arms like the trunk of the elephant of the gods and her breasts heavy like its cranial globes.

केक्कय तणय काइँ वण्णिज्जइ ॥
सयलकलाकलावसंपण्णी ।
णं पञ्चक्ख लच्छि अवइण्णी ॥
ताहें सयम्वरें मिलिय वर
हरिवाहणहेमप्पहपमुह ।
णाइँ समुद्दमहासिरिहें
थिय जलवाहिणिपवाह समुह ॥

३

तो करेणु आरुहेविं विणिग्गय ।
णं पञ्चक्ख महासिरिदेवय ॥
पेक्खन्तहँ णरवरसंघायहँ ।
भूगोयरविज्जाहररायहँ ॥
घित्त माल दससन्दणणामहों ।
मणहरगइएँ रइएँ णं कामहों ॥
तहिँ अवसरें विरुद्ध हरिवाहणु ।
धाइउ लेहु भणन्तु ससाहणु ॥
वरु आहणहों कण्ण उद्दालहों ।
रयणइँ जेम तेम महिपालहों ॥
सुहमइ रहुसुएण विण्णप्पइ ।
धीरउ होहि माम को चप्पइ ॥
मइँ जियन्तें अणरण्णहों नन्दणें ।
एउ भणेवि परिट्ठिउ सन्दणें ॥
केक्कइ धुरहिँ करेप्पिणु सारहि ।

8

She bore a son, Drona, and a daughter, Kaikeyi.
How can we describe her? She was accomplished in
the whole range of arts, as if Lakshmi herself had
descended from heaven.

At her *svayaṃvara* ceremony, suitors gathered, chief
among whom were Harivahana and Hemaprabha.[4] It
was as if streams of rivers stood before the great Lady
Ocean.

3

Then Kaikeyi mounted an elephant cow and came outside,
like the great goddess Lakshmi herself. As the
multitudes of great men—kings of earthbound people
and of Vidyadharas—watched, she threw the garland
to the one named Dasharatha, as if she were Rati, with
her breathtaking gait, throwing a garland at Kama. At
that moment Harivahana angrily rushed forth with
his army, saying, "Kill the suitor and seize the maiden,
as if she were the king's jewels!" Raghu's descendant
Dasharatha said to Sukhamati, "Be calm, my friend.
Who launches an attack when I, the son of Anaranya,
am alive?" With these words he set himself firm in his
chariot. He made Kaikeyi his charioteer at the yoke
and set out with all the great warriors.

तहिँ पयट्टु जहिँ सयल महारहि ॥
तो वोल्लिज्जइ दसरहेण
दूरयरणिवारियरवियरइँ ।
रहु वाहेवि तहिँ णेहि पिएँ
धयछत्तइँ जेत्थु णिरन्तरइँ ॥

४

तं णिसुणेॅवि परिओसियजणएं ।
वाहिउ रहवरु पिहुसिरितणएं ॥
तेण वि सरहिँ परज्जिउ साहणु ।
भग्गु सहेमप्पहु हरिवाहणु ॥
परिणिय केक्कइ दिण्णु महावरु ।
चवइ अउज्झापुरपरमेसरु ॥
सुन्दरि मग्गु मग्गु जं रुच्चइ ।
सुहमइसुयएँ णवेप्पिणु वुच्चइ ॥
दिण्णु देव पइँ मग्गमि जइयहुँ ।
णिययसच्चु पालिज्जइ तइयहुँ ॥
एम चवन्तइँ धणकणसंकुलें ।
थियइँ वे वि पुरें कउतुकमङ्गलें ॥
वहुवासरेहिँ अउज्झ पइट्ठइँ ।
सइवासव इव रज्जें वइट्ठइँ ॥
सयलकलाकलावसंपण्णा ।
ताम चयारि पुत्त उप्पण्णा ॥

Dasharatha then said, "Drive the chariot, my love, and
bring me to those flags and umbrellas clustered closely
together, keeping the rays of the sun far away."

4

At this Prithushri's daughter, to her father's delight, set
the great chariot in motion. Dasharatha vanquished
the army with arrows and defeated Harivahana along
with Hemaprabha. He married Kaikeyi and gave her
a great boon. The overlord of the city of Ayodhya
said, "Beautiful lady, ask. Ask what pleases you."
Sukhamati's daughter bowed and said, "If you give
it to me, lord, when I ask for it, your truthfulness
will be safeguarded." Speaking thus, the two resided
in Kautukamangala, abounding in riches and grain.
Many days later they entered Ayodhya. It was as if
Shachi and Indra settled in the kingdom. Then four
sons were born to Dasharatha, each accomplished in
the whole range of arts:

रामचन्दु अपरज्जियहें
सोमित्ति सुमित्तिहें एक्कु जणु ।
भरहु धुरन्धरु केक्कइहें
सुप्पहहें पुत्तु पुणु सत्तुहणु ॥

५

एय चयारि पुत्त तहों रायहों ।
णाइँ महासमुद्द महिभायहों ॥
णाइँ दन्त गिव्वाणगइन्दहों ।
णाइँ मणोरह सज्जणविन्दहों ॥
जणउ वि मिहिलाणयरें पइट्ठउ ।
समउ विदेहएँ रज्जें णिविट्ठउ ॥
ताहँ विहि मि वरविक्कमवीयउ ।
भामण्डलु उप्पण्णु ससीयउ ॥
पुव्ववइरु संभरेंवि अखेवें ।
दाहिण सेढि हरेंवि णिउ देवें ॥
तहिँ रहणेउरचक्कवालपुरें ।
वहलधवलछुहपङ्कापण्डुरें ॥
चन्दगइहें चन्दुज्जलवयणहों ।
णन्दणवणसमीवें तहों सयणहों ॥
घत्तिउ पिङ्गलेण अमरिन्दें ।
पुप्फवइहें अल्लविउ णरिन्दें ॥

12

moon-like Rama born from Aparajita, the unique man
  Lakshmana from Sumitri, noble Bharata from
  Kaikeyi, and last his son Shatrughna from Suprabha.

5

These four sons were to that king like the great oceans
  to the earth, like tusks to the great elephant of
  the gods, like wishes to an assembly of good folk.[5]
  Janaka entered the city of Mithila and settled in
  the kingship together with Videha. From these
  two, almighty Bhamandala was born, together with
  Sita. Before long a god remembered an old feud
  and abducted Bhamandala and brought him to the
  southern range of the Vaitadhya mountains. There, in
  Rathanupurachakravala, fair with thick white plaster
  and clay, the city of Chandragati, whose face was
  bright like the moon, near the pleasure grove of his
  home, that eminent god Pingala abandoned him. The
  king entrusted him to Pushpavati.

ताव रज्जु जणयहों तणउ
उद्दद्धु महाडइवासिऍहिँ ।
वव्वरसवरपुलिन्दऍहिँ
हिमवन्तविज्झसंवासिऍहिँ ॥

६

वेढिय जणयकणय दुप्पेच्छेहिँ ।
वव्वरसवरपुलिन्दामेच्छेहिँ ॥
गरुयासङ्कुऍ वालसहायहों ।
लेहु विसज्जिउ दसरहरायहों ॥
तूरइँ देवि सो वि सण्णज्झइ ।
रामु सलक्खणु ताव विरुज्झइ ॥
मइँ जीयन्तें ताय तुहुँ चल्लहि ।
हणमि वइरि छुड्डु हत्थुत्थल्लहि ॥
वुत्तु णराहिवेण तुहुँ वालउ ।
रम्भाखम्भगब्भसोमालउ ॥
किह आलग्गहि णरवरविन्दहुँ ।
किह घड भज्झहि मत्तगइन्दहुँ ॥
किह रिउरहहुँ महारहु चोयहि ।
किह वरतुरय तुरङ्घहुँ ढोयहि ॥
पभणइ रामु ताय पल्लट्टहि ।
हउँ जें पहुच्चमि काइँ पयट्टहि ॥

In the meantime, Janaka's kingdom was overrun by inhabitants of the great forests, Barbaras, Shabaras, Pulindas, and dwellers from the Himalaya and Vindhya mountains.

6

Janaka and Kanaka were besieged by unsightly Barbara, Shabara, and Pulinda barbarians. With profound hope they sent a letter to King Dasharatha and his sons. And that king sounded the drums and put on his armor. Then Rama and Lakshmana objected, "You depart, father, while I am alive? I will kill the enemy. Quickly dispatch me with a wave of your hand." The king said, "You are just a boy, soft like the core of a banana tree trunk. How could you pursue hordes of great men, crush a troop of rutting elephants, drive a grand chariot toward the enemy's chariots, or lead horses toward their horses?" Rama answered, "Father, turn back. I will go. Why do you proceed?

किं तमु हणइ ण वालु रवि
किं वालु दवग्गि ण डहइ वणु ।
किं करि दलइ ण वालु हरि
किं वालु ण डङ्कइ उरगमणु ॥

७

पहु पल्हट्टु पयट्टिउ राहउ ।
दूरासंघियमेच्छमहाहउ ॥
दूसहु सो जि अण्णु पुणु लक्खणु ।
एक्कु पवणु अण्णेक्कु हुआसणु ॥
विण्णि मि भिडिय पुलिन्दहों साहणें ।
रहवरतुरयजोहगयवाहणें ॥
दीहरसरेंहिँ वइरि संताविय ।
जणयकणय रणें उव्वेढाविय ॥
धाइउ समरङ्गणें तमु राणउ ।
वव्वरसवरपुलिन्दपहाणउ ॥
तेण कुमारहों चूरिउ रहवरु ।
छिण्णु छत्तु दोहाइउ धणुहरु ॥
तो राहवेण लइज्जइ वाणेंहिँ ।
णाइणिणायकायपरिमाणेंहिँ ॥
साहणु भग्गउ लग्गु उमग्गेंहिँ ।
करयलेहिँ ओलम्वियखग्गेंहिँ ॥

16

Does the young sun not defeat darkness? Does a fresh
   fire not burn a forest? Does a young lion not tear an
   elephant asunder? Does a young snake not bite?"

7

The king turned back, and Raghu's descendant Rama
   departed for the great fight with the barbarians
   from the distant wilds. So too did that unstoppable
   Lakshmana: one was the wind, the other was fire. The
   two attacked the Pulinda army, with its great chariots,
   horses, soldiers, elephants, and wagons. They afflicted
   the enemies with long arrows and in the battle freed
   Janaka and Kanaka from their siege. King Tama,
   the leader of the Barbaras, Shabaras, and Pulindas,
   rushed forth on the battlefield. He pulverized Prince
   Lakshmana's mighty chariot, cut his umbrella, and
   broke his bow in two. Then Rama, descendant of
   Raghu, showered him with arrows, each long like the
   bodies of snakes both female and male. The defeated
   army fell into disarray, their swords dropping low in
   their hands.

दसहिँ तुरङ्गहिँ णीसरिउ
भिल्लाहिउ भज्जेवि आहवहोँ ।
जाणइ जणयणराहिवेण
तहिँ कालेँ वि अप्पिय राहवहोँ ॥

८

वव्वरसवरवरूहिणि भग्गी ।
जणयहोँ जाय पिहिवि आवग्गी ॥
णाणारयणाहरणहिँ पुज्जिय ।
वासुएववलएव विसज्जिय ॥
सीयहेँ देहरिद्धि पावन्तिहेँ ।
एक्कु दिवसु दप्पणु जोयन्तिहेँ ॥
पडिमाछलेँण महाभयगारउ ।
आरिसवेसु णिहालिउ णारउ ॥
जणयतणय सहसत्ति पणट्ठी ।
सीहागमणेँ कुरङ्गि व तट्ठी ॥
हा हा माएँ भणन्तिहिँ सहियहिँ ।
कलयलु किउ सज्झसगहगहियहिँ ॥
अमरिसकुढुढ्ढाइय किङ्कर ।
उक्खयवरकरवालभयङ्कर ॥
मिलेवि तेहिँ कह कह वि ण मारिउ ।
लेवि अद्धचन्द्देहिँ णीसारिउ ॥

18

Escaping the battle, the tribal king fled with ten horses. At that time King Janaka gave his daughter Sita to Rama.

8

The army of the Barbaras and Shabaras was defeated. Janaka's dominion had been liberated. The Vasudeva and Baladeva were honored with various gems and ornaments and were sent away. As Sita's body matured, one day as she was looking into a mirror, through a trick of its reflection she saw Narada in his seer guise: this gave her quite a fright. Janaka's daughter quickly ran away, like a doe frightened at the arrival of a lion. Seized in terror's clutches, her friends caused a hubbub, saying, "Oh, oh, girl!" Livid with indignation, her servants rushed forth, striking fear with their great swords drawn. It was a miracle that Narada was not killed when they caught up with him. They grabbed him by the throat and threw him out.

गउ सपराहउ देवरिसि
पडें पडिम लिहेंवि सीयहें तणिय ।
दरिसाविय भामण्डलहों
विसजुत्ति णाइँ णरघारणिय ॥

९

दिट्ठु जं जें पडें पडिम कुमारें ।
पञ्चहिँ सरहिँ विद्धु णं मारें ॥
सुसियवयणु घुम्मइयणिडालउ ।
वलियअङ्गु मोडियभुवडालउ ॥
वद्धकेसु पक्खोडियवच्छउ ।
दरिसावियदसकामावत्थउ ॥
चिन्त पढमथाणन्तरें लग्गइ ।
वीयएँ पियमुहदंसणु मग्गइ ॥
तइयएँ ससइ दीहणीसासें ।
कणइ चउत्थएँ जरविण्णासें ॥
पञ्चमे डाहें अङ्गु ण मुच्चइ ।
छट्टुएँ मुहहों ण काइ मि रुच्चइ ॥
सत्तमें थाणें ण गासु लइज्जइ ।
अट्टमें गमणुम्माएँहिँ भिज्जइ ॥
णवमें पाणसंदेहहों ढुक्कइ ।
दसमएँ मरइ ण केम वि चुक्कइ ॥

The divine sage went away humiliated. He drew a picture
of Sita on a canvas and showed it to Bhamandala as if
he were applying a lethal poison.

9

As soon as the prince saw the picture on the canvas, it
was as if he was shot through by the god of love with
his five arrows. His mouth went dry, his forehead
trembled, his body burned, his arms were like broken
branches, his hair knotted, and his chest quivered. He
displayed the ten stages of love: in the first stage worry
arose; in the second he asked to see his beloved's face;
in the third he sighed deeply; in the fourth he whined
as his fever spread; in the fifth a burning pain clung
to his body; in the sixth nothing brought solace to his
mouth; in the seventh stage he could not take even
a mouthful of food; in the eighth he was pierced by
maddening thoughts about going to her; in the ninth
he came close to endangering his life; in the tenth he
narrowly managed to escape death.

कहिउ णरिन्दहों किङ्करेहिँ
पहु दुक्करु जीवइ पुत्तु तउ ।
काहें वि कण्णहें कारणेण
सो दसमी कामावत्थ गउ ॥

१०

णागणरामरकुलकलियारउ ।
चन्दगइएँ पडिपुच्छिउ णारउ ॥
कहि कहों तणिय कण्ण कहिँ दिट्ठी ।
जा महु पुत्तहों हियएँ पइट्ठी ॥
कहइ महारिसि मिहिलाराणउ ।
चन्दकेउण्णामेण पहाणउ ॥
तहों सुत जणउ तेत्थु मइँ दिट्ठउ ।
कण्णारयणु तिलोयवरिट्ठउ ॥
तं जइ होइ कुमारहों आयहों ।
तो सिय हरइ पुरन्दररायहों ॥
तं णिसुणेवि विज्जाहरणाहें ।
पेसिउ चवलवेउ असगाहें ॥
जाहि विदेहादइउ हरेवउ ।
मइँ विवाहसंवन्धु करेवउ ॥
गउ सो चन्दगइहें मुहु जोएँवि ।
मन्दुर ढुक्कु तुरङ्गमु होएँवि ॥
कोड्डेँ चडिउ णराहिउ जावेँहिँ ।

The servants told the king, "Lord, your son is barely alive. Because of some girl he has come to the tenth stage of love."[6]

10

Chandragati asked Narada, who stirs up strife in the families of demons, humans, and gods, "Tell me, whose daughter is she and where did you see her, the one who has entered my son's heart?" The great seer said, "The great king of Mithila is named Chandraketu. He has a son, Janaka. There I saw the gem of a girl, the most beautiful in the three worlds. If she would belong to this young man here, then he would steal Indra's luster." Hearing this, the Vidyadhara king sent out Chapalavega with a mean trick, "Go, you must abduct Videha's husband. He must strike a marriage agreement with me." He looked at Chandragati's face and departed. He turned himself into a horse and entered Janaka's stables. The king of Mithila marveled as he mounted the horse

दाहिण सेढि पराइउ तार्वेहिं ॥
मिहिलाणाहु मुएप्पिणु जिणहरें ।
चवलवेउ पइसइ पुरें मणहरें
आणिउ जणयणराहिवइ
णियणाहहों अक्खिउ सरहसेंण ।
वन्दणहत्तिएँ सो वि गउ
सहुँ पुत्तें विरहपरव्वसेंण ॥

११

विज्जाहरणरणयणाणन्देंहिं ।
किउ संभासणु विहि मि णरिन्देंहिं ॥
पभणइ चन्दगमणु तोसियमणु ।
विण्णि वि किण्ण करहुँ सयणत्तणु ॥
दुहिय तुहारी पुत्तु महारउ ।
होउ विवाहु मणोरहगारउ ॥
अमरिसु णवर पवद्धिउ जणयहों ।
दिण्ण कण्ण मइँ दसरहतणयहों ॥
रामहों जयसिरिरामासत्तहों ।
सवरवरूहिणिचूरियगत्तहों ॥
तहिँ अवसरें वद्धियअहिमाणें ।
वुत्तु णरिन्दु चन्दपत्थाणें ॥
कहिँ विज्जाहरु कहिँ भूगोयरु ।
गयमसयहुँ वड्ढारउ अन्तरु ॥

and set out for the southern range of the Vaitadhya
mountains. Chapalavega abandoned the king in a Jina
temple and entered the breathtaking city.

He hastily reported to Chandragati, "King Janaka has been
brought." Then Chandragati went to praise and revere
him, together with his son who was overpowered by
lovesickness.

11

The two kings, who each brought joy to the eyes of
Vidyadharas and humans, conversed. Chandragati
spoke with a delighted heart, "Why do we two not
create a bond? Your daughter, my son. Let there be
a wedding that will fulfill our wishes." But Janaka's
indignation grew, "I have given my daughter to the
son of Dasharatha, Rama, who is accompanied by
the charming woman, Lady Triumph, and whose
arms pulverized the Shabara army." As his arrogance
increased, Chandragati at that moment said to the
king, "What is the status of a Vidyadhara? And what
of an earthbound mortal? The difference is bigger
than that between an elephant and a mosquito.

माणुसखेत्तु जें ताम कणिट्ठउ ।
जीविउ तहिँ कहिँ तणउ विसिट्ठउ ॥
भणइ णराहिउ केत्तिऍण
जगें माणुसखेत्तु जें अग्गलउ ।
जसु पासिउ तित्थङ्करेहिँ
सिद्धत्तणु लद्धउ केवलउ ॥

१२

तं णिसुणेवि भामण्डलवप्पें ।
वुच्चइ विज्जावलमाहप्पें ॥
पगुणगुणइँ अइदुज्जयभावइँ ।
पुरें अच्छन्ति एत्थु वे चावइँ ॥
वज्जावत्तसमुद्दावत्तइँ ।
जक्खारक्खियरक्खियगत्तइँ ॥
किं भामण्डलेण किं रामें ।
ताइँ चडावइ जो आयामें ॥
परिणउ सो ज्जें कण्ण ऍउ पभणिउ ।
तं जि पमाणु करेवि पहु भणियउ ॥
गय ससरासण मिहिलापुरवरु ।९
वद्धु मञ्च आढत्तु सयम्वरु ॥
मिलिय णराहिव जे जगें जाणिय ।
सयल वि धणुपयावअवमाणिय ॥

The land of the humans is minuscule. Whose life is
superior there?"

King Janaka said, "How much more is the land of the
humans the best on earth; for the Tirthankaras
obtained Siddha-hood* and omniscience there!"

12

At this, Bhamandala's father, mighty from the power
of his *vidyās*,[7] said, "There are two bows here in
the city, with excellent bow-strings and an utterly
unconquerable nature, Vajravarta and Samudravarta;
their forms are protected by Yaksha guards. What of
Bhamandala, what of Rama? He who strings these
by his might, let him marry the girl! So it has been
declared." Now that this measure was arranged, it
was communicated to kings. Along with the bows,
they went to the city of Mithila. Platforms were
raised and the *svayaṃvara* ceremony commenced.
Kings renowned on earth gathered there. All were
humiliated by the might of the bows. There was no

---

* A state of enlightenment.

को वि णाहिँ जो ताइँ चडावइ ।
जक्खसहासहुँ मुहु दरिसावइ ॥
जाम ण गुणहिँ चडन्ताइँ ।
अहिजायइँ कउ सुहदंसणइँ ॥
अवसें जणहों अणिट्ठाइँ ।
कुकलत्तइँ जेम सरासणइँ ॥

१३

जं णरवइ असेस अवमाणिय ।
दसरहतणय चयारि वि आणिय ॥
हरिवलएव पढुक्किय तेत्तहें ।
सीयसयम्वरमण्डउ जेत्तहें ॥
दूरणिवारियणरवरलक्खेहिँ ।
धणुहराइँ अल्लवियइँ जक्खेहिँ ॥
अप्पणअप्पणाइँ सुपमाणइँ ।
णिव्वाडेवि लेहु वरचावइँ ॥
लइयइँ सायरवज्जावत्तइँ ।
गामहणा इव गुणेहिँ चडन्तइँ ॥
मेल्लिउ कुसुमवासु सुरसत्थें ।
परिणिय जणयतणय काकुत्थें ॥
जे जे मिलिय सयम्वरें राणा ।
णियणियणयरहों गय विद्दाणा ॥
दिवसु वारु णक्खत्तु गणेप्पिणु ।

28

one who could string them and dare to show his face
to the thousands of Yakshas.
How ominous were they to the crowd, those bows of
noble descent, a pleasure to behold, as no one could
string them with bow-strings? It was as if they were
disobedient wives!

13

As all the kings were being humbled, the four sons
of Dasharatha were brought near. The Vasudeva
and Baladeva approached the pavilion for Sita's
svayaṃvara. The Yakshas, as they held off myriads
of great men at a great distance, handed over the
bows, "You each make a choice, and take hold of these
grand, perfectly proportioned bows." They took hold
of Samudravarta and Vajravarta and strung them
with bow-strings as if they were ordinary bows. A
band of gods released a rain of flowers. Rama married
Janaka's daughter. All the kings who had gathered
at the ceremony left for their own cities, dejected.
Taking into account the day, the time, and the lunar

लग्गु जोग्गु गहदुत्थु णिएप्पिणु ॥
जोइसिएँहिँ आएसु किउ
जउ लक्खणरामहुँ सरहसहुँ ।
आयहें कण्णहें कारणेण
होसइ विणासु वहुरक्खसहुँ ॥

१४

ससिवद्धणेण ससिवयणियउ ।
कुवलयदलदीहरणयणियउ ॥
कलकोइलवीणावाणियउ ।
अट्ठारह कण्णउ आणियउ ॥
दस लहुभायरहुँ समप्पियउ ।
लक्खणहों अट्ठ परिकप्पियउ ॥
दोणेण विसल्लासुन्दरिय ।
कण्हहों चिन्तविय मणोहरिय ॥
वइदेहि अउज्झाणयरि णिय ।
दसरहेण महोच्छवसोह किय ॥
रहतिक्कचउक्कहिँ चच्चरहिँ ।
कुङ्कुमकप्पूरपवरवरहिँ ॥
चन्दनछडोहदिज्जन्तएँहिँ ।

mansion, and observing the favorable ascendant and
the inauspicious position of the planets,
astrologers foretold, "Because of this maiden, there will be
victory for the ferocious Lakshmana and Rama, and
destruction for many Rakshasas."

14

Shashivardhana brought his eighteen daughters with
moon-like faces, their eyes long like the petals of blue
water lilies and their voices like melodious cuckoos
and vinas. He gave ten to the younger brothers
and assigned eight to Lakshmana. Drona took the
breathtaking beauty Vishalya into consideration
for the Vasudeva. Videha's daughter Sita was taken
to the city of Ayodhya. Dasharatha arranged for
decoration worthy of a great feast on the highways,
at the junctions of three and four roads, and at every
crossing, with the best saffron and camphor, streams
of sandalwood juice were dispersed and songs were
sung by singers. Thresholds made of precious stones
were fashioned and frescos with pearls and gold.

गायणगीयहिँ गिज्जन्तऍहिँ ॥
मणिमइयउ रइयउ देहलिउ ।
मोत्तियकणऍहिँ रङ्गावलिउ ॥
सोवण्णदण्डमणितोरणइँ ।
वद्धइँ सुरवरमणचोरणइँ ॥
सीयवलइँ पइसारियइँ
जणें जयजयकारिज्जन्ताइँ ।
थियइँ अउज्झहें अविचलइँ
रइसोक्ख सयं भुञ्जन्ताइँ ॥

Golden stakes and jeweled arches were raised, stealing the hearts of the gods.

As cheers of victory resounded in the crowd, Sita and the Baladeva were led inside. They stayed firmly in Ayodhya, enjoying the happiness of lovemaking.

वावीसमो संधि

कोसलणन्दणेण
सकलत्तें णियघरु आएं ।
आसाढट्टमिहिँ
किउ ण्हवणु जिणिन्दहों राएं ॥

१

सुरसमरसहासेंहिँ दुम्महेण ।
किउ ण्हवणु जिणिन्दहों दसरहेण ॥
पट्टवियइँ जिणतणुधोवयाइँ ।
देविहिँ दिव्वइँ गन्धोवयाइँ ॥
सुप्पहहें णवर कज्झइ ण पत्तु ।
पहु पभणइ रहसुच्छलियगत्तु ॥
कहें काइँ णियम्विणि मणें विसण्ण ।
चिरचिंतिय भित्ति व थिय विवण्ण ॥
पणवेप्पिणु वुच्चइ सुप्पहाएँ ।
किर काइँ महु त्तणियएँ कहाएँ ॥
जइ हउँ जें पाणवल्लहिय देव ।
तो गन्धसलिलु पावइ ण केम ॥
तहिँ अवसरें कज्झइ ढुक्कु पासु ।
छणससि व णिरन्तरधवलियासु ॥

34

Chapter 22

When Rama, the son of Kosala's daughter, came home along with his wife, the king held a bathing ceremony for the great Jina during the Eight Day festival in the month of Ashadha.[*]

1

Dasharatha, indomitable in thousands of battles with the Gods,[1] held a bathing ceremony for the great Jina. He sent pleasantly perfumed water to the queens to bathe the Jina's body. However, the chamberlain did not come to Suprabha. As nervousness stiffened his limbs, the king said, "Tell me, lovely woman, why are you sad in your heart? You stand here washed-out like a wall painted long ago." Suprabha bowed and said, "Indeed, what of my story? Lord, if I am dear as life to you, then why did I not get perfumed water?" At that instant the chamberlain came near, his face completely white like the full moon, his teeth gone, ugly, with a stick

---

[*] In the traditional Indian calendar, mid-June to mid-July.

गयदन्तु अयंगमु दण्डपाणि ।
अणियच्छियपहु पक्खलियवाणि ॥
गरहिउ दसरहेॅण
पइँ कज्झुइ काइँ चिराविउ ।
जलु जिणवयणु जिह
सुप्पहहेॅ दवत्ति ण पाविउ ॥

२

पणवेप्पिणु तेण वि वुत्तु एम ।
गय दियहा जोव्वणु ल्हसिउ देव ॥
पढमाउसु जर धवलन्ति आय ।
पुणु असइ व सीसवलग्ग जाय ॥
गइ तुट्टिय विहडिय सन्धिवन्ध ।
ण सुणन्ति कण्ण लोयण णिरन्ध ॥
सिरु कम्पइ मुहेॅ पक्खलइ वाय ।
गय दन्त सरीरहोॅ णट्टु छाय ॥
परिगलिउ रुहिरु थिउ णवर चम्मु ।
महु एत्थु जें हुउ णं अवरु जम्मु ॥
गिरिणइपवाह ण वहन्ति पाय ।
गन्धोवउ पावउ केम राय ॥
वयणेण तेण किउ पहुवियप्पु ।
गउ परमविसायहोॅ रामवप्पु ॥

in his hand, not noticing his master, and his voice stammering.

Dasharatha scolded him, "Chamberlain, why were you absent for so long and why was the water, pure and bright like the face of the Jina, not immediately brought to Suprabha?"

2

He took a bow and spoke thus, "My days are over. Youth has retreated, my lord: old age has come for me, bleaching away what vitality I used to have. Like an unchaste woman she again appeared and took advantage of me. My gait is broken, and my joints are wrecked. My ears do not hear, and my eyes are completely blind. My head is trembling, my voice stammers in my mouth, my teeth have gone, and the luster of my body has vanished. My blood has seeped away. Only skin remains. It is as if another existence has now befallen me. My feet no longer carry me with the flow of a mountain river. How could the perfumed water reach here, my king?" Because of these words, anxiety overtook the king; Rama's father became

सच्चउ चलु जीविउ कवणु सोक्खु ।
तं किज्जइ सिज्झइ जेण मोक्खु ॥
सुहु महुविन्दुसमु
दुहु मेरुसरिसु पवियम्भइ ।
वरि तं कम्मु किउ
जं पउ अजरामरु लब्भइ ॥

३

कं दिवसु वि होसइ आरिसाहुँ ।
कज्झुइअवत्थ अम्हारिसाहुँ ॥
को हउँ का महि कहों तणउ दव्वु ।
सिंहासणु छत्तइँ अथिरु सव्वु ॥
जोव्वणु सरीरु जीविउ धिगत्थु ।
संसारु असारु अणत्थु अत्थु ॥
विसु विसय वन्धु दिढवन्धणाइँ ।
घरदारइँ परिहवकारणाइँ ॥
सुय सत्तु विढत्तउ अवहरन्ति ।
जरमरणहँ किंङ्कर किं करन्ति ॥
जीवाउ वाउ हय हय वराय ।
सन्दण सन्दण गय गय जें णाय ॥
तणु तणु जें खणड्ढें खयहों जाइ ।
धणु धणु जि गुणेण वि वङ्कु थाइ ॥

38

exceedingly sad, "Truly life is fleeting. What is the point of good health? I must do whatever it takes to obtain liberation.

Happiness is like a drop of honey, misfortune manifests in full glory like Mount Meru. It would be best that I act so that I achieve the condition of liberation without old age or death.

3

"What has befallen the chamberlain will happen to all of us, someday. Who am I? What is earth? To whom does wealth belong? The throne, umbrellas, it is all impermanent. Youth, the body, life: damn it all! Samsara is worthless, wealth is meaningless. Sensory objects are poison, relatives are firm fetters, houses and wives just bring about contempt. Sons are enemies who snatch away what one has accumulated. What do servants do against old age and death? The life span of a being is like the wind, horses are wretched and miserable, chariots melt away, elephants are known as diseases. The body is just a blade of grass: in half an instant it goes to waste. Riches are a bow: even with its merit—its string—it

दुहिया वि दुहिय माया वि माय ।
समभाउ लेन्ति किर तेण भाय ॥
आयइँ अवरइ मि
सव्वइँ राहवहों समप्पेवि ।
अप्पुणु तउ करमि
थिउ दसरहु एम वियप्पेवि ॥

४

तहिँ अवसरें आइउ सवणसङ्घु ।
परसमयसमीरणगिरिअलङ्घु ॥
दुम्महमहवम्महमहणसीलु ।
भयभङ्कुरभुअणुद्धरणलीलु ॥
अहिविसमविसयविसवेयसमणु ।
खमदमणिसेणिकियमोक्खगमणु ॥
तवसिरिवररामालिङ्घियङ्घु ।
कलिकलुससलिलसोसणपयङ्घु ॥
तित्थङ्करचरणम्बुरुहभमरु ।
कियमोहमहासुरणयरडमरु ॥
तहिँ सच्चभूइ णामेण साहु ।
जाणियसंसारसमुद्धथाहु ॥
मगहाहिउ विसयविरत्तदेहु ।
अवहत्थियपुत्तकलत्तणेहु ॥

remains crooked. A daughter is an enemy; a mother,
an illusion. Because of this, brothers indeed share the
same fate.
I will hand this and everything else to Rama: for my part,
I will practice asceticism." Such was Dasharatha's
intention.

4

At that time a group of mendicants arrived—invulnerable
as a mountain to the wind of other doctrines, skilled
at laying waste to indestructible lust, taking delight
in uplifting a world that is made fragile with fear,
like the bird Garuda* against the poison of the
dangerous snakes that are the sensory objects, and
making their way toward liberation via the ladder of
endurance and restraint, their bodies embraced by
the most charming Lady Austerity, a sun to dry the
dirty water of discord, bees on the lotus-like feet of
the Tirthankaras—causing a stir throughout the city
of the great demon Bewilderment. There was a sage
there named Satyabhuti, the king of Magadha, who
knew the ford through the ocean of samsara, his body
indifferent to the sensory objects, who had waved
away the affection of his sons and wives—

* Mythic bird, enemy of snakes.

गिव्वाणमहागिरि धीरिमाएँ ।
रयणायरगुरु गम्भीरिमाएँ ॥
रिसिसङ्घाहिवइ
सो आउ अउज्झ भडारउ ।
सिवपुरिगमणु करि
दसरहहों णाइँ हक्कारउ ॥

५

पडिवण्णएँ तहिँ तेत्तडएँ कालें ।
तो पुरें रहणेउरचक्कवालें ॥
भामण्डलु मण्डलु परिहरन्तु ।
अच्छइ रिसि सिद्धि व संभरन्तु ॥
वइदेहिविरहवेयण सहन्तु ।
दस कामावत्थउ दक्खवन्तु ॥
पडिहन्ति ण विज्जाहरतियाउ ।
णउ खाणपाणभोयणकियाउ ॥
ण जलद्द ण चन्दण कमलसेज्ज ।
ढुक्कन्ति जन्ति अण्णोण्ण वेज्ज ॥
वाहिज्जइ विरहें दूसहेण ।
णउ फिट्टइ केण वि ओसहेण ॥
णीसासु मुएप्पिणु दीहु दीहु ।
पुणरवि थिउ थक्केँवि जेम सीहुं ॥

like the great mountain of the gods in firmness and the venerable ocean in profundity.

So it was that, like an invitation to Dasharatha to enter into the city of bliss, this noble leader of a group of seers came to Ayodhya.

5

Just as he arrived, Bhamandala in the city of Rathanupurachakravala began to shun his social circle, and like a seer thinking of *siddhi*,* he endured the pain of lovesickness for Videha's daughter, Sita, and manifested the ten stages of love. Vidyadhara women did not appeal to him, nor did activities such as eating or drinking, nor a moist cloth, sandalwood paste, nor a bed of lotuses. Many different doctors came and went. He was afflicted by unbearable lovesickness. No medicine could make it disappear. Uttering a deep, deep sigh and halting, he stood once more as if he were a lion, "I will enjoy the earth-bound

---

* Ultimate liberation.

भूगोयरि भुञ्झमि मण्ड लेवि ।
णीसरिउ ससाहणु सण्णहेवि ॥
पत्तु वियड्ढपुरु
तं णिएॅवि जाउ जाईसरु ।
अण्णहिँ भवगहणें
हउँ होन्तु एत्थु रज्जेसरु ॥

६

मुच्छाविउ तं पेक्खेॅवि पएसु ।
संभरेॅवि भवन्तरु णिरवसेसु ॥
सब्भावें पभणिउ तेण ताउ ।
कुण्डलमण्डिउ णामेण राउ ॥
हउँ होन्तु एत्थु अखलियमरट्टु ।
पिङ्गलु णामेण कुवेरभट्टु ॥
ससिकेउदुहिय अवहरेॅवि आउ ।
परिवसइ कुडीरएॅ किर वराउ ॥
उद्दालिउ मइँ तहों तं कलत्तु ।
सों वि मरेॅवि सुरत्तणु कहिं मि पत्तु ॥
मुउ हउ मि विदेहहें देहें आउ ।
णिउ देवें जाणइजमलजाउ ॥
वर्णें घत्तिउ कण्टेण वि ण भिण्णु ।
पुप्फवइहें पइँ सायरेण दिण्णु ॥

woman by taking her by force." He put on his armor
and set out together with his army.

He reached the city of Vidagdha, and, seeing it, a memory
from a previous life came to him: "In another life
I used to be a king here."

6

When he saw that place and remembered his entire
previous existence, he fainted. He said to his
father with sincerity, "I used to be a king here with
unwavering pride, named Kundalamandita. Kubera's
teacher was named Pingala. He abducted the daughter
of Shashiketu and came here and lived in a hovel, the
poor wretch. I stole his wife away from him.[2] When
he died, he somehow acquired an existence as a god. I
also died and entered the body of Videha. Born a twin
with Janaka's daughter, I was taken away by the god. I
was left in the forest, though not even hurt by a thorn.
With care you gave me to Pushpavati.

वड्ढिउ तुम्ह घरें
जणु सयलु वि ऍउ परियाणइ ।
जणउ जणेरु महु
मायरि विदेह सस जाणइ ॥

७

वित्तन्तु कहेप्पिणु णिरवसेसु ।
गउ वन्दणहत्तिएँ तं पएसु ॥
जहिँ वसइ महारिसि सच्चभूइ ।
जहिँ जिणवरणहवणमहाविभूइ ॥
वइरग्गकालु जहिँ दसरहासु ।
जहिँ सीयरामलक्खणविलासु ॥
सत्तुहणभरह जहिँ मिलिय वे वि ।
गउ तहिँ भामण्डलु जणणु लेवि ॥
जिणु वन्दिउ मोक्खवलग्गजङ्कु ।
पुणु गुरुपरिवाडिएँ सवणसङ्कु ॥
पुणु किउ संभासणु समउ तेहिँ ।
सत्तुहणभरहवललक्खणेहिँ ॥
जाणाविउ सीयहें भाइ जेम ।
जिह हरिवल साला सावलेव ॥
सुउ परमधम्मु सुहभायणेण ।
तवचरणु लयउ चन्दायणेण ॥

46

I grew up in your home. All the people know this: Janaka is my father, Videha my mother, Janaka's daughter, Sita, my sister."

7

After he had narrated the entire story, he went to that place to praise and revere. There the great seer Satyabhuti resided, the grand splendor of the bathing ceremony of the Jina took place, the moment of Dasharatha's rejection of the material world was at hand, graced by the presence of Sita, Rama, and Lakshmana; both Shatrughna and Bharata were also there. Bhamandala approached, along with his father. He honored the Jina, whose legs had raced up to liberation, as well as the group of mendicants in order of their seniority. Then he conversed with Shatrughna, Bharata, the Baladeva, and Lakshmana. He revealed how he was Sita's brother, and how the Vasudeva and Baladeva were his proud brothers-in-law. Chandragati, a receptacle of happiness, heard the supreme doctrine and took up ascetic practice.

दसरहु अण्णदिणें
किर रामहॊ रज्जु समप्पइ ।
केक्कय ताव मणें
उण्हालएॕ धरणि व तप्पइ ॥

८

णरिन्दस्स सोऊण पव्वज्जयज्जं ।
सरामाहिरामस्स रामस्स रज्जं ॥
ससा दोणरायस्स भग्गाणुराया ।
तुलाकोडिकन्तीलयालिद्धपाया ॥
सपालम्वकञ्जीपहाभिण्णगुज्झा ।
थणुत्तुङ्गभारेण जा णिण्णमज्झा ॥
णवासोयवच्छच्छयाछायपाणी ।
वरालाविणीकोइलालाववाणी ॥
महामोरपिच्छोहसंकासकेसा ।
अणङ्गस्स भल्ली व पच्छण्णवेसा ॥
गया केक्कया जत्थ अत्थाणमग्गो ।
णरिन्दो सुरिन्दो व पीढं वलग्गो ॥
वरो मग्गिओ णाह सो एस कालो ।
महं णन्दणो ठाउ रज्जाणुपालो ॥
पिए होउ एवं तओ सावलेवो ।
समायारिओ लक्खणो रामएवो ॥

48

It was said that the following day Dasharatha would
    entrust the kingdom to Rama. Kaikeyi at once was
    scorched in her heart, like the earth in summer.

8

After a night's sleep, the king was set for his renunciation,
    and for Rama, the darling of his lovely wife, the
    kingship lay ahead. The affection of King Drona's
    sister, Kaikeyi, was crushed. Her feet enveloped by
    anklets like beautiful creepers, her private parts
    displayed by the radiance of her low-cut girdle, bent at
    the waist under the weight of her prominent breasts,
    her hands like the charming foliage of a young *aśoka*
    tree, her voice like the sound of a vina or a cuckoo,
    her hair like a large bundle of peacock feathers, as if
    she were the wife of Kama the bodiless, in disguise,
    Kaikeyi went toward the assembly hall, where the king
    had mounted his throne as if he were the king of the
    gods. She asked for the boon, "Lord, this is that time.
    Let my son stand as protector of the kingdom."—"So
    be it, my love." Then he summoned proud Lakshmana
    and Lord Rama:

जइ तुहुँ पुत्तु महु
तो एत्तिउ पेसणु किज्जइ ।
छत्तइँ वइसणउ
वसुमइ भरहहों अप्पिज्जइ ॥

९

अहवइ भरहु वि आसण्णभव्वु ।
सो चिन्तइ अथिरु असारु सव्वु ॥
घरु परियणु जीविउ सरीरु वित्तु ।
अच्छइ तवचरणणिहित्तचित्तु ॥
पइँ मुऍवि तासु जइ दिण्णु रज्जु ।
तो लक्खणु लक्खइँ हणइ अज्जु ॥
ण वि हउँ ण वि भरहु ण केक्कया वि ।
सत्तुहणु कुमारु ण सुप्पहा वि ॥
तं णिसुणेॅवि पप्फुल्लियमुहेण ।
वोल्लिज्जइ दसरहतणुरुहेण ॥
पुत्तहों पुत्तत्तणु एत्तिउं जें ।
जं कुलु ण चडावइ वसणपुञ्जें ॥
जं णियजणणहों आणाविहेउ ।
जं करइ विवक्खहों पाणछेउ ॥
किं पुत्तें पुणु पयपूरणेण ।
गुणहीणें हिययविसूरणेण ॥

"If you are my son, then execute this order: the umbrellas, throne, and the earth I entrust to Bharata.

9

"To be more precise: Bharata is destined to attain salvation in the near future. He considers everything impermanent and unessential: a house, a retinue, life, the body, wealth. His mind is set solely on asceticism. If I forsake you and give the kingship to him, then Lakshmana will kill lakhs this very day. Neither I, nor Bharata, nor Kaikeyi, nor prince Shatrughna, nor Suprabha will remain." Rama's face bloomed with a smile when he heard this; he spoke, "For a son, being a son means just this much: that he does not cause his family to ascend a great heap of misfortune, that he is obliged to obey the orders of his father, and that he cuts off the life of the enemy. What good is a useless[3] son, devoid of good qualities, who torments the heart?

लक्खणु ण वि हणइ
तवु भावहाँ सच्चु पयासहाँ ।
भुञ्जउ भरहु महि
हउँ जामि ताय वणवासहाँ ॥

हक्कारिउ भरहु णरेसरेण ।
पुणु वुच्चइ णेहमहाभरेण ॥
तउ छत्तइँ तउ वइसणउ रज्जु ।
साहेवउ मइँ अप्पणउ कज्जु ॥
तं वयणु सुणेॅवि दुम्मियमणेण ।
धिक्कारिउ केक्कयणन्दणेण ॥
तुहुँ ताय धिगत्थु धिगत्थु रज्जु ।
मायरि धिगत्थु सिरेँ पडउ वज्जु ॥
णउ जाणहुँ महिलहँ को सहाउ ।
जोव्वणमएण ण गणन्ति पाउ ॥
णउ वुज्झहि तुहु मि महामयन्धु ।
किं रामु मुऍॅवि महु पट्टवन्धु ॥
सप्पुरिस वि चञ्चलचित्त होन्ति ।
मणेँ जुत्ताजुत्तु ण चिन्तवन्ति ॥
माणिक्कु मुऍॅवि को लेइ कच्चु ।
कामन्धहाँ किर कहिँ तणउ सच्चु ॥

Lakshmana will not kill anyone. You should devote yourself to asceticism and let your truthfulness shine! Bharata may have the earth. I will go to stay in the forest, father."

10

The king summoned Bharata and, weighed down by the great burden of his affection, he spoke, "The royal parasols are now yours, the throne is yours, as is the kingdom. I must strive to work on my self." Hearing these words, Kaikeyi's son's heart grew distressed, and he cursed, "Damn you, father! Damn the kingdom! Damn my mother—may a thunderbolt fall on her head! We understand nothing of the nature of women. Intoxicated by their own youth, they fail to account for sin. Even you do not understand, blind as you are with passion. Why would you forsake Rama and tie the royal turban on me? Even good people have fickle minds: they do not deliberate on what is right and wrong in their heart. Who would give up a ruby and choose glass, instead? Indeed, where is the truthfulness of a man blinded by lust?

अच्छहुँ पुणु वि घरें
सत्तुहणु रामु हउँ लक्खणु ।
अलिउ म होहि तुहुँ
महि भुञ्जें भडारा अप्पुणु ॥

११

सुयवयणविरमें दससन्दणेण ।
वुच्चइ अणरण्णहों नन्दणेण ॥
केक्कयहें रज्जु रामहों पवासु ।
पव्वज्ज मज्झु ऍउ जगें पगासु ॥
तुहुँ पालें घरासउ परमरम्मु ।
णउ आयहों पासिउ को वि धम्मु ॥
दिज्जइ जइवरहुँ महप्पहाणु ।
सुअभेसहअभयाहारदाणु ॥
रक्खिवज्जइ सीलु कुसीलणासु ।
किज्जइ जिणपुज्ज महोववासु ॥
जिणवन्दण वारापेक्खवकरणु ।
सल्लेहणकालु समाहिमरणु ॥
ऍहु सव्वहुँ धम्महुँ परमधम्मु ।
जो पालइ तहों सुरमणुयजम्मु ॥
तं वयणु सुणेवि सइत्तणेण ।
वुच्चइ सुहमइदोहित्तएण ॥

What is more: we are staying in the house, Shatrughna, Rama, I, and Lakshmana. Do not be untrue! Rule the earth yourself, noble lord!"

11

When his son stopped speaking, Dasharatha, the son of Anaranya, said, "For Kaikeyi the kingdom, for Rama exile, and renunciation for me: this much is clear to all the world. You get to maintain the most enjoyable stage of life, that of a householder. No other stage of life comes near it. For great ascetics the best gift that is given is medicine for instruction and food for comfort.[4] For the householder, good conduct and the annihilation of immorality must be maintained, the Jina worshiped, a festival and a fast sponsored, the praise to the Jina offered, the duty of watching the door for passing mendicants observed, and a period of absolute abstention and a death in meditation ensured. This is the supreme of all ways of life. He who guards it will have a rebirth as a god or a human." At this, the self-assured grandson of Sukhamati said,

जइ घरवासें सुहु
एउं जें ताय पडिवज्जहि ।
तो तिणसमु गण्णेवि
कज्जेण केण पव्वज्जहि ॥

१२

तो खेडु मुऍवि दसरहेण वुत्तु ।
जइ सच्चउ तुहुँ महु तणउ पुत्तु ॥
तो किं पव्वज्जहें करहि विग्घु ।
कुलवंसधुरन्धरु होहि सिग्घु ॥
केक्कयहें सच्चु जं दिण्णु आसि ।
तं णिरिणु करहि गुणरयणरासि ॥
तो कोसलदुहियादुल्लहेण ।
वोल्लिज्जइ सीयावल्लहेण ॥
गुणु केवलु वसुहऍ भुत्तियाएँ ।
किं खणें खणें उत्तपउत्तियाएँ ॥
पालिज्जउ तायहों तणिय वाय ।
लइ महु उवरोहें पिहिवि भाय ॥
तो एम भणन्तें राहवेण ।
णिव्वूढाणेयमहाहवेण ॥
खीरोवमहण्णवणिम्मलेण ।
गिव्वाणमहागिरिअविचलेण ॥

"Father, if you accept that there is this much joy in staying at home, then why do you renounce the world, regarding it like grass?"

12

Dasharatha abandoned his playful approach and said, "If you are truly my son, then why do you create an impediment for my renunciation? Soon you will be the leader of our family and lineage. You, an ocean of virtues, must redeem the promise that I made to Kaikeyi." Then Sita's husband, the precious son of Kosala's daughter, spoke, "Your only virtue lies in ruling the earth. What's the point of talking back and forth, time and again? Let father's words be safeguarded. Accept the earth as a favor to me, brother." Speaking thus, Rama, the descendant of Raghu, successful in numerous great battles, spotless like the milk ocean, and unwavering like the great mountain of the gods,

पेक्खन्तहों जणहों
सुरकरिकरपवरपचण्डेहिँ ।
पट्टु णिवद्धु सिरें
रहुसुएॅण सयं भुवदण्डेहिँ ॥

Raghu's progeny, himself tied the turban to Bharata's head with his arms like clubs, eminent and formidable like the trunks of the elephant of the gods, as the people looked on.

तेवीसमो संधि

तहिँ मुणिसुव्वयतित्थे
बुहयणकण्णरसायणु ।
रावणरामहुँ जुज्झु
तं णिसुणहु रामायणु ॥

१

णमिऊण भडारउ रिसहजिणु ।
पुणु कव्वहों उप्परि करमि मणु ॥
जगें लोयहुँ सुयणहुँ पण्डियहुँ ।
सद्त्थसत्थपरिचट्ठियहुँ ॥
किं चित्तइँ गेण्हेँवि सक्कियइँ ।
वासेण वि जाइँ ण रञ्जियइँ ॥
तो कवणु गहणु अम्हारिसेँहिँ ।
वायरणविहूणेँहिँ आरिसेँहिँ ॥
कइ अत्थि अणेय भेयभरिय ।
जे सुयणसहासेँहिँ आयरिय ॥
चक्कलएँहिँ कुलएँहिँ खन्धएँहिँ ।
पवणुद्धुअरासालुद्धएँहिँ ॥
मञ्जरियविलसिणिणकुडेँहिँ ।
सुहछन्देँहिँ सद्देँहिँ खडहडेँहिँ ॥
हउँ किं पि ण जाणमि मुक्खु मणें ।

60

Chapter 23

Listen to this Ramayana, an elixir for the ears of the wise, the war between Ravana and Rama in the ford of Muni Suvrata.

1

Bowing to the noble Jina Rishabha, I again direct my
   mind to the poem. Could I captivate the minds of the
   common people on earth, of good folk, and of wise
   men, who mount handbooks for word meanings,
   minds whom even Vyasa[1] failed to charm? Then
   what to do for people such as us, who are wanting
   in grammar? There are numerous poets of different
   kinds, who are respected by thousands of good people,
   with *cakkalaka, kulaka, skandhaka, pavanoddhuta,*
   rāsālubdhaka, mañjarī, vilāsinī, narkuṭa, and
   khaḍahaḍa verses, and words in other beautiful
   meters.[2] I do not know anything, in my heart I am
   just a fool. Nevertheless I will disclose my views to

णिय बुद्धि पयासमि तो वि जणें ॥
जं सयलें वि तिहुवणें वित्थरिउ ।
आरम्भिउ पुणु राहवचरिउ ॥
भरहहों वड्ढएँ पट्टें
तो णिव्वूढमहाहउ ।
पट्टणु उज्झ मुएवि
गउ वणवासहों राहउ ॥

२

जं परिवड्ढु पट्टु परिओसें ।
जयमङ्गलजयतूरणिघोसें ॥
दसरहचरणजुयलु जयकारेवि ।
दाइयमच्छरु मणें अवहारेवि ॥
सम्पय रिद्धि विद्धि अवगण्णेवि ।
तायहों तणउ सच्चु परिमण्णेवि ॥
णिग्गउ वलु वलु णाइँ हरेप्पिणु ।
लक्खणो वि लक्खणइँ लएप्पिणु ॥
संचल्लेहिँ तेहिँ विद्दाणउ ।
ठिउ हेट्टामुहु दसरहु राणउ ॥
हियवएँ णाइँ तिसूलें सल्लिउ ।
राहउ किह वणवासहों घल्लिउ ॥

62

the people. I begin once more the deeds of Rama, the descendant of Raghu, which have spread throughout all the three worlds.

When he had tied the turban to Bharata, Rama, the victor of great battles, left the city of Ayodhya and went to live in the forest.

2

Once the Baladeva had happily tied on the turban to the sound of triumphant victory songs and drums, he extolled Dasharatha's two feet, banished anger toward his relatives from his heart, disregarded success, plenty, and prosperity, honored the promise of his father, and went away, as if removing his power, as did Lakshmana, taking away his good features. While they left, King Dasharatha stood dejected, his face cast down, as if pierced in the heart with a trident, "How is Rama banished to a life in the forest? Damn it! Damn

धिगधिगत्थु जणएण पवोल्लिउ ।
लज्झिउ कुलकमो वि सुमहल्लउ ॥
अहवइ जइ मइँ सच्चु ण पालिउ ।
तो णियणामु गोत्तु मइँ मइलिउ ॥
वरि गउ रामु ण सच्चु विणासिउ ।
सच्चु महन्तउ सव्वहाँ पासिउ ॥
सच्चें अम्बरें तवइ दिवायरु ।
सच्चें समउ ण चुक्कइ सायरु ॥
सच्चें वाउ वाइ महि पच्चइ ।
सच्चें ओसहि खयहाँ ण वच्चइ ॥
जो ण वि पालइ सच्चु
मुहें दाढियउ वहन्तउ ।
णिवडइ णरयसमुद्दें
वसु जेंम अलिउ चवन्तउ ॥

३

चिन्तावण्णु णराहिउ जावेंहिँ ।
वलु णियणिलउ पराइउ तावेंहिँ ॥
दुम्मणु एन्तु णिहालिउ मायएँ ।
पुणु णिहसेवि वुत्तु पियवायएँ ॥
दिवें दिवें चडहि तुरङ्गमणाएँहिँ ।
अज्जु काइँ अणुवाहणु पाएँहिँ ॥
दिवें दिवें वन्दिणविन्देंहिँ थुव्वहि ।

64

it!" The father said, "A most significant step in the family line is passed over. On the other hand, had I not guarded my promise, then I would have defiled our name and clan. It was for the best that Rama went and that my truthfulness did not go to waste. Truth is more important than anything. Because of truth the sun shines in the sky, the ocean does not go beyond its shore, the wind blows, and the earth is fertile, and medicine does no harm.

He who does not guard truth, though bearing the mustache on his face, falls into the ocean of hell, like Vasu who told a lie."[3]

3

While the king was immersed in worry, the Baladeva arrived at his quarters. His mother saw that his spirits were low as he approached. She smiled and then spoke with a loving voice, "Day after day you mount horses and elephants: why today are you shoeless and on foot? Day after day bands of bards praise you: why

अज्जु काइँ थुव्वन्तु ण सुव्वहिँ ॥
दिवें दिवें धुव्वहि चमरसहासेँहिँ ।
अज्जु काइँ तउ को वि ण पासेँहिँ ॥
दिवें दिवें लोयहिँ वुच्चहि राणउ ।
अज्जु काइँ दीसहि विद्दाणउ ॥
तं णिसुणेवि वलेण पजम्पिउ ।
भरहहों सयलु वि रज्जु समप्पिउ ॥
जामि माएँ दिढ हियवएँ होज्जहि ।
जं दुम्मिय तं सव्वु खमेज्जहि ॥
जें आउच्छिय माय
हा हा पुत्त भणन्ती ।
अपराइय महएवि
महियलें पडिय रुयन्ती ॥

४

रामें जणणि जं जें आउच्छिय ।
णिरु णिच्चेयण तक्खणें मुच्छिय ॥
लज्जियाहिँ हा माएँ भणन्तिहिँ ।
हरियन्दणेण सित्त रोवन्तिहिँ ॥
चमरुक्खेवेँहिँ किय पडिवायण ।
दुक्खु दुक्खु पुणु जाय सचेयण ॥
अज्झु वलन्ति समुट्ठिय राणी ।
सप्पि व दण्डाहय विद्दाणी ॥

today do we not hear your praise? Day after day you
are fanned with thousands of flywhisks: why today are
there none by your side? Day after day the people call
you king: why today do you seem so dejected?" At this,
the Baladeva answered, "The kingdom has entirely
been entrusted to Bharata. I am going, mother. Be
brave in your heart. Though you are distressed, please
forgive all of it!"

When he said goodbye to his mother, the chief queen
Aparajita fell weeping to the ground, crying out for
her son.

4

The moment that Rama bid his mother goodbye, she
instantly lost consciousness and fainted. The servant
girls, crying and saying, "Oh, mother," sprinkled her
with yellow sandalwood juice. They made a breeze by
waving flywhisks. With great difficulty she became
conscious again. The queen stood up, convulsing
her body, as distressed as a female snake beaten with
sticks. Her blue eyes were afflicted by the rawness of

णीलक्खण णीरामुम्माहिय ।
पुणु वि सदुक्खउ मेल्लिय धाहिय ॥
हा हा काइँ वुत्तु पइँ हलहर ।
दसरहवंसदीव जगसुन्दर ॥
पइँ विणु को पलङ्कें सुवेसइ ।
पइँ विणु को अत्थाणें वईसइ ॥
पइँ विणु को हयगयहुँ चडेसइ ।
पइँ विणु को झिन्दुऍण रमेसइ ॥
पइँ विणु रायलच्छि को माणइ ।
पइँ विणु को तम्बोलु समाणइ ॥
पइँ विणु को परवलु भञ्ञेसइ ।
पइँ विणु को मइँ साहारेसइ ॥
तं कूवारु सुणेवि
अन्तेउरु मुहवुण्णउ ।
लक्खणरामविओऍं
धाह मुएवि परुण्णउ ॥

her tears. Again she emitted howls full of sorrow, "Ah, ah, what did you say, Baladeva, light of Dasharatha's dynasty, most handsome boy in all the world? Who but you will sleep on this bed? Who but you will sit in the assembly hall? Who but you will mount horses and elephants? Who but you will play with the ball? Who but you will revel in the glory of kingship? Who but you will consume betel? Who but you will crush the enemy army? Who but you will comfort me?"

Hearing this lament, the harem, with alarm on their faces, moaned and wept at the departure of Lakshmana and Rama.

५

ता एत्थन्तरें असुरविमद्दें ।
धीरिय णियजणेरि वलहद्दें ॥
धीरिय होहि माऍ किं रोवहि ।
लुहि लोयण अप्पाणु म सोयहि ॥
जिह रविकिरणेहिँ ससि ण पहावइ ।
तिह मइँ होन्तें भरहु ण भावइ ॥
तें कज्जें वणवासें वसेवउ ।
तायहों तणउ सच्चु पालेवउ ॥
दाहिणदेसें करेविणु थत्ती ।
तुम्हहँ पासें एइ सोमित्ती ॥
एम भणेप्पिणु चलिउ तुरन्तउ ।
सयलु वि परियणु आउच्छन्तउ ॥
धवलकसणणीलुप्पलसामेहिँ ।
घरु मुञ्चन्तउ लक्खणरामेहिँ ॥
सोह ण देइ ण चित्तहों भावइ ।
णहु णिच्चन्दाइच्चउ णावइ ॥
णं कियउद्धहत्थु धाहावइ ।
वलहों कलत्तहाणि णं दावइ ॥
भरहणरिन्दहों णं जाणावइ ।
हरिवल जन्त णिवारहि णरवइ ॥
पुणु पाआरभुयउ पसरेप्पिणु ।
णाइँ णिवारइ आलिङ्गेप्पिणु ॥

70

5

Meanwhile the Baladeva, destroyer of demons, consoled
his mother, "Be brave, mother, why are you crying?
Wipe your eyes, do not feel sorry for yourself. Just
as the moon cannot shine because of the sun's rays,
Bharata cannot establish himself as long as I am
present. For that reason, I must go and live in the
forest. Father's truthfulness must be safeguarded.
Once we have taken up our abode in the southern
country, Sumitri's son will come to you." After these
words he quickly left, bidding farewell to the entire
retinue. The home that Lakshmana and Rama, a
white and dark blue lotus, had left behind ceased to
look beautiful; no longer did it please the mind, like
the sky without the moon and the sun. It was as if it
wailed with its hands held high, as if it showed the
Baladeva the coming loss of his wife, as if it said to
King Bharata, "King, stop the Vasudeva and Baladeva
from going!" Then, stretching out the arms that were
its high ramparts and embracing them, it was as if it
held them back.

चावसिलीमुहहत्थ
वे वि समुण्णयमाणा ।
तहों मन्दिरहों रुयन्तहों
णाइँ विणिग्गय पाणा ॥

६

तो एत्थन्तरें णयणाणन्दें ।
संचल्लन्तें राहवचन्दें ॥
सीयाएविहें वयणु णिहालिउ ।
णं चित्तेण चित्तु संचालिउ ॥
णियमन्दिरहों विणिग्गय जाणइ ।
णं हिमवन्तहों गङ्ग महाणइ ॥
णं छन्दहों णिग्गय गायत्ती ।
णं सद्दहों णीसरिय विहत्ती ॥
णाइँ किति सप्पुरिसविमुक्की ।
णाइँ रम्भ णियथाणहों चुक्की ॥
सुललियचलणजुयलमल्हन्ती ।
णं गयघड भडथड विहडन्ती ॥
णेउरहारडोरगुप्पन्ती ।
वहुतम्वोलपड्डें खुप्पन्ती ॥
हेट्ठामुह कमकमलु णियच्छेवि ।
अवराइयसुमित्ति आउच्छेवि ॥

With bow and arrows in hand, those two proud men went
away, as if they were the life-breaths of the palace, as
it cried.

6

Meanwhile, as moon-like Rama, the descendant of Raghu,
a joy to the eye, departed, he looked at the face of the
lady Sita. His focus was replaced by another focus, as
it were. Janaka's daughter emerged from her dwelling,
like the great river Ganga from the Himalaya, like
the *gāyatrī** arose from the Veda, like a case-ending
follows after a word, like the renown that is emitted by
good people, as if she were Rambha[†] who had strayed
from her abode. Pattering playfully with her most
charming pair of feet, she was like a troop of elephants
trampling a horde of soldiers; with her anklets,
necklace, and girdle tangled up, sinking in the mud
of abundant betel, her face cast down looking at her

---

* A Vedic meter.
† A famous celestial nymph.

णिग्गय सीयाएवि
सिय हरन्ति णियभवणहाँ ।
रामहाँ दुक्खुप्पत्ति
असणि णाइँ दहवयणहाँ ॥

रायवारु वलु वोलिउ जावेहिँ ।
लक्खणु मणें आरोसिउ तावेहिँ ॥
उट्ठिउ धगधगन्तु जसलुद्धउ ।
णाइँ घिएण सित्तु धूमद्धउ ॥
णाइँ मइन्दु महाघणगज्जिएँ ।
तिह सोमित्ति कुविउ गर्में सज्जिएँ ॥
के धरणिन्दफणामणि तोडिउ ।
के सुरकुलिसदण्डु भुएँ मोडिउ ॥
के पलयाणलें अप्पउ ढोइउ ।
के आरुट्ठउ सणि अवलोइउ ॥
के रयणायरु सोसेवि सक्किउ ।
के आइच्चहाँ तेउ कलङ्किउ ॥
के महिमण्डलु वाहहिँ टालिउ ।
के तइलोक्कचक्कु संचालिउ ॥
के जिउ कालु कियन्तु महाहवें ।
को पहु अण्णु जियन्तएँ राहवें ॥

lotus-like feet, Lady Sita said goodbye to Aparajita and Sumitri and set out, robbing her house of its luster, the origin of Rama's sorrow, and like a lightning bolt for ten-faced Ravana.

7

As the Baladeva passed through the royal gate, Lakshmana felt rage in his heart. He rose up, roaring and longing for glory. Just like a fire sprinkled with ghee, or a lion at the thundering of a great cloud, Sumitri's son grew angry now that the departure had been arranged: "Who tore out the jewel from Dharanendra's* hood? Who crushed Indra's thunderbolt in his hand? Who brought himself near the fire of destruction? Who has looked upon infuriated Saturn?[4] Who was capable of drying up the ocean? Who befouled the glow of the sun? Who disturbed the earth's sphere with his arms? Who made the wheel of the three worlds revolve? Who vanquished Yama, the god of death, in a great battle? Who else is king, so long as Raghu's descendant Rama is alive?

---

* Leader of the serpent gods.

अहवइ किं वहुएण
भरहु धरेप्पिणु अज्जु ।
रामहॊ णीसावण्णु
देमि सहत्थें रज्जु ॥

८

तो फुरन्तरत्तन्तलोयणो ।
कलिकियन्तकालो व्व भीसणो ॥
दुण्णिवारु दुव्वारवारणो ।
सुउ चवन्तु जं एम लक्खणो ॥
भणइ रामु तइलोक्कसुन्दरो ।
पइँ विरुद्धें किं को वि दुद्धरो ॥
जसु पडन्ति गिरि सिंहणाऍणं ।
कवणु गहणु तो भरहराऍणं ॥
कवणु चोज्जु जं दिवि दिवायरे ।
अमिउ चन्दें जलणिवहु सायरे ॥
सोक्खु मोक्खें दयधम्मु जिणवरे ।
विसु भुयङ्गें वर लील गयवरे ॥
धणऍं रिद्धि सोहग्गु वम्महे ।
गइ मरालें जयलच्छि महुमहे ॥
पउरुसं च पइँ कुविऍं लक्खणे ।
भणेॆवि एम करें धरिउ तक्खणे ॥

76

Or rather, why go on? Today, I will take Bharata and give
the kingdom over entirely to Rama with my own
hand."

8

When he heard what Lakshmana—his eyes throbbing
and red at their extremities, terrifying like Kali* and
Yama, the god of death, unrestrainable yet restrainer
of the unrestrainable—was saying, Rama, the most
handsome man in the three worlds, spoke: "When
you are angry, and your lion's roar can bring down
mountains, is there anyone who can stand against
you? What could be gained by King Bharata? Is it
any wonder that there is light in the sun, ambrosia in
the moon, water in the ocean, bliss in liberation, the
teaching of compassion in the great Jina, poison in a
snake, great vitality in a mighty elephant, prosperity
in wealth, pleasure in love, a particular gait in a duck,
victorious Lakshmi within Madhu's slayer,† and manly
valor in you, Lakshmana, when you are angry!" With
these words he immediately stopped him by the hand:

* The personified age of discord.
† Vishnu.

रज्जें किज्जइ काइँ
तायहाँ सच्चुविणासें ।
सोलह वरिसइँ जाम
वे वि वसहुँ वणवासें ॥

९

एह वोल्लु णिम्माइय जावेंहिँ ।
ढुक्कु भाणु अत्थवणहाँ तावेंहिँ ॥
जाय सज्झ आरत्त पदीसिय ।
णं गयघड सिन्दूरविहूसिय ॥
सूरमंसरुहिरावलिचच्चिय ।
णिसियरि व्व आणन्दु पणच्चिय ॥
गलिय सज्झ पुणु रयणि पराइय ।
जगु गिलेइ णं सुत्तु महाइय ॥
कहिं मि दिव्व दीवयसय वोहिय ।
फणिमणि व्व पजलन्त सुसोहिय ॥
तित्थु कालें णिरु णिज्झं दुग्गमें ।
णीसरन्ति रयणिहें चन्दुग्गमें ॥
वासुएववलएव महव्वल ।
साहम्मिय साहम्मियवच्छल ॥
रणभरणिव्वाहण णिव्वाहण ।
णिग्गय णीसाहण णीसाहण ॥

"What good is the kingdom, if it destroys father's truthfulness? Let us both pass the next sixteen years in the forest."

9

As these words resounded, the sun set. The twilight that arose appeared red like a troop of elephants decorated with vermilion, like a female demon dancing with delight, smeared with streaks of blood from the flesh of the sun. The twilight faded and almighty night arrived: it seemed to devour the slumbering world. In one place, hundreds of heavenly lamps were lit, like gleaming snake gems, shining brightly.[5] At that time, indeed by all means under difficult circumstances, at night as the moon came up, they set out. The mighty Vasudeva and Baladeva departed: sons of different mothers and affectionate toward people of their own faith, bearing the weight of war and without vehicles, without an army and without ornaments.[6]

विगयपओलि पवोलेंवि खाइय ।
सिद्धकूडु जिणभवणु पराइय ॥
जं पायारवारविप्फुरियउ ।
पोत्थासित्थगन्धवित्थरियउ ॥
गज्झतरङ्गहँ रङ्गसमुज्जलु ।
हिमइरिकुन्दचन्दजसणिम्मलु ॥
तहों भवणहों पासेहिँ
विविह महादुम दिट्ठा ।
णं संसारभएण
जिणवरसरणें पइट्ठा ॥

१०

तं णिएँवि भुवणु भुवणेसरहों ।
पुणु किउ पणिवाउ जिणेसरहों ॥
जय गयभय रायरोसविलय ।
जय मयणमहण तिहुवणतिलय ॥
जय खमदमतववयणियमकरण ।
जय कलिमलकोहकसायहरण ॥
जय कामकोहअरिदप्पदलण ।
जय जाइजरामरणत्तिहरण ॥
जय जय तवसूर तिलोयहिय ।
जय मणिविचित्तअरुणें सहिय ॥

80

Having crossed the moat away from the main road,
they reached Siddhakuta, a temple to the Jina, with
its sparkling ramparts and doors, abounding in
manuscripts and the smell of food offerings, splendid
with color like the waves of the Ganga, spotless and
beautiful like the Himalaya, downy jasmine, or the
moon.

At the sides of this temple various trees could be seen, as
if they sought refuge with the great Jina out of fear of
samsara.

10

When they saw that abode of the master of the world,
they bowed humbly to the lord Jina: "Hail, fearless
one, ruin to passion and rage. Hail, destroyer of
lust, ornament of the three worlds. Hail to you, who
accomplishes endurance, discipline, ascetic practice,
the vows, and restraint. Hail to you, remover of the
filth of discord, anger, and the passions. Hail to you,
crusher of the pride of the enemies, lust and anger.
Hail to you, who takes away the pain of birth, old
age, and death. Hail, hail, hero of ascetic practice,
benefactor of the three worlds. Hail to you, who are
accompanied by a mind like a brilliant sun. Hail to

जय धम्ममहारहवीढें ठिय ।
जय सिद्धिवरङ्गणरण्णपिय ॥
जय संजमगिरिसिहरुग्गमिय ।
जय इन्दणरिन्दचन्दणमिय ॥
जय सत्तमहाभयहयदमण ।
जय जिणरवि णाणम्वरगमण ॥
जय दुक्क्रियकम्मकुमुयडहण ।
जय चउगइरयणितिमिरमहण ॥
जय इन्दियदुद्दमदणुदलण ।
जय जक्खमहोरगथुयचलण ॥
जय केवलकिरणुज्जोयकर ।
जय भवियरविन्दाणन्दयर ॥
जय जय भुवणेक्कचक्कभमिय ।
जय मोक्खमहीहरें अत्थमिय ॥
भावें तिहि मि जणेहिँ
वन्दण करेवि जिणेसहों ।
पयहिण देवि तिवार
पुणु चलियइँ वणवासहों ॥

you, who sits on the seat of the great chariot of the doctrine. Hail Sun[7] to the lovely woman Siddhi. Hail to you, who has climbed to the top of the mountain of discipline. Hail to you, before whom Indra, kings, and the moon bow. Hail to you, who restrains those seven horses, the great fears.[8] Hail sun-like Jina, advancing in the sky of knowledge. Hail to you, who scorches the lotuses of karma from bad deeds. Hail to you, who dispels the darkness of night, the four modes of existence.[9] Hail to you, who crushes the invincible demons, the senses. Hail to you, whose feet are praised by Yakshas and Mahoragas. Hail to you, who brings light with the rays of your omniscience. Hail to you, who causes joy among those who are capable of salvation, as if they were lotuses and you the sun. Hail, hail to you, who revolves the unique wheel of the teaching in the world. Hail to you, who passed away on the mountain of liberation."

Sincerely praising the lord Jina and circling him thrice, the threesome then moved on to their stay in the forest.

११

रयणिहें मज्झें पयट्टइ राहवु ।
ताम णियच्छिउ परमु महाहवु ॥
कुद्धइँ विद्धइँ पुलयविसट्टइँ ।
मिहुणइँ वलइँ जेम अब्भिट्टइँ ॥
वलु वलु एक्कमेक्क कोक्कन्तइँ ।
मरु मरु पहरु पहरु जम्पन्तइँ ॥
सर हुङ्कारसार मेल्लन्तइँ ।
गरुअपहारहँ उरुउड्डुन्तइँ ॥
खणें ओवडियइँ अहर डसन्तइँ ।
खणें किलिविण्डिहिण्डि दरिसन्तइँ ॥
खणें वहु वालालुञ्चि करन्तइँ ।
खणें णिप्फन्दइँ सेउ फुसन्तइँ ॥
तं पेक्खेप्पिणु सुरयमहाहउ ।
सीयहें वयणु पजोयइ राहउ ॥
पुणु वि हसन्तइँ केलि करन्तइँ ।
चलियइँ हट्टमग्गु जोयन्तइँ ॥
जे वि रमन्ता आसि
लक्खणरामहुँ सड्ढेंवि ।
णावइ सुरयासत्त
आवण थिय मुहु ढड्ढेंवि ॥

11

In the middle of the night Rama, the descendant of
   Raghu, set out. At that time he observed a great war:
   fierce, exalted couples, swelling with erect body hair,
   attacked as if they were armies, calling each other,
   "Turn around! Turn around!" saying, "Die! Die! Hit
   me! Hit me," emitting sounds—chiefly moans—as
   arrows, bouncing up high from the intense thrusts.[10]
   At one time, they charged, biting their lips, then they
   demonstrated moving about as in a fight, then they
   pulled each other's hair again and again, then they
   were motionless, wiping away their sweat. Beholding
   that great war of lovemaking, Rama, the descendant
   of Raghu, looked at Sita's face. Laughing and
   frolicking they again moved on, observing the market
   road.
It was as if the shops, keen on sexual pleasure, had been
   making love, and now stood there covering their face,
   apprehensive of Lakshmana and Rama.

१२

उज्झहें दाहिणदिसएँ विणिग्गय ।
णाइँ णिरंकुस मत्त महागय ॥
ण सहइ पुरि वललक्खणमुक्की ।
मुक्क कुणारि व पेसणचुक्की ॥
पुणु थोवन्तरेँ वित्थयणामहों ।
तरुवर णमिय सुभिच्छ व रामहों ॥
उट्ठिय विहय वमालु करन्ता ।
णं वन्दिण मङ्गलइँ पढन्ता ॥
अद्धकोसु संपाइय जावेँहिँ ।
विमलु विहाणु चउद्दिसु तावेँहिँ ॥
णिसिणिसियरिएँ आसि जं गिलियउ ।
णाइँ पडीवउ जउ उग्गिलियउ ॥
रेहइ सूरविम्बु उग्गन्तउ ।
णावइ सुकइकव्वु पहवन्तउ ॥
पच्छएँ साहणु ताम पधाइउ ।
लहु हलहेइहेँ पासु पराइउ ॥
सीयसलक्खणु रामु
पणमिउ णरवरविन्देँहिँ ।
णं वन्दिउ अहिसेएँ
जिणु वत्तीसहिँ इन्देँहिँ ॥

12

They departed from Ayodhya in the southern direction,
    like great rutting elephants untrammeled by goads.
    Abandoned by the Baladeva and Lakshmana, the city
    did not look beautiful, but like an abandoned bad wife
    who had strayed from her duties. Then, a little farther,
    great trees like good servants bowed before Rama,
    with his widespread fame. Birds flew up causing a
    riot of sound, like bards reading out benedictory
    songs. When they reached half a *krośa** distance, the
    bright daybreak appeared all around. It was as if the
    world, which had been devoured by the female demon
    of the night, was regurgitated. The rising sun disk
    shone, like the poetry of a good poet, full of brilliance.
    Meanwhile, the army came after them. It quickly
    arrived near the Baladeva.
The troops bowed before Rama, Lakshmana, and Sita,
    just as the thirty-two Indras praised the Jina at his
    consecration.

---

* Approximately one mile.

१३

हेसन्ततुरङ्गमवाहणेण ।
परियरिउ रामु णियसाहणेण ॥
णं दिसगउ लीलएँ पयइँ देन्तु ।
तं देसु पराइउ पारियत्तु ॥
अण्णु वि थोवन्तरु जाइ जाम ।
गम्भीर महाणइ दिट्ठु ताम ॥
परिहच्छमच्छपुच्छुच्छलन्ति ।
फेणावलितोयतुसार देन्ति ॥
कारण्डडिम्भडुम्भियसरोह ।
वरकमलकरम्वियजलपओह ॥
हंसावलिपक्खवसमुल्लसन्ति ।२
कल्लोलवोलआवत्त दिन्ति ॥
सोहइ वहुवणगयजूहसहिय ।
डिण्डीरपिण्ड दरिसन्ति अहिय ॥
उच्छलइ वलइ पडिखलइ धाइ ।
मल्हन्ति महागयलील णाइँ ॥
ओहरमयररउद्द
सा सरि णयणकडक्खिय ।
दुत्तर दुप्पइसार
णं दुग्गइ दुप्पेक्खिय ॥

13

Rama was surrounded by his army, with neighing horses
as vehicles. Moving on with ease, as if he were a
cardinal elephant, he came to that area of Pariyatra.[11]
As he went a little farther still, he beheld the great
river Gambhira, rising up with the tails of rapid fish,
giving off rows of foam and sprays of water, its many
lakes rippling with *kāraṇḍa* ducklings, the flow of its
water beset with beautiful lotuses, shimmering with
the wings of rows of geese, exhibiting masses of waves
and whirls. It shone with multiple herds of forest
elephants, flourishing great gouts of foam. It flew up,
turned, held back, and rushed forth, as if playing the
sport of great elephants.

From the corner of his eyes he looked at that river,
terrifying with *oharas* and crocodiles, difficult to pass
or to enter and unsightly as if it were an evil fate.[12]

१४

सरि गम्भीर णियच्छिय जावेंहिँ ।
सयलु वि सेण्णु णियत्तिउ तावेंहिँ ॥
तुम्हें हि एवहिँ आणवडिच्छा ।³
भरहहों भिन्न होह हियइच्छा ॥
उज्झ मुएप्पिणु दाहिणएसहों ।
अम्हेंहिँ जाएवउ वणवासहों ॥
एम भणेप्पिणु समरसमत्था ।
सायरवज्जावत्तविहत्था ॥
पइसरन्ति तहिँ सलिलें भयङ्करें ।
रामहों चडिय सीय वामएँ करें ॥
सिय अरविन्दहों उप्परि णावइ ।
णावइ णिययकित्ति दरिसावइ ॥
णं उज्जोउ करावइ गयणहों ।
णाइँ पदरिसइ धण दहवयणहों ॥
लहु जलवाहिणिपुलिणु पवण्णइँ ।
णं भवियइँ णरयहों उत्तिण्णइँ ॥
वलिय पडीवा जोह
जे पहुपच्छलें लग्गा ।
कुमुणि कुवुद्धि कुसील
णं पव्वज्जहें भग्गा ॥

14

As they beheld the river Gambhira, Rama stopped the
entire army. "You must now become obedient,
caring servants to Bharata. Leaving Ayodhya,
we must now go to the southern country to stay
in the forest." Having spoken thus, Rama and
Lakshmana, competent in war and skilled with the
bows Samudravarta and Vajravarta, entered into
the terrifying water. Sita climbed onto Rama's left
hand, like Lakshmi on top of her lotus, as if he were
displaying his glory, as if he were creating light for
the sky, as if he were showing his wife to Ravana, the
ten-faced. They soon reached the opposite shore of
the river, like people capable of salvation escaping
from hell.

The soldiers who had come after their lord turned back,
like bad sages with bad thoughts and bad behavior,
abandoning their renunciation.

१५

वलु वोलावेंवि राय णियत्ता ।
णावइ सिद्धि कुसिद्धि ण पत्ता ॥
वलिय के वि णीसासु मुअन्ता ।
खणें खणें हा हा राम भणन्ता ॥
के वि महन्तें दुक्खें लइया ।
लोउ करेवि के वि पव्वइया ॥
के वि तिमुण्डधारि वम्भारिय ।
के वि तिकालजोइ वयधारिय ॥
के वि पवणधुयधवलविसालएँ ।
गम्पिणु तहिँ हरिसेणजिणालएँ ॥
थिय पव्वज्ज लएप्पिणु णरवर ।
सढकढोरवरमेरुमहीहर ॥
विजयवियड्डुविओयविमद्दण ।
धीरसुवीरसच्चपियवड्ढण ॥
पुञ्झमपुण्डरीयपुरिसुत्तम ।
विउलविसालरणुम्मियउत्तम ॥
इय एक्केक्कपहाण ।
जिणवरचलण णमंसेंवि ॥
संजमणियमगुणेहिँ ।
अप्पउ थिय सइँ भूसेंवि ॥

15

Summoning the army, the nobles turned back, like failed
Siddhas who had not achieved *siddhi:* some turned
back, sighing and saying again and again, "Ah, ah,
Rama;" some were seized by great sorrow; some
renounced the material world, performing the hair
pulling ceremony;[13] some became celibate, wearing
the *tripuṇḍra;*[14] some became yogis of the three times
and maintained vows. Some men went to that Jina
temple of Harishena,* white, vast, and stirred by
the wind, and stayed there, accepting renunciation:
Shatha, Kathora, Vara, Meru, Mahidhara, Vijaya,
Vidagdha, Viyoga, Vimardana, Dhira, Suvira, Satya,
Priyavardhana, Pungava, Pundarika, Purushottama,
Vipula, Vishala, Ranonmita, and Uttama.
Paying homage to the feet of the excellent Jina, these
noble men, one by one, stood there, adorning
themselves with the virtues of restraint and discipline.

* The tenth universal emperor.

चउवीसमो संधि

गएँ वणवासहों रामें
उज्झ ण चित्तहों भावइ ।
थिय णीसास मुअन्ति
महि उण्हालएँ णावइ ॥

१

सयलु वि जणु उम्माहिज्जन्तउ ।
खणु वि ण थक्कइ णामु लयन्तउ ॥
उव्वेल्लिज्जइ गिज्जइ लक्खणु ।
मुरववज्जें वाइज्जइ लक्खणु ॥
सुइसिद्धन्तपुराणेंहिँ लक्खणु ।
ओङ्कारेण पढिज्जइ लक्खणु ॥
अण्णु वि जं जं किं पि सलक्खणु ।
लक्खणणामें वुच्चइ लक्खणु ॥
का वि णारि सारङ्गि व वुण्णी ।
वड्ढी धाह मुएवि परुण्णी ॥
का वि णारि जं लेइ पसाहणु ।
तं उल्हावइ जाणइ लक्खणु ॥
का वि णारि जं परिहइ कङ्कणु ।
धरइ सुगाढउ जाणइ लक्खणु ॥

94

Chapter 24

When Rama had gone to stay in the forest, Ayodhya no longer stirred men's hearts: it stood there, sighing like the earth in the hot season.

1

All the people felt distressed. They did not cease to bring up his name for even a second: there was song and dance about Lakshmana; Lakshmana resounded in tambourine play; Lakshmana was in the scripture, the doctrine, and the ancient treatises; Lakshmana was recited with the sound Ohm. Whatever else was in any way "auspicious" was called "auspicious" with the name Lakshmana, "the auspicious one."[1] One woman, like a terrified doe, cried as she uttered a long moan. Another, when she applied her makeup, removed it again as she thought of Lakshmana. Another, when she put on a bracelet, tied it very tightly and thought

का वि णारि जं जोयइ दप्पणु ।
अण्णु ण पेक्खइ मेल्लेवि लक्खणु ॥
तो एत्थन्तरें पाणियहारिउ ।
पुरें वोल्हन्ति परोप्परु णारिउ ॥
सो पलङ्कु तं जें उवहाणउ ।
सेज्ज वि स ज्जें तं जें पच्छाणउ ॥
तं घरु रयणइँ ताइँ
तं चित्तयम्मु सलक्खणु ।
णवर ण दीसइ माएँ
रामु ससीयसलक्खणु ॥

२

ताम पडु पडह पडिपहय पहुपञ्झणे ।
णाइँ सुरदुन्दुही दिण्ण गयणञ्झणे ॥
रसिय सय सङ्ख जायं महागोन्दलं ।
टिविलटण्टन्तघुम्मन्तवरमन्दलं ॥
तालकंसालकोलाहलं काहलं ।
गीयसंगीयगिज्जन्तवरमङ्कलं ॥
डमरुतिरिडिक्किया झल्लरीरउरवं ।
भम्भभम्भीसगम्भीरभेरीरवं ॥
घण्टजयघण्टसंघट्टटूटङ्कारवं ।
घोलउल्लोलहलवोलमुहलारवं ॥

96

of Lakshmana. Another, when she looked in the mirror, did not see anything but Lakshmana. At that time, the women in the city who went to fetch water said to each other, "That couch, that pillow, even that bed and that cover,
that house, those jewels, that painting: all are of good quality.[2] But what is not seen, sister, is Rama, along with Sita and Lakshmana."

2

Meanwhile in the king's courtyard shrill drums were beaten, as if the kettledrum of the gods in heaven was struck. Hundreds of conches resounded. A great bustle arose of humming *ṭivila* tabors and excellent rolling *mardala* drums, the clatter of cymbals and gongs, the large *kāhala* drum, beautiful benedictions expressed in songs and harmonies, terrifying with *ḍamaru, tiriḍikkiya,*[3] and *jhallarī* drums,[4] the sound of *bhambha, bhambhīsa,* and heavy *bherī* kettledrums, ringing with the clashes of *ghaṇṭā* and *jayaghaṇṭā* bells, and the resonating noise of the swaying, uproar, and hubbub. All the warrior troops stood in the courtyard, puffed up in their armor, their hair

तेण सद्देण रोमञ्चकञ्झुद्धुआ ।
गोन्दलुद्दामवहुवहलअच्चब्भुआ ॥
सुहडसंघाय सव्वा य थिय पङ्गणे ।
मेरुसिहरेसु णं अमर जिणजम्मणे ॥
पणइफम्फावणडच्छत्तकइवन्दणं ।
नन्द जय भद्द जय जयहि वरसद्दणं ॥
लक्खणरामहुँ वप्पु ।
णियभिच्चेहिँ परियरियउ ॥
जिणअहिसेयहों कज्जें ।
णं सुरवइ णीसरियउ ॥

३

जं णीसरिउ राउ आणन्दें ।
वुत्तु णवेप्पिणु भरहणरिन्दें ॥
हउ मि देव पइँ सहुँ पव्वज्जमि ।
दुग्गइगामिउ रज्जु ण भुञ्जमि ॥
रज्जु असारु वारु संसारहों ।
रज्जु खणेण णेइ तम्वारहों ॥
रज्जु भयङ्करु इहपरलोयहों ।
रज्जें गम्मइ णिच्चणिगोयहों ॥
रज्जें होउ होउ महु सरियउ ।
सुन्दरु तो किं पइँ परिहरियउ ॥

bristling from that sound, brash in the bustle, in great
numbers and most extraordinary, like the gods on
the peaks of Mount Meru at the birth of the Jina. It
was a magnificent sound, the praise of supporters,
phamphāva singers,* actors, scholars, and poets,
"Rejoice! Hail, good sir! Hail, may you be victorious!"
Surrounded by his servants, the father of Lakshmana and
Rama set out, just like Indra, the lord of the gods, for
the consecration of the Jina.

3

When the king joyfully set out, King Bharata bowed and
said, "Lord, I also renounce the world together with
you. I do not enjoy kingship that leads to a bad mode
of existence: kingship is useless, a door to samsara;
all at once, kingship leads to destruction; kingship
is terrible for this and the other world; because of
kingship one reaches the state of eternal *nigoda*.⁵ If
the path of kingship were so thoroughly appealing
for me, then why did you give it up? Clever sages call

---

* A class of dwarf bards or minstrels.

रज्जु अकज्जु कहिउ मुणिछेयहिँ ।
दुट्ठकलत्तु व भुत्तु अणेयहिँ ॥
दोसवन्तु मयलउच्छणविम्बु व ।
वहुदुक्खाउरु दुग्गकुडुम्बु व ॥
तो वि जीउ पुणु रज्जहों कङ्खइ ।
अणुदिणु आउ गलन्तु ण लक्खइ ॥
जिह महुविन्दुहें कज्जें
करहु ण पेक्खइ कक्करु ।
तिह जिउ विसयासत्तु
रज्जें गउ सयसक्करु ॥

४

भरहु चवन्तु णिवारिउ राएं ।
अज्ज वि तुज्झु काइँ तववाएं ॥
अज्ज वि रज्जु करहि सुहु भुञ्जहि ।
अज्ज वि विसयसुक्खु अणुहुञ्जहि ॥
अज्ज वि तुहुँ तम्वोलु समाणहि ।
अज्ज वि वरउज्जाणइँ माणहि ॥
अज्जु वि अङ्कु सइच्छएँ मण्डहि ।
अज्ज वि वरविलयउ अवरुण्डहि ॥
अज्ज वि जोगउ सव्वाहरणहों ।
अज्ज वि कवणु कालु तवचरणहों ॥

100

kingship improper, enjoyed by multiple men like a wife of the worst kind; stained like the disk of the moon; pained by manifold sorrows like a family in dire straits. Nevertheless a living being again desires kingship. He does not see that his life span wanes every day.

Just as a camel does not see a rock because of a honey drop,[6] a living being attached to sensory objects is broken into a thousand pieces because of kingship."

4

The king stopped Bharata from speaking: "Why do you talk of asceticism now? For now, you exercise kingship and experience happiness, enjoy the pleasure of sensory objects, chew betel, relish beautiful gardens, adorn your body at your pleasure, and embrace gorgeous women. For now you are fit for every embellishment. What time is there for ascetic practice now? The Jina's path of renunciation is very hard to endure. Who tolerated the twenty-two afflictions?[7]

जिणपव्वज्ज होइ अइदुसहिय ।
कें वावीस परीसह विसहिय ॥
कें जिय चउकसायरिउ दुज्जय ।
कें आयामिय पञ्च महव्वय ॥
कें किउ पञ्चहुँ विसयहुँ णिग्गहु ।
कें परिसेसिउ सयलु परिग्गहु ॥
को दुममूलें वसिउ वरिसालएँ ।
को एक्कझें थिउ सीयालएँ ॥
कें उण्हालएँ किउ अत्तावणु ।
एॅउ तवचरणु होइ भीसावणु ॥
भरह म वड्ढिउ वोल्लि
तुहुँ सो अज्ज वि वालु ।
भुञ्जहि विसयसुहाइँ
को पव्वज्जहें कालु ॥

तं णिसुणेवि भरहु आरुट्ठउ ।
मत्तगइन्दु व चित्तें दुट्ठउ ॥
विरुयउ ताव वयणु पइँ वुत्तउ ।
किं वालहाें तवचरणु ण जुत्तउ ॥
किं वालत्तणु सुहेहिँ ण मुञ्चइ ।
किं वालहाें दयधम्मु ण रुच्चइ ॥
किं वालहाें पव्वज्ज म होओ ।

Who vanquished the invincible enemies, the four
passions?[8] Who pursued the five great vows?[9] Who
waged war against the five objects of the senses? Who
forsook all possession? Who stayed at the root of a
tree in the rainy season? Who stood with only his
naked body in the cold season? Who performed self-
mortification in the hot season? This ascetic practice
is horrifying.

Bharata, do not talk like an old man. For now you are a
boy. Enjoy the pleasures of sensory objects. What
time is this for renunciation?"

5

Hearing this, Bharata was enraged, like a rutting elephant,
vicious in his heart, "What you said just now is
offensive. Why is ascetic practice not suitable for a
boy? Why should boyhood not be free of pleasures?
Why is the teaching of compassion not agreeable for a
boy? Why should there be no renunciation for a boy?

किं वालहों दूसिउ परलोओ ॥
किं वालहों सम्मत्तु म होओ ।
किं वालहों णउ इट्टविओओ ॥
किं वालहों जरमरणु ण ढुक्कइ ।
किं वालहों जमु दिवसु वि चुक्कइ ॥
तं णिसुणेवि भरहु णिब्भच्छिउ ।
तो किं पहिलउ पट्टु पडिच्छिउ ॥
एवहिँ सयलु वि रज्जु करेवउ ।
पच्छलें पुणु तवचरणु चरेवउ ॥
एम भणेप्पिणु राउ
सच्चु समप्पेवि भज्जहें ।
भरहहों वन्धेवि पट्टु
दसरहु गउ पव्वज्जहें ॥

६

सुरवरवन्दिएँ धवलविसालएँ ।
गम्पिणु सिद्धकूडें चइतालएँ ॥
दसरहु थिउ पव्वज्ज लएप्पिणु ।
पञ्च मुट्ठि सिरें लोउ करेप्पिणु ॥
तेण समाणु सणेहें लइयउ ।
चालीसोत्तरु सउ पव्वइयउ ॥

104

Why is the other world bad for a boy? Why should what is proper not be for a boy? Is there not the loss of precious things for a boy? Does a death of old age not loom for a boy? Does Yama stay away from a boy even for just a day?" At this, Dasharatha rebuffed Bharata, "Then why did you first accept the royal turban? You must now fully exercise kingship; only afterward may you practice asceticism."

Delivering his promise to his wife with these words, King Dasharatha tied the royal turban to Bharata and set out for his renunciation.

6

After he went to the Siddhakuta temple, lauded by the great gods, white and vast, Dasharatha stood there, accepting renunciation and pulling out the hair on his head in five fistfuls. Seized by affection, one hundred forty men renounced the world together with him.

कण्ठाकडयमउड अवयारेंवि ।
दुद्धर पञ्च महव्वय धारेंवि ॥
थिय णीसङ्ग णाग णं विसहर ।
अहवइ समयवाल णं विसहर ॥
णं केसरि गयमासाहारिय ।
णं परदारगमण परदारिय ॥
केण वि कहिउ ताम भरहेसहों ।
गय सोमित्तिराम वणवासहों ॥
तं णिसुणेवि वयणु धुयवाहउ ।
पडिउ महीहरो व्व वज्जाहउ ॥
जं मुच्छाविउ राउ
सयलु वि जणु मुहकायरु ।
पलयाणलसंतत्तु
रसेंवि लग्गु णं सायरु ॥

७

चन्दणेण पव्वालिज्जन्तउ ।
चमरुक्खेवेंहिँ विज्जिज्जन्तउ ॥
दुक्खु दुक्खु आसासिउ राणउ ।
जरढमियङ्कु व थिउ विद्दाणउ ॥
अविरलअंसुजलोल्लियणयणउ ।
एम पजम्पिउ गग्गरवयणउ ॥
णिवडिय अज्जु असणि आयासहों ।

Laying down their pendants, bracelets, and crowns
and taking up the five severe great vows, they stood
there desireless and supporting the doctrine, like
snakes holding poison.[10] Or rather, they protected
the teaching like rain clouds control the season.[11]
Like lions after eating the meat of an elephant, they
fasted for a month.[12] Like adulterers approaching
another man's wife, they were on their way to Lady
Liberation.[13] Meanwhile someone said to King
Bharata, "Rama and Sumitri's son have gone to stay
in the forest." Hearing those words, he fell down, his
arms shaking, like a mountain struck by lightning.
When the king fainted, all the people, with despair in their
faces, began to howl, like the ocean heated by the fire
of destruction.

7

Sprinkled with sandalwood water and fanned with
flywhisks, with great difficulty the king was brought
back to his senses. He stood as dejected as the waning
moon. His eyes soaked in the water of incessant
tears, he spoke with a stammering voice, "Today a
thunderbolt struck down from the sky. Today there

अज्जु अमङ्गलु दसरहवंसहों ॥
अज्जु जाउ हउँ सूडियपक्खउ ।
दुहभायणु परमुहहँ उवेक्खउ ॥
अज्जु णयरु सियसम्पयमेल्लिउ ।
अज्जु रज्जु परचक्कें पेल्लिउ ॥
एम पलाउ करेवि सहग्गएँ ।
राहवजणणिहें गउ ओलग्गएँ ॥
केसविसण्ठुल दिट्ठु रुअन्ती ।
अंसुपवाह धाह मेल्लन्ती ॥
धीरिय भरहणरिन्दें
होउ माएँ महु रज्जें ।
आणमि लक्खणराम
रोवहि काइँ अकज्जें ॥

एम भणेवि भरहु संचल्लिउ ।
तुरिउ गवेसहों हत्थुत्थल्लिउ ॥
दिण्णु सङ्खु जयपडहु पवज्जिउ ।
णं चन्दुग्गमें उवहि पगज्जिउ ॥
पहुमग्गेण णराहिउ लग्गउ ।
जीवहों कम्मु जेम अणुलग्गउ ॥

is misfortune for Dasharatha's lineage. Today I have
become a man who has had half of his body destroyed,
a vessel of sorrow, indifferent to the faces of others.
Today the city is deserted by its luster and fortune.
Today the kingdom is besieged by the army of the
enemy." Complaining thus in front of the assembly,
he went to serve the mother of Rama. He saw her
crying, her hair disheveled, emitting howls and floods
of tears.
King Bharata comforted her, "Mother, enough with my
being king: I will bring back Lakshmana and Rama.
Why do you cry for no reason?"

8

At these words, she signaled Bharata with her hand,
saying, "Quickly search for them," and he departed.
The horn was blown and the victory drum struck,
like the ocean thundering at moonrise. The king went
in pursuit along the royal road, like karma pursuing

छट्टएँ दिवसें पराइउ तेत्तहें ।
सीय सलक्खणु राहउ जेत्तहें ॥
छुडु छुडु सलिलु पिएवि णिविट्ठइँ ।
सरवरतीरें लयाहरें दिट्ठइँ ॥
चलणेहिँ पडिउ भरहु तग्गयमणु ।
णाइँ जिणिन्दहों दससयलोयणु ॥
थक्कु देव मं जाहि पवासहों ।
होहि तरण्डउ दसरहवंसहों ॥
हउँ सत्तुहणु भिच्च तउ वे वि ।
लक्खणु मन्ति सीय महएवि ॥
जिह णक्खत्तेहिँ चन्दु
इन्दु जेम सुरलोएं ।
तिह तुहुँ भुञ्जहि रज्जु
परिमिउ वन्धवलोएं ॥

९

तं वयणु सुणेवि दसरहसुएण ।
अवगूढु भरहु हरिसियभुएण ॥
सच्चउ मायापियपरमदासु ।
पइँ मेल्लेवि अण्णहों विणउ कासु ॥
अवरोप्परु ए आलाव जाम ।
तहिँ जुवइसयहिँ परियरिय ताम ॥

110

a soul. On the sixth day he arrived where Sita and
Raghu's descendant Rama were together with
Lakshmana. In due course he saw them sitting down
in an arbor at the shore of a great lake after drinking
some water. His heart devoted to them, Bharata fell
at their feet, like Indra the thousand-eyed at the feet
of the lord Jina, "Stay, lord, do not go into exile. You
are the raft of Dasharatha's family. I and Shatrughna
are both your servants, Lakshmana your minister, and
Sita chief queen.
Like the moon by the stars, like Indra by the gods, you
should rule the kingdom surrounded by your kin."

9

Hearing those words, Dasharatha's son Rama, the hair
on his arms bristling, embraced Bharata, "You are
truly the ultimate servant of our parents. Who else
but you demonstrates such decency?" As they spoke
thus, they saw Bharata's mother, accompanied by
hundreds of young women, arriving like a troop of

लक्खिवज्जइ भरहहों तणिय माय ।
णं गयघड भड भञ्जन्ति आय ॥
णं तिलयविहूसिय वच्छराइ ।
सपओहर अम्बरसोह णाइँ ॥
णं भरहहों सम्पयरिद्धिविद्धि ।
णं रामहों गमणहों तणिय सिद्धि ॥
णं भरहहों सुन्दरसोक्खखाणि ।
णं रामहों इट्टुकलत्तहाणि ॥
णं भणइ भरहु तुहुँ आउ आउ ।
वणवासहों राहउ जाउ जाउ ॥
सुपय सुसन्धि सुणाम
वयणविहत्तिविहूसिय
कह वायरणहों जेम ।
केक्कय एन्ति पदीसिय ॥

१०

सहुँ सीयऍ दसरहणन्दणेहिँ ।
जोक्कारिय रामजणद्दणेहिँ ॥
पुणु वुच्चइ सीरप्पहरणेण ।
किं आणिउ भरहु अकारणेण ॥
सुणु माऍ महारउ परमतञ्चु ।
पालेवउ तायहों तणउ सच्चु ॥

elephants crushing soldiers. She was adorned with a forehead mark, like a row of trees with *tilakas*.[14] With her breasts she was like the splendor of the sky with its clouds.[15] To Bharata she was like fortune, wealth, and abundance, to Rama like the verdict of banishment. To Bharata she was like a mine of agreeable comfort, to Rama like the loss of his beloved wife. It was as if she said to Bharata, "You come, come. Let Rama go, let him go to stay in the forest."

As Kaikeyi approached, they beheld her, with beautiful feet, joints, and good fame, and adorned with embellishments on her face, like an eloquent tale has good verse-feet, good sandhi, and good substantives, and is adorned with number and case.[16]

10

She was praised by Dasharatha's sons, Rama and the Vasudeva, together with Sita. Then the Baladeva asked her, "Why was Bharata brought here for no reason? Mother, listen to my highest truth: father's truthfulness must be safeguarded. There is no need

णउ तुरऍहिँ णउ रहवरेहिँ कज्जु ।
णउ सोलह वरिसइँ करमि रज्जु ॥
जं दिण्णु सच्चु ताएं तिवार ।
तं मइ मि दिण्णु तुम्ह सयवार ॥
ऍउ वयणु भणेप्पिणु सुहसमिद्धु ।
सइँ हत्थें भरहहों पट्टु वद्धु ॥
आउच्छेवि परवलमइयवट्टु ।
वणवासहों राहउ पुणु पयट्टु ॥
गउ भरहु णियत्तु सुपुज्जमाणु ।
जिणभवणु पत्तु भिन्नेहिँ समाणु ॥४
विहुँ मुणिधवलहुँ पासें
भरहें लइउ अवग्गहु ।
दिट्ठएँ राहवचन्दें
मह णिविन्ति हयरज्जहों ॥

११

एम चर्वेवि उच्चलिउ महाइउ ।
राहवजणणिहें भवणु पराइउ ॥
विणउ करेप्पिणु पासु पढुक्किउ ।
रामु माऍ मइँ धरेवि ण सक्किउ ॥
हउँ तुम्हेवहिँ आणवडिच्छउ ।
पेसणयारउ चलणणियच्छउ ॥

for horses or great chariots. For sixteen years I
will not exercise kingship. The promise that father
delivered to you threefold, that I too have delivered
to you hundredfold." With these words, he tied the
royal turban, endowed with pleasures, to Bharata
with his own hands. Bidding them farewell, Rama,
the descendant of Raghu, destroyer of enemy armies,
again set out for his stay in the forest. Bharata went
and returned, and together with his servants reached
the much-venerated Jina temple.
In the company of two immaculate sages Bharata took
a pledge, "When I behold moon-like Rama, the
descendant of Raghu, escape from this wretched
kingship will be mine."

11

With these words the noble man set out and reached the
home of Rama's mother. He approached her, while
showing propriety, "Mother, I have not been able to
stop Rama. Now I am your obedient servant, looking
down to your feet." Thus comforting the mother
of the demon-slayer Rama, King Bharata went to
his quarters. Roaming around, the three, Janaka's

धीरेंवि एम जणणि दणुदमणहों ।
भरहु णराहिउ गउ णियभवणहों ॥
जाणइ हरि हलहरु विहरन्तइँ ।
तिण्णि मि तावसवणु संपत्तइँ ॥
तावस के वि दिट्ठ जडहारिय ।
कुजण कुगाम जेम जडहारिय ॥
के वि तिदण्डि के वि धाडीसर ।
कुविय णरिन्द जेम धाडीसर ॥
के वि रुद्द रुद्दङ्कुसहत्था ।
मेट्टु जेम रुद्दङ्कुसहत्था ॥
तहिँ पइसन्ती सीय
लक्खणरामविहूसिय ।
विहिँ पक्खेहिँ समाण
पुण्णिम णाइँ पदीसिय ॥

१२

अण्णु वि थोवन्तरु विहरन्तइँ ।
वणु धाणुक्कहँ पुणु संपत्तइँ ॥
जहिँ जणवउ मयवत्थणियत्थउ ।
वरहिणपिच्छपसाहियहत्थउ ॥
कन्दमूलवहुवणफलभुञ्जउ ।
सिरें वडमाल वद्ध गलें गुञ्जउ ॥

daughter, the Vasudeva, and the Baladeva, came to
a forest of ascetics:[17] they saw some ascetics bearing
matted locks, like lowly communities and villages
contain dullness;[18] some *tridaṇḍin* ascetics and some
dhāḍīsara ascetics,[19] like angry kings who are intent
on assault;[20] some Rudra* worshipers holding Rudra's
trident, like an elephant keeper holding a frightful
goad.[21]
Entering there, together with Lakshmana and Rama, Sita
appeared like the full moon with its two halves.[22]

12

As they roamed a little farther, they then came to a forest
    of archers, where the people were dressed in animal
    hides, their hands decorated with peacock feathers,
    eating bulbs, roots, and many kinds of forest fruits;
    where they tied a garland from the banyan tree to the
    head and crab's-eye beans to the neck; where young

---

* A terrifying form of Shiva.

जहिँ जुवइउ छुडु जायविवाहउ ।
मयकरिरयवलयङ्क्रियवाहउ ॥
मयकरिकुम्भु करेप्पिणु उक्खलु ।
लेवि विसाणमुसलु धवलुज्जलु ॥
मोत्तियचाउलदलणोवइयउ ।
चुम्वियवयणउ मयणब्भइयउ ॥
तं तेहउ वणु भिल्लहुँ केरउ ।
हरिवलएर्वेंहिँ किउ विवरेरउ ॥
तं मेल्लेंवि घरवारु
लोयहिँ हरिसियदेहेंहिँ ।
छाइय लक्खणराम
चन्दसूर जिम मेहेंहिँ ॥

१३

सहरि सभज्जउ रामु धणुद्धरु ।
अण्णु वि जाम जाइ थोवन्तरु ॥
दिट्ठइँ गोट्ठय णाइँ सुवेसइँ ।
णं णरवइमन्दिरइँ सुवेसइँ ॥
जुज्झन्तइँ ढेक्कार मुअन्तइँ ।
णलिणिमुणालसण्ड तोडन्तइँ ॥
कत्थइ वच्छहणइँ णीसङ्झइँ ।
पव्वइयाइँ व णिरु णीसङ्झइँ ॥

girls, their arms decorated with bracelets of elephant ivory, were arranged to marry quickly, making a mortar out of the frontal globe of an elephant and taking the white, shiny tusk as a pestle, dexterous in the crushing of grain like pearls, their faces kissed, extremely exhilarating. Such was that forest of the Bhillas.* The Vasudeva and the Baladeva considered it peculiar.

Like the sun and the moon by clouds, Rama and Lakshmana were overwhelmed by the people who abandoned their household, their bodies covered in bristling hair.

13

When the bowman Rama, together with Lakshmana and his wife, went a little farther still, he beheld cow stations with good settlers, like the palaces of a king with good concubines:[23] here herds of calves were fighting, mooing, and trampling bunches of lotus fibers, without horns, like renunciants who are indeed passionless;[24] there the people, smeared with curd,

---

* A tribal community.

कत्थइ जणवउ सिसिरें चच्छिउ ।
पढमसूइ सिरें धरेंवि पणच्छिउ ॥
कत्थइ मन्थामन्थियमन्थणि ।
कुणइ सद्दु सुरए व विलासिणि ॥
कत्थइ णारिणियम्वें सुहासिउ ।
णावइ कुडउ कुणइ मुहवासिउ ॥
कत्थइ डिम्भउ परियन्दिज्जइ ।
अम्माहिरउ गेउ झुणिज्जइ ॥
तं पेक्खेप्पिणु गोट्टु
णारीयणपरियरियउ ।
णावइ तिहिं मि जणेहिँ
वालत्तणु संभरियउ ॥

१४

तं मेल्लेप्पिणु गोट्टु रवण्णउ ।
पुणु वणु पइसरन्ति आरण्णउ ॥
जं फलपत्तरिद्धिसंपण्णउ ।
तरलतमालतालसंछण्णउ ॥
वणं जिणालयं जहा सचन्दणं ।
जिणिन्दसासणं जहा ससावयं ॥
महारणङ्गणं जहा सवासणं ।
मइन्दकन्धरं जहा सकेसरं ॥

started to dance, holding the first crop on their heads;
there a churning pot stirred with a churning stick
made a noise like a wanton lady during lovemaking;
there the beautiful conessi tree failed to reach up
to the hips of the women, but still perfumed their
mouths; there a child was being cradled and a nursery
rhyme sung.
Seeing that cow station attended by the womenfolk, it was
as if all three of them remembered their childhood.

14

Leaving behind that charming cow station, they then
entered the wild forest, abounding in a wealth of fruits
and leaves, covered with jimsonweeds, *tamāla* trees,
and palmyras: it was as full of sandalwood trees as a
Jina temple with sandalwood paste; with beasts of
prey like the Jain order with laymen;[25] with cries like a
vast battlefield is a place of corpses;[26] with pollen like
the neck of a lion has a mane;[27] with *māuya* trees like

णरिन्दमन्दिरं जहा समाउयं ।
सुसञ्झणच्छियं जहा सतालयं ॥
जिणेसण्हाणयं जहा महासरं ।
कुतावसे तवं जहा मयासवं ॥
मुणिन्दजीवियं जहा समोक्खयं ।
महाणहङ्गणं जहा ससोमयं ॥
मियङ्कबिम्वयं जहा मयासयं ।
विलासिणीमुहं जहा महारसं ॥
तं वणु मेल्लेवि ताइँ
इन्ददिसएँ आसण्णइँ ।
मासेहिँ चउरद्धेहिँ
चित्तकूडु वोलीणइँ ॥

१५

तं चित्तउडु मुएवि तुरन्तइँ ।
दसउरपुरसीमन्तरु पत्तइँ ॥
दिट्ठु महासर कमलकरम्बिय ।
सारसहंसावलिवगचुम्विय ॥
उज्जाणइँ सोहन्ति सुपत्तइँ ।
मुणिवर इव सुहलाइँ सुपत्तइँ ॥
सालिवणइँ पणमन्ति सुभत्तइँ ।
णं सावयइँ जिणेसरभत्तइँ ॥

the palace of a king contains anklets;[28] with palmyras
like a dance performance has rhythm;[29] with grand
lakes like the bathing ceremony of the lord Jina is
accompanied by great noises;[30] with flowing elephant
ichor like the austerities of a false ascetic go hand-
in-hand with flowing alcohol;[31] with weaver's beam
trees like the life of a great sage is associated with
liberation;[32] with soma plants like the great firmament
is furnished with the moon;[33] a refuge for deer, like
the disk of the moon;[34] with abundant fluids like the
charm of the face of a wanton woman.[35]
Leaving behind that forest, they reached Indra's
region,* and in four and a half months, they went to
Chitrakuta.

15

Passing Chitrakuta, they quickly came to the outskirts
of the city of Dashapura. They saw great lakes filled
with lotuses and kissed by rows of sarus cranes and
geese and storks. Gardens shone bright with beautiful
foliage and nice fruits, like great sages with good
karmic fruition and fine begging bowls.[36] The stalks in
the fertile rice fields bent low, as if they were laymen
devoted to the lord Jina. Sugarcane fields with tall

* The east.

उच्छुवणइँ दलदीहरगत्तइँ ।
णियवइलङ्घणइँ व दुकलत्तइँ ॥
पङ्कयणवणीलुप्पलसामेहिँ ।
तहिँ पइसन्तेहिँ लक्खणरामेहिँ ॥
सीरकुडुम्बिउ मणुसु पदीसिउ ।
वुण्णु कुरङ्कु व वाहुत्तासिउ ॥
हडहडफुट्टसीसु चलणयणउ ।
पाणक्कन्तु समुब्भडवयणउ ॥
सो णासन्तु कुमारेँ
सुरवरकरिकरचण्डेँहिँ ।
आणिउ रामहाँ पासु
धरेँवि सइं भुवदण्डेँहिँ ॥

stems and leaves were growing beyond their own enclosure, like bad wives who insult their husbands.[37] When Lakshmana and Rama entered there, like a pink and fresh blue lotus, they beheld a terrified man, Sirakutumbika, like a deer frightened by a tiger, his head completely in disarray, his eyes trembling, agitated in his breathing, and his face showing great distress.

When the youth Lakshmana, with his club-like arms, fierce like the trunks of the elephant of the great gods, caught him as he fled, he brought him near Rama.

Encounters on the Road

पञ्चवीसमो संधि

धणुहरहत्थेण
दुव्वारवइरिआयामें ।
सीरकुडुम्विउ
मम्भीसेंवि पुच्छिउ रामें ॥

१

दुद्दमदाणविन्दमद्दणमहाहवेणं ।
भो भो किं विसन्थुलो वुत्तु राहवेणं ॥
तं णिसुणेवि पजम्पिउ गहवइ ।
वज्जयण्णु णामेण सुणरवइ ॥
सीहोयरहों भिच्चु हियइच्छिउ ।
भरहु व रिसहहों आणवडिच्छिउ ॥
दसउरणाहु जिणेसरभत्तउ ।
पियवद्धणहों पासें उवसन्तउ ॥
जिणवरपडिमझुट्टएँ लेप्पिणु ।
अण्णहों णवइ ण णाहु मुएप्पिणु ॥
ताम कुमन्तिहिँ कहिउ णरिन्दहों ।
पइँ अवगण्णेंवि णवइ जिणिन्दहों ॥
तं णिसुणेवि वयणु पहु कुद्धउ ।
णं खयकालें कियन्तु विरुद्धउ ॥

128

Chapter 25

Exerting himself against unstoppable enemies, Rama, his bow in hand, reassured Sirakutumbika and questioned him.

1

Rama, who crushes the implacable demon lords in great
    battles, spoke, "Sir, why are you frightened?"[1]
    Hearing this, Sirakutumbika answered, "There
    is a good ruler named Vajrakarna, subservient to
    Simhodara and dear to his heart, like Bharata who
    obeyed the orders of Rishabha. He is the king of
    Dashapura, a devotee of the lord Jina, who attained
    inner peace through Priyavardhana.* He wore an
    icon of the great Jina on his thumb and did not bow
    to anyone except his lord.[2] Vicious ministers then
    reported to the king, 'He bows to the lord Jina, and
    dishonors you.' When the king heard this, he grew
    angry, like an enraged Yama, the god of death, at the

* A Jain sage.

कोवाणलपलित्तु सीहोयरु ।
णं गिरिसिहरें मइन्दकिसोयरु ॥
जो मइँ मुऍवि अण्णु जयकारइ ।
सो किं हय गय रज्जु ण हारइ ॥
अह किं वहुऍण
कलऍ दिणयरें अत्थन्तऍ ।
जइ ण वि मारमि
तो पइसमि जलणें जलन्तऍ ॥

२

पइज करेवि जाम पहु आहवे अभग्गो ।
ताम पइट्ठु चोरु णामेण विज्जुलङ्गो ॥
पइसन्तें रयणिहें मज्झयालें ।
अलिउलकज्जलसण्णिहतमालें ॥
तें दिट्ठु नराहिउ विप्फुरन्तु ।
पलयाणलो व्व धगधगधगन्तु ॥
रोमञ्चकञ्चुकञ्चुइयदेहु ।
जलगब्भिणु णं गज्जन्तु मेहु ॥
सण्णद्धवद्धपरियरणिवन्धु ।
रणभरधुरधोरिउ दिण्णखन्धु ॥
वलिवण्डमण्डणिड्डुरियणयणु ।
दट्ठोट्ठु सुट्टुविप्फुरियवयणु ॥

time of destruction. Simhodara was incensed by
the fire of anger, like a slim-waisted lion on a
mountaintop. 'He who praises any other except
me, does he not cause his horses, elephants, and
kingship to be taken away?
Or rather, what more is there to add? If I do not kill him
tomorrow by the time the sun sets, then I enter a
blazing fire.'

2

"As the king, unbeaten in battle, made that promise, a
thief named Vidyudanga came in.
As he entered in the middle of the night, black like a
bee swarm or kohl, he saw the king: flashing like
a sizzling fire of destruction; his body covered in
an armor of bristling body hair; like a thundering
cloud filled with water; his fetters and belts all
fastened and tied; capable of bearing the weight
of battle and offering his shoulders for it; his eyes
tremendously fierce and terrifying; biting his lips
and his face flashing even more; saying, 'The enemy
must be killed'; enraged like Saturn at the time of
destruction. Seeing that, long-armed Vidyudanga

मारेवउ रिउ जम्पन्तु एम ।
खयकालें सणिच्छरु कुविउ जेम ॥
तं पेक्खेवि चिन्तइ भुअविसालु ।
किं मारमि णं णं सामिसालु ॥
साहम्मियवच्छलु किं करेमि ।
सव्वायरेण गम्पिणु कहेमि ॥
गउ एम भणेवि कण्टइयगत्तु ।
णिविसड्ढें दसउरणयरु पत्तु ॥
छुडु अरुणुग्गमें
सो विज्जुलङ्कु धावन्तउ ।
दिट्ठु णरिन्देण
जसपुञ्जु णाइँ आवन्तउ ॥

३

पुच्छिउ वज्जयण्णेण हसेवि विज्जुलङ्को ।
भो भो कहिँ पयट्टु वहुवहलपुलइयङ्को ॥
तं णिसुणेप्पिणु वयणविसालें ।
वुच्चइ वज्जयण्णु कुसुमालें ॥
कामलेह णामेण विलासिणि ।
तुङ्कपओहर जणमणभाविणि ॥
तहें आसत्तउ अत्थविवज्जिउ ।
कारणें मणिकुण्डलहँ विसज्जिउ ॥
पुणु विज्जाहरकरणु करेप्पिणु ।

thought, 'Do I kill him? No, no, he is an important lord. What act of kindness do I undertake toward Vajrakarna, who follows the same teachings as I do? I will go and tell him every concern.' With these words, he set out, his limbs bristling with excitement. In half a wink he reached the city of Dashapura.

As the sun rose, the king observed that Vidyudanga, running quickly like a mass of glory, was approaching.

3

"Vajrakarna smiled and asked Vidyudanga, 'Sir, where do you come from, your limbs bristling so profusely and densely?'

Hearing this, the wide-faced thief said to Vajrakarna, 'There is a wanton, buxom lady named Kamalekha, pleasing to people's minds. I am fond of her, but wanting in wealth, and she sent me away because of some pearl earrings. Then, doing what Vidyadharas do—flying—I set out, and crossed the seven

गउ सत्त वि पायार कमेप्पिणु ॥
किर वरभवणु पईसमि जावेंहिँ ।
पइज करन्तु राउ सुउ तावेंहिँ ॥
हउँ वयणेण तेण आदण्णउ ।
वट्टइ वज्जयण्णु उच्छण्णउ ॥
साहम्मिउ जिणसासणदीवउ ।
एम भणेप्पिणु वलिउ पडीवउ ॥
पुणु वि वियडपयछोहेंहिँ धाइउ ।
णिविसें तुम्हहुँ पासु पराइउ ॥
किं ओलग्गएँ
जाणन्तु वि राय म मुज्झहि ।
पाण लएप्पिणु
जेम णासहि जेम रणें जुज्झहि ॥

४

अहवइ काइँ एण वहुजम्पिएण राया ।
परवलें पेक्खु पेक्खु उट्ठन्ति धूलिछाया ॥
पेक्खु पेक्खु आवन्तउ साहणु ।
गलगज्जन्तु महागयवाहणु ॥
पेक्खु पेक्खु हिंसन्ति तुरङ्गम ।
णहयलें विउलें भमन्ति विहङ्गम ॥
पेक्खु पेक्खु चिन्धइँ धुव्वन्तइँ ।
रहचक्कइँ महियलें खुप्पन्तइँ ॥

134

ramparts. When I entered the beautiful palace,
you see, I heard the king making a promise. I was
troubled by those words. Surely Vajrakarna, my
fellow layman, a light for the teachings of the Jina, is
doomed, I said to myself and came back. I then ran
with many giant strides and reached your side in an
eyewink.
What is the use of serving him? King, do not be a fool now
you are in the know. To save your life, either flee or
face him in battle.

4

"'Why should I go on, king? Look, look: a row of dust is
rising up from the enemy army.
Look, look: the army is coming, thundering with great
elephants as vehicles. Look, look: the horses are
neighing and birds fly about in the expansive sky.
Look, look: the standards are shaking, and the
chariot wheels are sinking into the earth. Look, look:

पेक्खु पेक्खु वज्जन्तइँ तूरइँ ।
णाणाविहणिणायगम्भीरइँ ॥
पेक्खु पेक्खु सय सङ्ख रसन्ता ।
णाइँ सदुक्खउ सयण रुअन्ता ॥
पेक्खु पेक्खु पचलन्तउ णरवइ ।
गहणक्खत्तमज्झें सणि णावइ ॥
दसउरणाहु णिहालइ जावेहिँ ।
परवलु सयलु विहावइ तावेहिँ ॥
साहु साहु तो एम भणेप्पिणु ।
विज्जुलङ्कु णिउ आलिङ्गेप्पिणु ॥
थिउ रणभूमि पसाहेवि जावेहिँ ।
सयलु वि सेण्णु पराइउ तावेहिँ ॥
अमरिसकुद्धेहिँ
चउपासेहिँ णरवरविन्दहिँ ।
वेढिउ पट्टणु
जिम महियलु चउहिँ समुद्दहिँ ॥

the drums are beating, deep with all kinds of noises.
Look, look: hundreds of horns resound, like family
members crying mournfully. Look, look: the king is
advancing like Saturn amid the planets and stars.'
As Vajrakarna, the lord of Dashapura, looked closely,
he observed the entire enemy army. With the words,
'Well done! Well done!' he embraced Vidyudanga
and led him away. As he stood there, adorning the
battlefield, the whole army arrived.
The city was besieged from four sides by troops of great
men, furious with indignation, like the earth's
surface by the four oceans.

५

किय गय सारिसज्ज पक्खरिय वरतुरङ्गा ।
कवयणिवद्ध जोह अब्भिट्टु पुलइयङ्गा ॥
अब्भिट्टु जुज्झु विण्ह वि वलाहँ ।
अवरोप्परु वड्ढियकलयलाहँ ॥
वज्जन्ततूरकोलाहलाहँ ।
उवसोहचडावियमयगलाहँ ॥
मुक्केक्कमेक्कसरसव्वलाहँ ।
भुअच्छिण्णभिण्णवच्छत्थलाहँ ॥
लोट्टावियधयमालाउलाहँ ।
पडिपहरविहुरविहलङ्घलाहँ ॥
णिड्डुरियणयणडसियाहराहँ ।
असिझससरसत्तिपहरणधराहँ ॥
सुपमाणचावकड्ढियकराहँ ।
गुणदिट्ठिमुट्ठिसन्धियसराहँ ॥
दुग्घोट्टथट्टलोट्टावणाहँ ।
कायरणरमणसंतावणाहँ ॥
जयकारहों कारणें दुद्धराहँ ।
रणु वज्जयण्णसीहोयराहँ ॥
विहि मि भिडन्तहिँ
समरङ्गणें दुन्दुहि वज्जइ ।
विहि मि णरिन्दहँ
रणें एक्कु वि जिणइ ण जिज्जइ ॥

138

5

"Elephants were harnessed; excellent horses were
equipped. Soldiers, fitted out with coats of mail,
their body hair bristling with excitement, charged
into battle.

A war was waged between the two armies: the hubbub
increasing on both sides; with the clatter of
drums resounding; with elephants furnished with
decorations; with arrows and javelins fired at each
other; with arms broken and chests pierced; with
heaps of ruined flags and garlands; some miserable
and stunned from counterblows, their eyes terrifying
and biting their lips; some bearing swords, daggers,
arrows, and *śaktis* as weapons, their hands bending
good-sized bows; arrows were brought together
with bowstrings, eyes, and fists; squashing troops of
elephants and tormenting the minds of fainthearted
men. Thus is the war between Vajrakarna and
Simhodara, unstoppable for the sake of victory.

As the two fight on the battlefield, the kettledrum
resounds. Neither of the two kings is victorious or
defeated.

६

हणु हणु <हणु> भणन्ति हम्मन्ति आहणन्ति ।
पउ वि ण ओसरन्ति मारन्ति रणे मरन्ति ॥
उहयवलेहिँ पडियग्गिमखन्धइँ ।
उहयवलेहिँ णच्चन्ति कवन्धइँ ॥
उहयवलेहिँ मुसुमूरिय धयवड ।
उहयवलेहिँ लोट्टाविय भडथड ॥
उहयवलेहिँ हय गय विणिवाइय ।
उहयवलेहिँ रुहिरोह पधाइय ॥
उहयवलेहिँ णित्तंसिय खग्गइँ ।
उहयवलेहिँ डेवन्ति विहङ्झइँ ॥
उहयवलेहिँ णीसद्दइँ तूरइँ ।
उहयवलइँ पहरणखरविहुरइँ ॥
उहयवलइँ गयदन्तेहिँ भिण्णइँ ।
उहयवलइँ रणभूमिणिसण्णइँ ॥
उहयवलइँ रुहिरोल्लियगत्तइँ ।
हक्कडक्कलल्क्क मुअन्तइँ ॥
एम पक्खु वट्टइ सङ्गमहों ।
अक्खइ सीरकुडुम्बिउ रामहों ॥
तं णिसुणेप्पिणु
मणिमरगयकिरणफुरन्तउ ।
दिण्णु सहत्थेण
कण्ठउ कडउ कडिसुत्तउ ॥

6

"'Kill! Kill! Kill!' they say, and they kill or perish. Not even
  a foot do they give way. They murder and they die in
  the battle.

In both armies the divisions at the front have attacked,
  headless corpses dance, flags are torn, troops of
  soldiers are crushed, horses and elephants are struck
  down, streams of blood flow, swords flicker, arrows
  fly past, and the drums are silent. Both armies are
  harsh and hostile with their weapons, injured by
  elephants' tusks, firmly set on the battlefield, with
  bodies soaked in blood, exclaiming defiance, battle
  cries, and screams. Thus for a fortnight the war
  wages on," Sirakutumbika told Rama.

Hearing this, Rama with his own hand offered him a
  pendant, a bracelet, and a belt, flashing with pearl
  and emerald rays.

पुणु संचल्लु वे वि वलएववासुएवा ।
जाणइकरिणिसहिय गय गिल्लगण्ड जेवा ॥
चावविहत्थ महत्थ महाइय ।
सहसक्कूडु जिणभवणु पराइय ॥
जं इट्टालधवलछुहपङ्क्रिउ ।
सज्जणहियउ जेम अकलङ्क्रिउ ॥
जं उत्तुङ्गसिहरु सुरकित्तिउ ।
वण्णविचित्तचित्तचिररचित्तिउ ॥
तं जिणभवणु णियवि परितुट्टुइँ ।
पयहिण देवि तिवार वइट्टुइँ ॥
तहिँ चन्दप्पहविम्बु णिहालिउ ।
जं सुरवरतरुकुसुमोमालिउ ॥
जं णागेन्दसुरेन्दणरिन्दहिँ ।
वन्दिउ मुणिविज्जाहरविन्दहिँ ॥
दिट्ठु सुसोहिउ सोम्मु सुदंसणु ।
अण्णु मि सेयचमरु सिंहासणु ॥
छत्तत्तउ असोउ भामण्डलु ।
लच्छिविहूसिउ वियडउरत्थलु ॥
किं वहु[एं]चविऍण
जग्गें को पडिविम्बु ठविज्जइ ।
पुणु वि पडीवउ
जइ णाहें णाहुवमिज्जइ ॥

7

Then the two, the Baladeva and the Vasudeva, set out,
    like elephants with cheeks streaked with rut ichor,
    accompanied by the elephant cow, Janaka's daughter.
These dignified, noble men, skilled with bows, came to
    Sahasrakuta, a temple to the Jina, constructed in
    brick and coated in white plaster, spotless like the
    heart of good folk, with lofty turrets, celebrated
    among the gods, painted long ago with frescos varied
    in color. As they beheld that Jina temple, they felt
    delight. Circling it thrice, they went inside. There
    they saw the icon of Chandraprabha, garlanded with
    flowers from the *arjuna* tree, praised by the leaders
    of the Nagas, gods, and humans, and by groups
    of sages and Vidyadharas. They further observed
    his most splendid, pleasant, good-looking white
    flywhisk, throne, triple umbrella, *aśoka* tree, halo,
    and broad chest adorned with the *śrīvatsa* sign.[3]
Why elaborate? What on earth can reflect him?[4] Only if
    one again and again compares the lord with a lord.

जं जगणाहु दिट्ठु वलसीयलक्खणेहिं ।
तिहि मि जणेहिं वन्दिओ विविहवन्दणेहिं ॥
जय रिसह दुसहपरिसहसहण ।
जय अजिय अजियवम्महमहण ॥
जय संभव संभवणिद्दलण ।
जय अहिणन्दण णन्दियचलण ॥
जय सुमइभडारा सुमइकर ।
पउमप्पह पउमप्पहपवर ॥
जय सामि सुपास सुपाससहण ।
चन्दप्पह पुण्णचन्दवयण ॥
जय जय पुप्फयन्त पुप्फच्छिय ।
जय सीयल सीयलसुहसंचिय ॥
जय सेयङ्कर सेयंसजिण ।
जय वासुपुज्ज पुज्जियचलण ॥
जय विमलभडारा विमलमुह ।
जय सामि अणन्त अणन्तसुह ॥
जय धम्मजिणेसर धम्मधर ।
जय सन्तिभडारा सन्तिकर ॥
जय कुन्थु महत्थुइथुअचलण ।
जय अरअरहन्त महन्तगुण ॥
जय मल्लि महल्लमल्लमलण ।
मुणि सुव्वय सुव्वय सुद्धमण ॥

8

When the threesome, Baladeva, Sita, and Lakshmana,
    beheld the lord of the world, they honored him with
    manifold praises,
"Hail Rishabha, endurer of the unbearable afflictions!
    Hail Ajita, crusher of invincible Kama, the god
    of love! Hail Sambhava, eradicator of rebirth!
    Hail Abhinandana, at whose feet we rejoice! Hail
    noble Lord Sumati, generator of good thoughts,
    and Padmaprabha, excellent like the splendor of a
    lotus! Hail Master Suparshva, annihilator of karmic
    nooses, and Chandraprabha, your face like the
    full moon! Hail, hail Pushpadanta, honored with
    flowers! Hail Shitala, full of temperate happiness!
    Hail wholesome Jina Shreyamsa! Hail Vasupujya,
    whose feet are revered! Hail noble Lord Vimala,
    with your radiant face! Hail Master Ananta, with
    your eternal bliss! Hail Lord Jina Dharma, supporter
    of the doctrine! Hail noble Lord Shanti, bringer
    of peace! Hail Kunthu, whose feet are praised in
    great eulogies! Hail venerable Ara, with your grand
    virtues! Hail Malli, crusher of the great athlete,
    Kama, and Muni Suvrata, with your good vows and
    pure heart!"

वीस वि जिणवर
वन्देप्पिणु रामु वईसइ ।
जहिँ सीहोयरु
तं णिलउ कुमारु पईसइ ॥

९

ताम णरिन्दवारें थिरथोरवाहुजुअलो ।
सो पडिहारु दिट्ठु सद्त्थदेसिकुसलो ॥
पइसन्तु सुहडु तें धरिउ केम ।
णियसमएं लवणसमुद्दु जेम ॥
तं कुविउ वीरु विप्फुरियवयणु ।
विहुणन्तु हत्थ णिट्ठुरियणयणु ॥
मणें चिन्तइ वइरिसमुद्दमहणु ।
किं मारमि णं णं कवणु गहणु ॥
गउ एम भणेविं भुअदण्डचण्डु ।
णं मत्तमहागउ गिल्गण्डु ॥
तं दसउरणयरु पइट्ठु केम ।
जणमणमोहन्तु अणङ्गु जेम ॥
दुव्वारवइरिसयपाणचोरु ।
णीसरिउ णाइँ केसरिकिसोरु ॥
जं लक्खणु लक्खिउ रायवारें ।
पडिहारु वुत्तु मं मं णिवारें ॥

After they had praised the twenty great Jinas, Rama sat
down. Young Lakshmana entered that place where
Simhodara resided.

9

Then, at the king's door, he saw that gatekeeper, both
his arms firm and strong, skilled in the meaning of
words in the local language.
How was the warrior Lakshmana halted by him as he
entered? Like the saline ocean by his own shore. The
warrior, his face trembling, shaking his hands and
his eyes terrifying, churner of the ocean of enemies,
then angrily thought to himself, "Do I kill him?
No, no, what would be the use?" With these words,
he went away, fierce with his club-like arms, like a
grand rutting elephant with cheeks streaked with rut
ichor. How did he enter that city of Dashapura? Like
Kama, the bodiless god, bewildering the hearts of
the people. He who had stolen the lives of hundreds
of irresistible enemies, stepped forth like a young
lion. When Lakshmana appeared at the royal gate,
the gatekeeper received the instruction, "No, do not

तं वयणु सुणेवि पइट्टु वीरु ।
चक्कवइलच्छिलच्छियसरीरु ॥
दसउरणाहेंण
लक्खिवज्जइ एन्तउ लक्खणु ।
रिसहजिणिन्देंण
णं धम्मु अहिंसालक्खणु ॥

हरिसिउ वज्जयण्णु दिट्ठेण लक्खणेणं ।
पुणु पुणु णेहणिब्भरो चविउ तक्खणेणं ॥
किं देमि हत्थि रह तुरयथट्टु ।
विच्छुरियफुरियमणिमउडपट्टु ॥
किं वत्थेंहिँ किं रयणेहिँ कज्जु ।
किं णरवरपरिमिउ देमि रज्जु ॥
किं देमि सविब्भमु पिण्डवासु ।
किं ससुउ सकन्तउ होमि दासु ॥
तं वयणु सुणेवि हरिसियमणेण ।
पडिवुत्तु णराहिउ लक्खणेण ॥
कहिँ मुणिवरु कहिँ संसारसोक्खु ।
कहिँ पावपिण्डु कहिँ परममोक्खु ॥
कहिँ पायउ केत्थु कुडुक्कवयणु ।

stop him." At these words, the warrior entered, his
    body marked with the glory of a universal emperor.[5]
Vajrakarna, the lord of Dashapura, beheld Lakshmana as
    he entered, as the lord Jina Rishabha observed the
    doctrine characterized by nonviolence.

10

When he saw Lakshmana, Vajrakarna was delighted.
    Instantly he spoke, again and again, filled with
    affection:
"Do I give you elephants, chariots, herds of horses,
    glittering crowns and turbans inlaid with jewels?
    Is there any need for clothes? For gems? Do I give
    you the kingdom, regulated by excellent men? Do I
    give you my harem, with all its allures? Do I become
    your servant with my children and wives?" At those
    words, Lakshmana with a delighted heart answered
    the king, "Where is a great sage, and where is
    happiness in samsara? Where a ball of sin, and where
    supreme liberation? Where is Prakrit, and where

कहिँ कमलसण्डु कहिँ विउलु गयणु ॥
कहिँ मयगलें हलु कहिँ उट्टें घण्ट ।
कहिँ पन्थिउ कहिँ रहतुरयथट्टृ ॥
तं वोल्लहि जं ण चडइ कलाएँ ।
अम्हइँ वाहिय भुक्खएँ खलाएँ
तुहुँ साहम्मिउ
दयधम्मु करन्तु ण थक्कहि ।
भोयणु मग्गिउ
तिहुँ जणहुँ देहि जइ सक्कहि ॥

११

वुच्चइ वज्जयण्णेणं सजललोयणेणं ।
मग्गिउ देमि रज्जु किं गहणु भोयणेणं ॥
एम भणेप्पिणु अण्णुच्चाइउ ।
णिविसें रामहों पासु पराइउ ॥
खणें कञ्चोल थाल ओयारिय ।
परियलसिप्पिसङ्ख वित्थारिय ॥
वहुविहखण्डपयारेहिँ वड्ढिउ ।
उच्छुवणं पिव मुहरसियड्ढिउ ॥
उज्जाणं पिव सुट्टु सुअन्धउ ।
सिद्धहों सिद्धिसुहं पिव सिद्धउ ॥
रेहइ असणवेल वलहद्दहों ।
णाइँ विणिग्गय अमयसमुद्दहों ॥

gibberish? Where is a cluster of lotuses, and where
the expansive sky? Where is a plow to an elephant?
Where a bell to a camel? Where is a traveler, and
where chariots and herds of horses?[6] What you
mention is not proper, even in the slightest. We are
afflicted by wretched hunger.
You, a follower of the same teachings as we, are not
exercising the doctrine of compassion: I request a
meal for three people. Give it, if you can."

11

With tear-filled eyes, Vajrakarna said, "I would give you
the kingdom if you had requested it. How much
more so for a meal?"
After he had said this, food was taken up and, in an instant,
arrived near Rama. At once dishes and bowls were
laid down and plates, shells, and conches were
distributed. The meal swelled with many different
sorts of things. Like a thicket of sugarcane, it was
rich in juices for the mouth. Like a garden it was
truly fragrant. Like the bliss of Siddhi for a Siddha, it
was well prepared. This meal pleased the Baladeva,
as if it had come forth from an ocean of ambrosia,

धवलप्पउरकूरफेणुज्जल ।
पेज्जावत्त दिन्ति चल चञ्चल ॥
घियकल्लोलवोल पवहन्ती ।
तिम्मणतोयतुसार मुअन्ती ॥
सालणसयसेवालकरम्विय ।
हरिहलहरजलयरपरिचुम्विय ॥
किं वहुचविॲण
सच्छाउ सलोणु सविञ्जणु ।
इट्ठकलत्तु व
तं भुत्तु जहिच्छएँ भोयणु ॥

१२

भुञ्जेिवि रामचन्देंणं पभणिओ कुमारो ।
भोयणु ण ॲउ होइ उवयारगरुअभारो ॥
पडिउवयारु किं पि विण्णासहि ।
उभयवलेहिँ अप्पाणु पगासहि ॥
तं सीहोयरु गम्पि णिवारहि ।
अद्धें रज्जहों सन्धि समारहि ॥
वुच्चइ भरहें दूउ विसज्जिउ ।
दुज्जउ वज्जयण्णु अपरज्जिउ ॥
तेण समाणु कवणु किर विग्गहु ।
जें आयामिउ समरें परिग्गहु ॥

152

radiant with abundant white rice for foam, yielding
up unsteady, wavering whirlpools of rice gruel,
bearing masses of waves of ghee, emitting sprays of
curry for water, mixed with hundreds of pickles for
mud, covered with kisses from the Vasudeva and the
Baladeva for aquatic animals.

Why elaborate? They enjoyed the colorful, tasty, well-
seasoned meal with pleasure, as if it were a virtuous
wife who was lovely, charming, and full of clever
ways.[7]

12

When they had eaten, moon-like Rama said to the youth
Lakshmana, "This is not a meal; this is the heavy
burden of service.

You must arrange for some favor in return. Show yourself
to both armies. You go to that Simhodara and stop
him. Broker a peace with half of the kingdom. You
should say this, 'I am an envoy sent by Bharata.
Vajrakarna is invincible and unsurpassed. Indeed,
why fight with him, since he always seizes control in
battle?'" At those words, the Vasudeva, crusher of

तं णिसुणेवि वयणु रिउमद्दणु ।
रामहों चलणेहिँ पडिउ जणद्दणु ॥
अज्जु कियत्थु अज्जु हउँ धण्णउ ।
जं आएसु देव पइँ दिण्णउ ॥
एम भणेवि पयट्टु महाइउ ।
गउ सीहोयरभवणु पराइउ ॥
मत्तगइन्दु जेम गलगज्जेंवि ।
तं पडिहारु करग्गें तज्जेंवि ॥
तिणसमु मण्णेंवि ।
अत्थाणु सयलु अवगण्णेंवि ॥
पइठु भयाणणु ।
गयजूहें जेम पञ्चाणणु ॥

१३

अमरिसकुद्दूरएण वहुभरियमच्छरेणं ।
सीहोयरु पलोइओ जिह सणिच्छरेणं ॥
कोवाणलसयजालजलन्तें ।
पुणु पुणु जोइउ णाइँ कयन्तें ॥
जउ जउ लक्खणु लक्खइ संमुहु ।
तउ तउ सिमिरु थाइ हेट्टामुहु ॥
चिन्तिउ को वि महावलु दीसइ ।
णउ पणिवाउ करइ णउ वइसइ ॥

enemies, fell at Rama's feet, "Today I am satisfied.
Today I am fortunate, lord, that you have given me
an order." Speaking thus, the noble man departed.
He went and reached the palace of Simhodara.
Roaring like an enormous rutting elephant,
threatening that gatekeeper with his finger,
considering the entire assembly to be as useless as grass
and disregarding it, he entered, instilling fear like a
lion in a herd of elephants.

13

Furious with indignation and brimming with wrath like
Saturn, he beheld Simhodara.
Ablaze with hundreds of flames from the fire of anger,
he looked at him again and again, as if he were
Yama, the god of death. Wherever Lakshmana sent
his glance, the army cast their faces down. They
thought, "Some very formidable man has appeared.
He bows to no one and refuses to sit." Taking this as a

तं जि णिमित्तु लएवि कुमारें ।
वुत्तु राउ किं वहुवित्थारें ॥
एम विसज्जिउ भरहणरिन्दें ।
करइ केलि को समउ मइन्दें ॥
को सुरकरिविसाण उप्पाडइ ।
मन्दरसेलसिङ्घु को पाडइ ॥
को ऽमयवाहु करग्गें ढङ्कइ ।
वज्जयण्णु को मारेंवि सक्कइ ॥
सन्धि करहों परिभुञ्जहों मेइणि ।
हिययसुहङ्करि जिह वरकामिणि ॥
अहवइ णरवइ
जइ रज्जहों अड्डु ण इच्छहि ।
तो समरङ्गणें
सरधोरणि एन्ति पडिच्छहि ॥

१४

लक्खणवयणदूसिओ अहरविप्फुरन्तो ।
मरु मरु मारि मारि <मारि> हणु हणु भणन्तो ॥
उट्ठिउ पहु करवालविहत्थउ ।
अच्छउ ताम भरहु वीसत्थउ ॥
दूवहों दूवत्तणु दरिसावहों ।
छिन्दहों णासु सीसु मुण्डावहों ॥

sign, young Lakshmana said to the king, "Do I really need to say it? King Bharata has announced the following, 'Who plays with a lion? Who pulls out the tusks of the elephant of the gods? Who throws down the peak of Mount Meru? Who hides the moon, the vessel of ambrosia, with his finger? Who is capable of killing Vajrakarna? Make peace! Rule the land, that brings joy to the heart, as if it were a beautiful, loving woman.

Or rather, king, if you do not assent to half of the kingdom, then you invite a stream of arrows to come at you on the battlefield.'"

14

Sullied by Lakshmana's words, his lips quivering as he cried, "Die! Die! Kill! Kill! Kill! Hit him! Hit him!" King Simhodara, skilled with the sword, rose up. "Let Bharata rest assured then! Show the envoy what it means to be an envoy! Cut off his nose and shave

लुणहों हत्थ विच्छारेंवि धाडहों ।
गद्दहें चडियउ णयरें भमाडहों ॥
तं णिसुणेवि समुट्टिय णरवर ।
गलगज्जन्त णाइँ णव जलहर ॥
हणु हणु हणु भणन्त वहुमच्छर ।
णं कलिकालकियन्तसणिच्छर ॥
णं णियसमयचुक्क रयणायर ।
णं उम्मेट्टु पधाइय कुञ्जर ॥
करें करवालु को वि उग्गामइ ।
भीसण को वि गयासणि भामइ ॥
को वि भयङ्कुरु चाउ चडावइ ।
सामिहें भिच्चत्तणु दरिसावइ ॥
एव णरिन्देहिँ
फुरियाहरभिउडिकरालेहिँ ।
वेढिउ लक्खणु
पञ्जाणणु जेम सियालेहिँ ॥

his head! Chop off his hands! Cover him with ashes, bring him outside, and drive him around in the city mounted on a donkey!" Hearing this, the great men stood up, thundering like fresh rainclouds, saying with deep wrath, "Hit him! Hit him! Hit him!" as if they were Kali, Yama, and Saturn, or oceans overrunning their shores. Like driverless elephants they rushed at him. One raised the sword in his hand, another wielded a horrifying club like a thunderbolt, another strung his terrifying bow and demonstrated his servitude to his master.

Thus Lakshmana was surrounded by great men with quivering lips and horrifying eyebrows, like a lion by jackals.

१५

सूरु व जलहरेहिँ जं वेढिओ कुमारो ।
उट्ठिउ धर दलन्तु दुव्वारवइरिवारो ॥
रोक्कइ वलइ धाइ रिउ रुम्भइ ।
णं केसरिकिसोरु पवियम्भइ ॥
णं सुरवरगइन्दु मयविम्भलु ।
सिरकमलइँ तोडन्तु महावलु ॥
दरमलन्तु मणिमउड णरिन्दहुँ ।
सीहु पढुक्किउ जेम गइन्दहुँ ॥
कों वि मुसुमूरिउ चूरिउ पाऍहिँ ।
को वि णिसुम्भिउ टक्करघाऍहिँ ॥
को वि करग्गेहिँ गयणें भमाडिउ ।
को वि रसन्तु महीयलें पाडिउ ॥
को वि जुज्झविउ मेसझडक्कऍ ।
कों वि कडुवाविउ हक्कदडक्कऍ ॥
गयवरलग्गणखम्भुप्पाडेंवि ।
गयणमग्गें पुणु भुअहिँ भमाडेंवि ॥
णाइँ जमेण दण्डु पम्मुक्कउ ।
वइरिहिँ णं खयकालु पढुक्कउ ॥
आलणखम्भेंण
भामन्तें पुहइ भमाडिय ।
तेण पडन्तेंण
दस सहस णरिन्दहुँ पाडिय ॥

160

15

When young Lakshmana, tamer of unstoppable enemies,
    was surrounded like the sun by rainclouds, he rose
    up, cracking the earth.
He stopped, turned, advanced, and checked the enemy.
    Like a young lion he appeared in full glory; like
    the mighty, enormous elephant of the great gods,
    agitated with ichor, as it tears off heads as if they
    were lotuses. Shattering the jeweled crowns of the
    kings, he closed on them like a lion toward enormous
    elephants. One was crushed and pulverized by his
    feet; another was struck down by punches and blows
    to the head; another was hurled into the air by his
    hands; another was thrown to the ground crying;
    another was challenged to fight by a thrust as of a
    ram; another felt afflicted by the shouting of war
    cries. Tearing out the post to which great elephants
    were attached and then heaving it with his arms
    along the path of the sky, he released it, like Yama
    throwing his club. For the enemies it was as if the
    time of destruction had come near.
As the tying post moved by, it made the earth shake. When
    it fell, ten thousand kings perished.

१६

जं पडिवक्खु सयलु णिद्दलिउ लक्खणेणं ।
गयवरें पट्टवन्धणे चडिउ तक्खणेणं ॥
अहिमुहु सीहोयरु संचल्लिउ ।
पलयसमुद्दु णाइँ उत्थल्लिउ ॥
सेण्णावत्त दिन्तु गज्जन्तउ ।
पहरणतोयतुसारमुअन्तउ ॥
तुझ्झतुरङ्गतरङ्गसमाउलु ।
मत्तमहागयघडवेलाउलु ॥
उब्भियधवलछत्तफेणुज्जलु ।
धयकल्लोलचलन्तमहावलु ॥
रिउसमुद्दु जं दिट्ठु भयङ्करु ।
लक्खणु ढुक्कु णाइँ गिरि मन्दरु ॥
चलइ वलइ परिभमइ सुपच्चलु ।
णाइँ विलासिणिगणु चलु चञ्चलु ॥
गेण्हेंवि पहउ णरिन्दु णरिन्दें ।
तुरएं तुरउ गइन्दु गइन्दें ॥
रहिएं रहिउ रहङ्गु रहङ्गें ।
छत्तें छत्तु धयग्गु धयग्गें ॥
जउ जउ लक्खणु
परिसक्कइ भिउडिभयङ्करु ।
तउ तउ दीसइ
महिमण्डलु रुण्डणिरन्तरु ॥

162

16

When Lakshmana had completely crushed the opposition,
  Simhodara immediately climbed onto the seat of his
  great elephant,
and set out toward him. It was as if the ocean of
  destruction rose up: triggering whirlpools—the
  army; roaring and emitting sprays of water—the
  weapons; abounding in waves—the lofty horses;
  agitated at its shores—his troop of great rutting
  elephants; radiant with foam—the raised, white
  umbrellas; formidable and unsteady with its
  waves—his flags. Seeing the terrifying ocean of
  enemies, Lakshmana came toward it as if he were
  Mount Meru.[8] The army advanced, turned, and
  moved about most skillfully, like an unsteady,
  tottering group of lovely ladies. A king was seized
  and beaten by another king; a horse by a horse; an
  enormous elephant by an enormous elephant; a
  charioteer by a charioteer; a chariot by a chariot; an
  umbrella by an umbrella; the tip of a standard by the
  tip of a standard.
Wherever Lakshmana, instilling fear with his eyebrows,
  walked around, the earth's surface appeared
  completely covered in corpses.

१७

जं रिउउअहि महिउ सोमित्तिमन्दरेणं ।
सीहोयरु पधाइओ समउ कुञ्जरेणं ॥
अब्भिट्टु जुज्झु विण्णि वि जणाहँ ।
उज्जेणिणराहिवलक्खणाहँ ॥
दुव्वारवइरिगेण्हणमणाहँ ।
उग्गामियभामियपहरणाहँ ॥
मयमत्तगइन्दुद्दारणाहँ ।
पडिवक्खपक्खसंघारणाहँ ॥
सुरवहुअसत्थतोसावणाहँ ।
सीहोयरलक्खणणरवराहँ ।
भुअदण्डचण्डहरिसियमणाहँ ॥
एत्थन्तरेँ सीहोयरधरेण ।
उरेँ पेल्लिउ लक्खणु गयवरेण ॥
रहसुब्भडु पुलयविसट्टदेहु ।
णं सुक्केँ खीलिउ सजलु मेहु ॥
तेँ लेवि भुअग्गेँ थरहरन्त ।
उप्पाडिय दन्तिहेँ वे वि दन्त ॥
कडुआविउ मयगलु मरणेण तट्टु ।
विवरम्मुहु पाण लएवि णट्टु ॥
ताम कुमारेण
विज्जाहरकरणु करेप्पिणु ।
धरिउ णराहिउ
गयमत्थएँ पाउ थवेप्पिणु ॥

164

17

When Sumitri's son like Mount Meru churned the ocean
of enemies, Simhodara charged with his elephant.
A war was waged between the two men, the king of
Ujjayini and Lakshmana, their minds focused on
capturing the unstoppable enemy, their weapons
raised and cast around, devastating enormous
elephants, intoxicated with ichor, trashing the army
of the opposition, delighting assemblies of wives of
the gods, the great men Simhodara and Lakshmana,
their hearts fierce and excited with their club-like
arms. Then, the exceptionally violent Lakshmana,
his body distended with bristling hair, was struck
in the chest by the great elephant that was carrying
Simhodara, like a raincloud pinned by bright light.
He took the two throbbing tusks of the elephant
with his hand and pulled them out. Afflicted and
trembling in its heart, the elephant turned its head
and fled to save its life.
At that moment, the youth Lakshmana, doing what
Vidyadharas do, captured the king, placing his foot
on the head of the elephant.

१८

णरवइ जीवगाहि जं धरिउ लक्खणेणं ।
केण वि वज्जयण्णहो कहिउ तक्खणेणं ॥
हे णरणाहणाह अच्छरियउ ।
परवलु पेक्खु केम जज्जरियउ ॥
रुण्डणिरन्तरु सोणियचच्छिउ ।
णाणाविहविहङ्गपरियञ्छिउ ॥
को वि पयण्डवीरु वलवन्तउ ।
भमइ कियन्तु व रिउजगडन्तउ ॥
गयघड भडथड सुहड वहन्तउ ।
करिसिरकमलसण्ड तोडन्तउ ॥
रोक्कइ कोक्कइ ढुक्कइ थक्कइ ।
णं खयकालु समरें परिसक्कइ ॥
भिउडिभयङ्कुरु कुरुडु समच्छरु ।
थिउ अवलोयणें णाइँ सणिच्छरु ॥
णउ जाणहुँ किं गणु किं गन्धवु ।
किं पच्छण्णु को वि तउ वन्धवु ॥
किण्णरु किं मारुवु विज्जाहरु ।
किं वम्भाणु भाणु हरि हलहरु ॥
तेण महाहवें माणमइन्दहँ ।
विणिवाइय दस सहस णरिन्दहँ ॥
अण्णु वि दुज्जउ मच्छरभरियउ ।
जीवगाहि सीहोयरु धरियउ ॥

166

18

When Lakshmana had captured the king alive, someone
      immediately spoke to Vajrakarna:
"King of kings, it is a miracle! Look at how the enemy
      army is shattered, the battlefield teeming with
      corpses, smeared with blood, circled by different
      kinds of birds. Some mighty, fierce warrior walks
      about tormenting our enemy as if he were Yama, the
      god of death, slaying the elephant troop and throngs
      of soldiers and warriors, tearing off the heads of
      elephants as if they were lotus clusters. He stopped,
      called out, came on, halted, and walked around in the
      battle as if he were the time of destruction. Instilling
      fear with his eyebrows, ferocious and wrathful,
      he stood there, as if he were Saturn standing right
      before our eyes. We do not know if he is a Gana or
      a Gandharva, or some relative of yours in disguise,
      or a Kinnara, or the god of wind, a Vidyadhara, or
      Brahma, the sun, the Vasudeva or the Baladeva.[9] Ten
      thousand kings, like lions in arrogance, were struck
      down by him in the great battle. Moreover, he has
      captured the invincible Simhodara, full of wrath,
      alive.

एक्कें होन्तेण
वलु सयलु वि आहिन्दोलिउ ।
मन्दरवीढेण
णं सायरसलिलु विरोलिउ ॥

१९

तं णिसुणेवि को वि परितोसिओ मणेणं ।
को वि णिएहुँ लग्गु उद्धेण जम्पणेणं ॥
को वि पजम्पिउ मच्छरभरियउ ।
चङ्कउ जं सीहोयरु धरियउ ॥
जो मारेवउ वइरि सहत्थें ।
सो परिवड्ढु पाउ परहत्थें ॥
वन्धवसयणहिँ परिमिउ अज्जु ।
वज्जयण्णु अणुहुञ्जउ रज्जु ॥
को वि विरुद्धउ पुणु पुणु णिन्दइ ।
धम्मु मुएवि पाउ किं णन्दइ ॥
को वि भणइ जें मग्गिउ भोयणु ।
दीसइ सो ज्जें णाइँ ऍहु वम्भणु ॥
ताम कुमारें रिउ उक्खन्धेँवि ।
चोरु व राउलेण णिउ वन्धेँवि ॥
सालङ्कारु सदोरु सणेउरु ।
दुम्मणु दीणवयणु अन्तेउरु ॥

One man on his own razed the entire army, just like the
    surface of Mount Meru that churned the water of
    the ocean."

19

Hearing this, one man felt delight in his heart. Another
    started to look round as he chattered with
    excitement.
Another spoke, filled with wrath, "It is good that
    Simhodara is captured. The enemy who should
    have been killed by our own hand, that criminal was
    seized by the hand of a stranger. May Vajrakarna
    now rule the kingdom, surrounded by his relatives
    and kin." Another was enraged and scolded again
    and again, "Does the sinner rejoice, having forsaken
    righteousness?" Another said, "The one who
    requested a meal, it is he who we see there, that one
    who was like a Brahman." Meanwhile, the youth
    Lakshmana, having attacked and captured the
    enemy like a thief, brought him into the palace. With
    their ornaments, ropes, and anklets, the dejected,
    sad-faced harem ran toward him, their eyes wet with

धाइउ अंसुजलोल्लियणयणउ ।
हिमहयकमलवणु व कोमाणउ ॥
केसविसन्थुलु
मुहकायरु करुणु रुअन्तउ ।
थिउ चउपासेँहिँ
भत्तारभिक्ख मग्गन्तउ ॥

२०

ताम मणेण सङ्किया राहवस्स घरिणी ।
णं भयभीय काणणे वुण्णुयण्ण हरिणी ॥
पेक्खु पेक्खु वलु वलु आवन्तउ ।
सायरसलिलु जेम गज्जन्तउ ॥
लइ धणुहरु म अच्छि णिच्छिन्तउ ।
मज्छुदु लक्खणु रणें अत्थन्तउ ॥
तं णिसुणेँवि णिव्वूढमहाहवु ।
जाम चाउ किर गिण्हइ राहवु ॥
ताम कुमारु दिट्ठु सहुँ णारिहिँ ।
परिमिउ हत्थि जेम गणियारिहिँ ॥
तं पेक्खेप्पिणु सुहडणिसामें ।
भीय सीय मम्भीसिय रामें ॥
पेक्खु केम सीहोयरु वड्ढउ ।
सीहेण व सियालु उट्टुब्भउ ॥

170

water from their tears, like a withered lotus cluster
struck by frost.

Their hair tousled and their faces frightened, crying
mournfully, they stood on all sides, begging for their
husband as alms.

20

In the meantime, Rama's wife felt fear in her heart, like a
doe, horror-struck in a forest, with trembling, erect
ears,

"Look, look: an army! An army is coming, roaring like
the water of the ocean. Seize your bow, do not stay
unperturbed: maybe Lakshmana is perishing in
the fight." At this, as soon as Rama, successful in
great wars, grabbed his bow, he beheld the youth
Lakshmana together with the women, like an
elephant surrounded by elephant cows. When he
saw this, Rama, the destroyer of warriors, reassured
frightened Sita, "See how Simhodara is captured,
like a jackal vanquished by a lion." Indeed, while this

एव वोल्ल किर वट्टइ जार्वेहिँ ।
लक्खणु पासु पराइउ तार्वेहिँ ॥
चलणेहिँ पडिउ वियावडमत्थउ ।
भविउ व जिणहोँ कियञ्जलिहत्थउ ॥
साहु भणन्तेण
सुरभवणविणिग्गयणामें ।
सइँ भुअफलिहेँहिँ
अवरुण्डिउ लक्खणु रामें ॥

conversation was taking place, Lakshmana drew
near them. He fell to Rama's feet, his head bent and
his hands cupped in reverence, like a man capable of
salvation before the Jina.

With the words "Well done," Rama, whose fame
resounded in the palaces of the gods, embraced
Lakshmana himself, with his arms like iron clubs.

छव्वीसमो संधि

लक्खणरामहुँ
धवलुज्जलकसणसरीरइँ ।
एक्कहिँ मिलियइँ
णं गङ्गाजउणहें णीरइँ ॥

अवरोप्परु गज्जोल्लियगत्तेहिँ ।
सरहसु साइउ देवि तुरन्तेहिँ ॥
सीहोयरु णमन्तु वइसारिउ ।
तक्खणें वज्जयण्णु हक्कारिउ ॥
सहुँ णरवरजणेण णीसरियउ ।
णाइँ पुरन्दरु सुरपरियरियउ ॥
रेहइ विज्जुलङ्कु अणुपच्छएँ ।
पडिवाइन्दु व सूरहों पच्छएँ ॥
तं इट्टालधूलिधुअधवलउ ।
सहसकूडु गय पत्त जिणालउ ॥
चउदिसु पयहिण देवि तिवारएँ ।
पुणु अहिवन्दण करइ भडारएँ ॥
तं पियवड्ढणमुणि पणवेप्पिणु ।
वलहों पासें थिउ कुसलु भणेप्पिणु ॥

Chapter 26

The splendid white and black bodies of Lakshmana and Rama came together as one, like the waters of the Ganga and Yamuna.

1

Quickly giving each other a tight embrace, their limbs covered in bristling hair, they invited Simhodara, who took a bow, to sit. Immediately they summoned Vajrakarna. He came outside with a group of great men, like Indra surrounded by the gods. Vidyudanga shone behind him, like the new moon behind the sun. They went and reached that temple to the Jina, Sahasrakuta, white, free from all dust, and made of brick. Circling its four sides three times, Vajrakarna then made respectful salutations before the noble lord. He bowed to that sage Priyavardhana and stood near the Baladeva, speaking in a proper manner.

दसउरपुरपरमेसरु रामें ।
साहुक्कारिउ सुहडणिसामें ॥
सच्चउ णरवइ
मिच्छत्तसरेहिँ णउ भिज्जहि ।
दिढसम्मत्तेण
पर तुज्झु जें तुहुँ उवमिज्जहि ॥

२

तं णिसुणेवि पयम्पिउ राएं ।
एउ सव्वु महु तुम्ह पसाएं ॥
पुणु वि तिलोयविणिग्गयणामें ।
विज्जुलङ्घु पोमाइउ रामें ॥
भो दिढकढिणवियडवच्छत्थल ।
साहु साहु साहम्मियवच्छल ॥
सुन्दरु किउ जं णरवइ रक्खिउ ।
रणें अच्छन्तु ण पइँ उव्वेक्खिउ ॥
तो एत्थन्तरें वुत्तु कुमारें ।
जम्पिएण किं वहुवित्थारें ॥
हे दसउरणरिन्द विसगइसुअ ।
जिणवरचलणकमलफुल्लन्धुअ ॥
जो खलु खुद्दु पिसुणु मच्छरियउ ।
अच्छइ ऍहु सीहोयरु धरियउ ॥

176

Rama, destroyer of warriors, praised the supreme
      lord of the city of Dashapura,
"King, you are truly not pierced by the arrows of false
      doctrines. Through resolute righteousness you are
      only measured against yourself."

2

The king listened, then replied, "All this is mine, thanks
      to you." Thereupon Rama, whose name went forth
      in the three worlds, praised Vidyudanga, "Oh, you
      with your firm, strong, broad chest, well done! Well
      done, you who shows affection to your fellow Jains!
      You did well when you protected the king and did
      not disregard him while he was at war." Then young
      Lakshmana spoke, "What with all this elaborate
      talk? Hey, king of Dashapura, son of Vishvagati, a
      bee at the lotus-like feet of the great Jina: we have
      captured this mean, vile, wrathful wretch, this
      Simhodara here, have we not? Shall I kill him? Will

किं मारमि किं अप्पुणु मारहि ।
णं तो दय करि सन्धि समारहि ॥
आणवडिच्छउ
ऍहु एवहिँ भिच्चु तुहारउ ।
रिसहजिणिन्दहों
सेयंसु व पेसणयारउ ॥

३

पभणइ वज्जयण्णु वहुजाणउ ।
हउँ पाइक्कु पुणु वि ऍहु राणउ ॥
णवर एक्कु वउ मइँ पालेवउ ।
जिणु मेल्लेवि अण्णु ण णमेवउ ॥
तं णिसुणेविणु लक्खणरामेहिँ ।
सुरवरभवणविणिग्गयणामेहिँ ॥
दसउरपुरउज्जेणिपहाणा ।
वज्जयण्णसीहोयरराणा ॥
वेण्णि वि हत्थें हत्थु धराविय ।
सरहसु कण्ठग्गहणु कराविय ॥
अद्धोअद्धिऍ महि भुञ्जाविय ।
अण्णु वि जिणवरधम्मु सुणाविय ॥
कामिणि कामलेह कोक्काविय ।
विज्जुलङ्गहों करयलें लाविय ॥

you kill him yourself? If not, then take pity on him
and make peace.

This Simhodara here is now your servant, obeisant to
your orders, like Shreyamsa serving the great Jina
Rishabha."

3

Wise Vajrakarna said, "I am a foot soldier; he, on the other
hand, is a king. I must only safeguard one vow: I
will not bow to anyone but the Jina." Hearing this,
Rama and Lakshmana, whose names went forth to
the palaces of the great gods, made the two kings,
Vajrakarna and Simhodara, rulers of the cities of
Dashapura and Ujjayini, hold each other's hand and
embrace firmly. They let them rule the land, each
in his half, and hear the teachings of the great Jina.
They summoned the lovely Kamalekha and gave
her hand in marriage to Vidyudanga. He gave her

दिण्णइँ मणिकुण्डलइँ फुरन्तइँ ।
चन्दाइच्चहुँ तेउ हरन्तइँ ॥
ताम कुमारु वुत्तु विक्खाएँहिँ ।
वज्जयण्णसीहोयरराएँहिँ ॥
णवकुवलयदलदीहरणयणहुँ ।
मयगलगइगमणहुँ ससिवयणहुँ ॥
उच्छिणिलाडालङ्क्ष्यतिलयहुँ ।
वहुसोहग्गभोग्गगुणणिलयहुँ ॥
विब्भमभाउब्भिण्णसरीरहुँ ।
तणुमज्झहुँ थणहरगम्भीरहुँ ॥
अहिणवरूवहुँ
लायण्णवण्णसंपुण्णहुँ ।
लइ भो लक्खण
वर तिण्णि सयइँ तुहुँ कण्णहुँ ॥

४

तं णिसुणेप्पिणु दसरहणन्दणु
एम पजम्पिउ हर्सेवि जणद्दणु ॥
अच्छउ तियणु ताम विलवन्तउ ।
भिसिणिणिहाउ व रवियरछित्तउ ॥
मइँ जाएवउ दाहिणदेसहों ।
कोङ्कणमलयपण्डिउद्देसहों ॥

jeweled earrings, robbing the moon and sun of their glance. Then the celebrated kings Vajrakarna and Simhodara said to Prince Lakshmana, "Girls with eyes wide like the petals of fresh blue water lilies, walking with an elephant's gait, their faces like the moon, with marks adorning their high foreheads, abodes of abundant happiness, pleasure, and virtue, their bodies bursting with charm and deep feeling, with slim waists and heavy bosoms,
with youthful beauty, and furnished with loveliness and a good complexion, well Lakshmana, you may take three hundred such girls as your wives."

4

Hearing this, the Vasudeva, son of Dasharatha, laughed and answered thus, "For now the women will have to keep on crying, like a lotus cluster struck by the sun's rays. I must go to the land in the south, to the region of Konkana, Malaya, and Pandi. There I will

तहिँ वलहद्दहों णिलउ गवेसमि ।
पच्छएँ पाणिग्गहणु करेसमि ॥
एम कुमारु पजम्पिउ जं जे ।
मणें विसण्णु कण्णायणु तं जे ॥
दट्ठु हिमेण व णलिणिसमुच्चउ ।
मुहें मुहें णाइँ दिण्णु मसिकुञ्चउ ॥
जाम ताम तूरेहिँ वज्जन्तेहिँ ।
विविहेहिँ मङ्गलेहिँ गिज्जन्तेहिँ ॥
वन्दिणेहिँ जय जय पभणन्तेहिँ ।
खुज्जयवामणेहिँ णच्चन्तेहिँ ॥
सीय सलक्खणु वलु पइसारिउ ।
वीयाइन्दु व जयजयकारिउ ॥
तहिँ णिवसेप्पिणु णयरें रवण्णएँ ।
अद्धरत्तिअवसरें पडिवण्णएँ
वलणारायण
गय दसउरु मुएँवि महाइय ।
चेत्तहों मासहों
तं कुव्वरणयरु पराइय ॥

find a home for the Baladeva. Afterward, I will get
married." When the youth Lakshmana answered
thus, the group of girls was saddened in their heart,
like a bundle of lotuses scorched by frost. It was as if
a heap of soot was applied to each of their faces. In
the meantime, while drums were sounded, different
sorts of auspicious songs were sung, bards were
proclaiming, "Hail! Hail!" and hunchbacks and
dwarves were dancing, the Baladeva, together with
Lakshmana and Sita, was taken inside and praised
as if he were a second Indra. Staying in that pleasant
city, when the hour of midnight arrived,
those two noble men, the Baladeva and the Vasudeva,
departed from Dashapura and marched on. In the
month of Chaitra* they came to the city of Kubara.

* March to April.

५

कुव्वरणयरु पराइय जावेंहिँ ।
फग्गुणमासु पवोलिउ तावेंहिँ ॥
पइठु वसन्तराउ आणन्दें ।
कोइलकलयलमङ्गलसद्दें ॥
अलिमिहुणेंहिँ वन्दिणेंहिँ पढन्तेंहिँ ।
वरहिणवावणेहिँ णच्चन्तेंहिँ ॥
अन्दोलासयतोरणवारेंहिँ ।
ढुक्कु वसन्तु अणेयपयारेंहिँ ॥
कत्थइ चूअवणइँ पल्लवियइँ ।
णवकिसलयफलफुल्लब्भहियइँ ॥
कत्थइ गिरिसिहरइँ विच्छायइँ ।
खलमुहइँ व मसिवण्णइँ णायइँ ॥
कत्थइ माहवमासहों मेइणि ।
पियविरहेण व सूसइ कामिणि ॥
कत्थइ गिज्जइ वज्जइ मन्दलु ।
णरमिहुणेंहिँ पणच्चिउ गोन्दलु ॥
तं तहों णयरहों उत्तरपासेंहिँ ।
जणमणहरु जोयणउद्देसेंहिँ ॥
दिट्ठु वसन्ततिलउ उज्जाणउ ।
सज्जणहियउ जेम अपमाणउ ॥

5

As they came to the city of Kubara, the month of
Phalguna* had passed. King Spring joyfully entered
to the auspicious sound of the cuckoo's coos. Spring
approached in different ways: in pairs of bees like
bards reciting; in peacocks like dwarves dancing;
in hundreds of swings like archways; in one place,
mango forests stretched with an extraordinary
amount of fruits and flowers on their new sprouts;
in another, dull mountain peaks with sooty color
resembled the faces of rogues; in another, the earth
of the month of spring was parched like a lovely lady
separated from her beloved; in another, there was
singing, a *mardala* drum played, and couples danced
and murmured to each other. On the northern sides
of the city, a *yojana* away, they beheld that park
Vasantatilaka, taking people's breath away, as vast as
the heart of a good person.[1]

* February to March.

सुहलु सुयन्थउ
डोल्लन्तु वियावडमत्थउ ।
अग्गएँ रामहों
णं थिउ कुसुमञ्जलिहत्थउ ॥

६

तहिँ उववणें पइसेॢवि विणु खेवें ।
पभणिउ वासुएवु वलएवें ॥
भो असुरारिवइरिमुसुमूरण ।
दसरहवंसमणोरहपूरण ॥
लक्खण कहिं मि गवेसहि तं जलु ।
सज्जणहियउ जेम जं णिम्मलु ॥
दूरागमणें सीय तिसाइय ।
हिमहयणवणलिणि व विच्छाइय ॥
तं णिसुणेॢवि वडदुमसोवाणेॢहिँ ।
चडिउ महारिसि व्व गुणथाणेॢहिँ ॥
ताव महासरु दिट्ठु रवण्णउ ।
णाणाविहतरुवरसंछण्णउ ॥
सारसहंसकुञ्जवगचुम्विउ ।
णवकुवलयदलकमलकरम्बिउ ॥
तं पेक्खेॢवि कुमारु पधाइउ ।
णिविसें तं सरतीरु पराइउ ॥

186

It stood before Rama, swaying, with its beautiful fruits and
pleasant smells, and bowing its head, as if cupping
the hands of its blossoms in reverence.

6

Entering that garden without hesitation, the Baladeva
said to the Vasudeva, "You have ground to dust the
opposition of our demon enemies, and fulfilled the
wishes of Dasharatha's lineage, Lakshmana, find
water somewhere, pure like the heart of a good
person. Sita is thirsty from walking such a distance.
She is pale like a fresh lotus struck by frost." At this,
Lakshmana climbed onto a banyan tree ladder, like
a great seer mounting the stages of purification.
Then he beheld a lovely great lake, hidden by trees
of different kinds, kissed by sarus cranes, geese,
curlews, and storks, scattered with petals of fresh
blue water lilies and pink lotuses. Seeing this, Prince
Lakshmana ran toward it. In an instant he reached
the lake's shore.

पइठु महावलु
जलें कमलसण्डु तोडन्तउ ।
माणससरवरें
णं सुरगइन्दु कीलन्तउ ॥

७

लक्खणु जलु आडोहइ जार्वेहिँ ।
कुव्वरणयरणराहिउ तार्वेहिँ ॥
छुडु छुडु वणकीलएँ णीसरियउ ।
मयणदिवसें णरवरपरियरियउ ॥
तरुवरें तरुवरें मञ्जु णिवद्धउ ।
मञ्झें मञ्झें थिउ जणु समलद्धउ ॥
मञ्झें मञ्झें आरूढ णरेसर ।
मेरुणियम्वें णाइँ विज्जाहर ॥
मञ्झें मञ्झें आलावणि वज्जइ ।
महु पिज्जइ हिन्दोलउ गिज्जइ ॥
मञ्झें मञ्झें जणु रसयविहत्थउ ।
घुम्मइ घुलइ वियावडमत्थउ ॥
मञ्झें मञ्झें कीलन्ति सुमिहुणइँ ।
णवमिहुणइँ कहिँ णेहविहूणइँ ॥
मञ्झें मञ्झें अन्दोलइ जणवउ ।
कोइल वासइ भज्जइ दमणउ ॥

The formidable man entered into the water, tearing up
   lotus clusters, like the great elephant of the gods at
   play in the Manasa lake.*

7

While Lakshmana was stirring the water, the ruler of
   the city of Kubara went out in slow stages for some
   repose in the forest on that spring day, accompanied
   by noblemen. Near every tree a platform was fixed.
   On every platform someone stood appointed; kings
   ascended them like Vidyadharas on the flank of
   Mount Meru; an *ālāpinī* vina was played, liquor
   was drunk, and the raga *hindola*† was sung; people
   overpowered by alcohol rolled and stumbled,
   bending their heads; lovely couples relaxed—where
   are new couples wanting in affection?—people
   rocked to and fro; a cuckoo called; and self-restraint
   was shattered.

---

* A sacred lake in the Himalayas.
† Associated with spring.

कुव्वरणाहेंण
किउ मञ्झारोहणु जावेंहिं ।
सूरु व चन्देंण
लक्खिज्जइ लक्खणु तावेंहिं ॥

८

लक्खिउ लक्खणु लक्खणभरियउ ।
णं पञ्चक्खु मयणु अवयरियउ ॥
रूउ णिऍवि सुरभवणाणन्दहों ।
मणु उल्लोलेंहिं जाइ णरिन्दहों ॥
मयणसरासणि धरेंवि ण सक्किउ ।
वम्महु दसथाणेहिं पढुक्किउ ॥
पहिलऍ कहों वि समाणु ण वोल्लइ ।
वीयऍ गुरु णीसासु पमेल्लइ ॥
तइयऍ सयलु अङ्गु परितप्पइ ।
चउथऍ णं करवत्तेंहिं कप्पइ ॥
पञ्चमें पुणु पुणु पासेइज्जइ ।
छट्टुऍ वारवार मुच्छिज्जइ ॥
सत्तमें जलु वि जलद्द ण भावइ ।
अट्ठमें मरणलील दरिसावइ ॥
णवमऍ पाण पडन्त ण वेयइ ।
दसमऍ सिरु छिज्जन्तु ण चेयइ ॥

When the ruler of Kubara mounted a platform, she
    spotted Lakshmana, like the sun beholding the
    moon.[2]

8

She saw Lakshmana abounding in auspicious signs, as
    if he were Kama, the god of love himself, who had
    descended from heaven. Observing his beauty, the
    heart of the monarch, who brought joy to the palaces
    of the gods, was in turmoil.[3] The thunderbolt-like
    arrow of the god of love could not be stopped. Kama,
    tormentor of hearts, approached in ten stages: in the
    first, she no longer spoke with anyone; in the second,
    she emitted deep sighs; in the third, her entire body
    felt pain; in the fourth, it was as if she was being cut
    with saws; in the fifth, she continuously broke out
    in a sweat; in the sixth, she fainted over and over; in
    the seventh, neither water nor a moist cloth brought
    relief; in the eighth, she played at being dead; in the
    ninth, she did not realize that her life was fading; and
    in the tenth, she did not see that her head was being
    cut off.

एम वियम्भिउ

कुसुमाउहु दसहि मि थाणेहिँ ।

तं अच्छरियउ

जं मुक्कु कुमारु ण पाणेहिँ ॥

जं कण्ठट्ठिउ जीवु कुमारहों ।

सण्णएँ वुत्तु पहिउ हक्कारहों ॥

पहुआणएँ पाइक्क पधाइय ।

णिविसड्ढें तहों पासु पराइय ॥

पणवेविँ वुत्तु तिखण्डपहाणउ ।

तुम्हहँ काइ मि कोक्कइ राणउ ॥

तं णिसुणेविँ उच्चलिउ जणद्दणु ।

तिहुअणजणमणणयणाणन्दणु ॥

वियड पओह देन्तु णं केसरि ।

कन्दइ भारक्कन्त वसुन्धरि ॥

दिट्ठु कुमारु कुमारें एन्तउ ।

मयणु जेम जणमणमोहन्तउ ॥

खणें कल्लाणमालु रोमञ्चिउ ।

णडु जिह हरिसविसाएँहिँ णच्चिउ ॥

पुणु वइसारिउ हरि अद्धासणें ।

भविउ जेम थिउ दिट्ठु जिणसासणें ॥

Thus Kama, with flowers for weapons, manifested himself in ten stages. It was a miracle that the youth did not lose her life.

9

When the youth was about to perish,[4] she said with a gesture, "Summon the traveler." On their ruler's order the foot soldiers rushed forth and in an instant arrived near him. With a bow they said to Lakshmana, lord of the three parts of Bharata,[5] "The king calls you for some reason." At this, the Vasudeva, who brought joy to the eyes and hearts of the people of all three worlds, set out, taking long strides, like a lion. Overcome by his weight, the earth moaned. The youth saw Prince Lakshmana approaching, bewildering everyone's hearts, as if he were Kama. Immediately Kalyanamala's hair bristled. She danced, like an actor, with both joy and sadness. Then she invited the Vasudeva to share half of her seat. He remained firm, like a person capable of salvation in the teaching of the Jina.

वइठु जणद्दणु
आलीढएँ मज्झें रवणएँ ।
णववरइत्तु व
पच्छण्णु मिलिउ सहुँ कण्णएँ ॥

१०

वे वि वइठु वीर एक्कासणें ।
चन्दाइच्च जेम गयणङ्गणें ॥
एक्कु पचण्डु तिखण्डपहाणउ ।
अण्णेक्कु वि कुव्वरपुरराणउ ॥
एक्कहॉ चलणजुअलु कुम्मुणउ ।
अण्णेक्कहॉ रत्तुप्पलवण्णउ ॥
एक्कहॉ ऊरूजुअलु सुवित्थरु ।
अण्णेक्कहॉ सुकुमारु सुमच्छरु ॥
पज्झाणणकडिमण्डलु एक्कहॉ ।
णारिणियम्ब्विबिम्बु अण्णेक्कहॉ ॥
एक्कहॉ सुललिउ सुन्दरु अङ्गउ ।
अण्णेक्कहॉ तणुतिवलितरङ्गउ ॥
एक्कहॉ सोहइ वियडु उरत्थलु ।
अण्णेक्कहॉ जोव्वणु थणचक्कलु ॥
एक्कहॉ वाहउ दीहविसालउ ।
अण्णेक्कहॉ णं मालइमालउ ॥
वयणकमलु पप्फुल्लिउ एक्कहॉ ।

The Vasudeva sat on the lovely platform that had been
fixed there, like a young suitor meeting a girl in
secret.

10

The two heroes sat on one seat, like the moon and the
sun in the sky: one was the fierce lord of the three
parts of Bharata, the other, the monarch of the city
of Kubara; one had feet curved like a tortoise, the
other's were the color of red lotuses; one's thighs
were well developed, the other's were very soft
and delicate; one's buttocks were like a lion's, the
other had the hips of a woman; one's body was very
charming and handsome, the other's was slender
and billowed with three belly folds; one's broad chest
looked radiant, the other possessed a youthfulness,
rounded with breasts; one's arm was long and wide,
the other's resembled jasmine garlands; one's
blooming face was like a lotus, the other's was round

पुण्णिमचन्दरुन्दु अण्णेक्कहों ॥
एक्कहों गोकमलइँ वित्थरियइँ ।
अण्णेक्कहों वहुविब्भमभरियइँ ॥
एक्कहों सिरु वरकुसुमेहिँ वासिउ ।
अण्णेक्कहों वरमउडविहूसिउ ॥
एक्कु सलक्खणु
लक्खिवज्जइ जण्णेण असेसें ।
अण्णेक्कु वि पुणु
पच्छण्ण णारि णरवेसें ॥

११

दणुदुग्गाहगाहअवगाहें ।
पुणु पुणरुत्तेहिँ कुव्वरणाहें ॥
णयणकडक्खिउ लक्खणसरवरु ।
जो सुरसुन्दरिणलिणिसुहङ्करु ॥
जो कत्थूरियपङ्कप्पङ्किउ ।
जो अरिकरिहिँ ण डोहेवि सक्किउ ॥
जो सुरसउणसहासेहिँ मण्डिउ ।
जो कामिणिथणचक्केहिँ चड्डिउ ॥
तहिँ तेहएँ सरें सेयजलोल्लिउ ।
लक्खणवयणकमलु पप्फुल्लिउ ॥

like the full moon; one had wide, lotus-like eyes, the other's charmingly twinkled; one's head smelled of beautiful flowers, the other's was embellished with a lovely crown.

All the people recognized the first one with these characteristics. The second one, however, was secretly a woman disguised as a man.

11

Obsessed with that catcher of uncatchable demons, the ruler of Kubara again and again eyed the great lake that was Lakshmana: he who pleased the beautiful women of the gods—its lotuses; who was smeared with musk ointment—its mud; who could not be restrained by his enemies—its elephants; who was adorned by thousands of his divine virtues—its birds;[6] whom the breasts of lovely ladies—its ruddy shelducks—rubbed against. In the midst of lake Lakshmana bloomed the lotus of his face: moist with

कण्ठमणोहरदीहरणालउ ।
वररोमञ्झकञ्झुकण्टालउ ॥
दसणसकेसरु अहरमहादलु ।
वयमयरन्दउ कण्णावत्तलु ॥
लोयणफुल्लन्धुयपरिचुम्बिउ ।
कुडिलवालसेवालकरम्बिउ ॥
लक्खणसरवरु
हउ भुक्खमहाहिमवाएं ।
तं मुहपङ्कउ
लक्खिवज्जइ कुव्वरराएं ॥

१२

जं मुहकमलु दिट्ठु ओहुल्लिउ ।
वालिखिल्लतणएण पवोल्लिउ ॥
हे णरणाहणाह भुवणाहिव ।
भोयणु भुञ्झहु सुकलत्तं पिव ॥
सगुलु सलोणउ सरसु सइच्छउ ।
महुरु सुअन्धु सणेहु सुपच्छउ ॥
तं भुञ्झेप्पिणु पढमपियासणु ।
पच्छलें किं पि करहु संभासणु ॥
तं णिसुणेवि पजम्पिउ लक्खणु ।

sweat for water; with a breathtaking, long stalk for
his neck; with prickly thorns that were his bodice of
bristling body hair; with filaments for his teeth and
large petals for his lips; with pollen for his voice and
whirlpools for his ears; kissed passionately by bees
for his eyes; and covered in the moss of his curly hair.
The ruler of Kubara noticed that that great lake
Lakshmana, his face like a lotus, was struck by a
severe, icy wind of hunger.

12

Seeing his wilted lotus-like face, Valikhilya's daughter*
said, "King of kings, lord of the world, enjoy a meal
like a good wife: with molasses as her kisses, salt as
her charm, juices as her affection, your wishes as her
desires, sweet, with nice aromas for her perfume,
oiliness for her tenderness, and good for you, just
like her beautiful buttocks.[7] Once you have eaten this
exquisite, lovely food, you may talk a bit." At this,

* Kalyanamala.

अमरवरङ्गणणयणकडक्खणु ॥
उहु जो दीसइ रुक्खु रवण्णउ ।
पत्तलवहलडालसंछण्णउ ॥
आयहों विउलें मूलें दणुदारउ ।
अच्छइ सामिसालु अम्हारउ ॥
लक्खणवयर्णेहिँ
वलु कोक्किउ चलिउ सकन्तउ ।
करिणिविहूसिउ
णं वणगइन्दु मल्हन्तउ ॥

१३

गुलुगुलन्तु हलहेइ महग्गउ ।
तरुवरगिरिकन्दरहों विणिग्गउ ॥
सेयपवाहगलियगण्डत्थलु ।
तोणाजुयलविउलकुम्भत्थलु ॥
पिच्छावलिअलिउलपरिमालिउ ।
किङ्किणिगेज्जामालोमालिउ ॥
वित्थियवाणविसाणभयङ्करु ।
थोरपलम्बववाहुलम्वियकरु ॥
धणुवरलग्गणखम्भुम्मूलणु ।
दुट्ठारुट्ठमेट्टपडिकूलणु ॥
सरसिक्कार करन्तु महावलु ।
तिसभुक्खएँ खलन्तु विहलङ्घलु ॥

Lakshmana, eyed by the beautiful wives of the gods,
answered, "That pleasant tree that you see over
there, covered with dense foliage and branches, near
the thick root of that one sits our supreme master, a
destroyer of demons."
At Lakshmana's words, she summoned the Baladeva. He
set out together with his wife, like a great playful
forest elephant, accompanied by his elephant cow.

13

The Baladeva departed from the great tree as a huge
roaring elephant comes out from a mountain cave:
his cheeks trickling with streams of sweat for ichor;
his two quivers for frontal lobes; garlanded with
rows of fletched arrows for bee swarms; festooned
with tinkling bells for a neck chain; terrifying with
the arrows he brandished for tusks; his firm, long
arms for his pendulous trunk; pulling out his bow
like a tying post; opposing the lure of sin as if it were
a cruel mahout; emitting words like trumpetings;
formidable, stumbling, and confused from thirst
and hunger; angrily taking aim at his shadow, but

छाहिहें वेज्झइँ देन्तु विरुद्धउ ।
जिणवरवयणङ्कुसेण णिरुद्धउ ॥
जाणइवरगणियारिविहूसिउ ।
तं पेक्खेंवि जणवउ उद्धूसिउ ॥
मञ्झारुहणहों
उत्तिण्णु असेसु वि रायगणु ।
मेरुणियम्वहों
णं णिवडिउ गहतारायणु ॥

१४

हरिकल्लाणमाल दणुदलणेहिँ ।
पडिय वे वि वलएवहों चलणेहिँ ॥
अच्छहुँ ताव देव जलकीलएँ ।
पच्छएँ भोयणु भुञ्झहुँ लीलएँ ॥
एम भणेप्पिणु दिण्णइँ तूरइँ ।
झल्लरितुणवपणवदडिपहरइँ ॥
पइठ ससाहण सरवरणहयलें ।
फुलन्धुअभमन्तगहमण्डलें ॥
धवलकमलणक्खत्तविहूसिएँ ।
मीणमयरकक्कडएँ पदीसिएँ ॥
उत्थल्लन्तसफरिचलविज्जुलें ।
णाणाविहविहङ्घघणसङ्कुलें ॥
कुवलयदलतमोहदरिसावणें ।

subdued by the goad of the great Jina's words;
accompanied by Janaka's daughter as a beautiful
elephant cow. When the people saw him, they were
delighted.

The entire band of kings descended from their elevated
seats. It was as if a multitude of planets and stars flew
down from the flank of Mount Meru.

14

Both the Vasudeva and Kalyanamala fell at the demon-
crushing feet of the Baladeva, "Lord, first let us pass
some time with water play. Then, we can dine at
pleasure." At these words, drums were struck, along
with the beating of the *jhallarī, tuṇava, paṇava,* and
daḍi drums.[8] Together with the army, they entered
into the great lake that resembled the sky: with
bees as its revolving planetary spheres; embellished
with white lotuses for stars; with fish, crocodiles,
and crabs appearing for Pisces, Capricorn, and
Cancer;[9] with darting *śaphari*[10] fish for unsteady
lightning bolts; flocked by manifold birds for clouds;
displaying the petals of blue water lilies like a flood

सीयरणियरवरिसवरिसावर्णे ॥
जलतरङ्गसुरचावारम्भिएँ ।
वलजोइसियचक्कपवियम्भिएँ ॥
तहिँ सरणहयलें
सकलत्त वे वि हरिहलहर ।
रोहिणिरण्णहिँ
णं परिमिय चन्ददिवायर ॥

१५

तहिँ तेहएँ सरें सलिलें तरन्तइँ ।
संचरन्ति चामीयरजन्तइँ ॥
णाइँ विमाणइँ सग्गहों पडियइँ ।
वण्णविचित्तरयणवेयडियइँ ॥
णत्थि रयणु जहिँ जन्तु ण घडियउ ।
णत्थि जन्तु जहिँ मिहुणु ण चडियउ ॥
णत्थि मिहुणु जहिँ णेहु ण वड्ढिउ ।
णत्थि णेहु जो णउ सुरयड्ढिउ ॥
तहिँ णरणारिजुवइ जलकीलएँ ।
कीलन्ताइँ ण्हन्ति सुरलीलएँ ॥
सलिलु करग्गेहिँ अप्फालन्तइँ ।
मुरववज्जघायइँ दरिसन्तइँ ॥
खलिएँहिँ वलिएँहिँ अहिणवगेँहिँ ।

of darkness; raining down showers of abundant
sprays; generating waves on the water for rainbows;
appearing in full glory with the army for the zodiac.
In that firmament-like lake, both the Vasudeva and the
Baladeva together with their women resembled
the moon and the sun accompanied by Rohini* and
Ranna.

15

There in that lake golden machines were moving about,
floating in the water. They resembled celestial
chariots, fallen from heaven, inlaid with gems
of diverse colors. There was no gem with which
a machine had not been fashioned; no machine
onto which a couple had not climbed; no couple in
whom love had not intensified; no love that was not
accompanied by lovemaking. During that repose in
the water, men, women, and young ladies bathed as
they frolicked with divine ease, tossing up water with
their hands, marking a beat with tambourines. With
all the twisting and turning, and playing new songs,

---

* Asterism personified as the moon's favorite wife.

वन्धहिँ सुरयक्खित्तियभेऍहिँ ॥
छन्देंहिँ तालेंहिँ वहुलयभङ्ग्रेंहिँ ।
करणुच्छित्तेंहिँ णाणाभङ्ग्रेंहिँ ॥
चोक्खु सरागउ
सिङ्गारहारदरिसावणु ।
पुक्खरजुज्झु व
तं जलकीलणउ सलक्खणु ॥

१६

जलें जयजयसद्देँ ण्हाय णर ।
पुणु णिग्गय हलसारङ्गधर ॥
एत्थन्तरेँ समरेँ समत्थऍण ।
सिरणमियकयञ्जलिहत्थऍण ॥
तणुलुहणइँ देवि पहाणऍण ।
पुणु तिण्णि वि कुव्वरराणऍण ॥
पच्छण्णें भवणें पइसारियइँ ।
चामियरवीढें वइसारियइँ ॥
वित्थारिउ वित्थरु भोयणउ ।
सुकलत्तु व इच्छ ण भञ्जणउ ॥
रज्जं पिव पट्टविहूसियउ ।
तूरं पिव थालालङ्कियउ ॥
सुरयं पिव सरसु सतिम्मणउ ।

and positions and wounds caused by lovemaking, the
pleasures, the hand claps, the frequent breaks in the
rhythm, abandoning hand signals and all the many
contortions,
that lovely, passionate water play, a display of erotic
gestures, bore all the signs of a war waged in the lake.

16

With cheers of triumph the people bathed in the water.
Then the Baladeva and the Vasudeva came out.
After their bodies had been rubbed dry, the principal
ruler of Kubara, skilled in battle, her hands cupped
in reverence and bowing her head, led the three of
them into her private dwelling and invited them
each to sit on a golden seat. She had an elaborate
meal spread out, which, like a good wife, did not
disappoint their desires. It was adorned by dishes,
like kingship by the turban.[11] Like a drum, it was
adorned with metal plates. With its flavors and
sauces, it was like lovemaking, passionate and with
the mind directed toward the woman.[12] It shone with

वायरणु व सहइ सविण्णउ ॥
तं भुत्तु सइच्छऍ भोयणउ ।
णं किउ जगणाहें पारणउ ॥
दिण्णु विलेवणु
दिण्णइँ देवङ्गइँ वत्थइँ ।
सालङ्कारइँ
णं सुकइकियइँ सुइसत्थइँ ॥

१७

तीहि मि परिहियाइँ देवङ्गइँ ।
उवहिजलाइँ व वहलतरङ्गइँ ॥
दुल्लहलम्भइँ जिणवयणाइँ व ।
पसरियपट्टइँ उच्छवणाइँ व ॥
दीहरछेयइँ अत्थाणाइँ व ।
फुल्लियडालइँ उज्जाणाइँ व ॥
णिच्छिद्दइँ कइकव्वपयाइँ व ।
हलुवइँ चारणजणवयणाइँ व ॥
लण्हइँ कामिणिमुहकमलाइँ व ।
वड्डुइँ जिणवरधम्मफलाइँ व ॥
समसुत्तइँ किण्णरमिहुणाइँ व ।
अहसंमत्तइँ वायरणाइँ व ॥

its seasoning, like grammar with consonants.[13] They
enjoyed that meal at pleasure, like the Jina, the lord
of the world, when he broke his fast.
They were given ointments and ornate, divine garments,
like faultless treatises composed by good poets with
figures of speech.[14]

17

The three put on the divine garments: with their dense
cloth they were like the waters of the ocean with
abundant waves;[15] difficult to procure like the words
of the Jina; with ribbons issuing from them like
sugarcane forests with widespread foliage;[16] with
long slits like assemblies with long interruptions;[17]
with wide borders like gardens with flowering
branches;[18] they were unblemished, just as the feet in
a poem by a good poet do not have imperfections;[19]
light like the words of bards; soft like the lotus-like
faces of lovely ladies; ample like the fruits of the
teachings of the great Jina; made with smooth yarn
like couples of Kinnaras that have fallen asleep
together;[20] finished at the bottom like grammars

तो एत्थन्तरें कुव्वरसारें ।
ओयारिउ सण्णाहु कुमारें ॥
सुरवरकुलिसमज्झतनुअङ्घें ।
णावइ कञ्चुउ मुक्कु भुअङ्घें ॥
तिहुअणणाहेण
सुरजणमणणयणाणन्दें ।
मोक्खहों कारणें
संसारु व मुक्कु जिणिन्दें ॥

१८

तहिँ एक्कन्तभवणें पच्छण्णऍ ।
जं अप्पाणु पगासिउ कण्णऍ ॥
पुच्छिय राहवेण परिओसें ।
अक्खु काइँ तुहुँ थिय णरवेसें ॥
तं णिसुणेप्पिणु पगलियणयणी ।
एम पजम्पिय गग्गिरवयणी ॥
रुद्दभुत्तिणामेण पहाणउ ।
दुज्जउ विज्झमहीहरराणउ ॥
तेण धरेप्पिणु कुव्वरसारउ ।
वालिखिल्लु णिउ जणणु महारउ ॥
तें कज्जें थिय हउँ णरवेसें ।
जिह ण मुणिज्जमि जणेण असेसें ॥

made complete with words like *atha,* "now."[21] Then
the young woman, the chief of Kubara, took off
her armor, her body slender at the waist like the
thunderbolt of Indra, leader of the gods, as if she
were a snake that had shed its skin,
like the great Jina, the lord of the three worlds, a joy to the
hearts and eyes of the gods, who abandoned samsara
for the sake of liberation.

18

When the girl revealed herself in those private, secluded
quarters, Rama, the descendant of Raghu,
questioned her with delight, "Tell us, why do you live
disguised as a man?" At this, her eyes dripping with
tears and her voice stuttering, she answered, "There
is a king named Rudrabhuti, the invincible ruler of
the Vindhya mountains. He captured and took away
the leader of Kubara named Valikhilya, my father.
For that reason I live here disguised as a man, so
that no one recognizes me." When the Vasudeva

तं णिसुणेवि वयणु हरि कुद्धउ ।
णं पञ्चाणणु आमिसलुद्धउ ॥
अच्चन्तन्तणेत्तु फुरियाहरु ।
एम पजम्पिउ कुरुडु समच्छरु ॥
जइ समरङ्गणें
तं रुद्दभुत्ति णउ मारमि ।
तो सहुँ सीयएँ
सीराउहु णउ जयकारमि ॥

१९

जं कल्लाणमाल मम्भीसिय ।
लहु णरवेसु लइउ आसासिय ॥
ताव दिवायरु गउ अत्थवणहों ।
लोउ पढुक्कउ णियणियभवणहों ॥
णिसिणिसियरि दसदिसहिँ पधाइय ।
महिगयणोट्टु डसेँवि संपाइय ॥
गहणक्खत्तदन्तउद्दन्तुर ।
उवहिजीहगिरिदाढाभासुर ॥
घणलोयणससितिलयविहूसिय ।
सज्झालोहियदित्तपदीसिय ॥
तिहुयणवयणकमलु दरिसेप्पिणु ।
सुत्त णाइँ रविमडउ गिलेप्पिणु ॥

heard this, he became furious, like a lion longing
for prey. With bloodshot eyes and trembling lips he
ferociously and wrathfully answered thus:
"If I do not kill that Rudrabhuti on the battlefield, then I
will not cheer for the Baladeva and Sita."

19

When Kalyanamala was reassured and consoled, she
quickly put on her male disguise. Meanwhile the
sun set and people went to their homes. Like a
female demon, night advanced in the ten directions:
biting with the earth and the sky as her lips, she
approached; horrifying with the planets and stars
as her teeth; dreadful with the ocean as her tongue
and the mountains as her tusks; adorned with clouds
as her eyes, and the moon as her forehead mark;
appearing as if on fire with the redness of twilight.
Showing her lotus-like face to the three worlds and
devouring the corpse of the sun, she fell asleep, as it
were. Having chased away her powerful army,[22] and

ताव महावलवलु विण्णासेंवि ।
तालवत्तें णियणामु पगासेंवि ॥
सीयएँ सहुँ वलकण्ह विणिग्गय ।
णित्तुरङ्ग णीसन्दण णिग्गय ॥
ताव विहाणउ
रवि उट्ठिउ रयणिविणासउ ।
गय अच्छन्ति व
णं दिणयरु आउ गवेसउ ॥

२०

उट्ठेंवि कुव्वरपुरपरमेसरु ।
जाव सहत्थें वायइ अक्खरु ॥
ताव तिलोयहों अतुलपयावइँ ।
सुरवरभवणविणिग्गयणावइँ ॥
दुद्दमदाणवेन्दआयामइँ ।
दिट्ठइँ लक्खणरामहुँ णावइँ ॥
खणें कल्लाणमाल मुच्छंगय ।
णिवडिय केलि व खरपवणाहय ॥
दुक्खु दुक्खु आसासिय जावेंहिँ ।
हाहाकारु पमेल्लिउ तावेंहिँ ॥
हा हा राम राम जगसुन्दर ।
लक्खण लक्खणलक्खसुहङ्कर ॥

clearly leaving behind their name on a palm leaf, the
Baladeva and Vasudeva, together with Sita, went
forth, without horses, chariots, or elephants.
Then at daybreak the sun, destroyer of night, arose. It
was as if the sun came to inquire whether they had
departed.

20

When the supreme ruler of the city of Kubara got up and
herself read out what they'd written, she saw the
names of Rama and Lakshmana, of unequaled glory
for the three worlds, their fame going forth to the
palaces of the great gods, restrainers of unstoppable
kings of demons. Immediately Kalyanamala fainted,
like a banana tree that fell down, struck by a fierce
wind. When she was brought to with great difficulty,
she emitted howls, "Ah, ah, Rama, Rama, the most
handsome man on earth! Lakshmana, whose lakhs

हा हा सीऍं सीऍं उप्पेक्खमि ।
तिहि मि जणहुँ एक्कं पि ण पेक्खमि ॥
एम पलाउ करन्ति ण थक्कइ ।
खणें णीससइ ससइ खणें कोक्कइ ॥
खणें खणें जोयइ
चउदिसु लोयणेंहिँ विसालेंहिँ ।
खणें खणें पहणइ
सिरकमलु सइं भुवडालेंहिँ ॥

of fine features are a joy to behold! Ah, ah, Sita, Sita! I look up, but I do not see any of you three." As she mourned thus, she could not stand still. One instant she sighed and panted, the next she was calling.

All the time she was looking in the four directions with her wide eyes and all the time she was striking her lotus-like head with her branch-like arms.

सत्तवीसमो संधि

तो सायरवज्जावत्तधर
सुरडामर असुरविणासयर ।
णारायणराहव रणें अजय
णं मत्त महागय विज्झु गय ॥

१

ताणन्तरें णम्मय दिट्ठु सरि ।
सरि जणमणणयणाणन्दकरि ॥
करिमयरकराहयउहयतड ।
तडयड पडन्ति णं वज्जझड ॥
झडभीमणिणाएं गीढभय ।
भयभीयसमुट्ठियचक्कहय ॥
हयहिंसियगज्जियमत्तगय ।
गयवरअणवरयविसट्टमय ॥
मयमुक्ककरम्विय वहइ महु ।
महुयर रुण्टन्ति मिलन्ति तहु ॥
तहों धाइय गन्धवपवहगण ।
गणभरियकरञ्जलि तुट्ठमण ॥
मणहर ढेक्कार मुअन्ति वल ।
वलकमलकरम्विय सङ्कदल ॥

Chapter 27

Then the Vasudeva and Rama, the descendant of Raghu, bearers of the bows Samudra and Vajravarta, causing turmoil among the gods and destruction for the demons, invincible in battle, each like a grand rutting elephant, went to the Vindhya mountains.

1

In the meantime they saw the river Narmada: the river,
    bringing joy to the hearts and eyes of the people;
    both its banks pounded by the trunks and snouts
    of elephants and crocodiles; crackling like a falling
    lightning strike; gripped by fear from the terrible
    noise of the rapids; its terrified ruddy shelducks
    stirred up together; with neighing horses and
    roaring rutting elephants; filled with ichor issuing
    continuously from the heads of great elephants.
    Covered in deer musk she flowed sweetly. Bees
    hummed and met with her. A cluster of streams
    moved toward her, as if they were Gandharvas,
    delighted in their hearts, with the flocks fulfilling
    the cupping of the hands in reverence. Bulls were
    mooing breathtakingly. She was surrounded by bulls
    like lotuses, their horns like petals. On a petal, bees
    were hovering near a filament, the filament that was
    brought to the lord Jina.[1]

दलें भमर परिट्टिय केसरहों ।
केसरु णिउ णवर जिणेसरहों ॥
तो सीराउहसारङ्गधर
सहुँ सीयएँ सलिलें पइट्ठु णर ।
उवयारु करेप्पिणु रेवयएँ
णं तारिय सासणदेवयएँ ॥

२

थोवन्तरें महिहर भुअणसिरि ।
सिरिवच्छें दीसइ विज्झइरि ॥
इरिणप्पहु ससिपहु कण्हपहु ।
पिहुलप्पहु णिप्पहु झीणपहु ॥
मुखो व्व सतालु सवंसहरु ।
विसहो व्व ससिङ्कु महन्तडरु ॥
मयणो व्व महाणलदद्धतणु ।
जलउ व्व सवारि भडु [व्]व सवणु ॥
तहिं तेहएँ सेलें अहिट्ठियइँ ।
दुणिमित्तइँ ताव समुट्ठियइँ ॥
फेक्कारइ सिव वायसु रसइ ।
भीसावणु भण्डणु अहिलसइ ॥
सरु सुणेवि पकम्पिय जणयसुअ ।
थिय विहि मि धरेप्पिणु भुऍहिँ भुअ ॥

Then the men, the Baladeva and the Vasudeva, entered
into the water together with Sita. By offering them
her service, the Narmada, like the goddess of the
doctrine, helped them cross over.

2

A bit farther on, king,[2] Lakshmana beheld the world-
renowned Vindhya mountain range: Iranaprabha,
Shashiprabha, Krishnaprabha, Prithulaprabha,
Nishprabha, and Kshinaprabha. With its palmyras
and bamboo forests it was like a tambourine,
following talas and supporting the bamboo flute;[3]
with peaks and most terrifying, like a large, horned
dara bull;[4] its grasses scorched by great fires, like
Kama, the god of love, whose body was incinerated
by a great fire;[5] like a raincloud with its water; and
like an injured soldier with its forests.[6] There on that
mountain range they halted. Then bad omens arose:
a jackal cried, a crow cawed and terrifyingly spoiled
for a fight. When Janaka's daughter heard that

किं ण सुउ चवन्तु वि को वि णरु ।
जिह सउणउ माणिउ देइ वरु ॥
तं णिसुणॆवि असुरविमद्दणॆण
मम्भीसिय सीय जणद्दणॆण ।
सिय लक्खणु वलु पञ्चक्खु जहिँ
कउ सउणविसउणॆहिँ गण्णु तहिँ ॥

३

एत्थन्तरें रहससमुच्छलिउ ।
आहेडएँ रुद्दभुत्ति चलिउ ॥
तिसहासॆहिँ रहवरगयवरॆहिँ ।
तद्दूणतुरङ्ॆहिँ णरवरॆहिँ ॥
संचल्लें विज्झपहाणॆण ।
लक्खिज्जइ जाणइ राणॆण ॥
पप्फुल्लियधवलकमलवयण ।
इन्दीवरदलदीहरणयण ॥
तणु मज्झें णियम्वें वच्छें गरुअ ।
जं णयणकडक्खिय जणयसुअ ॥
उम्मायणमयणॆहिँ मोहणॆहिँ ।
वाणॆहिँ संदीवणसोसणॆहिँ ॥
आयल्लिउ सल्लिउ मुच्छियउ ।
पुणु दुक्खु दुक्खु ओमुच्छियउ ॥

sound, she trembled. Clasping her arms, she stood
there, "Did you not hear some person talking? We
should consider this an ill omen."
Hearing this, the Vasudeva, crusher of demons, reassured
Sita, "What do good or bad omens count for when
noble Lakshmana and the Baladeva stand before
you?"

3

Meanwhile Rudrabhuti eagerly rose up and set out for
the hunt with three thousand mighty chariots
and elephants, twice as many horses, and with his
noblemen. As the eminent king of the Vindhyas
departed, he noticed Janaka's daughter, her face like
a blooming white lotus, her eyes wide like the petals
of a blue water lily, slender at the waist and heavy at
the hips and bosom. As he eyed Janaka's daughter,
he was tormented and pierced by the maddening,
intoxicating, bewildering, inflaming, and scorching
arrows of Kama, and fainted.[7] Then with great
difficulty he came back to his senses. He squeezed

कर मोडइ अङ्गु वलइ हसइ ।
ऊससइ ससइ पुणु णीससइ ॥
मयरद्धयसरजज्जरियतणु
पहु एम पजम्पिउ कुइयमणु ।
वलिमण्डएँ वणवसि वणवसहुँ
उद्दालेवि आणहों पासु महु ॥

४

तं वयणु सुणेप्पिणु णरणियरु ।
उत्थरिउ णाइँ णवअम्बुहरु ॥
गज्जन्तमहागयघणपवलु ।
तिक्खग्गखग्गविज्जुलचवलु ॥
हयपडहपगज्जियगयणयलु ।
सरधाराधोरणिजलवहलु ॥
धुअधवलछत्तडिण्डीरवरु ।
मण्डलियचावसुरचावकरु ॥
सयसन्दणवीढभयावहलु ।
सियचमरवलायपन्तिविउलु ॥
ओरसियसङ्खदद्दुरपउरु ।
तोणीरमोरणच्छणगहिरु ॥
तं पेक्खेवि गुञ्जपुञ्जणयणु ।
दद्दोट्टरुद्दरोसियवयणु ॥

his hands, twisted his body, smiled, gasped, panted, and again sighed.

His body torn to pieces by Kama's arrows, the king's heart grew enraged, and he spoke thus: "Seize that forest-dwelling woman from those forest-dwellers by force, and bring her to me!"

4

Hearing those words, the band of men attacked like a new rainstorm: awesome with their roaring grand elephants for clouds; flickering with their sharp-edged swords for lightning; the firmament thundering with their resounding drums; dense with streams of arrows for rain showers; with trembling white umbrellas for beautiful foam; creating rainbows with the bent bows; accompanied by the radiance of hundreds of chariot seats; with white flywhisks for impressive flocks of cranes; abounding in reverberating horns for frogs; with deep quivers for the solemn dancing of peacocks. When the

आवद्धतोणु धणुहरु अभउ ।
धाइउ लक्खणु लहु लद्धजउ ॥
तं रिउकङ्कालविणासयरु
हलहेइहें भायरु सीयवरु ।
जणमणकम्पावणु सरपवणु
हेमन्तु पढुक्किउ महुमहणु ॥

५

अप्फालिउ महुमहणेण धणु ।
धणुसद्दें समुट्ठिउ खरपवणु ॥
खरपवणपहय जलयर रडिय ।
रडियागमें वज्जासणि पडिय ॥
पडिया गिरि सिहर समुच्छलिय ।
उच्छलिय चलिय महि णिद्दलिय ॥
णिद्दलिय भुअङ्ग विसग्गि मुक्क ।
मुक्कन्त णवर सायरहँ ढुक्क ॥
ढुक्कन्तेहिँ वहल फुलिङ्ग चित्त ।
घण सिप्पिसङ्कसंपुड पलित्त ॥
धगधगधगगन्ति मुत्ताहलाइँ ।
कढकढकढढन्ति सायरजलाइँ ॥
हसहसहसन्ति पुलिणन्तराइँ ।
जलजलजलन्ति भुअणन्तराइँ ॥

226

triumphant, fearless archer Lakshmana saw this, his
eyes turned red like a heap of crab's-eye beans, his
face grew furious and, fuming as he bit his lips, he
tightly tied on his quiver and he rushed at them.
The brother of the Baladeva, cherished by Sita, the
Vasudeva advanced like the cold season, bringing
about the end of the monsoon of his enemies and
sending shivers through the hearts of people with
the wind of his arrows.

5

The Vasudeva shot his bow: with the twang of the
bow-string a sharp wind arose. Struck by the sharp
wind, the clouds howled. As the howling erupted,
a lightning bolt fell. Mountains crashed, peaks flew
up, the earth rose up, shook, and went to pieces.
Snakes were hit and vomited burning poison. As they
vomited, it went all the way to the oceans. When it
approached, it gave off dense sparks and the hard
exteriors of shells and conches burst into flames.
Pearls were hissing, the ocean's waters were sizzling,
the spaces between sandbanks were fizzing, the
spaces between the worlds were blazing. Because of

तें धणुहरसद्दें णिट्ठुरेण ।
रिउ मुक्क पयावमडप्फरेण ॥
भयभीय विसण्ठुल णर पवर
लोट्टाविय हय गय धय चमर ।
धणुहरटङ्कारपवणपहय
रिउतरुवर णं सयखण्ड गय ॥

एत्थन्तरें तो विज्झाहिवइ ।
सहुँ मन्तिहिँ रुद्दभुत्ति चवइ ॥
इमु काइँ होज्ज तइलोक्कभउ ।
किं मेरुसिहरु सयखण्ड गउ ॥
किं दुन्दुहि हय सुरवरजणेण ।
किं गज्जिउ पलयमहाघणेण ॥
किं गयणमग्गें तडि तडयडिय ।
किं महिहरें वज्जासणि पडिय ॥
किं कालु कयन्तमित्तु हसिउ ।
किं वलयामुहु समुद्दु रसिउ ॥
किं इन्दहों इन्दत्तणु टलिउ ।
खयरक्खसेण किं जगु गिलिउ ॥
किं गउ पायालहों भुवणयलु ।
वम्भण्डु फुट्टु किं गयणयलु ॥

that harsh sound of the bow, his enemies' dignity and pride deserted them.

The great men were terrified and confused. The horses, elephants, flags, and flywhisks were left to wallow in chaos. Struck by the wind of the twanging of the bow, the immense tree of the enemy forces went to hundreds of pieces.

6

Then the king of the Vindhyas, Rudrabhuti, spoke with his ministers, "What could be terrifying all the three worlds? Has the peak of Mount Meru gone to hundreds of pieces? Have the great gods struck their kettledrum? Is it the thundering of the great cloud of destruction? Is it crackling lightning on the path of the sky? Has a lightning bolt fallen onto a mountain? Is it Kala, the time of death, friend of Yama, the terminator, who is laughing? Is it the ocean or the Mare's Mouth* that is resounding? Has Indra ceased to be Indra? Has the earth been devoured by a demon of destruction? Has the surface of the earth become a Patala?[8] Did the universe or the sky burst open? Did the wind of destruction set off from its place? Did a lightning strike hit?

---

* The entrance to the lower regions, situated in the ocean.

किं खयमारुउ ठाणहों चलिउ ।
किं असणिणिहाउ समुच्छलिउ ॥
किं सयल ससायर चलिय महि
किं दिसिगय किं गज्जिय उवहि ।
ऍउ अक्खु महन्तउ अच्छरिउ
कहों सद्दें तिहुअणु थरहरिउ ॥

७

जं णरवइ एव चवन्तु सुउ ।
पभणइ सुभुत्ति कण्टइयभुउ ॥
सुणि अक्खमि जं तइलोक्कभउ ।
णउ मेरुसिहरु सयखण्ड गउ ॥
णउ दुन्दुहि हय सुरवरजणेण ।
णउ गज्जिउ पलयमहाघणेण ॥
णउ गयणमग्गें तडि तडयडिय ।
णउ महिहरें वज्जासणि पडिय ॥
णउ कालु कियन्तमित्तु हसिउ ।
णउ वलयामुहु समुद्दु रसिउ ॥
णउ इन्दहों इन्दत्तणु टलिउ ।
खयरक्खसेण णउ जगु गिलिउ ॥
णउ गउ पायालहों भुवणयलु ।
वम्भण्डु फुट्टु णउ गयणयलु ॥

230

Did the entire earth shake with its oceans? Did the
cardinal elephants roar? Or the oceans? Explain this
great wonder. Whose sound has disturbed the three
worlds?"

7

As he heard the king speaking thus, Subhuti answered,
as the hair on his arms bristled with excitement,
"Listen, I will explain the terror of the three worlds:
it is not the peak of Mount Meru that has gone to
hundreds of pieces; nor did the great gods strike
their kettledrum; nor the thundering of the great
cloud of destruction; nor crackling lightning on the
path of the sky; nor did a lightning bolt fall onto a
mountain; nor is Kala, the time of death, friend of
Yama, the terminator, laughing; nor is the ocean or
the Mare's Mouth resounding; nor has Indra ceased
to be Indra; nor has the earth been devoured by the
demon of destruction; nor has the earth's surface
become a Patala; nor did the universe or the sky
burst open; nor did the wind of destruction set off

णउ खयमारुउ थाणहों चलिउ ।
णउ असणिणिहाउ समुच्छलिउ ॥
णउ सयल ससायर चलिय महि ।
णउ दिसिगय णउ गज्जिय उवहि ॥
सियलक्खणवलगुणवन्तएँण
णीसेसु वि जउ धवलन्तएँण ।
सुकलत्तें जिम जणमणहरेँण
एँउ गज्जिउ लक्खणधणुहरेँण ॥

८

सुण्णे णरवइ असुरपरायणहुँ ।
जं चिण्हइँ वलणारायणहुँ ॥
तं अत्थि असेसु वि वणवसहुँ ।
सुरभुवणुच्छलियमहाजसहुँ ॥
एक्कहों ससिणिम्मलधवलु तणु ।
अण्णेक्कहों कुवलयघणकसणु ॥
एक्कहों महिमाणदण्ड चलण ।
अण्णेक्कहों दुद्दमदणुदलण ॥
एक्कहों तणु मज्झु पदीसियउ ।
अण्णेक्कहों कमलविहूसियउ ॥
एक्कहों वच्छत्थलु सियसहिउ ।
अण्णेक्कहों सीयाणुग्गहिउ ॥
एक्कहों भीसावणु हेइ हलु ।

232

from its place; nor did a lightning strike hit; nor did
the entire earth with its oceans shake; nor did the
cardinal elephants roar, nor did the oceans.
This roaring is caused by the archer Lakshmana, who
brightens up the entire world, endowed with
splendor, auspicious characteristics, might, and
virtue, and as lovely for people to behold as a good
wife.

8

"Listen, king: these forest-dwellers, whose great fame
shot up to the world of the gods, possess all the
characteristics of the demon-vanquishing Baladeva
and Vasudeva. One has a body, shining and white
like the moon; the other's is dark like blue water
lilies or clouds. One has feet that are clubs against
the earth's arrogance; the other's crush unstoppable
demons. One is seen with a slender waist; the other's
is adorned with lotuses. One has a chest bearing the
śrīvatsa mark; the other's is cherished by Sita. One
has the horrifying plow for a weapon; the other a

अण्णेक्कहों धणुहरु अतुलवलु ॥
एक्कहों मुहु ससिकुन्दुज्जलउ ।
अण्णेक्कहों णवघणसामलउ ॥
तं वयणु सुणेप्पिणु विगयमउ
णीसन्दणु णिग्गउ णित्तुरउ ।
वलएवहों चलणेहिँ पडिउ किह
अहिसेएँ जिणिन्दहों इन्दु जिह ॥

९

जं रुद्दभुत्ति चलणेहिँ पडिउ ।
तं लक्खणु कोवाणलें चडिउ ॥
धगधगधगगन्तु ।
थरथरथरन्तु ॥
हणु हणु भणन्तु ।
णं कलि कियन्तु ॥
करयल धुणन्तु ।
महि णिद्दलन्तु ॥
विप्फुरियवयणु ।
णिट्ठुरियणयणु ॥
महिमाणदण्डु ।
परवलपचण्डु ॥

bow of unmatched might. One's face is luminous like
the moon or jasmine flowers; the other's is dark like a
fresh cloud."

What was it like when Rudrabhuti fell without pride,
chariots, elephants, or horses at the feet of the
Baladeva, once he had heard those words? It was like
Indra at the consecration of the lord Jina.

9

As Rudrabhuti fell at Rama's feet, Lakshmana ascended
a fire of anger. Sizzling and crackling, saying, "Kill!
Kill!" he was like Kali or Yama, the terminator.
Shaking his hands, tearing up the earth, his face
flashing, and his eyes terrifying, a club to the
arrogance of the earth, ferocious against the enemy

सो चविउ एव ।
रिउ मेल्लि देव ॥
जं पइज एण ।
पुज्जइ हएण ॥
तं वयणु सुणेप्पिणु अतुलवलु
सुणु लक्खण पचविउ एव वलु ।
मुक्काउहु जो चलणेहिँ पडइ
तें णिहएं को जसु णिव्वडइ ॥

१०

थिउ लक्खणु वलेण णिवारियउ ।
णं वरगइन्दु कण्णारियउ ॥
णं सायरु मज्जायएँ धरिउ ।
पुणु पुणु वि चविउ मच्छरभरिउ ॥
खल खुद्द पिसुण तउ सिरकमलु ।
एत्तडेण चुक्कु जं णविउ वलु ॥
वरि वालिखिल्लु मुएँ वन्दि लहु ।
णं तो जीवन्तु ण जाहि महु ॥
तं णिसुणेवि णिविसें मुक्कु पहु ।
णं जिणवरेण संसारपहु ॥
णं गहकल्लोलें अमियतणु ।
णं गरुडविहड्डें उरगमणु ॥

army, he spoke thus, "Lord, dismiss the enemy so
that I fulfill my promise by killing him."
Hearing those words, the Baladeva, of unmatched might,
answered thus, "Listen, Lakshmana, what glory
befalls you by killing a man who has discarded his
weapons and has fallen at my feet?"

10

Lakshmana stood there, restrained by the Baladeva, like
a fine bull elephant goaded at the ears, or like the
ocean held back by the coast. He then spoke again,
filled with wrath, "Mean, vile wretch, thus far your
lotus-like head has escaped, because it bows to the
Baladeva. Better release the prisoner Valikhilya
quickly! If not, you will not get away from me alive."
At this, Rudrabhuti released the king in the blink
of an eye, like the great Jina forsaking the path of
samsara, like Rahu, enemy of the planets, releasing
the ambrosia-bodied moon, like the bird Garuda
releasing a snake. Like a good person who has

णं मुक्कु सुअणु दुज्जणजणहों ।
णं वारणु वारिणिवन्धणहों ॥
णं मुक्कु भविउ भवसायरहों ।
तिह वालिखिल्लु दुक्खोयरहों ॥
ते रुद्भुत्तिवलमहुमहण
सहुँ कुव्वरणिवेंण चयारि जण ।
थिय जाणइ तेहिँ समाणु किह
चउसायरपरिमिय पुहइ जिह ॥

११

तो वालिखिल्लविज्झाहिवइ ।
अवरोप्परु णेहणिवद्धमइ ॥
कमकमलेंहिँ णिवडिय हलहरहों ।
णमिविणमि जेम चिरु जिणवरहों ॥
सइँ हत्थें वलेण समुट्ठविय ।
उवहि व समएहिँ परिट्ठविय ॥
भरहहों पाइक्क वे वि थविय ।
लहु णियणियणिलयहुँ पट्ठविय ॥
उत्तिण्णइँ तिण्णि वि महिहरहों ।
णं भवियइँ भवदुक्खोयरहों ॥
णं मेरुणियम्वहों किण्णरइँ ।
णं सग्गहों चवियइँ सुरवरइँ ॥

escaped a crowd of bad folk, like an elephant from an elephant trap, like a person capable of salvation escaping the ocean of existence, Valikhilya came out of the prison.

How did Janaka's daughter stand with them, these four men, Rudrabhuti, the Baladeva, and the Vasudeva, together with the king of Kubara? Like the earth enclosed by the four oceans.

11

Then Valikhilya and the king of the Vindhyas, their minds fixed on mutual affection, fell at the Baladeva's lotus-like feet, like long ago Nami and Vinami did before the great Jina.[9] The Baladeva then lent them his hands and had them stand up, like oceans directed by the tides. He appointed them both as foot soldiers of Bharata and quickly sent them to their abodes. The three* came down from the mountain, like persons capable of salvation escaping from the prison of existence, like Kinnaras from the flank of Mount Meru, like great gods descending from heaven.

* Rama, Lakshmana, and Sita.

विणु खेवें तावि पराइयइँ ।
किर सलिलु पियन्ति तिसाइयइँ ॥
णवरुण्हउ रवियरतावियउ ।
सुकुडुम्बु व खलसंतावियउ ॥
दिणयरवरकिरणकरम्बियउ
जलु लेवि भुऍहिँ परिचुम्बियउ ।
पइसन्तु ण भावइ मुहहों किह
अण्णाणहों जिणवरवयणु जिह ॥

१२

पुणु तावि तरेप्पिणु णिग्गयइँ ।
णं तिण्णि मि विज्झमहागयइँ ॥
वइदेहि पजम्पिय हरिवलहों ।
सुरवरकरिकरथिरकरयलहों ॥
जलु कहि मि गवेसहों णिम्मलउ ।
जं तिसहरु हिमससिसीयलउ ॥
तं इच्छमि भविउ व जिणवयणु ।
णिहि णिद्धणु जच्चन्धु व णयणु ॥
वलु धीरइ धीरी होहि धणें ।
मं कायरु मुहु करि मिगणयणें ॥
थोवन्तरु पुणु विहरन्तऍहिँ ।
मल्हन्तेंहिँ पउ पउ देन्तऍहिँ ॥

Without delay they arrived at the river Tapi. Being
thirsty, they drank deep of its water. It was definitely
hot, warmed by the rays of the sun, like a good family
afflicted by a scoundrel.

They took the water that was beset with beautiful sunrays
in their hands and kissed it. How was it unpleasant
to their mouths as it entered? Like the words of the
great Jina to a benighted man.

12

Crossing the Tapi, they then emerged like three great
Vindhya elephants. Videha's daughter said to the
Vasudeva and the Baladeva, their hands firm like
the trunks of the elephant of the great gods, "Find
clean water somewhere to take away my thirst, cool
like snow or the moon. I long for it, like a person
capable of salvation longs for the words of the Jina,
like a pauper longs for treasure, and like a man who
is blind from birth longs for an eye." The Baladeva
assured her, "Be brave, my love. Do not look
frightened, deer-eyed woman." Wandering a little
farther and enjoying themselves at every step, they

लक्खिवज्जइ अरुणगामु पुरउ ।
वयवन्धविहूसिउ जिह मुरउ ॥
कप्पदुमो व्व चउद्दिसु सुहलु ।
णट्टावउ व्व णाडयकुसलु ॥
तं अरुणगामु संपाइयइँ
मुणिवर इव मोक्खतिसाइयइँ ।
सो णउ जणु जेण ण दिट्ठाइँ
घरु कविलहों गम्पि पइट्ठाइँ ॥

१३

णिज्झाइउ तं घरु दियवरहों ।
णं परमथाणु थिरु जिणवरहों ॥
णिरवेक्खु णिरक्खरु केवलउ ।
णिम्माणु णिरञ्जणु णिम्मलउ ॥
णिव्वत्थु णिरत्थु णिराहरणु ।
णिद्दुणु णिब्भत्तउ णिम्महणु ॥
तहिँ तेहएँ भवणें पइट्ठाइँ ।
छुडु छुडु जलु पिएँवि णिविट्ठाइँ ॥
कुञ्जर इव गुहें आवासियइँ ।
हरिणा इव वाहुत्तासियइँ ॥
अच्छन्ति जाव तहिँ एक्कु खणु ।
दिउ ताव पराइउ कुइयमणु ॥

came upon Arunagrama in front of them, adorned
with arrangements of enclosed pieces of land like
a tambourine is embellished with leather straps,[10]
successful all around like a wishing tree bears good
fruits on all sides,[11] as familiar with yoking ropes as a
dance master is skilled in dancing.[12]
They reached that Arunagrama, thirsty like great sages
longing for liberation. There was no one who did not
notice them. They went to the house of Kapila and
entered.

13

They beheld that house of the prominent Brahman, firm
like the ultimate abode of the great Jina: there were
no wants, no sounds; and it stood isolated, humble,
colorless, and clean, without valuable objects, riches,
or ornaments, without wealth, food, or the churning
of dairy.[13] There in that house they entered.
Drinking some water, they gradually settled there,
like elephants dwelling in a cave, or deer frightened
by a tiger. As they were sitting there for a moment,
the Brahman arrived, with a furious temper, saying,

मरु मरु णीसरु णीसरु भणन्तु ।
धूमद्धूउ व्व धगधगधगगन्तु ॥
भयभीसणु कुरुडु सणिच्छरु व्व ।
वहुउवविसविण्णउ विसहरु व्व ॥
किं कालु कियन्तु मित्तु वरिउ
किं केसरि केसरग्गेँ धरिउ ।
को जममुहकुहरहों णीसरिउ
जो भवणें महारएँ पइसरिउ ॥

१४

तं वयणु सुणेप्पिणु महुमहणु ।
आरुट्टु समरभरउव्वहणु ॥
णं धाइउ करि थिरथोरकरु ।
उम्मूलिउ दियवरु जेम तरु ॥
उग्गामेवि भामेवि गयणयलें ।
किर घिवइ पडीवउ धरणियलें ॥
करें धरिउ ताव हलपहरणेँण ।
मुएँ मुएँ मा हणहि अकारणेँण ॥
दियवालगोलपसुतवसितिय ।
छ वि परिहरु मेल्लेवि माणकिय ॥
तं णिसुणेवि दियवरु लक्खणेँण ।
णं मुक्कु अलक्खणु लक्खणेँण ॥

"Die! Die! Get out! Get out!" like a sizzling fire,
    terrifying and fierce like Saturn, highly skilled in
    poisonous substances like a snake:
"Have Kala, the time of death, and his friend Yama, the
    terminator, been restrained? Has a lion been caught
    by the tip of its mane? Who are you, who have
    entered my house, having escaped from Yama's
    gaping mouth?"

14

Hearing those words, the Vasudeva, who could bear the
    weight of battle, was enraged. He rushed forth with
    his firm, strong arms—like an elephant with a firm,
    strong trunk—and uprooted the Brahman like a
    great tree. Lifting him and hurling him in the air,
    he smashed him back onto the ground. Then the
    Baladeva stopped him by the hand, "Leave him,
    leave him, do not kill for no reason! Forsake your
    haughty actions and spare these six: the Brahman,
    the child, the cow, the wild animal, the ascetic,
    and the woman." At this, Lakshmana released the

ओसरिउ वीरु पच्छामुहउ ।
अङ्कुसणिरुद्धु णं मत्तगउ ॥
पुणु हियएँ विसूरइ खणें जें खणें ।
सयखण्डखण्डु वरि हूउ रणें ॥
वरि पहरिउ वरि किउ तवचरणु
वरि विसु हालाहलु वरि मरणु ।
वरि अच्छिउ गम्पिणु गुहिलवणें
णवि णिविसु वि णिवसिउ अवुहयणें ॥

१५

तो तिण्णि वि एम चवन्ताइं ।
उम्माहउ जणहों जणन्ताइं ॥
दिणपच्छिमपहरें विणिग्गयाइँ ।
कुञ्जर इव विउलवणहों गयाइँ ॥
वित्थिण्णु रण्णु पइसन्ति जाव ।
णग्गोहु महादुमु दिट्ठु ताव ॥
गुरुवेसु करेंवि सुन्दरसराइँ ।
णं विहय पढावइ अक्खराइँ ॥
वुक्कणकिसलय कक्का रवन्ति ।
वाउलिविहङ्ग किक्की भणन्ति ॥
वणकुक्कुड कुक्कू आयरन्ति ।

246

Brahman, like a good characteristic forsaking a
person who is without auspicious signs. Averting
his face, the valiant man stepped aside, like a rutting
elephant checked by a goad. Again and again
Lakshmana felt distress in his heart, "It is better
to have been shattered into thousands of pieces in
battle,
better to have been struck, better to have practiced
asceticism, *hālāhala* poison* is better, death is better,
it is better to go into an impenetrable forest and live
out one's days, than to dwell even for a moment in
the company of fools."

15

Speaking thus, the three, who caused a stir among the
people, departed in the last *prahara*† of the day.
Like elephants, they went toward a vast forest.
As they entered the immense forest, they saw a great
banyan tree. Taking on the guise of a teacher, it was
as if it made birds recite beautiful sounding syllables.
Twigs with crows echoed, "Ka-kaa," sky-going flying
foxes said, "Kee-keeee," forest cocks went, "Ku-koo,"

---

* Mythological poison generated by the churning of the ocean.
† The eighth part of a day, about three hours.

अण्णु वि कलाव केक्कइ चवन्ति ॥
पियमाहवियउ कोक्कउ लवन्ति ।
कंका वप्पीह समुल्लवन्ति ॥
सो तरुवरु गुरुगणहरसमाणु ।
फलपत्तवन्तु अक्खरणिहाणु ॥
पइसन्तेहिँ असुरविमद्दणेहिँ
सिरु णामेवि रामजणद्दणेहिँ ।
परिअञ्चेवि दुमु दसरहसुऍहिँ
अहिणन्दिउ मुणि व सइं भुऍहिँ ॥

peacocks moreover said, "Kay-kaay," female cuckoos called, "Ko-kow." Herons and pied cuckoos sang together. That great tree with its fruits and foliage, that treasure of sounds, was like the Master and his first disciples with their good karma and begging bowls, a treasure of sacred words.[14]

As Rama and the Vasudeva, the crushers of demons, the sons of Dasharatha, came closer, bowing their heads, they embraced the tree with their encircling arms, as if it were a sage.

अट्ठावीसमो संधि

सीय सलक्खणु दासरहि
तरुवरमूलें परिट्ठिय जावेंहिँ ।
पसरइ सुकइहें कव्वु जिह
मेहजालु गयणङ्गणें तावेंहिँ ॥

१

पसरइ मेहविन्दु गयणङ्गणें ।
पसरइ जेम सेण्णु समरङ्गणें ॥
पसरइ जेम तिमिरु अण्णाणहों ।
पसरइ जेम वुद्धि वहुजाणहों ॥
पसरइ जेम पाउ पाविट्ठहों ।
पसरइ जेम धम्मु धम्मिट्ठहों ॥
पसरइ जेम जोण्ह मयवाहहों ।
पसरइ जेम कित्ति जगणाहहों ॥
पसरइ जेम चिन्त धणहीणहों ।
पसरइ जेम कित्ति सुकुलीणहों ॥
पसरइ जेम सद्दु सुरतूरहों ।
पसरइ जेम रासि णहें सूरहों ॥
पसरइ जेम दवग्गि वणन्तरें ।
पसरइ मेहजालु तिह अम्वरें ॥

250

Chapter 28

While Sita, Lakshmana, and Rama, the son of Dasharatha, stood at the base of the great tree, a cover of clouds spread out across the sky, like poetry that issues forth from a good poet.

1

The mass of clouds spread out in the sky, like an army on
    the battlefield, like darkness out of ignorance, like
    insight from a learned man, like sin from the greatest
    sinner, like righteousness from the most righteous,
    like moonlight from the ambrosia-bearing moon, like
    fame from the lord of the world, like anxiety from
    a pauper, like fame from a person of noble birth,
    like sound from the drum of the gods, like a ray of
    light from the sun in the sky, like a wildfire within
    a forest. Like this the cover of clouds spread in the

तडि तडयडइ पडइ घणु गज्जइ ।
जाणइ रामहों सरणु पवज्जइ ॥
अमरमहाधणुगहियकरु
मेहगइन्दें चडेंवि जसलुद्धउ ।
उप्परि गिम्भणराहिवहों
पाउसराउ णाइँ सण्णद्धउ ॥

२

जं पाउसणरिन्दु गलगज्जिउ ।
धूलीरउ गिम्भेण विसज्जिउ ॥
गप्पिणु मेहविन्दें आलग्गउ ।
तडिकरवालपहारेंहिँ भग्गउ ॥
जं विवरम्मुहु चलिउ विसालउ ।
उट्ठिउ हणु भणन्तु उण्हालउ ॥
धगधगधगधगगन्तु उद्धाइउ ।
हसहसहसहसहसन्तु संपाइउ ॥
जलजलजलजलजल पचलन्तउ ।
जालावलिफुलिङ्ग मेल्लन्तउ ॥
धूमावलिधयदण्डुब्भेंप्पिणु ।
वरवाउल्लिखग्गु कड्ढेप्पिणु ॥
झडझडझडझडझडन्तु पहरन्तउ ।
तरुवररिउभडथड भज्जन्तउ ॥
मेहमहागयघड विहडन्तउ ।

sky. Lightning crackled and fell. A cloud thundered.
Janaka's daughter took to Rama for protection.
It was as if King Monsoon, his hand clenching his grand
rainbow, mounted on his elephant of clouds and,
eager for glory, was ready for battle against King
Summer.

2

When King Monsoon thundered, Summer released a
cloud of dust. It went and latched onto the mass of
clouds but was crushed by sword strikes of lightning.
As the vast cloud of dust ran away with its face
averted, Summer rose up, saying, "Kill!" He rushed
forth sizzling and came near hissing. Blazing as he
advanced; discharging rows of flames and sparks;
raising wreaths of smoke—his flagstaffs; pulling
out a fierce wind—his sword; howling, attacking,
and shattering great trees—the hordes of enemy
soldiers; tearing into the clouds—the troop of grand

जं उण्हालउ दिट्टु भिडन्तउ ॥
धणु अप्फालिउ पाउसेण ।
तडिटङ्कारफार दरिसन्तें ॥
चोऍवि जलहरहत्थिहड ।
णीरसरासणि मुक्क तुरन्तें ॥

३

जलवाणासणिघायहिँ घाइउ ।
गिम्भणराहिउ रणें विणिवाइउ ॥
दद्दुर रडेँवि लग्ग णं सज्जण ।
णं णच्चन्ति मोर खल दुज्जण ॥
णं पूरन्ति सरिउ अक्कन्दें ।
णं कइ किलिकिलन्ति आणन्दें ॥
णं परहुय विमुक्क उग्घोसें ।
णं वरहिण लवन्ति परिओसें ॥
णं सरवर वहुअंसुजलोल्लिय ।
णं गिरिवर हरिसें गज्जोल्लिय ॥
णं उण्हविअ दवग्गि विओएं ।
णं णच्चिय महि विविहविणोएं ॥
णं अत्थमिउ दिवायरु दुक्खें ।
णं पइसरइ रयणि सइँ सुक्खें ॥
रत्तपत्त तरु पवणाकम्पिय ।

elephants. When he saw Summer was attacking,
Monsoon shot his bow, generating loud blasts with
his twanging of lightning. He urged on his
elephant troop of clouds and quickly discharged a
thunderbolt-like arrow of water.

3

Struck down by the hits of the water arrows, King
Summer perished in the war. Frogs began to croak as
if they were his relatives. Peacocks danced as if they
were wicked scoundrels. Rivers filled up as if from
crying. Monkeys screeched as if with joy. Cuckoos
were robbed of their cooing, as it were. Peacocks
screamed as if with delight. Great lakes were wet as if
with the water from their abundant tears. Enormous
mountains seemed to bristle with excitement. Forest
fires grew thin as if from lovesickness. The earth
danced as if with many kinds of play. The sun set as
if from sorrow. Night herself came forth as if with
pleasure. Trees with blood red leaves were stirred

केण वि वहिउ गिम्भु णं जम्पिय ॥
तेहएँ कालें भयाउरएँ ।
वेण्णि मि वासुएववलएव ॥
तरुवरमूलें ससीय थिय ।
जोगु लएविणु मुणिवर जेम ॥

४

हरिवल रुक्खमूलें थिय जावेर्हिँ ।
गयमुहु जक्खु पणासेवि तावेर्हिँ ॥
गउ णियणिवहों पासु वेवन्तउ ।
देव देव परिताहि भणन्तउ ॥
णउ जाणहुँ किं सुरवर किं णर ।
किं विज्जाहरगण किं किण्णर ॥
धणुधर धीर पडायउ उब्भेवि ।
सुत्त महारउ णिलउ णिरुम्भेवि ॥
तं णिसुणेविणु वयणु महाइउ ।
पूवणु मम्भीसन्तु पधाइउ ॥
विज्झमहीहरसिहरहों आइउ ।
तक्खणें तं उद्देसु पराइउ ॥
ताम णिहालिय वेण्णि वि दुद्धर ।
सायरवज्जावत्तधणुद्धर ॥

256

by the wind and seemed to say, "Someone killed
Summer."
At that moment of anguish, both the Vasudeva and the
Baladeva stayed at the base of the great tree, along
with Sita, like great sages taking up yoga.

4

While the Vasudeva and the Baladeva stood at the base of
the tree, the trembling Yaksha Gajamukha fled and
went to his king, saying, "Lord, lord, help! We do not
know if they are gods, humans, Vidyadharas, Ganas,
or Kinnaras. Some bold archers raised their banners,
besieged my house, and fell asleep there." Hearing
those words, the magnanimous Putana reassured
him and set out. He came from a peak of the Vindhya
mountains and immediately arrived in that area.
Then he observed the two unstoppable bearers of the

अवहीणाणु पउञ्जइ जार्वेहिँ ।
लक्खणराम मुणिय मणें तार्वेहिँ ॥
पेक्खेँवि हरिवल वे वि जण ।
पूवणजक्खें जयजसलुद्धें ॥
मणिकङ्कणधणजणपउरु ।
पट्टणु किउ णिमिसद्धहोँ अद्धें ॥

५

पुणु रामउरि पघोसिय लोएं ।
णं णारिहेँ अणुहरिय णिओएं ॥
दीहरपन्थपसारियचलणी ।
कुसुमणियत्थवत्थसाहरणी ॥
खाइयतिवलितरङ्गविहूसिय ।
गोउरथणहरसिहरपदीसिय ॥
विउलारामरोमरोमञ्चिय ।
इन्दगोवसयकुङ्कुमअञ्चिय ॥
गिरिवरसरियपसारियवाही ।
जलफेणावलिवलयसणाही ॥
सरवरणयणघणञ्झणअञ्जिय ।
सुरधणुभउहपदीसियपञ्जिय ॥
देउलवयणकमलु दरिसेप्पिणु ।
वरमयलञ्छणतिलउ छुहेप्पिणु ॥

bows Samudravarta and Vajravarta. With the help of
his *avadhi** knowledge, he understood that they were
Lakshmana and Rama.

Beholding the two, the Vasudeva and the Baladeva, the
Yaksha Putana, eager for victory and glory, instantly
built a city overflowing in gems, gold, riches, and
people.

5

The people then named it Ramapuri, the city of Rama. It
certainly resembled a woman: with long roads for
her extended feet; with flowers as the garments and
ornaments that she wore; embellished with moats as
the swells of her three belly folds; with distinct city
gates as the tips of her full breasts; bristling with vast
gardens as her erect body hair; honored by hundreds
of lac insects as saffron; with rivers coming from the
great mountains as her extended arms; endowed
with rows of foam on the water as her bracelets;
covered with clouds of kohl near the great lakes of
her eyes; appearing painted on with rainbows for
her eyebrows. It was as if she displayed the temple
as her lotus-like face, removed the beautiful moon

---

* Clairvoyance.

णाइँ णिहालइ दिणयरदप्पणु ।
एम विणिम्मिउ सयलु वि पट्टणु ॥
वइसेंवि वलहों पासें वीसत्थउ ।
आलावइ आलावणिहत्थउ ॥
एक्कवीसवरमुच्छणउ
सत्त वि सर तिगाम दरिसन्तउ ।
वुज्झि भडारा दासरहि
सुप्पहाउ तउ एव भणन्तउ ॥

६

सुप्पहाउ उच्चारिउ जावेहिँ ।
रामें वलेंवि पलोइउ तावेंहिँ ॥
दिट्ठु णयरु जं जक्खसमारिउ ।
णाइँ णहङ्गणु सूरिविहूसिउ ॥
सघणु सकुम्भु ससवणु ससङ्कउ ।
सवुहु सतारउ सगुरुससङ्कउ ॥
पुणु वि पडीवउ णयरु णिहालिउ ।
णाइँ महावणु कुसुमोमालिउ ॥
णाइँ सुकइहें कव्वु पयइत्तिउ ।
णाइँ णरिन्दचित्तु वहुचित्तउ ॥
णाइँ सेण्णु रहवरहँ अमुक्कउ ।
णाइँ विवाहगेहु सचउक्कउ ॥
णाइँ सुरउ चञ्चरिचरियालउ ।

260

as her forehead mark, and looked into the sun as her mirror. Thus the entire city was constructed. Sitting down near the Baladeva, bold Putana sang as he held his *ālāpinī* vina,

demonstrating twenty-one beautiful scales, seven notes, and three tone systems, saying, "Wake up, noble lord Rama, son of Dasharatha, there is a beautiful morning for you."

6

As Putana bid him good morning, Rama turned around and looked. When he saw the city built by the Yaksha, it was like the sky adorned by the sun: with its crowds for clouds, its water pots for the sign Aquarius, its wandering mendicants for the lunar mansion Shravana, with its uncertainties for the passage of planets through the zodiac, with its learned men for the planet Mercury, its ferrymen for stars, its teachers for Jupiter, and bridges for the moon.[1] He then looked at the city again. Like a great forest it was garlanded with flowers. It had subjects like the poetry of a good poet has all the right words.[2] It had many colors like the mind of a king has many thoughts.[3] Like an army there was no want of great chariots. It had four-road junctions like a wedding hall has a courtyard.[4] Like lovemaking it was full of merriment and action. Like a young child

णावइ डिम्भउ अहियच्छुहालउ ॥
अह किं वण्णिएण खणे जे खणें ।
तिहुअणे णत्थि जं पि तं पट्टणें ॥
तं पेक्खेप्पिणु रामउरि
भुअणसहासविणिग्गयणामहों ।
मच्छुडु उज्झाउरिणयरु
जाय महन्त भन्ति मणें रामहों ॥

जं किउ विम्भउ सासयलक्खें ।
वुत्तु णवेप्पिणु पूअणजक्खें ॥
तुम्हारउ वणवसणु णिएप्पिणु ।
किउ मइँ पट्टणु भाउ धरेप्पिणु ॥
एम भणेवि सुवित्थयणामहों ।
दिण्ण सुघोस वीण तें रामहों ॥
दिण्णु मउडु साहरणु विलेवणु ।
मणिकुण्डल कडिसुत्तउ कङ्कणु ॥
पुणु वि पजम्पिउ जक्खपहाणउ ।
हउँ तउ भिच्चु देव तुहुँ राणउ ॥
एव वोल्ल णिम्माइय जावेंहिँ ।
कविलें णयरु णिहालिउ तावेंहिँ ॥

is a receptacle of abundant hunger, it was an abode
of profuse plaster.[5] Indeed, why describe it time and
again? Whatever did not exist anywhere else in the
three worlds, that was there in the city.
Beholding that Ramapuri, great confusion arose in Rama's
mind, whose name went forth thousandfold in the
world, "Is it Ayodhya?"

7

Because the Yaksha Putana, whose qualities endured, had
astonished them, he took a bow and said, "When I
observed that you were residing in the forest, I built
a city, out of my affection for you." Speaking thus, he
gave the vina called Sughosha to far-famed Rama. He
offered a crown along with ornaments, ointments,
jeweled earrings, a belt, and a bracelet. Then the
master of the Yakshas said, "I am your servant, lord,
you are my king." As they spoke, Kapila saw the
amazing city, which resembled the heavens of the

जणमणहरु सुरसग्गसमाणउ ।
वासवपुरहों वि खण्डइ माणउ ॥
तं पेक्खेविवि आसङ्घिउ वम्भणु ।
कहिँ वित्थिण्णु रण्णु कहिँ पट्टणु ॥
थरहरन्तु भयमारुऍण
समिहउ घिर्वेवि पणासइ जार्वेहिँ ।
मम्भीसन्ति मियङ्कमुहि
पुरउ समाय जक्खि थिय तार्वेहिँ ॥

८

हे दियवर चउवेयपहाणा ।
किण्ण मुणहि रामउरि अयाणा ॥
जणमणवल्लहु राहवराणउ ।
मत्तगइन्दु व पगलियदाणउ ॥
तक्कुवभमरसएहिँ ण मुच्चइ ।
देइ असेसु वि जं जसु रुच्चइ ॥
जो घइँ जिणवरणामु लएइ ।
तहों कड्ढेप्पिणु पाणइँ देइ ॥
ऍउ जं वासवदिसऍ विसालउ ।
दीसइ तिहुअणतिलउ जिणालउ ॥
तहिँ जो गम्पि करइ जयकारु ।
पट्टणें णवरि तासु पइसारु ॥
तं णिसुणेप्पिणु दियवरु धाइउ ।

gods. It crushed the pride of Indra's city. Beholding
   it, the Brahman felt anxious, "Where is the vast
   forest? Where is the city?"
As he fled, shivering from the wind of fear and dropping
   his firewood, a moon-faced Yaksha lady by magic
   appeared before him, reassuring him,

8

"Hey great Brahman, master in the four Vedas, don't
   you know Ramapuri, silly man? King Rama,
   descendant of Raghu, the darling of the people's
   hearts, is handing out gifts like a great elephant
   in rut drops down ichor.[6] Hundreds of beggars
   and libertines never leave his side. He gives away
   everything, whatever anyone desires. For anyone
   who truly accepts the name of the great Jina, he
   draws out and offers his life. That vast Jina temple,
   Tribhuvanatilaka, that one sees in the East? Anyone
   who goes and sings praise there, he alone is allowed
   to enter into the city." At this, the great Brahman
   ran and in an instant reached the temple of the great

णिविसें जिणवरभवणु पराइउ ॥
तं चारित्तसूरु मुणि वन्देवि ।
विणउ करेवि अप्पाणउ णिन्देवि ॥
पुच्छिउ मुणिवरु दियवरेंण
दाणहों कारणें विणु सम्मत्तें ।
धम्में लइएं कवणु फलु
एउ देव महु अक्खि पयत्तें ॥

९

मुणिवरु कहेवि लग्गु विउलाइं ।
किं जणें ण णियहि धम्मफलाइं ॥
धम्में भडथड हय गय सन्दण ।
पावें मरणविओयक्कन्दण ॥
धम्में सग्गु भोगु सोहग्गु ।
पावें रोगु सोगु दोहग्गु ॥
धम्में रिद्धि विद्धि सिय संपय ।
पावें अत्थहीण णर विद्दय ॥
धम्में कडयमउडकडिसुत्ता ।
पावें णर दालिद्दें भुत्ता ॥
धम्में रज्जु करन्ति णिरुत्ता ।
पावें परपेसणसंजुत्ता ॥

266

Jina. After he had greeted the sage Charitrasura,
acted politely, and confessed his sins,
the great Brahman asked that great sage, "What is the
fruit in accepting a doctrine for the sake of a gift
without righteousness? Explain this to me with care,
lord."

9

The great sage began to speak, "Do you not see the fruits
of the doctrine among the people? Because of
the doctrine, there are troops of soldiers, horses,
elephants, and chariots; because of sin, there is
death, deprivation, and mourning. Because of the
doctrine, there is heaven, pleasure, and welfare;
because of sin, disease, sorrow, and misfortune.
Because of the doctrine, there is abundance, growth,
luster, and success; because of sin, people are
destitute and merciless. Because of the doctrine,
there are bracelets, crowns, and belts; because of
sin, people are consumed by poverty. Because of the

धम्में वरपल्लङ्कें सुत्ता ।
पावें तिणसंथारें विभुत्ता ॥
धम्में णर देवत्तणु पत्ता ।
पावें णरयघोरें संकन्ता ॥
धम्में णर रमन्ति वरविलयउ ।
पावें दूहविउ दुहणिलयउ ॥
धम्में सुन्दरु अङ्गु णिवड्ढउ ।
पावें पङ्गुलउ वि वहिरन्धउ ॥
धम्मपावकप्पदुमहुँ
आयइँ जसअवजसवहुलाइं ।
वेण्णि मि असुहसुहङ्करइँ
जाइँ पियइँ लइ ताइँ फलाइं ॥

१०

मुणिवरवयणेहिँ दियवरु वासिउ ।
लइउ धम्मु जो जिणवरें भासिउ ॥
पञ्चाणुव्वय लेवि पधाइउ ।
णियमन्दिरु णिविसेण पराइउ ॥
गम्पिणु पुणु सोम्महें वज्जरियउ ।
अज्जु महन्तु दिट्ठु अच्छरियउ ॥
कहिँ वणु कहिँ पट्टणु कहिँ राणउ ।
कहिँ मुणि दिट्ठु अणेयइँ जाणउ ॥

doctrine, people rule without question; because of
sin, they are appointed to serve another. Because
of the doctrine, people sleep in an excellent bed;
because of sin, they wind up on a bed of grass.
Because of the doctrine, people are reborn as a god;
because of sin, they pass into the horrors of hell.
Because of the doctrine, people enjoy beautiful
women; because of sin, a painful abode of sorrow.
Because of the doctrine, a handsome body is formed;
because of sin, a lame, deaf, and blind one.
Accept these two fruits, whichever you like, of the wishing
trees of doctrine and sin, abounding in fame and
infamy, and bringing misfortune and happiness."

10

The words of the excellent sage affected the great
Brahman, and he accepted the doctrine proclaimed
by the grand Jina. Receiving the five minor vows,
he ran off and in an instant arrived at his house.[7] He
then went to his wife Saumya and told her, "Today
I beheld a great miracle. Where did I see a forest?
Where a city? Where a king? Where a sage, who
knew many things? Where was my mind? Where

कहिँ मइ कहिँ लद्धइँ जिणवयणइँ ।
वहिरें कण्ण ऽन्धेण व णयणइँ ॥
तं णिसुणेवि सोम्म गज्जोल्लिय ।
जाहुँ णाह तहिँ एम पवोल्लिय ॥
पुणु संचल्लइँ वे वि तुरन्तइँ ।
तिहुयणतिलउ जिणालउ पत्तइँ ॥
साहु णवेप्पिणु पासें णिविट्ठइँ ।
धम्मु सुणेप्पिणु णयरें पइट्ठइँ ॥
दिट्ठु णरिन्दत्थाणु णहु
जाणइमन्दाइणिपरिचड्डिउ ।
णरणक्खत्तहिँ परियरिउ
हरिवलचन्ददिवायरमण्डिउ ॥

११

हरि अत्थाणमग्गें जं दिट्ठउ ।
दियवरु पाण लएवि पणट्ठउ ॥
णट्ठु कुरङ्गु व वारणवारहों ।
णट्ठु जिणिन्दु व भवसंसारहों ॥
णट्ठु मियङ्कु व अब्भपिसायहों ।
णट्ठु दवग्गि व णीरणिहायहों ॥
णट्ठु भुअङ्गु व गरुडविहङ्गहों ।
णट्ठु खरो व्व मत्तमायङ्गहों ॥

did I receive the words of the Jina, like a deaf person
receiving ears, or a blind person eyes?" Hearing
this, Saumya's body hair bristled. "Let us go there,
husband," she answered. The two then quickly set
out and reached the Jina temple, Tribhuvanatilaka.
Bowing to the sage, they sat near him, and after
hearing the doctrine, they went into the city.
They beheld the king's assembly hall, as if it were the
sky, frequented by Janaka's daughter—the Ganga,
attended by men—the stars, and adorned by the
Vasudeva and the Baladeva—the sun and the moon.

11

When, on the way to the assembly hall, the great Brahman
saw the Vasudeva, he fled to save his life. He fled like
a deer from a lion, like the lord Jina from the cycle
of rebirth, like the moon from Rahu, the demon in
the sky, like a forest fire from a mass of water, like
a snake from the bird Garuda, like an ass from a

णट्टु अणङ्कु व सासयगमणहों ।
णट्टु महाघणो व्व खरपवणहों ॥
णट्टु महीहरो व्व सुरकुलिसहों ।
णट्टु तुरङ्गमो व्व जममहिसहों ॥
तिह णासन्तु पदीसिउ दियवरु ।
मम्भीसन्तु पधाइउ सिरिहरु ॥
मण्ड धरेवि करेण करगऍं ।
गम्पि चित्तु वलएवहों अग्गऍं ॥
दुक्खु दुक्खु अप्पाणउ धीरेंवि ।
सयलु महब्भउ मणें अवहेरेंवि ॥
दुद्दमदाणविन्दवलमद्दहों ।
पुणु आसीस दिण्ण वलहद्दहों ॥
जेम समुद्दु महाजलेण
जेम जिणेसरु सुक्किरयकम्में ।
चन्दकुन्दजसणिम्मलेण
तिह तुहुँ वड्ढु णराहिव धम्में ॥

१२

तो एत्थन्तरें परवलमद्दणु ।
कहकहसद्दें हसिउ जणद्दणु ॥
भवणें पइट्ठु तुहारऍं जइयहुँ ।
पइँ अवगण्णेवि घल्लिय तइयहुँ ॥

rutting elephant, like bodiless Kama from the way
to eternity, like a great cloud from a sharp wind,
like a mountain from the divine thunderbolt, like a
horse from Yama's buffalo. Thus the great Brahman
seemed as he ran away. Saying reassuring words, the
Vasudeva rushed after him. Stopping him by forcibly
grabbing him by the hand, he went and threw him
before the Baladeva. With much difficulty the
Brahman braced himself, and disregarding all the
great fear welling up in his heart, he gave blessings
to the Baladeva, destroyer of armies of unassailable
demon-kings,

"Like the ocean with abundant water, like the lord Jina
with karma from good deeds, thus you, lord, are
filled with the doctrine, splendid and pure like the
moon or a jasmine."

12

Thereupon the Vasudeva, crusher of enemy armies, let
out a great laugh,[8] "When we entered your house,
you mistreated us and threw us out. And how is it
that the great Brahman here now gives blessings
and is acting so politely?" At this, the Brahman who

एत्थु कालें पुणु दियवरु कीसा ।
विणउ करेंवि पुणु दिण्ण असीसा ॥
तं णिसुणेवि भणइ वेयायरु ।
अत्थहों को ण वि करइ महायरु ॥
जिह आणन्दु जणइ सीयालएँ ।
तिह किं ण रुच्चइ रवि उण्हालएँ ॥
कालवसेण कालु वि सहेवउ ।
एत्थु ण हरिसु विसाउ करेवउ ॥
अत्थु विलासिणिजणमणवल्लहु ।
अत्थविहूणउ वुच्चइ घल्लहु ॥
अत्थु वियड्डु अत्थु गुणवन्तउ ।
अत्थविहूणु भमइ मग्गन्तउ ॥
अत्थु अणग्घु अत्थु जगें सूहउ ।
अत्थविहूणु दीणु णरु दूहउ ॥
अत्थु सइच्छिउ भुञ्जइ रज्जु ।
अत्थविहूणें किं पि ण कज्जु ॥
साहु भणन्तें राहवेंण
इन्दणीलमणिकञ्झणखण्डेंहिँ ।
कडयमउडकडिसुत्तयहिँ
पुज्जिउ कविलु सइं भुवदण्डेंहिँ ॥

honored the Vedas spoke, "Who does not show respect for wealth? Why is the sun not pleasant in the hot season, even though it brings joy in the cold season? One must tolerate time as time demands. This is no reason to feel happy or sad. Wealth is what the minds of wanton women crave. When a man has no wealth they say, 'Throw him out!' Wealth is clever; wealth is virtuous. A man without wealth can only wander around begging. Wealth is love. Wealth is blessed in the world. A poor man, one without wealth, is reviled. Wealth enjoys power however it wants. What can anyone do without wealth?"[9]

Saying, "Well done," Rama with his massive arms, himself honored Kapila with bracelets, crowns, and belts with sapphire, pearl, and gold.

एगुणतीसमो संधि

सुरडामररिउडमरकर
कोवण्डधर
सहुँ सीयएँ चलिय महाइय ।
वलणारायण वे वि जण
परितुट्ठमण
जीवन्तणयरु संपाइय ॥

पट्टणु तिहि मि तेहिँ आवज्जिउ ।
दिणयरविम्बु व दोसविवज्जिउ ॥
णवर होइ जइ कम्पु धएसु ।
हउ तुरएसु जुज्झु सुरएसु ॥
घाउ मुरवेसु ।
भज्जु चिहुरेसु ॥
जडउ रुद्देसु ।
मलिणु चन्देसु ॥
खलु खेत्तेसु ।
दण्डु छत्तेसु ॥
[वहु]कर गहणेसु ।
पहरु दिवसेसु ॥

Chapter 29

The two noble men, the Baladeva and the Vasudeva, terrifying the enemies who frightened the gods, together with Sita were delighted to reach the city of Jivanta.

1

These three observed the city. It was as flawless as the
   disc of the sun is devoid of darkness.[1] If there was
   shaking, it was only in flags, killing only in horses,
   fighting only in sexual encounters, a blow only on
   tambourines, decay only as the wave of hair, idiocy
   only as the matted locks on Rudra worshipers, sin
   only as the stain on the moon,[2] a villain only as a
   threshing floor in the fields, the rod only as the stick
   of umbrellas, high taxes only in the frequent taking
   of the hand in marriage, a blow only as a *prahara* in

धणु दाणेसु ।

चिन्त झाणेसु ॥

सुर सग्गेसु ।

सीहु रण्णेसु ॥

कलहु गएसु ।

अङ्कु कव्वेसु ॥

डरु वसहेसु ।

वेलु गयणेसु ॥

वणु रुक्खेसु ।

झाणु मुक्खेसु ॥

अहवइ कित्तिउ णिव वण्णिज्जइ ।

जइ पर तं जि तासु उवमिज्जइ

तहों णयरहों अवरुत्तरेंण

कोसन्तरेंण

उववणु णामेण पसत्थउ ।

णाइँ कुमारहों एन्ताहों

पइसन्ताहों

थिउ णवकुसुमञ्जलिहत्थउ ॥

days, a bow only as riches in gifts, anxiety only as thought in meditation, alcohol only as the gods in the heavens, a lion only in the forests, strife only as an elephant calf among adults, crime only as an act in drama compositions, fear only as a *ḍara* bull among bulls, a thief only as the edge of the skies, a wound only as a forest in trees, dullness only as meditation among eminent men.[3] Or rather, king,* how can it be portrayed? Perhaps only this place here† is comparable to it?

Less than a *krośa*‡ to the northwest of this city there was a park named Prashasta. With its fresh flowers, it seemed to stand with hands cupped in reverence for Prince Lakshmana as he entered it.

* Shrenika.
† Rajagriha, the city of Shrenika.
‡ Distance of 1¼ to 2 miles.

२

तहिँ उववणें थिय हरिवल जार्वेहिँ ।
भरहें लेहु विसज्जिउ तार्वेहिँ ॥
अग्गएँ चित्तु णरेण णरिन्दहों ।
भविउ व चलणेहिँ पडिउ जिणिन्दहों ॥
लइउ महीहरेण सइँ हत्थें ।
जिणवरधम्मु व मुणिवरसत्थें ॥
वारिणिवन्धहों मुक्कु गइन्दु व ।
दिट्ठु अङ्कु तहिँ णहयलें चन्दु व ॥
रज्जु मुएवि वे वि रिउमद्दण ।
गय वणवासहों रामजणद्दण ॥
को जाणइ हरि कद्दिउ आवइ ।
तहों वणमाल देज्ज जसु भावइ ॥
लेहु चिवेप्पिणु णरवइ महिहरु ।
णाइँ दवेण दड्डु थिउ महिहरु ॥
णाइँ मियङ्को कमिउ विडप्पें ।
तिह महिहरु णरिन्दु माहप्पें ॥
जाय चिन्त मणें दुद्धरहों
धरणीधरहों
सिंहिगलतमालघणवण्णहों ।
लक्खणु लक्खणलक्खधरु
तं मुएँवि वरु
मइँ दिण्ण कण्ण किं अण्णहों ॥

2

While the Vasudeva and the Baladeva settled in that park,
Bharata sent a letter. A man placed it before the king,
as a person capable of salvation falls at the feet of
the lord Jina. Mahidhara took it with his own hand,
like a band of excellent sages accepting the doctrine
of the great Jina. He took it out of its envelope, like
a grand elephant that is released from a trap, and
looked at its seal as if it were the moon in the sky,
"Those two crushers of enemies, Rama and the
Vasudeva, have left the kingdom behind and gone for
a stay in the forest. Who knows when the Vasudeva
arrives? Please give Vanamala to him, if it pleases
him." Tossing aside the letter, King Mahidhara stood
there like a mountain scorched by forest fire. Like
the moon is devoured by Rahu, King Mahidhara was
consumed by his arrogance.

A thought arose in the mind of the implacable Mahidhara,
whose complexion was like a peacock's neck or a
mass of dense darkness, "Shall I give my daughter to
someone else, forsaking that Lakshmana, bearer of
lakhs of auspicious signs, as a groom?"

३

तो एत्थन्तरें णयणविसालऍ ।
एह वत्त जं सुय वणमालऍ ॥
आउलिहुय हियएण विसूरइ ।
दुक्खें महणइ व्व आऊरइ ॥
सिरें पासेउ चडइ मुहु सूसइ ।
कर विहुणइ पुणु दइवहॉं रूसइ ॥
मणु धुगुधुगइ देहु परितप्पइ ।
वम्महॉं णं करवत्तें कप्पइ ॥
ताव णहङ्कणेण घणु गज्जिउ ।
णाइँ कुमारें दूउ विसज्जिउ ॥
धीरी होहि माऍ णं भासिउ ।
उहु लक्खणु उववणें आवासिउ ॥
गरहिउ मेहु तो वि तणुअङ्गिऍ ।
दोस वि गुण हवन्ति संसग्गिऍ ॥
तुहुँ किर जणमणणयणाणन्दणु ।
महु पुणु जलहर णाइँ हुआसणु ॥
तुज्झु ण दोसु दोसु कुलहॉं
हयदुहकुलहॉं
जलें जलणें पवणें जं जायउ ।
तं पासेउ दाहु करहु
णीसासु महु
तिण्णि वि दक्खवणहॉं आयउ ॥

3

When wide-eyed Vanamala heard those words, she
    became agitated and distressed in her heart. Like a
    great river she filled up with sadness. Sweat welled
    up on her head, her mouth became dry, and she
    shook her hands. Then she felt anger toward fate.
    Her mind was buzzing, her body burning with pain.
    It was as if Kama was cutting her with a saw. Then
    a cloud thundered in the sky, like a messenger sent
    by the youth Lakshmana. "Be brave, girl," it seemed
    to say, "for Lakshmana is residing in the park."
    Nevertheless the girl with her slender frame rebuked
    the cloud—qualities become faults in confusion,
    "They say that you bring joy to the hearts and eyes of
    the people. For me, cloud, you are like fire.
It is not your fault, it is the fault of your family—your
    lowly, miserable family—that you were born from
    water, heat, and wind. That is why you cause sweat,
    fever, and sighing. You have come to me, who is
    exhibiting all three."

४

दोच्छिउ मेहु पणट्ठु णहङ्गणें।
पुणु वणमालएँ चिन्तिउ णियमणें॥
किं पइसरमि वलन्तें हुआसणें।
किं समुद्दें किं रण्णें सुभीसणें॥
किं विसु भुञ्जमि किं अहि चप्पमि।
किं अप्पउ करवत्तें कप्पमि॥
किं करिवरदन्तहिँ उरु भिन्दमि।
किं करवालेहिँ तिलु तिलु छिन्दमि॥
किं दिस लङ्घमि किं पव्वज्जमि।
कहों अक्खमि कहों सरणु पवज्जमि॥
अहवइ एण काइँ गमु सज्जमि।
तरुवरडालएँ पाण विसज्जमि॥
एम भणेप्पिणु चलिय तुरन्ती।
कङ्क्रेल्लीथड उग्घोसन्ती॥
गन्धधूववलिपुप्फविहत्थी।
लीलएँ चिक्कमन्ति वीसत्थी॥
चउविहसेण्णें परियरिय
धण णीसरिय
को विहिँ आलिङ्गणु देसइ।
एम चवन्ति पइट्ठु वणें
रविअत्थवणें
कहिँ लक्खणु णाइँ गवेसइ॥

284

4

The scorned cloud disappeared in the sky. Then Vanamala
reflected in her mind, "Do I enter into a blazing fire?
Or into the ocean? Or into a terrifying forest? Do I
ingest poison? Do I go up to a snake? Do I cut myself
with a saw? Do I pierce my chest with the tusks of
a great elephant? Do I chop myself into tiny pieces
with swords? Do I go abroad? Do I renounce the
world? Whom should I tell? To whom should I go for
refuge? Or rather, what is the use of any of this? I am
ready to go. I will relinquish my life on the branch of
a great tree." With these words, she quickly set out,
announcing that she was going to the *asoka* grove.[4]
Feigning confidence as she walked, skilled with
perfume, incense, sacrificial food, and flowers,
accompanied by a fourfold army, the lovely girl went
outside. Saying, "Who of the two will embrace me?"[5]
she went into the forest as the sun set, as if it were
itself searching, wondering, "Where is Lakshmana?"

५

दिट्ठु असोयवच्छु परिअञ्चिउ ।
जिणवरो व्व सब्भावें अञ्चिउ ॥
पुणु परिवायणु कियउ असोयहाँ ।
अण्णु ण इहलोयहाँ परलोयहाँ ॥
जम्में जम्में मुअमुअहें सलक्खणु ।
पियभत्तारु होज्ज महु लक्खणु ॥
पुणु पुणु एम णमंसइ जार्वेहिँ ।
रयणिहें वे पहरा हुय तार्वेहिँ ॥
सयलु वि साहणु णिद्दोणल्लउ ।
णावइ मोहणजालें पेल्लिउ ॥
णिग्गय पुणु वणमाल तुरन्ती ।
हारडोरणेउरेंहिँ खलन्ती ॥
हरिविरहम्बुपूरें उब्भन्ती ।
वुण्णकुरङ्गि व चित्तुब्भन्ती ॥
णिविसद्धें णग्गोहें वलग्गी ।
रमणचवल णं गोहवलग्गी ॥
रेहइ दुमें वणमाल किह
घणें विज्जु जिह
पहवन्ती लक्खणकङ्घिणि ।
किलिकिलन्ति कोड्डावणिय
भीसावणिय
पन्चक्ख णाइँ वडजक्खिणि ॥

286

5

She saw an *aśoka* tree and walked around it, as if it were
the great Jina being honored with sincerity. Then
she cried to the *aśoka*, "There is no other in this
world and the next. In birth upon birth, from death
upon death, may Lakshmana, with his auspicious
characteristics, be my beloved husband!" As she
was paying homage again and again, the first two
praharas of the night passed by. The entire army
sank into slumber, as if afflicted by bewildering
magic. Vanamala then quickly set out, tottering with
all of her necklaces, strings, and anklets, wading
forth in an overflow of lovesickness for the Vasudeva,
distressed in her heart like a frightened doe. In half
an eyewink she climbed into a banyan tree, like a
charming, fickle woman approaching her paramour.
How did Vanamala appear in the tree? Like lightning in
a cloud, radiant in her longing for Lakshmana. It
was as if she were the genuine female Yaksha of the
banyan tree, screeching, marvelous, and terrifying.

तहिँ वालएँ कलुणु पकन्दियउ ।
वणडिम्भउ णं परिअन्दियउ ॥
आयण्णहों वयणु वणस्सइहों ।
गञ्झाणइजउणसरस्सइहों ॥
गहभूयपिसायहों विन्तरहों ।
वणजक्खहों रक्खहों खेयरहों ॥
गयवग्घहों सिद्धहों सम्वरहों ।
रयणायरगिरिवरजलयरहों ॥
गणगन्धव्वहों विज्जाहरहों ।
सुरसिद्धमहोरगकिण्णरहों ॥
जमखन्दकुवेरपुरन्दरहों ।
वुहभेसइसुक्कसणिच्छरहों ॥
हरिणङ्कहों अक्कहों जोइसहों ।
वेयालदइच्चहों रक्खसहों ॥
वइसाणरवरुणपहञ्झणहों ।
तहों एम कहिज्जहों लक्खणहों ॥
वुच्चइ धीय महीहरहों
दीहरकरहों
वणमालणाम भयवज्जिय ।
लक्खणपइ सुमरन्तियएँ
कन्दन्तियएँ
वडपायवें पाण विसज्जिय ॥

6

There the girl sobbed mournfully, as if she were the
forest's newborn that was crying: "Hear my words,
plants, Rivers Ganga, Yamuna, and Sarasvati,
Grahas, Bhutas, Pishachas, and Vyantaras, Yakshas
of the forest, Rakshasas who fly through the sky,
elephants, tigers, lions, and sambars, oceans,
great mountains, and clouds, Ganas, Gandharvas,
and Vidyadharas, gods, Siddhas, Mahoragas,
and Kinnaras, Yama, Skanda, Kubera, and Indra,
Mercury, Jupiter, Venus, and Saturn, moon, sun, and
heavenly bodies, Vetalas, Daityas, and Rakshasas,
Agni, Varuna, and Vayu![6] Please say this to that
Lakshmana,
'It is said that long-armed Mahidhara had a fearless
daughter named Vanamala. Thinking of Lakshmana
as her husband and crying, she relinquished her life
in a banyan tree.'"

७

एम भणेप्पिणु णयणविसालएँ ।
अंसुअपासउ किउ वणमालएँ ॥
सो ज्ज्ञें णाइँ सइँ मम्भीसावइ ।
णाइँ विवाहलील दरिसावइ ॥
णं दियवरु दाणहों हक्कारिउ ।
णाइँ कुमारें हत्थु पसारिउ ॥
गलें लाएँवि हल्लावइ जावेंहिँ ।
कण्ठें धरियालिङ्ग्रेंवि तावेंहिँ ॥
एम पजम्पिउ मम्भीसन्तउ ।
हउँ सो लक्खणु लक्खणवन्तउ ॥
दसरहतणउ सुमित्तिएँ जायउ ।
रामें सहुँ वणवासहों आयउ ॥
तं णिसुणेंवि विम्भाविय णियमणें ।
कहिँ लक्खणु कहिँ अच्छिउ उववणें ॥
ताम हलाउहु कोक्कइ लग्गउ ।
भो भो लक्खण आउ कहिँ गउ ॥
तं णिसुणेंवि महिहरसुअएँ
पुलइयभुअएँ
णडु जिह णच्चाविउ णियमणु ।
सहल मणोरह अज्जु महु
परिहूउ सुहु
भत्तारु लद्धु जं लक्खणु ॥

290

7

Speaking thus, wide-eyed Vanamala made a noose with
a garment. It itself appeared to reassure her, as
if it staged a pretend marriage, as if it were the
great Brahman summoned for the giving away
ceremony, as if it were the hand stretched out
by the groom. As she shuddered when she put it
around her neck, she was held by her throat while
it embraced her. Reassuring words were uttered,
"I am that Lakshmana, endowed with auspicious
characteristics, son of Dasharatha, born from
Sumitri, come for a stay in the forest together with
Rama." When she heard this, she felt astonishment
in her heart, "Where is Lakshmana? Where is he
settled in the park?" Then the Baladeva called close
by, "Hey, hey, Lakshmana, come! Where did you
go?"
At this, Mahidhara's daughter, her arms covered with
bristling body hair, allowed her heart to dance like
an actor, "Today all my wishes bear fruits. Happiness
has prevailed, for I have gotten Lakshmana as a
husband."

तो एत्थन्तरें भुवणाणन्दें ।
दिट्ठु जणद्दणु राहवचन्दें ॥
णावइ तमु दीवयसिहसहियउ ।
णावइ जलहरु विज्जुपगहियउ ॥
णावइ करि करिणिहें आसत्तउ ।
चलणेहिं पडिउ वलहों सकलत्तउ ॥
चारु चारु भो णयणाणन्दण ।
कहिं पइं कण्ण लद्ध रिउमद्दण ॥
वुत्तु कुमारें विज्ज व सगुणिय ।
धरणीधरहों धीय किं ण मुणिय ॥
जा महु पुव्वयण्णउवदिट्ठी ।
सा वणमाल एह वण्णें दिट्ठी ॥
हरि अप्फालइ जाव कहाणउ ।
ताम रत्ति गय विमलु विहाणउ ॥
सुहड विउद्ध कुद्ध जसलुद्धा ।
केण वि लइय कण्ण सण्णद्धा ॥
ताव णिहालिय दुज्जऍहिं
पुणु रहगयऍहिं
चाउद्दिसु चवलतुरङ्गेंहिं ।
वेढिय रणउहें वे वि जण
वलमहुमहण
पञ्चाणण जेम कुरङ्गेंहिं ॥

292

8

Thereupon moon-like Rama, the descendant of
Raghu, beheld the Vasudeva: it was like darkness
accompanied by the flame of a lamp, like a raincloud
seized by lightning, like an elephant clinging to an
elephant cow. Together with his consort, he fell at
the Baladeva's feet. "Dear brother, who brings joy to
my eyes, crusher of enemies, where did you find the
girl?" Prince Lakshmana spoke, "Do you not know
Mahidhara's daughter, virtuous like a *vidyā*? The one
who was pointed out to me before, this Vanamala
here, I saw her in the forest." While the Vasudeva
told his story, the night had passed and a pure dawn
had come. The warriors woke up, and angry and
eager for glory they put on their armor: "Someone
has taken the girl."
Then they observed the two men, the Baladeva and the
Vasudeva, and surrounded them on the battlefront
with unassailable chariots, elephants, and swift
horses on all sides, like deer surrounding lions.

९

अब्भिडु सेण्णु कलयलु करन्तु ।
जिह लइय कण्ण तिह हणु भणन्तु ॥
तं वयणु सुणेप्पिणु हरि पलित्तु ।
उद्धाइउ सिहि णं घिएँण सित्तु ॥
एक्कल्लउ लक्खणु वलु अणन्तु ।
आलग्गु तो वि तिणसमु गणन्तु ॥
परिसक्कइ थक्कइ चलइ वलइ ।
तरुवर उम्मूलेँवि सेण्णु दलइ ॥
उव्वडइ भिडइ पाडइ तुरङ्ग ।
महि कमइ भमइ भामइ रहङ्ग ॥
अवगाहइ साहइ धरइ जोह ।
दलवट्टइ लोट्टइ गयवरोह ॥
विणिवाइय धाइय सुहडथट्ट ।
कडुआविय विवरामुह पयट्ट ॥
णासन्ति के वि जे समरेँ चुक्क ।
कायरणरकरपहरणइँ मुक्क ॥
गम्पिणु कहिउ महीहरहों
एक्कहों णरहों
आवटु सेण्णु भुवदण्डएँ ॥
जिह णासहि जिम भिडु समरेँ
विहिँ एक्कु करेँ
वणमाल लइय वलिमण्डएँ ॥

9

The army was in an uproar as it attacked, with shouts
of, "Kill him, for he took the girl!" When he heard
those words, the Vasudeva became incensed. Like
a fire sprinkled with ghee, he attacked. Lakshmana
was alone; the army was boundless. Nevertheless he
engaged with it, considering it as useless as grass. He
ran around, halted, moved, and turned. Uprooting
great trees, he routed the army. He jumped up,
attacked, and toppled the horses. He walked over
the earth, roamed about, and left chariot wheels
spinning. He dove in between soldiers, overpowered
them, and captured them. He crushed and rolled
droves of great elephants. The troops of warriors
ran off defeated. Distressed and averting their faces,
they left. Some who had escaped in battle, fled. The
weapons lay abandoned where they fell from the
hands of the disheartened men.

Someone went and told Mahidhara, "The army has been
laid to waste by the club-like arm of a single man.
Either you flee or attack him in battle. You must do
one of the two. He has taken Vanamala by force."

तं वयणु सुणेप्पिणु थरहरन्तु ।
धरणीधरु धाइउ विप्फुरन्तु ॥
आरूढु महारहें दिण्णु सहु ।
सण्णद्धु कुद्धु जयलच्छिकहु ॥
तो दुज्जय दुद्धर दुण्णिवार ।
हणु हणु भणन्त णिग्गय कुमार ॥
वणमालकुसुमकल्लाणमाल ।
जयमालसुमालसुवण्णमाल ॥
गोपालपाल इय अट्ठ भाइ ।
सहुँ राएं णव गह कुइय णाइँ ॥
एत्थन्तरें रणें वहुमच्छरेण ।
हक्कारिउ लक्खणु महिहरेण ॥
वलु वलु समरङ्गणें देहि जुज्झु ।
णियणामु गोत्तु कहें कवणु तुज्झु ॥
तं णिसुणेँवि वोल्लिउ लच्छिगेहु ।
कुलणामहों अवसरु कवणु एहु ॥
पहरु पहरु जं पइँ गुणिउ
किण्ण वि मुणिउ
जसु भाइ महन्तउ रामु ।
रहुकुलणन्दणु लच्छिहरु
तउ जीवहरु
णरवइ महु लक्खणु णामु ॥

10

When Mahidhara heard those words, he set out, roaring
   and trembling with rage. He climbed into his
   great chariot, blew his conch, and angrily put on
   his armor, eager for the glory of victory. Then the
   unconquerable, unrestrainable, and unstoppable
   princes came out, saying, "Kill! Kill!" Vanamala,
   Kusuma, Kalyanamala, Jayamala, Sumala,
   Suvarnamala, Gopala, and Pala, these eight brothers
   together with the king were like the nine enraged
   planets. Then, full of wrath, Mahidhara challenged
   Lakshmana in battle, "Turn around, turn around,
   stand and fight on the battlefield! Tell me your name
   and your lineage." At this, Lakshmana, the abode
   of luster spoke, "Is this the moment to speak of my
   family name?
Strike! Strike! The one who was on your mind—do you not
   know?—whose brother is the great Rama, illustrious
   son from the family of Raghu, who will take away
   your life: king, my name is Lakshmana."

११

कुलु णामु कहिउ जं सिरिहरेण ।
धणु घत्तेवि महिहें महीहरेण ॥
सुरकरिकरसमभुअपञ्जरेण ।
अवरुण्डिउ णेहमहाभरेण ॥
हवि सक्खिकरेंवि अपरायणासु ।
सइँ दिण्ण कण्ण णारायणासु ॥
आरूढु महीहरु एक्करहें ।
अट्ठ वि कुमार अण्णेक्करहें ॥
वणमाल सलक्खण एक्करहें ।
थिय सवल सीय अण्णेक्करहें ॥
पडुपडहसङ्खवद्धावणेहिँ ।
णच्चन्तेंहिँ खुज्जयवामणेहिँ ॥
उच्छाहेंहिँ धवलेंहिँ मङ्गलेंहिँ ।
कंसालेंहिँ तालेंहिँ मद्दलेंहिँ ॥
आणन्दें णयरें पइट्ठाइँ ।
लीलएँ अत्थाणें वइट्ठाइँ ॥
सहुँ वणमालएँ महुमहणु
परितुट्ठमणु
जं वेइहें जन्तु पदीसिउ ।
लोएँहिँ मङ्गलु गन्तएँहिँ
णच्चन्तएँहिँ
जिणु जम्मणें जिह सइं भूसिउ ॥

11

When the Vasudeva revealed his family and name,
 Mahidhara threw his bow to the ground and
 embraced him with a heavy burden of affection
 within the cage of his arms that resembled the
 trunks of Indra's elephant. Calling on fire as his
 witness, he himself gave his daughter away to the
 insurmountable Vasudeva. Mahidhara climbed into
 one chariot, the eight princes into another, Vanamala
 with Lakshmana into one chariot, and Sita stood
 with the Baladeva in another. With the rejoicing
 of shrill drums and conches, dancing hunchbacks
 and dwarves, energetic, heroic, and benedictory
 songs, gongs, cymbals, and *mardala* drums, they
 joyfully entered into the city and sat at leisure in the
 assembly hall.

When the Vasudeva appeared together with Vanamala,
 going up to the wedding altar with delighted spirit,
 the people themselves adorned him, singing a
 benedictory song and dancing, as if he were a Jina at
 his birth.

तीसमो संधि

तहिँ अवसरें आणन्दभरें
उच्छाहकरें
जयकारहों कारणें णिक्किउ ।
भरहहों उप्परि उच्चलिउ
रहसुच्छलिउ
णरु णन्दावत्तणराहिउ ॥

१

जो भरहहों दूउ विसज्जियउ ।
आइउ सम्माणविवज्जियउ ॥
लहु णन्दावत्तणराहिवहों ।
वज्जरिउ अणन्तवीरणिवहों ॥
हउँ पेक्खु केम विच्छारियउ ।
सिरु मुण्डेवि कह वि ण मारियउ ॥
सो भरहु ण इच्छइ सन्धि रणें ।
जं जाणहों तं चिन्तवहों मणें ॥
अण्णु वि उक्खन्धें आइयउ ।
सहुँ सेण्णें विज्झु पराइयउ ॥
तहिँ णरवइ वालिखिल्लु वलिउ ।
सीहोयरु वज्जयण्णु मिलिउ ॥

Chapter 30

At that joyful, delighting moment, the king of Nandavarta, a merciless man, advanced upon Bharata and jumped up with passion, all for the sake of victory.

1

The messenger whom he had sent to Bharata returned without having been treated with respect. He immediately told the ruler of Nandavarta, King Anantavirya, "Look how I have been covered with ashes. After shaving my head, for some reason or other they did not kill me. Bharata does not desire a treaty in war. Reflect on what you know in your mind. Moreover, he has come to attack: he has reached the Vindhya with an army. There he met the powerful King Valikhilya, Simhodara, and

तहिँ रुद्रभुत्ति सिरिवच्छधरु ।
मरुभुत्ति सुभुत्ति विभुत्तिकरु ॥
अवरेहि मि समउ समावडिउ ।
पेक्खेसहि कल्लएँ अब्भिडिउ ॥
ताम अणन्तवीरु खुहिउ
पइजारुहिउ
जइ कल्लएँ भरहु ण मारमि ।
तो अरहन्तभडाराहाँ
सुरसाराहाँ
णउ चलणजुअलु जयकारमि ॥

२

पइजारूढु णराहिउ जावेहिँ ।
साहणु मिलिउ असेसु वि तावेहिँ ॥
लेहु लिहेप्पिणु जगविक्खायहाँ ।
तुरिउ विसज्जिउ महिहररायहाँ ॥
अग्गएँ चित्तु वड्ढु लम्मिक्कु व ।
हरिणक्खरहिँ लीणु णण्डिक्कु व ॥
सुन्दरु पत्तवन्तु वरसाहु व ।
णाववहुलु सरिगङ्गपवाहु व ॥
दिट्ठु राय तहिँ आय अणन्त वि ।
सल्लविसल्लसीहविक्कन्त वि ॥

Vajrakarna. Rudrabhuti, Shrivatsadhara, Marubhuti, Subhuti, and Vibhutikara, along with others, joined him there too. You will see when you are attacked tomorrow."

Then the agitated Anantavirya vowed, "I will not praise the two feet of the venerable, noble lord, the master of the gods, unless I kill Bharata tomorrow!"

2

When the king had made this vow, he gathered his entire army. Writing a letter, he quickly sent it to the world-renowned King Mahidhara. It was thrown before him in its envelope[1] like a thief in shackles; completely covered in fawn-colored letters like a camouflaged hunter; beautiful and made out of leaves, like a great sage with a begging bowl;[2] abounding in names like the stream of the river Ganga in boats.[3] Mahidhara saw these countless names of kings in it: Shalya, Vishalya, Simhavikranta, Durjaya, Ajaya, Vijaya,

दुज्जयअजयविजयजयजयमुह ।
णरसद्दूलविउलगयगयमुह ॥
रुद्दवच्छमहिवच्छमहद्दय ।
चन्दणचन्दोयरगरुडद्दय ॥
केसरिमारिचण्डजमघण्टा ।
कोङ्कणमलयपण्डियाणट्टा ॥
गुज्जरगङ्गवङ्गमङ्गाला ।
पइवियपारियत्तपञ्झाला ॥
सिन्धवकामरूवगम्भीरा ।
तज्जियपारसीयपरतीरा ॥
मरुकण्णाडलाडजालन्धर ।
टक्काहीरकीरखसवव्वर ॥
अवर वि जे एक्केक्कपहाणा ।
केण गणेप्पिणु सक्किय राणा ॥
ताम णराहिउ कसणतणु
थिउ विमणमणु
णं पडिउ सिरत्थलें वज्जु ।
किह सामियसम्माणभरु
विसहिउ दुद्धरु
किह भरहहों पहरिउ अज्जु ॥

304

Jaya, Jayamukha, Narashardula, Vipula, Gaja,
Gajamukha, Rudravatsa, Mahivatsa, Mahadhvaja,
Chandana, Chandrodara, Garudadhvaja, Kesarin,
Marichanda, and Yamaghanta; and kings of the
Konkanas, Malayas, Pandyas, Anartas, Gurjaras,
Gangas, Vangas, Mangalas, Paiviyas, Pariyatras,
Panchalas, Saindhavas, Kamarupas, Gambhiras,
Tajikas, Parasikas, Paratiras, Marus, Karnatas,
Latas, Jalandharas, Takkas, Abhiras, Kiras, Khasas,
Barbaras; and others too, one by one eminent kings.
Who could count them?

Then the black-bodied king stood there with dejected
spirit, as if lightning had fallen on top of his head,
"How do I endure the unbearable weight of respect
to my lord? How can I now fight against Bharata?"

३

जं णरवइ मणें चिन्तावियउ ।
हलहरु एक्कन्तपक्खें थियउ ॥
अट्टु वि कुमार कोक्किय खणेण ।
वइदेहि आय सहुँ लक्खणेण ॥
मेल्लेप्पिणु मन्तिउ मन्तणउ ।
वलु भणइ म दरिसहों अप्पणउ ॥
रहतुरयमहागय परिहरेंवि ।
तियचरणगायणवेंसु करेंवि ॥
तं रिउअत्थाणु पईसरहों ।
णच्चन्त अणन्तवीरु धरहों ॥
तं वयणु सुणेंवि परितुट्ठमण ।
थिय कामिणिवेस कियाहरण ॥
वलएवें जोइउ पियवयणु ।
किं होइ ण होइ वेसगहणु ॥
लइ सुन्दरि ताव तिट्ठु णयरें ।
अम्हेंहिँ पुणु जुज्झेवउ समरें ॥
लग्ग कडच्छएँ जणयसुय
कण्टइयभुय
लहु णरवरणाह ण एसहि ।
मइं मेल्लेवि भासुरएँ
रणसासुरएँ
मा कित्तिवहुअ परिणेसहि ॥

3

As the king reflected in his mind, the Baladeva stood
   on one side. He immediately summoned the eight
   princes. Videha's daughter, Sita, came, together with
   Lakshmana. The Baladeva rejected the advice they
   had thought of, and said, "Do not reveal yourself.
   Abandon your chariots, horses, and great elephants
   and adopt the guise of female bards and singers:
   then you can enter that assembly of enemies and
   take Anantavirya prisoner as you dance." Hearing
   those words, they stood there with delighted
   hearts, disguised as lovely ladies with their apparel
   completed. The Baladeva looked at the face of his
   beloved: was this a disguise that someone had put on
   or not? "Well, beautiful lady, you stay in the city. We
   must now fight in battle."
He pursued Janaka's daughter with a sidelong look, her
   arms covered in bristling body hair, "Will you not
   quickly return, lord of great men? Do not marry
   the bride Fame in the terrible house of War, your
   in-laws, and leave me behind."

खेड्डु करेंवि संचल्ल महाइय ।
णिविसें णन्दावत्तु पराइय ॥
दिट्ठु जिणालउ खण्णें परिअञ्चेंवि ।
अग्गएँ गाएँवि वाएँवि णच्चेंवि ॥
सीय ठवेंवि पइट्टु पुरसरवरें ।
रहवरतुरयमहागयजलयरें ॥
देउलवहलधवलकमलायरें ।
णन्दणवणघणतीरलयाहरें ॥
चारुविलासिणिणलिणिकरम्विएँ ।
छप्पण्णयछप्पयपरिचुम्विएँ ॥
सज्जणणिम्मलसलिलालङ्किएँ ।
पिसुणवयणघणपङ्कुप्पङ्किएँ ॥
कामिणिचलमणमच्छुत्थलिएँ ।
णरवरहंससएहिँ अमेल्लिएँ ॥
तहिँ तेहएँ पुरसरवरें दुज्जय ।
लीलएँ णाइँ पइट्टु दिसागय ॥
कामिणिवेस कियाहरण
विहसियवयण
गय पत्त तेत्थु पडिहारु ।
वुच्चइ आयइँ चारणइँ
भरहहों तणइँ
जिव कहें जिव देइ पइसारु ॥

4

Plotting their scheme, the magnanimous men set out and
in the blink of an eye reached Nandavarta. They soon
saw the temple of the Jina and after they had circled
it and had sung, played music and danced before
it, they left Sita behind and entered the city as if it
were a great lake: with great chariots, horses, and
grand elephants as aquatic animals; with temples as
thick, white bundles of lotuses; with pleasure groves
as dense arbors on the shore; dotted with beautiful
seductive ladies as lotuses; frequented by learned
men as insects; adorned with good people as pure
water; smeared by the words of slanderers as thick
mud; rising up with the fickle minds of lovely ladies
as fish; swarmed by hundreds of great men as geese.
In that city there, that was like a great lake, the
invincible men artfully entered as if they were the
elephants of the directions.

In the guise of lovely ladies, their apparel complete
and their faces smiling, they went and met with
the gatekeeper there. They said to him, "We are
Bharata's bards who have arrived. Tell him, so that
he may allow us to enter!"

५

तं वयणु सुणेविं पडिहारु गउ ।
विण्णत्तु नराहिउ रणें अजउ ॥

पहु एत्तइँ गायण आयाइँ ।
फुडु माणुसमेत्तेण जायाइँ ॥

णउ जाणहुँ किं विज्जाहरइँ ।
किं गन्धव्वइँ किं किण्णरइँ ॥

अइसुसरइँ जणमणमोहणइँ ।
मुणिवरहु मि मणसंखोहणइँ ॥

तं वयणु सुणेवि नराहिवेण ।
दे दे पइसारु वुत्तु णिवेण ॥

पडिहारु पधाइउ तुट्ठमणु ।
पइसरहों भणन्तु कण्टइयतणु ॥

तं वयणु सुणेवि समुच्चलिय ।
णं दस दिसिवह एक्कहिँ मिलिय ॥

पइठ नरिन्दत्थाणवणें
रिउरुक्खवघणें
सिंहासणगिरिवरमण्डिएँ ।
पोढविलासिणिलयवहलें
वरवेल्लहलें
अइवीरसीहपरिचड्डिएँ ॥

310

5

Hearing those words, the gatekeeper went and informed
the king who was unbeatable in war, "Lord, some
singers have come. It is clear that they have appeared
as mere humans, but we do not know if they are
Vidyadharas, Gandharvas, or Kinnaras, with the
most beautiful voices, charming the hearts of the
people and even disturbing the minds of great
sages." When he heard those words, the king, leader
of men, said, "Let them enter." With a satisfied mind
the gatekeeper ran toward them, the hair on his body
bristling, saying, "Enter!" Hearing those words they
set out together, as if they were the ten directions
having come together in one point.
They entered into the assembly hall of the king as if it were
a forest, thick with enemies as trees, adorned with
a throne as a great mountain, dense with impudent
seductive ladies as creepers, beautiful and agreeable
as with excellent wood apples, and presided over by
Anantavirya as a lion.[4]

तहिँ तेहएँ रिउअत्थाणवण्णें ।
पञ्झाणण जेम पइट्टु खण्णें ॥
णन्दियडणराहिउ दिट्टु किह ।
णक्खत्तहँ मज्झें मियङ्कु जिह ॥
आरम्भिउ अग्गएँ पेक्खणउ ।
सुकलत्तु व सवलु सलक्खणउ ॥
सुरयं पिव वन्धकरणपवरु ।
कव्वं पिव छन्दसद्दगहिरु ॥
रण्णं पिव वंसतालसहिउ ।
जुज्झं पिव रायसेयसहिउ ॥
जिह जिह उव्वेल्लइ हलवहणु ।
तिह तिह अप्पाणु णवेइ जणु ॥
मयरद्धयसरसंखोहियउ ।
मिगणिवहु व गेएं मोहियउ ॥
वलु पढइ अणन्तवीरु सुणइ ।
को सीहें समउ केलि कुणइ ॥
जाम ण रणमुहें उत्थरइ
पहरणु धरइ
पइँ जीवगाहु सहुँ राएँहिँ ।
ताम अयाण मुएवि छलु
परिहरेवि वलु
पडु भरहणरिन्दहों पाएँहिँ ॥

6

Into that forest that was the assembly hall of the enemy
they instantly entered as if they were lions. How
did they see the king of Nandavarta? As if he were
the moon in the midst of the stars. The spectacle
commenced before him with the Baladeva and
Lakshmana, like a good wife with energy and
auspicious characteristics.[5] Like lovemaking is
exceptional with positions and postures, it excelled
with *bandhakaraṇa* songs.[6] As a literary composition
is profound in its meter and language, it was dense
with pleasing sounds.[7] Like a forest contains bamboo
and palmyras, it was accompanied by a flute and
cymbals.[8] Just as war goes together with the sweat
of kings, there was passion and perspiration there.[9]
The more the Baladeva rose up, the more the people
stooped themselves, afflicted by the arrows of Kama
and bewildered by the singing as if they were a
herd of deer. The Baladeva recited as Anantavirya
listened, "Who sports with a lion?
"Before he attacks on the battlefront, grasps a weapon, or
captures you alive together with your kings, fool, you
fall at King Bharata's feet, forsaking your wickedness
and quitting your army."

७

राहवचन्दु मणेण ण कम्पिउ ।
पुणु पुणरुत्तेंहिँ एव पजम्पिउ ॥
भो भो णरवइ भरहु णमन्तहुँ ।
कवणु पराहउ किर अणुणन्तहुँ ॥
जो परवलसमुद्दें महणायइ ।
जो परवलमियङ्केँ गहणायइ ॥
जो परवलगयणेँहिँ चन्दायइ ।
जो परवलगइन्दें सीहायइ ॥
जो परवलरयणिहिँ हंसायइ ।
जो परवलतुरङ्गेँ महिसायइ ॥
जो परवलभुयङ्गेँ गरुडायइ ।
जो परवलवणोहें जलणायइ ॥
जो परवलघणोहें पवणायइ ।
जो परवलपवणोहें धरायइ ॥
जो परवलधरोहें वज्जायइ ॥
तं णिसुणेवि विरुद्धॲण
मणें कुद्धॲण
अइवीरें अहरफुरन्तें ।
रत्तुप्पलदललोयणेँण
जगभोयणेँण
णं किउ अवलोउ कियन्तें ॥

7

Moon-like Rama, the descendant of Raghu, did not
tremble in his heart. In repeated utterances he spoke
again thus, "King, what humiliation is there really
for those who bow to Bharata and appease him, he
who is like the churning stick to the ocean that is
the enemy army, he who is like Rahu, the eclipser,
to the moon that is the enemy army, he who is like
the moon to the heavens that is the enemy army, he
who is like a lion to the enormous elephant that is the
enemy army, he who is like the sun to the night that
is the enemy army, he who is like a buffalo to a horse
that is the enemy army, he who is like Garuda to a
snake that is the enemy army, he who is like fire to a
band of forests that is the enemy army, he who is like
wind to a cluster of clouds that is the enemy army, he
who is like a mountain to a surge of wind that is the
enemy army, he who is like lightning to a mountain
chain that is the enemy army!"
Hearing this, infuriated and enraged in his heart,
Anantavirya, with trembling lips and his eyes like the
petals of a red lotus, cast an angry look, as if he were
Yama who consumes the world.

८

भयभीसणु अमरिसकुइयदेहु ।
गज्जन्तु समुट्ठिउ जेम मेहु ॥
करें असिवरु लेइ ण लेइ जाम ।
णहें उड्डेंवि रामें धरिउ ताम ॥
सिरें पाउ देवि चोरु व णिवड्डु ।
णं वारणु वारिणिवन्धें छुड्डु ॥
रिउ चम्पेंवि परवलमइयवट्टु ।
जिणभवणहों सम्मुहु वलु पयट्टु ॥
एत्थन्तरें महुमहणेण वुत्तु ।
जो ढुक्कइ तं मारमि णिरुत्तु ॥
तं सुणेंवि परोप्परु रिउ चवन्ति ।
किं एय परक्कम तियहँ होन्ति ॥
एत्तडिय वोल्ल पडिवक्खें जाम ।
णर दस वि जिणालउ पत्त ताम ॥
जे गिलिय आसि पुररक्खसेण ।
णं मुक्क पडीवा भयवसेण ॥
तावन्तेउरु विमणमणु
गयगइगमणु
वहुहारदोरखुप्पन्तउ ।
आयउ पासु जियाहवहों
तहों राहवहों
दे दइयभिक्ख मग्गन्तउ ॥

316

8

Horrifying and his body incensed with intolerant rage, he
   rose up, thundering like a cloud. As he tried to take
   his great sword in his hand,[10] Rama leapt into the air
   and caught him. Placing his foot on his head, he tied
   him up as if he were a thief, agitated like an elephant
   in a trap. After he had suppressed the enemy, the
   Baladeva, the destroyer of the enemy army, set
   out toward the abode of the Jina. Thereupon the
   Vasudeva said, "I defiantly kill the one who comes
   near!" Hearing this, the enemies said to each other,
   "Are these the heroic deeds of women?" While such
   words were being spoken on the opposite side, the
   ten men reached the temple of the Jina. It was as if
   they who had been swallowed by the demon of the
   city, were now released again through the power of
   fear.

Meanwhile, with a dejected heart, going with the gait of
   an elephant and overwhelmed by their abundant
   necklaces and strings, the harem came to Rama,
   the descendant of Raghu, who had won the battle,
   begging, "Give us back our husband as alms!"

॰ ९

जं एव वुत्तु वणियायणेण ।
पहु पभणिउ दसरहणन्दणेण ॥
जइ भरहहों होहि सुभिच्छु अज्जु ।
तो अज्जु वि लइ अप्पणउ रज्जु ॥
तं वयणु सुणेवि परलोयभीरु ।
विहसेप्पिणु भणइ अणन्तवीरु ॥
पाडेवउ जो चलणेहिँ णिच्चु ।
तहों केम पडीवउ होमि भिच्छु ॥
वलिमण्डएँ तवचरणेण जो वि ।
पाडेवउ पायहिँ भरहु तो वि ॥
तं वयणु सुणेप्पिणु तुट्ठु रामु ।
सच्चउ जें तुज्झु अइवीरु णामु ॥
पुणरुत्तेहिँ वुच्चइ साहु साहु ।
हक्कारिउ तहों सुउ सहसवाहु ॥
सो णियसंताणहों रइउ राउ ।
अण्णु वि भरहहों पाइक्कु जाउ ॥
रिउ मेल्लेप्पिणु दस वि जण
गय तुट्ठमण
णियणयरु पराइय जावेंहिँ ।
णन्दावत्तणराहिवइ
जिणें करेवि मइ
दिक्खहं समुट्ठिउ तावेंहिँ ॥

9

When the womenfolk spoke thus, the son of Dasharatha said to the king, "If today you become a good servant to Bharata, then you may have your kingship for yourself." When he heard those words, Anantavirya, who was fearful of the hereafter, spoke as he burst into laughter, "How could I now become the servant of one who by all means will have to fall at my feet? For that Bharata still forcibly has to fall at someone else's feet due to their ascetic practice." When he heard those words, Rama was pleased, "Your name is truly Anantavirya, 'infinitely brave.'" He said repeatedly, "Well done! Well done!" His son Sahasrabahu was summoned. He was appointed king in accordance with his family line. Moreover, he became a foot soldier for Bharata.

While the ten men, leaving behind their enemy, went with satisfied hearts and reached their own city, the king of Nandavarta rose up to be initiated, directing his mind toward the Jina.

एत्थन्तरें पुरपरमेसराहँ ।
दिक्खाएँ समुट्ठिउ सउ णराहँ ॥
सद्दूलविउलवरवीरभद्द ।
मुणिभद्दसुभद्दसमन्तभद्द ॥
गरुडद्धयमयरद्धयपचण्ड ।
चन्दणचन्दोयरमारिचण्ड ॥
जयघण्टमहद्धयचन्दसूर ।
जयविजयअजयदुज्जयकुकूर ॥
इय एत्तिय पहु पव्वइय तेत्थु ।
लाहणपव्वएँ जयणन्दि जेत्थु ॥
थिय पञ्च मुट्ठि सिरें लोउ देवि ।
सइँ वाहहिँ आहरणइँ मुएवि ॥
णीसङ्ग वि थिय रिसिसङ्घसहिय ।
संसार वि भवसंसाररहिय ॥
णिम्माण वि जीवसयहुँ समाण ।
णिग्गन्थ वि गन्थपयत्थजाण ॥
इय एक्केक्कपहाण रिसि
भवतिमिरससि
तवसूर महावयधारा ।
छट्ठट्ठमदसवारसेँहिँ
वहुउववसेँहिँ
अप्पाणु खवन्ति भडारा ॥

10

Then a hundred men, supreme lords of the city, rose up
for initiation: Shardula, Vipula, Varavirabhadra,
Munibhadra, Subhadra, Samantabhadra,
Garudadhvaja, Makaradhvaja, Prachanda,
Chandana, Chandrodara, Marichanda, Jayaghanta,
Mahadhvaja, Chandra, Shura, Jaya, Vijaya, Ajaya,
Durjaya, and Kukura, such men renounced the world
there, where Jayanandin was near a mountain of
donated food. They stood there, pulling out their
hair in five fistfuls and removing the ornaments
on their arms by themselves. Free from desires,
they stayed there together with the community of
seers, wandering and having forsaken the cycle of
existence, prideless and with respect for hundreds
of life forms, without possessions and knowing the
meaning of the words in texts.

These seers, each of them eminent men, like the moon
in the darkness of existence, heroes in asceticism
who bore the great vows, noble men, chastised
themselves with frequent fasts of six, eight, ten, or
twelve meals.

११

तवचरणें परिट्ठिउ जं जि राउ ।
तहों वन्दणहत्तिएँ भरहु आउ ॥
तें दिट्ठु भडारउ तेयपिण्डु ।
जो मोहमहीहरें वज्जदण्डु ॥
जो कोहहुवासणें जलणिहाउ ।
जो मयणमहाघणें पलयवाउ ॥
जो दप्पगइन्दें महामइन्दु ।
जो माणभुअङ्गमें वरखगिन्दु ॥
सो मुणिवरु दसरहणन्दणेण ।
वन्दिउ णियगरहणणिन्दणेण ॥
भो साहु साहु गम्भीर धीर ।
पइँ पूरिय पइज्जा ऽणन्तवीर ॥
जं पाडिउ हउँ चलणेहिँ देव ।
तं तिहुअणु कारावियउ सेव ॥
गउ एम पसंसेॅवि भरहु राउ ।
णियणयरु पत्तु साहणसहाउ ॥
हरिवल पइठ जियन्तपुरें
धणकणपउरें
जयमङ्गलतूरवमालेँहिँ ।
लक्खणु लक्खणवन्तियएँ
णियपत्तियएँ
अवगूढु सइं भुवडालेँहिँ ॥

322

11

Just as the king was engaged in ascetic practice, Bharata
came to praise and revere him. He beheld the noble
lord, a ball of splendor. He who was a lightning bolt
for the mountain of bewilderment, who was a mass
of water for the fire of anger, who was the wind of
destruction for the great cloud of lust, who was a
great lion for the enormous elephant of arrogance,
who was Garuda, the grand king of birds, for the
snake of pride, that great seer was praised by the
son of Dasharatha, reproaching and rebuking
himself, "Well done! Well done! Solemn, composed
Anantavirya—you have fulfilled your promise, and so
I am obliged to fall at your feet, lord. This threefold
world is rendered into your service." After lauding
him thus, King Bharata went and returned to his own
city together with his army.
The Vasudeva and the Baladeva entered into the city of
Jivanta, abounding in riches and grain, accompanied
by the clamor of triumphant, festive drums.
Lakshmana was himself embraced by his wife,
who possessed auspicious characteristics, with her
branch-like arms.

Meetings with Sages
and a Bird

एक्कतीसमो संधि

धणधण्णसमिद्धहों
पुहइपसिद्धहों
जणमणणयणाणन्दणहों ।
वणवासहों जन्तेंहिँ
रामाणन्तेंहिँ
किउ उम्माहउ पट्टणहों ॥

१

छुडु छुडु उहय समागमलुद्धइँ ।
रिसिकुलइँ व परमागमलुद्धइँ ॥
छुडु छुडु अवरोप्परु अणुरत्तइँ ।
सज्झदिवायरइँ व अणुरत्तइँ ॥
छुडु छुडु अहिणववहुवरइत्तइँ ।
सोमपहा इव सुन्दरचित्तइँ ॥
छुडु छुडु चुम्वियतामरसाइं ।
फुलन्धय इव लुद्धरसाइं ॥
ताम कुमारें णयणविसाला ।
जन्तें आउच्छिय वणमाला ॥
हे मालूरपवरपीवरथणे ।
कुवलयदलपप्फुल्लियलोअणे ॥

Chapter 31

When Rama and the Vasudeva went on for their stay in the forest, they caused trepidation for the world-renowned city of Jivanta, that abounded in riches and grain and brought joy to the hearts and minds of its people.

1

In good time, both Lakshmana and Vanamala had
    grown desirous of making love, like communities
    of seers who long to reach the supreme; attached
    to each other, as Sun is enamored of Twilight;* the
    young bride and groom had become beautiful and
    bright like the moon and its radiance; like bees,
    kissing lotuses and longing for nectar. Then the
    youth Lakshmana, as he went on his way, bade
    farewell to the wide-eyed Vanamala: "Your perfect,
    round breasts are like *mālūra* fruits, your blooming
    eyes like the petals of blue water lilies, your gait

---

* Twilight is personified as the wife of the Sun.

हंसगमणें गयलीलविलासिणि ।
चन्दवयणें णियणामपगासिणि ॥
जामि कन्तें हउँ दाहिणदेसहों ।
गिरिकिक्किन्थणयरउद्देसहों ॥
सुरवरवरइत्तें
णववरइत्तें
जं आउच्छिय णियय धण ।
ओहुल्लियवयणी
पगलियणयणी
थिय हेट्टामुह विमणमण ॥

२

कज्जलवहलुप्पीलसणाहें ।
महि पव्वालिय अंसुपवाहें ॥
एत्तिउ विरुवउ माणुसलोउ ।
जं जरजम्मणमरणविओउ ॥
धीरिय लक्खणेण एत्थन्तरें ।
रामहों णिलउ करेवि वणन्तरें ॥
कइहि मि दिणेहिँ पडीवउ आवमि ।
सयल ससायर महि भुञ्जावमि ॥
जइ पुणु कहवि तुलग्गें णायउ ।
हउँ ण होमि सोमित्तिएँ जायउ ॥

328

like a goose, you are playful with all the charm of an
elephant, your face is as bright as the moon, you bring
luster to your name. My love, I am going to a land in
the south, to the region of the mountain and city of
Kishkindha."
When the young groom, favored by the excellent gods,
bade farewell to his beloved, she stood looking
downward, her face dejected, her eyes streaming, and
her heart discouraged.

2

The earth was inundated with the flow of her tears,
furnished with dense masses of kohl. So monstrous is
the world of humans that there is old age, birth, death,
and separation. Thereupon Lakshmana reassured
her, "After I have built a dwelling for Rama inside
the forest, in a few days I will come back and make
sure you enjoy the entire earth, with oceans and all.
If somehow I have not returned by the entrance of
the sun in Libra, I am not the son of Sumitri! What is

अण्णु वि रयणिहें जो भुञ्जन्तउ ।
मंसभक्खि महु मज्जु पियन्तउ ॥
जीव वहन्तउ अलिउ चवन्तउ ।
परधणें परकलत्तें अणुरत्तउ ॥
जो नरु आऍहिँ वसणेहिँ भुत्तउ ।
हउँ पावेण तेण संजुत्तउ ॥
जइ एम वि णावमि
वयणु ण दावमि
तो णिव्वूढमहाहवहों ।
णवकमलसुकोमल
णहपहउज्जल
छित्त पाय मइँ राहवहों ॥

३

वणमाल णियत्तेंवि भग्गमाण ।
गय लक्खणराम सुपुज्जमाण ॥
थोवन्तरें मच्छुत्थल्ल देन्ति ।
गोलाणइ दिट्ठु समुव्वहन्ति ॥
सुंसुअरघोरघुरुघुरुहुरन्ति ।
करिमयरड्डोहियडुहुडुहन्ति ॥
डिण्डीरसण्डमण्डलिउ देन्ति ।
दद्दुरयरडियदुरुदुरुदुरन्ति ॥

more, one who consumes food at night, who eats meat and drinks honey and alcohol, who kills living beings and tells a lie, who is desirous for another man's riches or wife, a man who is possessed by these sins, with such a sinner I am then associated.

Thus if I do not return and show my face, then I have disrespected the feet of Rama, the descendant of Raghu, successful in battle, most tender like fresh lotuses and bright like the path of the sky."

3

When Vanamala returned, her sulkiness thwarted, the well-revered Lakshmana and Rama went off. A little farther they saw the river Godavari, allowing fish to fly up and carrying them along, grunting vehemently with porpoises, booming with the stirrings of elephants and crocodiles, making circles out of heaps of foam, croaking with the sound of frogs, flowing

कल्लोलुल्लोलहिँ उव्वहन्ति ।
उग्घोसघोसघवघवघवन्ति ॥
पडिखलणवलणखलखलखलन्ति ।
खलखलियखडक्कझडक्कु देन्ति ॥
ससिसङ्खकुन्दधवलोज्झरेण ।
कारण्डुड्डावियडम्बरेण ॥
फेणावलिवङ्किय
वलयालङ्किय
णं महिकुलवहुअहेँ तणिय ।
जलणिहिभत्तारहो
मोत्तियहारहो
वाह पसारिय दाहिणिय ॥

४

थोवन्तरेँ वलणारायणेहिँ ।
खेमञ्जलिपट्टणु दिट्ठु तेहिँ ॥
अरिदमणु णराहिउ वसइ जेत्थु ।
अइचण्डु पयण्डु ण को वि तेत्थु ॥
रज्जेसरु जो सव्वहँ वरिट्ठु ।
सो पहु पहियाह मि मूलेँ दिट्ठु ॥
णहभासुरु जो लङ्कूलदीहु ।
सो मायङ्गेहि मि लइउ सीहु ॥

along with billows and waves, swashing with loud
rumbling, halting, turning, and gurgling, gushing and
thrusting toward the rocks, with a waterfall, white like
the moon, a conch, or jasmine flowers, and with the
commotion of *kāraṇḍa* ducks that she chased away.
It was as if she were the right arm of the virtuous Lady
   Earth, adorned with rows of foam for wavy bracelets,
   stretched out toward her husband, Ocean, for a pearl
   necklace.

4

A little farther, that Baladeva and Vasudeva beheld the
   city of Kshemanjali, where king Aridamana lived. No
   one there was as ferocious and formidable. He who
   was the chief in the kingdom, the most excellent of
   all, that lord was always seen marching at the head
   of his followers;[1] splendid like the sky and wielding
   a lofty *lāṅgūla* weapon, clung to by the limbs of
   Lady Glory, a lion with terrible claws and a long tail,
   followed by elephants;[2] who pulverized the royal
   camp of unstoppable demons, the sun who quivered

जो दुद्दमदाणवसिमिरचूरु ।
सो तियमुहयन्दहों तसइ सूरु ॥
जं रायहँ तं छत्तह मि छित्तु ।
जं सुहडहँ तं कुडुह मि चित्तु ॥
तहों णयरहों थिउ अवरुत्तरेण ।
उज्जाणु अद्धकोसन्तरेण ॥
सुरसेहरु णामें जगें पयासु ।
णं अग्घविहत्थउ थिउ वलासु ॥
तहिँ तेहएँ उववणें
णवतरुवरघणें
जहिं अमरिन्दु रइ करइ ।
तहिँ णिलउ करेप्पिणु
वे वि थवेप्पिणु
लक्खणु णयरें पईसरइ ॥

५

पइसन्तें पुरवाहिरें करालु ।
भडमडयपुञ्जु दीसइ विसालु ॥
ससिसङ्खकुन्दहिमदुद्धधवलु ।
हरहारहंससरयब्भविमलु ॥
तं पेक्खेविवि लहु हरिसियमणेण ।
गोवाल पपुच्छिय लक्खणेण ॥

for the moon-like face of his woman. Within half a
krośa to the northwest of that city lay a park, touched
by as many kings as scholars and notable for as many
warriors as marvels, world-renowned, by the name of
Surashekhara, it was as if it stood before the Baladeva,
skilled with welcoming offerings.
After he had set up a place to stay there in that park, dense
with new great trees, where the king of the gods found
pleasure, and had settled the two there, Lakshmana
entered into the city.

5

As he entered, he observed on the outside of the city
a terrifying, vast heap of soldiers' corpses, white
like the moon, conches, jasmine flowers, or milk,
and bright like the necklace of Shiva,* a goose, or
an autumn cloud. Seeing this, Lakshmana, with an
excited heart, quickly asked the cowherds, "What is

* A necklace made of skulls.

इउ दीसइ काइँ महापयण्डु ।
णं णिम्मलु हिमगिरिसिहरखण्डु ॥
तं णिसुणेंवि गोवहिँ वुत्तु एम ।
किं एह वत्त पइँ ण सुअ देव ॥
अरिदमणधीय जियपउमणाम ।
भडथडसंघारणि जिह दुणाम ॥
सा अज्ज वि अच्छइ वरकुमारि ।
पच्चक्ख णाइँ आइय कुमारि ॥
तहें कारणें जो जो मरइ जोहु ।
सो चिप्पइ तं हडुइरि एहु ॥
जो घइँ अवगण्णेवि
तिणसमु मण्णेवि
पञ्च वि सत्तिउ धरइ णरु ।
पडिवक्खविमद्दणु
णयणाणन्दणु
सो पर होसइ ताहें वरु ॥

६

तं वयणु सुणेप्पिणु दुण्णिवारु ।
रोमञ्चिउ खणें लक्खणकुमारु ॥
वियडप्पयछोहेंहिँ पुणु पयट्टु ।
णं केसरि मयगलमइयवट्टु ॥

this great horrifying thing I must look upon, white like a shining fragment from the top of a Himalayan mountain?" At this, the herdsmen said, "Have you not heard this story, sir? Aridamana's daughter, named Jitapadma, is the slayer of hordes of soldiers like a female Durnama.[3] Today this beautiful young girl is like none other than the wicked goddess of pestilence herself come among us. Every soldier that perished because of her is thrown out. This is the mountain of their bones.

He who truly halts five *śaktis*,* disregarding them and considering them futile as grass, a crusher of hostile armies and bringer of joy to the eyes, he alone will be her groom."

6

Hearing these words, the unrestrainable youth Lakshmana instantly was covered in bristling body hair. Thereupon he set out with countless giant strides, like an elephant-butchering lion. In one place

---

* A missile or projectile weapon; here, without magic properties.

कत्थइ कप्पद्रुम दिट्ठु तेण ।
णं पन्थिय थिय णयरासएण ॥
कत्थइ मालइकुसुमइँ खिवन्ति ।
सीस व सुकइहें जसु विक्खिरन्ति ॥
कत्थइ लक्खइ सरवर विचित्त ।
अवगाहिय सीयल जिह सुमित्त ॥
कत्थइ गोरसु सव्वहँ रसाहुँ ।
णं णिग्गउ माणु हरेवि ताहुँ ॥
कत्थइ आवाह डज्झन्ति केम ।
दुज्जणदुव्वयणेहिँ सुयण जेम ॥
कत्थइ अरहट्ट भमन्ति केम ।
संसारिय भवसंसारें जेम ॥
णं धउ हक्कारइ एहि एहि ।
भो लक्खण लहु जियपउम लेहि ॥
वारुब्भडवयणें
दीहियणयणें
देउलदाढाभासुरेण ।
णं गिलिउ जणद्दणु
असुरविमद्दणु
एन्तउ णयरणिसायरेण ॥

338

he saw wishing trees, like travelers settled in the
refuge of the city; in another, people were scattering
jasmine flowers, just as students of a good poet
spread his fame; in another he saw wonderful great
lakes in which people bathed, cool like good friends;
elsewhere, buttermilk of all flavors, as if arisen while
stealing these flavors' pride; elsewhere, the sugarcane
fields—how did they burn? Like good people through
the evil words of the wicked; elsewhere, the wheels
of the wells—how did they revolve? Like migrating
souls in the cycle of existence. A flag summoned him,
as it were, "Come, come. Lakshmana, quickly take
Jitapadma."

As he entered, it was as if the demon-crushing Vasudeva
was swallowed by the demon city: with its gate for
its exceptional mouth, oblong tanks for eyes, and
splendid with temples for fangs.

पायारभुऍहिँ पुरणाईंतेण ।
अवरुण्डिउ लक्खणु णाइँ तेण ॥
कत्थइ कुम्भा सहु णाडएहिँ ।
णं णड णाणाविहणाडएहिँ ॥
कत्थइ वंसारि समुद्धवंस ।
णावइ सुकुलीण विसुद्धवंस ॥
कत्थइ धयवड णच्चन्ति एम ।
वरि अम्हि सुरायर सग्गें जेम ॥
कत्थइ लोहारेहिँ लोहखण्डु ।
पिट्टिज्जइ णरऍ व पावपिण्डु ॥
तं हट्टमग्गु मेल्लेवि कुमारु ।
णिविसेण पराइउ रायवारु ॥
पडिहारु वुत्तु कहि गम्मि एम ।
वरु वुच्चइ आइउ एक्कु देव ॥
जियपउमहें माणमरट्टदलणु ।
परवलमसक्कु दरियारिदमणु ॥
रिउसंघायहों संघायकरणु ।
सहुँ सत्तिहिँ तुज्झु वि सत्तिहरणु ॥

7

With its ramparts for arms, that city embraced Lakshmana
like a merchant. In one place there were pitchers with
handles, like actors in different kinds of spectacles;
in another elephants were holding up bamboo, like
people from noble birth with a virtuous lineage;[4] in
another, flags danced like troupes of gods above us in
heaven; elsewhere blacksmiths were forging a piece
of metal, like a ball of sin in hell. Leaving that market
road, the youth Lakshmana in an instant reached
the royal gate. He said to the gatekeeper, "You go
and say thus, 'It is said that a groom has arrived,
lord, a crusher of Jitapadma's pride and arrogance,
pulverizing hostile armies and vanquishing proud
enemies, giving battle to foes in great numbers and
robbing you of your power along with the *śaktis.*'

[अह] किं वहुएं जम्पिएॅण
णिप्फलचविएॅण
एम भणहि तं अरिदमणु ।
दसवीस ण पुच्छइ
सउ वि पडिच्छइ
पञ्चहँ सत्तिहिँ को गहणु ॥

तं णिसुणेॅवि गउ पडिहारु तेत्थु ।
सहमण्डवेॅ सो अरिदमणु जेत्थु ॥
पणवेप्पिणु वुच्चइ तेण राउ ।
परमेसर विण्णत्तिएॅ पसाउ ॥
भडु कालें चोइउ आउ इक्कु ।
ण मुणहुँ किं अक्कु मियङ्कु सक्कु ॥
किं कुसुमाउहु अतुलियपयाउ ।
पर पञ्च वाण णउ एक्कु चाउ ॥
तहोॅ णरहोॅ णवल्ही भङ्गि का वि ।
फिटृइ ण लच्छि अम्हहोॅ कयावि ॥
सो चवइ एम जियपउम लेमि ।
किं पञ्चहिँ दस सत्तिउ धरेमि ॥
तं णिसुणेॅवि पभणइ सत्तुदमणु ।
पेक्खमि कोक्कहि वरइत्तु कवणु ॥

Or rather, what with elaborate talk and useless chatter?
Say this to that Aridamana, 'He does not ask for ten
or twenty, he wants a hundred. What is catching five
śaktis?'"

8

At this, the gatekeeper went where that Aridamana was
in the assembly hall. With a bow he said to the king,
"Supreme master, some news, if you please:[5] a soldier
has arrived, urged on by Death. We do not know if he
is the sun, the moon, or Indra, or the flower-armed
Kama, of unequaled splendor. He only has five arrows,
and not one bow. This man has a fresh way about
him. The luster never strays from his body. He said
this, 'I am taking Jitapadma. What with five? I can
stop ten *śaktis*.'" Hearing this, Aridamana said, "I
see. Call him. Who is the suitor?" Summoned by the
gatekeeper, the Vasudeva came, adorned by the luster
of triumph and thirsty for a fight.

पडिहारें सद्दिउ आउ कण्हु ।
जयलच्छिपसाहिउ जुज्झतण्हु ॥
अच्चुब्भडवयणेहिँ
दीहरणयणेहिँ
णरवइविन्दहिँ दुज्जऍहिँ ।
लक्खिज्जइ लक्खणु
एन्तु सलक्खणु
जेम मइन्दु महागऍहिँ ॥

९

लक्खणु पासु पराइउ जं जे ।
वुत्तु णिवेण हसेप्पिणु तं जे ॥
को जियपउम लएवि समत्थु ।
केण हुवासणें ढोइउ हत्थु ॥
केण सिरेण पडिच्छिउ वज्जु ।
केण कियन्तु वि घाइउ अज्जु ॥
केण णहङ्गणु छित्तु करग्गें ।
केण सुरिन्दु परज्जिउ भोगें ॥
केण वसुन्धरि दारिय पाएं ।
केण पलोट्टिउ दिग्गउ घाएं ॥
केण सुरेहहोँ भग्गु विसाणु ।
केण तलप्पएँ पाडिउ भाणु ॥
लद्धिउ केण समुद्दु असेसु ।

Bands of invincible kings, with most exceptional faces and
wide eyes, looked at Lakshmana as he approached
with his auspicious characteristics, like great
elephants observing a lion.

9

While Lakshmana came closer, the king said as he
laughed, "Who is capable of taking Jitapadma?
Who has stuck his hand into this fire? Who asks for
lightning onto his head? Who has attacked Yama, the
terminator, today? Who touched the sky with a finger?
Who overcame the lord of the gods in enjoyment?
Who tore open the earth with his foot? Who threw
down a cardinal elephant with a blow? Who broke off
a tusk of the elephant of the gods? Who struck down
the sun with a slap? Who crossed the entire ocean?

के फणमण्डवें चूरिउ सेसु ॥
केण पहञ्झणु वड्ढु पडेण ।
मेरुमहागिरि टालिउ केण ॥
जिह तुहुँ तिह अण्ण वि
णीसावण्ण वि
गरुयइँ गज्जिय वहुय णर ।
महु सत्तिपहारेंहिँ
रणें दुव्वारेंहिँ
किय सयसक्कर दिट्ठु पर ॥

१०

अरिदमणें भडु जं अहिखित्तु ।
महुमहु जेम दवग्गि पलित्तु ॥
हउँ जियपउम लएवि समत्थु ।
मइँ जि हुआसणें ढोइउ हत्थु ॥
मइँ जि सिरेण पडिच्छिउ वज्जु ।
मइँ जि कियन्तु वि घाइउ अज्जु ॥
मइँ जि णहञ्झणु छिंतु करग्गें ।
मइँ जि सुरिन्दु परज्जिउ भोग्गें ॥
मइँ जि वसुन्धरि दारिय पाएं ।
मइँ जि पलोट्टिउ दिग्गउ घाएं ॥
मइँ जि सुरेहहों भग्गु विसाणु ।
मइँ जि तलप्पएँ पाडिउ भाणु ॥

Who crushed Shesha[6] in his pavilion-like hood? Who
tied up the wind with a piece of cloth? Who disturbed
great Mount Meru?
Just like you, many other extraordinary, venerable men
have roared. But I saw them all broken into hundreds
of pieces by the blows of my *śaktis,* unstoppable in
battle."

10

When Aridamana had insulted the soldier Vasudeva,
he grew enraged like a forest fire: "I am capable of
taking Jitapadma. I stuck my hand into the fire. I
requested lightning onto my head. I attacked Yama,
the terminator, today. I touched the sky with a finger.
I overcame the lord of the gods in enjoyment. I tore
open the earth with my foot. I threw down a cardinal
elephant with a blow. I broke off a tusk of the elephant
of the gods. I struck down the sun with a slap.

लद्धिउ मइँ जि समुद्दु असेसु ।
मइँ फणमण्डवें चूरिउ सेसु ॥
मइँ जि पहञ्जणु वद्धु पडेण ।
मेरुमहागिरि टालिउ जेण ॥
हउँ तिहुअणडामरु
हउँ अजरामरु
हउँ तेत्तीसहुँ रणें अजउ ।
खेमञ्जलिराणा
अवुह अयाणा
मेल्लि सत्ति जइ सत्ति तउ ॥

११

तं णिसुणेंवि खेमञ्जलिराणउ ।
उट्ठिउ गलगज्जन्तु पहाणउ ॥
सत्तिविहत्थउ सत्तिपगासणु ।
धगधगधगधगगन्तु सहुआसणु ॥
अम्बरें तेयपिण्डु णउ दिणयरु ।
णियमज्जायचत्तु णउ सायरु ॥
जणें अणवरयदाणु णउ मयगलु ।
परमण्डलविणासु णउ मण्डलु ॥

348

I crossed the entire ocean. I crushed Shesha in his
pavilion-like hood. I tied up the wind with a piece of
cloth. I disturbed great Mount Meru.
I am the scourge of the three worlds, I am free of old age
and death; in a war with the thirty-three gods, I am
invincible. Foolish, ignorant king of Kshemanjali,
release a *śakti*, if you have the power."

11

At this, the eminent king of Kshemanjali, skilled with
śaktis, rose up roaring, revealing a *śakti*, sizzling with
fire: like the sun, a ball of light in the sky, like the
ocean that went beyond its shore, like an elephant
with ichor flowing uninterrupted among people,
like a planet destroying another planet, like Ravana

रामायणहों मज्झें णउ रामणु ।
भीमसरीरु ण भीमु भयावणु ॥
तेण विमुक्क सत्ति गोविन्दहों ।
णं हिमवन्तें गङ्ग समुद्दहों ॥
धाइय धगधगन्ति समरङ्गणें ।
णं तडि तडयडन्ति णहअङ्गणें ॥
सुरवर णहें वोल्हन्ति परोप्परु ।
एण पहारें जीवइ दुक्करु ॥
एत्थन्तरें कण्हें
जयजसतण्हें
धरिय सत्ति दाहिणकरेंण ।
संकेयहों ढुक्की
थाणहों चुक्की
णावइ परतिय परणरेंण ॥

१२

धरिय सत्ति जं समरें समत्थें ।
मेल्लिउ कुसुमवासु सुरसत्थें ॥
पुण्णिमइन्दुरुन्दमुहसोमहें ।
केण वि कहिउ गम्पि जियपोमहें ॥
सुन्दरि पेक्खु पेक्खु जुज्झन्तहों ।
णोखी का वि भङ्गि वरइत्तहों ॥

350

in the Ramayana, like the terrifying Bhima[7] with his tremendous body. He discharged the *śakti* toward the Vasudeva, like the Himalaya releases the Ganga toward the ocean. It rushed forth sizzling on the battlefield, like crackling lightning in the sky. The great gods in heaven said to each other, "It will be hard to survive such a blow."

Then the Vasudeva, thirsty for the fame of victory, caught the *śakti* with his right hand, like a stranger catching the wife of another man, who had approached for a rendezvous and left her home.

12

When Lakshmana, skilled in battle, caught the *śakti*, a group of gods released a rain of flowers. Someone went and told Jitapadma, whose face was round like the full moon, "Beautiful lady, look, look: the battling suitor has an unprecedented way about him. The

जा तउ ताएं सत्ति विसज्जिय ।
लग्ग हत्थें असइ व्वालज्जिय ॥
णरभमरेण एण अकलङ्कउ ।
पर चुम्बेवउ तुह मुहपङ्कउ ॥
तं णिसुणेप्पिणु विहसियवयणऍ ।
णवकुवलयदलदीहरणयणऍ ॥
जालगवक्खऍ जो अन्तरपडु ।
णाइँ सहत्थें फेडिउ मुहवडु ॥
लक्खणु णयणकडक्खिवउ कण्णऍ ।
णं जुज्झन्तु णिवारिउ सण्णऍ ॥
ताम कुमारें दिट्ठु सुदंसणु ।
धवलहरम्वरें मुहमयलञ्छणु ॥
सुहणक्खत्तें सुजोग्गें सुहङ्करु ।
णयणामेलउ जाउ परोप्परु ॥
एत्थन्तरें दुट्टें
मुक्कारुट्टें
लहु अण्णेक्क सत्ति णरेंण ।
स वि धरिय सरग्गें
वामकरग्गें
णावइ णववहु णववरेंण ॥

śakti that your father discharged clung to his hand like a shameless adulteress. This man will soon kiss your unstained lotus-like face like a bee." At this, the maiden, her face smiling and her eyes wide like the petals of fresh blue water lilies, with her own hand removed the piece of cloth that was between them on the lattice window as if it were a veil, and cast a glance at Lakshmana, as if stopping him from fighting with a signal. Then the youth Lakshmana beheld the lovely moon-like face in the sky-like upper story of the palace. Under a most suitable, favorable constellation, a fortunate meeting of their eyes occurred.

Thereupon the wicked, furious man quickly released another *śakti*. That too he caught at the tip of the missile with the top of his left hand, like a new groom holding a new bride.

अण्णेक्क मुक्क वहुमच्छरेण ।
वज्जासणि णाइँ पुरन्दरेण ॥
स हि दाहिणकक्खहिँ छुड्ढ तेण ।
अवरुण्डिय वेस व कामुएण ॥
अण्णेक्क विसज्जिय धगधगन्ति ।
णं सिहिसिह जालासय मुअन्ति ॥
स वि धरिय एन्ति णारायणेण ।
वामद्धें गोरि व तिणयणेण ॥
णं महिहरु देवइणन्दणेण ।
पञ्चमिय मुक्क वहुमच्छरेण ॥
पम्मुक्क पधाइय णरवरासु ।
णं कन्त सुकन्तहोँ सुहयरासु ॥
स विसाणेहिँ एन्ति णिरुद्ध केम ।
णवसुरयसमागमें जुवइ जेम ॥
एत्थन्तरें देवहिँ लक्खणासु ।
सिरें मुक्क पडीवउ कुसुमवासु ॥
अरिदमणु ण सोहइ सत्तिहीणु ।
खलकुपुरिसु व्व थिउ सत्तिहीणु ॥

13

Wrathfully he released another, like Indra hurling a
thunderbolt. This one he caught in his right armpit,
as if it were a prostitute embraced by a lover. Another
sizzling one was discharged, like a fire plume
emitting hundreds of flames. This one the Vasudeva
caught as it neared his left side, like the three-eyed
Shiva holding dazzling Parvati. Like a mountain by
Devaki's son,* he wrathfully released the fifth. As it
was discharged it sped toward the great man, like a
wife to her beloved, gratifying husband. How did he
stop it with his teeth[8] as it approached? As if it were a
young woman in the union of a first sexual encounter.
Thereupon the gods again released a rain of flowers
on Lakshmana's head. Bereft of his *śaktis,* Aridamana
did not look good. He stood there like a powerless,
wretched, lowly man.

---

* Krishna.

हरि रोमञ्चियतणु
सहइ सपहरणु
रणमुहें परिसक्कन्तु किह ।
रत्तुप्पललोयणु
रसवसभोयणु
पञ्चाउहु वेयालु जिह ॥

१४

समरङ्गणें असुरपरायणेण ।
अरिदमणु वुत्तु णारायणेण ॥
खल खुद्द पिसुण मच्छरिय राय ।
मइँ जेम पडिच्छिय पञ्च घाय ॥
तिह तुहु मि पडिच्छहि एक्क सत्ति ।
जइ अत्थि का वि मरणे मणुससत्ति ॥
किर एम भणेप्पिणु हणइ जाम ।
जियपउमएँ घत्तिय माल ताम ॥
भो साहु साहु रणें दुण्णिरिक्ख ।
मं पहरु देव दइ जणणभिक्ख ॥
जें समरें परज्जिउ सत्तुदमणु ।
पइँ मुएँवि अण्णु वरइत्तु कवणु ॥
तं वयणु सुणेप्पिणु लक्खणेण ।
आउद्धइँ घित्तइँ तक्खणेण ॥

How did the Vasudeva shine, his body covered in bristling body hair, as he walked around on the battlefront with the weapons? As if he were a Vetala with five weapons, with eyes like red lotuses, feasting on bodily juices and fat.

14

The demon-vanquishing Vasudeva spoke to Aridamana on the battlefield, "Wretched, mean, vile, wrathful king, just as I received five blows, you receive one *śakti*, if there is any manliness in your heart." Speaking thus, as he indeed attacked, Jitapadma threw him a garland, "Well done, well done: you who are difficult even to behold in battle. Cease your attack, lord, and give me my father as alms. What other bridegroom is there except you, who overthrew Aridamana in battle?" Hearing those words, Lakshmana immediately threw

मुक्काउहु गउ अरिदमणपासु।
सहसक्खु व पणविउ जिणवरासु॥
जं अमरिसकुद्धें
जयजसलुद्धें
विप्पिउ किउ तुम्हेहिँ सहुँ।
अण्णु वि रेकारिउ
कह वि ण मारिउ
तं मरुसेज्जहि माम महु॥

१५

खेमझलिपुरपरमेसरेण।
सोमित्ति वुत्तु रज्जेसरेण॥
किं जम्पिएण वहुअमरिसेण।
लइ लइय कण्ण पइँ पउरिसेण॥
तुहुँ दीसहि दणुमाहप्पचप्पु।
कहें कवणु गोत्तु का माय वप्पु॥
महुमहणु पवोल्लिउ णिसुणि राय।
महु दसरहु ताउ सुमित्ति माय॥
अण्णु वि पयडउ इक्खक्कुवंसु।
वड्डारउ जिह तरुवरहों वंसु॥
वे अम्हइँ लक्खणराम भाय।
वणवासहों रज्जु मुएवि आय॥

down his weapons. Unarmed he went to Aridamana
and like the thousand-eyed Indra before the great Jina
he bowed,

"That I, furious with indignation and longing for the fame
of victory, committed an offense against you, that
I moreover reproached you and all but killed you,
please forgive me, dear friend!"

15

The chief of the kingdom, the supreme lord of the city of
Kshemanjali, said to Sumitri's son, "What with talk
full of indignation? Indeed, you have won the girl
with valor. You appear to be a crusher of demons'
pride. Tell me, what is your lineage? Who are your
mother and father?" The Vasudeva answered,
"Listen, king, Dasharatha is my father, Sumitri my
mother. Moreover, our famous Ikshvaku dynasty is
exceptional, like the trunk of an excellent tree. We
two brothers, Lakshmana and Rama, have come for

उज्जाणें तुहारऍ असुरमद्दु ।
सहुँ सीयऍ अच्छइ रामभद्दु ॥
वयणेण तेण कण्टइउ राउ ।
संचल्लु णवर साहणसहाउ ॥
जणमणपरिओसें
तूरिणघोसें
णरवइ कहिं मि ण माइयउ ।
जहिं रामु सभज्जउ
वाहुसहेज्जउ
तं उद्देसु पराइयउ ॥

१६

एत्थन्तरें परवलभडणिसामु ।
उट्ठिउ जणणिवहु णिएवि रामु ॥
करें धणुहरु लेइ ण लेइ जाम ।
सकलत्तउ लक्खणु दिट्ठु ताम ॥
सुरवइ व सभज्जउ रहें णिविट्ठु ।
अण्णेक्कु पासें अरिदमणु दिट्ठु ॥
सन्दणहों तरेप्पिणु दुण्णिवारु ।
रामहों चलणेहिं णिवडिउ कुमारु ॥
जियपउम सविब्भम पउमचलण ।
पउमच्छि पफुल्लियपउमवयण ॥

a stay in the forest, after forsaking the kingship.
Blessed demon-slaying Rama resides together with
Sita in your park." The king's body hair bristled with
these words. He set out immediately accompanied by
his army.

With the sound of drums, a delight to the hearts of the
people, the king could not be contained anywhere.
He reached that area where Rama, whose arms were
his allies, was together with his wife.

16

When Rama, destroyer of soldiers of enemy armies,
observed the crowd of people, he rose up. As he
hesitated taking up his bow in the hand,[9] he saw
Lakshmana with his wife, seated in a chariot like the
lord of the gods with his consort. He saw someone
else beside him: it was Aridamana. Descending from
the chariot, the unstoppable youth Lakshmana fell at
Rama's feet. The charming girl Jitapadma, her feet
like lotuses, her eyes like lotuses and her face like

पउमहों पयपउमेंहिँ पडिय कण्ण ।
तेण वि सुपसत्थासीस दिण्ण ॥
एत्थन्तरें मामें ण किउ खेउ ।
कणयरहें चडाविउ रामएउ ॥
पडु पडह पहय कियकलयलेहिँ ।
उच्छाहेंहिँ धवलेंहिँ मङ्गलेहिँ ॥
रहें एक्कें णिविट्ठइँ
णयरें पइट्ठइँ
सीयवलइँ वलवन्ताइँ ।
णारायणु णारि वि
थियइँ चयारि वि
रज्जु सइं भुञ्जन्ताइँ ॥

a blossoming lotus, fell at the lotus-like feet of Rama, the lotus. He blessed her most sincerely. Then the dear man did not hesitate and let Lord Rama climb into the golden chariot. Shrill drums were struck, accompanied by energetic, heroic, and benedictory songs that stirred up excitement.

The mighty Sita and Rama sat in one chariot and entered into the city. The four, the Vasudeva and his wife too, remained there, ruling the kingdom themselves.

वत्तीसमो संधि

हलहरचक्कहर
परचक्कहर
जिणवरसासणे अणुराइय ।
मुणिउवसग्गु जहिँ
विहरन्त तहिँ
वंसत्थलु णयरु पराइय ॥

१

ताम विसन्थुलु पाणक्कन्तउ ।
दिट्ठु असेसु वि जणु णासन्तउ ॥
दुम्मणु दीणवयणु विद्दाणउ ।
गउ विच्छत्त व गलियविसाणउ ॥
पण्णयणिवहु व फणिमणितोडिउ ।
गिरिणिवहु व वज्जासणिफोडिउ ॥
पङ्कयसण्डु व हिमपवणाहउ ।
उब्भडवयणु समुब्भियवाहउ ॥
जणवउ जं णासन्तु पदीसिउ ।
राहवचन्दें पुणु मम्भीसिउ ॥
थक्कहों मं भज्जहों मं भज्जहों ।
अभउ अभउ भउ सयलु विवज्जहों ॥

364

Chapter 32

As the Baladeva and Vasudeva, who had held back the enemy army and were devoted to the teaching of the Jina, roamed onward, they reached the city of Vamshasthala, where a calamity had struck the sages.

1

They saw all the people fleeing, frightened and breathing
  heavily, in low spirits, with sad faces, despondent,
  and defenseless like a tuskless elephant, like a
  heap of snakes whose forehead-jewels had been
  broken, like a cluster of mountains shattered by
  thunderbolts, like a bunch of lotuses struck by an icy
  wind, their faces impassioned and with their arms
  held high. When he saw the populace fleeing, moon-
  like Rama, the descendant of Raghu, offered them
  reassurance, "Stop, do not run, do not run. Be calm,

ताम दिट्ठु ओखण्डियमाणउ ।
णासन्तउ वंसत्थलराणउ ॥
तेण वुत्तु मं णयरें पईसहों ।
तिण्णि मि पाण लएप्पिणु णासहों ॥
एत्तिउ एत्थु पुरें
गिरिवरसिहरें
जो उट्ठइ णाउ भयङ्करु ।
तेण महन्तु डरु
णिवडन्ति तरु
मन्दिरइँ जन्ति सयसक्करु ॥

२

एॅउ दीसइ गिरिवरसिहरु जेत्थु ।
उवसग्गु भयङ्करु होइ तेत्थु ॥
वाओलि धूलि दुव्वाइ एइ ।
पाहण पडन्ति महि थरहरेइ ॥
धर भमइ समुट्ठइ सीहणाउ ।
वरिसन्ति मेह णिवडइ णिहाउ ॥
तें कज्जें णासइ सयलु लोउ ।
मं तुम्ह वि उहु उवसग्गु होउ ॥
तं णिसुणेवि सीय मणें कम्पिय ।
भीयविसन्थुल एव पजम्पिय ॥

be calm, abandon all fear." Then they saw the king of
Vamshasthala fleeing, his pride broken to pieces. He
said, "Do not enter the city. You three run away to
save your lives!

All this anxiety is due to that terrifying sound that rises
up in this city on top of the great mountain, as trees
are falling down and houses collapse into hundreds
of pieces.

2

"There is a terrifying calamity underway there, where you
can see the top of the great mountain. A fierce storm,
dust, and a harsh wind have set in, rocks are falling,
the earth is shaking, the mountain moves, the roar of
a lion rises up, clouds pour down rain, and a tremor
occurs. For this reason all the people are fleeing.
Do not let that calamity affect you too." Hearing this,
Sita shivered in her heart; frightened and agitated

अम्हहुँ देसें देसु भमन्तहुँ ।
कवणु पराहउ किर णासन्तहुँ ॥
तं णिसुणेवि भणइ दामोयरु ।
वोल्लिउ काइँ माएँ पइँ कायरु ॥
विहि मि जाम करें अतुलपयावइँ ।
सायरवज्जावत्तइँ चावइँ ॥
जाम विहि मि जयलच्छि परिट्ठिय ।
तोणीरहिँ णाराय अहिट्ठिय ॥
ताम माएँ तुहुँ कहों आसङ्कहि ।
विहरु विहरु मा मुहु ओवङ्कहि ॥
धीरेंवि जणयसुय
कोवण्डभुय
संचल्ल वे वि वलकेसव ।
सग्गहों अवयरिय
सइपरियरिय
ते इन्दपडिन्दसुरेस व ॥

३

पहन्तरे भयङ्करो ।
झसालछिण्णकक्करो ॥
वलो व्व सिझ्ददीहरो ।
णियच्छिओ महीहरो ॥

368

she spoke, "Indeed, what humiliation is it for us to
flee, as we roam from country to country?" At this,
the Vasudeva said, "Why do you speak so cowardly,
girl? As long as we both have the bows of unequaled
splendor, Samudravarta and Vajravarta, in our hands,
as long as Lady Triumph stands near us, and arrows sit
in our quivers, girl, what do you fear? Go on, go on, do
not avert your face."
Once they had reassured Janaka's daughter, the Baladeva
and the Vasudeva both set out with their bows in
their hands, as if those lords of the gods, Indra and
Pratindra,* had descended from heaven, accompanied
by Shachi.

3

Along the road they observed the terrifying mountain,
with bamboo trees and cleft rocks, with lofty peaks
like a bull with long horns:[1] in one place it had

* Indra's second-in-command, vice-Indra.

कहिं जें भीमकन्दरो ।
झरन्तणीरणिज्झरो ॥
कहिं जि रत्तचन्दणो ।
तमालतालवन्दणो ॥
कहिं जि दिट्ठु छारया ।
लवन्त मत्तमोरया ॥
कहिं जि सीहगण्डया ।
धुणन्तपुच्छदण्डया ॥
कहिं जि मत्तणिब्भरा ।
गुलुग्गुलन्ति कुञ्जरा ॥
कहिं जि दाढभासुरा ।
घुरुग्घुरन्ति सूयरा ॥
कहिं जि पुच्छदीहरा ।
किलिक्किलन्ति वाणरा ॥
कहिं जि थोरकन्धरा ।
परिब्भमन्ति सम्वरा ॥
कहिं जि तुझ्झअङ्गया ।
हयारि तिक्खसिङ्गया ॥
कहिं जि आणणुण्णया ।
कुरङ्ग वुण्णकण्णया ॥

dreadful cliffs and waterfalls with surging water; in another, red sandalwood trees, *tamālas,* palmyras, and sacred fig trees; here they saw bears and frantically calling peacocks; there lions and rhinoceroses, shaking their club-like tails; here rutting, violent elephants were roaring; there boars with terrible tusks were grunting; here monkeys with long tails were screeching; there sambars with massive necks were moving about; here there were buffaloes with tall bodies and sharp horns; there deer with their heads elevated and their ears alert.

तहिँ तेहएँ सइलें
तरुवरवहलें
आरूढ वे वि हरिहलहर ।
जाणइविज्जुलएँ
धवलुज्जलएँ
चिञ्झइय णाइँ णव जलहर ॥

४

पिहुलणियम्वविम्बरमणीयहें ।
राहउ दुम दरिसावइ सीयहें ॥
ऍहु सो धरणें णग्गोहपहाणु ।
जहिँ रिसहहों उप्पण्णउ णाणु ॥
ऍहु सो सत्तवन्तु किं ण मुणिउ ।
अजिउ सणाणदेहु जहिँ पथुणिउ ॥
ऍहु सो इन्दवच्छु सुपसिद्धउ ।
जहिँ संभवजिणु णाणसमिद्धउ ॥
ऍहु सो सरलु सहलु संभूअउ ।
अहिणन्दणु सणाणु जहिँ हूअउ ॥
ऍहु पीयङ्गु सीएँ सच्छायउ ।
सुमइ सणाणपिण्डु जहिँ जायउ ॥

Those two, the Vasudeva and the Baladeva, ascended
that very mountain, dense with great trees, like fresh
rainclouds adorned by the white, luminous lightning
bolt that was Janaka's daughter.

4

Rama, the descendant of Raghu, showed the trees to the
lovely woman with her wide, round hips, Sita, "This,
my love, is the eminent banyan tree, under which
Rishabha's knowledge* came to be. This here is the
devil tree—did you not know?—under which Ajita,
whose body was knowledge, was venerated. This here
is the well-renowned tree of Indra,[2] under which
the Jina Sambhava was gifted with knowledge. This
is a spreading chir pine, under which Abhinandana
became a possessor of knowledge. This is the shady
priyaṅgu, Sita, under which Sumati became endowed
with the great mass of knowledge. This is the *śāla* tree,

* Omniscience.

एहु सालु सो सीएँ णियच्छिउ ।
पउमप्पहु सणाणु जहिँ अच्छिउ ॥
एँहु सो सिरिसु महद्दुमु जाणइ ।
णाणु सुपासें भणेंवि जगु जाणइ ॥
एँहु सो णागरुक्खु चन्दप्पहें ।
णाणुप्पत्ति जेत्थु चन्दप्पहें ॥
एँहु सो मालइरुक्खु पदीसिउ ।
पुप्फयन्तु जहिँ णाणविहूसिउ ॥
एँहु सो पक्खतरु
फलफुल्लभरु
तेन्दुइसमाणु दुहणासहुँ ।
जहिँ परिहूयाइँ
संभूयाइँ
णाणइँ सीयलसेयंसहुँ ॥

५

एँह सा पाडलि सुहल सुपत्ती ।
वासुपुज्जें जहिँ णाणुप्पत्ती ॥
एँसु सो जम्बू एहु असत्थु ।
विमलाणन्तहुँ णाणसमत्थु ॥
उहु दहिवण्णणन्दि सुपसिद्धा ।
धम्मसन्ति जहिँ णाणसमिद्धा ॥

374

Sita, that you see, under which Padmaprabha became
a bearer of knowledge. This is the great *śirīṣa* tree,
daughter of Janaka. The world knows of it, because
the knowledge was proclaimed under it in Suparshva.
This is that *nāga* tree, lady with your moon-like
radiance, where the knowledge came into being for
Chandraprabha. Here you can see the jasmine tree,
under which Pushpadanta became adorned with
knowledge.
This is the Chinese banyan tree together with the
persimmon, with their abundance of fruits and
flowers, under which knowledge was grasped and
came to be for Shitala and Shreyamsa, vanquishers of
sorrow.

5

"This is the trumpet flower tree with its beautiful
fruits and leaves, under which knowledge arose for
Vasupujya. This here is the *jambū* tree and this the
sacred fig tree, related to the knowledge of Vimala
and Ananta. These are the famed *dadhiparṇa* and
crepe jasmin, under which Dharma and Shanti were

उहु साहारतिलउ दीसन्ति ।
कुन्थुअरहुँ जहिँ णाणुप्पत्ति ॥
ऍहु सो तरु कङ्केलिपहाणु ।
मल्लिजिणहों जहिँ केवलणाणु ॥
ऍहु सो चम्पउ किण्ण णियच्छिउ ।
मुणि सुव्वउ सणाणु जहिँ अच्छिउ ॥
इय उत्तिमतरु इन्दु वि वन्दइ ।
जणु कज्जेण तेण अहिणन्दइ ॥
एम चवन्त पत्त वललक्खण ।
जहिँ कुलभूसणदेसविहूसण ॥
दिवस चयारि अणङ्गवियारा ।
पडिमाजोगें थक्क भडारा ॥
वेन्तरघोणसेंहिँ
आसीविसेंहिँ
अहिविच्छियवेल्लिसहासेंहिँ ।
वेढिय वे वि जण
सुहलुद्धमण
पासण्डिय जिह पसुपासेंहिँ ॥

bestowed with knowledge. Here you can see a mango
and a *tilaka* tree, under which knowledge arose for
Kunthu and Ara. This is the eminent *aśoka* tree, under
which omniscience manifested for the Jina Malli.
Have you not seen this champac here, under which
Muni Suvrata became the bearer of knowledge? Even
Indra praises these notable trees. For that reason the
people honor them." As they were speaking thus, the
Baladeva and Lakshmana reached the place where
the noble men Kulabhushana and Deshavibhushana,
destroyers of lust, had been standing for four days in
the *pratimāyoga* position.*

The two men were surrounded by Vyantaras, *ghoṇasa*³ and
āśīviṣa snakes, and thousands of serpents, scorpions,
and creepers, just like heretics, whose hearts long for
comfort, are ensnared by the fetters of everyday life.

* A standing meditative position with the arms hanging loose.

६

जं दिट्ठु असेसु वि अहिणिहाउ ।
वलएउ भयङ्करु गरुडु जाउ ॥
तोणीरपक्खु वइदेहिचञ्चु ।
पक्खुज्जलसररोमञ्चकञ्चु ॥
सोमित्तिवियडविप्फुरियवयणु ।
णारायतिक्खणिडुरियणयणु ॥
दोण्णि वि कोवण्डइँ कण्ण दो वि ।
थिउ राहउ भीसणु गरुडु होवि ॥
तं णयणकडक्खेंवि दुग्गमेहिँ ।
परिचिन्तिउ कज्जु भुअङ्गमेहिँ ॥
लहु णासहुँ किं णरसंगमेण ।
खज्जेसहुँ गरुडविहङ्गमेण ॥
एत्थन्तरें विहडिय अहि मयन्ध ।
गय खयहोँ णाइँ मुणिकम्मवन्ध ॥
भयभीय विसन्थुल मरणेण तट्टु ।
खरपवणपहय घण जिह पणट्टु ॥
वेल्हीसङ्कुलहोँ
वंसत्थलहोँ
विसहरफुक्कारकरालहोँ ।
जाय पगास रिसि
णहेँ सूरससि
उम्मिल्ल णाइँ घणजालहोँ ॥

6

When the Baladeva saw that great mass of snakes, he
    became the terrifying Garuda, with quivers for wings,
    Videha's daughter for his beak, arrows with splendid
    fletchings for his bristling feathers, Sumitri's son
    for his wide, flashing face, and sharp arrows for his
    horrific eyes. The two bows were his two ears. Thus
    Rama, the descendant of Raghu, stood there, having
    become the Garuda. Eyeing him, the formidable
    snakes reflected on their cause, "Let us quickly flee.
    What good would an encounter with those humans
    do? We will be devoured by the bird Garuda."
    Thereupon the snakes, blind with pride, scattered
    like the annihilated karmic fetters of a sage. Horror-
    struck, agitated, and frightened in their heart, they
    fled like clouds struck by a fierce wind.
From out of the profusion of creepers of Vamshasthala,
    terrifying with the snakes' hisses, the seers became
    visible, like the sun and the moon in the sky appearing
    out of a cloudbank.

७

अहिणिवहु जं जें गउ ओसरेंवि ।
मुणि वन्दिय जोगभत्ति करेंवि ॥
जे भवसंसारारिहें डरिय ।
सिवसासयगमणहों अइतुरिय ॥
विहिँ दोसहिँ जे ण परिग्गहिय ।
विहिँ वज्जिय विहिँ झाणहिँ सहिय ॥
तिहिँ जाइजरामरणेंहिँ रहिय ।
दंसणचारित्तणाणसहिय ॥
जे चउगइचउकसायमहण ।
चउमङ्गलकर चउसरणमण ॥
जे पञ्चमहव्वयदुधरधर ।
पञ्चेन्दियदोसविणासयर ॥
छत्तीसगुणड्ढिगुणेँहिँ पवर ।
छज्जीवणिकायहुँ खन्तिकर ॥
जिय जेहिँ सभय सत्त वि णरय ।
जे सत्तसिवङ्कर अणवरय ॥
कम्मट्ठमयट्ठदुट्ठदमण ।
अट्ठविहगुणड्ढीसरसवण ॥

7

As soon as the mass of snakes had fled and gone, they
praised the sages, showing their devotion for their
yoga, "You who fear the cycle of existence like an
enemy, quickly hastening to go to blissful eternity, not
caught by the two sins,[4] devoid of both, endowed with
the two forms of meditation,[5] free of the three—birth,
old age, and death—accompanied by the correct view
of reality, proper conduct, and correct knowledge,
you who have annihilated the four modes of existence
and the four passions, who perform the fourfold
auspicious practice,[6] whose minds are focused on
the Four Refuges,[7] bearing the unbearable five great
vows, destroying the sins of the five senses, who excel
in the abundance and merit of the thirty-six virtues,[8]
patient toward the six categories of life forms,[9] you
who have overcome the seven terrible hell regions,[10]
continuously executing the seven elements of bliss,[11]
destroying the eight wicked forms of karma and
the eight arrogances,[12] oceans of the eight virtuous,
miraculous phenomena!"

एक्केक्कोत्तरिय
इय गुणभरिय
पुणु वन्दिय वलगोविन्देहिँ ।
गिरिमन्दरसिहरें
वरवेइहरें
जिणजुवलु व इन्दपडिन्देहि ॥

८

भावें तिहि मि जणेहिँ धम्मज्जणु ।
किउ चन्दणरसेण सम्मज्जणु ॥
पुप्फच्चणिय छुद्धसयवत्तेहिँ ।
पुणु आढत्तु गेउ मुणिभत्तेहिँ ॥
रामु सुघोस वीण अप्फालइ ।
जा मुणिवरहु मि चित्तइँ चालइ ॥
जा रामउरिहिँ आसि रवण्णी ।
तूसेवि पूयणजक्खें दिण्णी ॥
लक्खणु गाइ सलक्खणु गेउ ।
सत्त वि सर तिगामसरभेउ ॥
एक्कवीस वरमुच्छणठाणइँ ।
एक्कुणपञ्चास वि सरताणइँ ॥
तालविताल पणच्चइ जाणइ ।
णव रस अट्ठ भाव जा जाणइ ॥

Each of these men who had escaped, laden with virtues,
   was then thus praised by the Baladeva and the
   Vasudeva, like a pair of Jinas atop Mount Meru, the
   home of beautiful pedestals,[13] by Indra and Pratindra.

8

The three people cleansed them with sandalwood water,
   which procured them righteousness, and offered an
   homage of flowers by scattering lotuses. Then the
   devotees of the sages began to sing. Rama played
   the vina Sughosha, which moved the minds even
   of those excellent sages, the agreeable one that
   was given in Ramapuri by the Yaksha Putana in
   gratitude. Lakshmana sang a song with auspicious
   characteristics, of seven notes, three tone systems,
   tonal change, twenty-one scales and registers, and
   forty-nine tonal patterns. Janaka's daughter, who
   knew the nine moods and eight emotions, danced
   with talas and breaking times, the ten glances and

दस दिट्ठिउ वावीस लयाइं ।
भरहें भरहगविटुइँ जाइं ॥
भावें जणयसुय
चउसट्ठि भुय
दरिसन्ति पणच्चइ जावेंहिँ ।
दिणयरअत्थवर्णे
गिरिगुहिलवर्णे
उवसग्गु समुट्ठिउ तावेंहिँ ॥

९

तो कोवग्गिकरम्वियहासइँ ।
दिट्ठइँ णहयलें असुरसहासइँ ॥
अण्णइँ विप्फुरियाहरवयणइँ ।
अण्णइँ रत्तुम्मिल्लियणयणइँ ॥
अण्णइँ पिङ्कङ्कइँ पिङ्कक्खइँ ।
अण्णइँ णिम्मंसइँ दुप्पेक्खइँ ॥
अण्णइँ णहें णच्चन्ति विवत्थइँ ।
अण्णइँ तहिँ चामुण्डविहत्थइँ ॥
अण्णइँ कङ्कालइँ वेयालइँ ।
कत्तियमडयकरइँ विकरालइँ ॥
अण्णइँ मसिवण्णइँ अपसत्थइँ ।
णरसिरमालकवालविहत्थइँ ॥

twenty-two tempos, that Bharata laid down in his
Bharatanāṭyaśāstra.[14]
While Janaka's daughter danced, succinctly
demonstrating the sixty-four hand gestures, a
calamity arose in the dense forest of the mountain as
the sun set.

9

All at once in the sky they saw thousands of demons,
laughing and engulfed by the fire of anger: some
had faces with quivering lips; others blood-red eyes
opened wide; others yellow bodies and yellow eyes;
others were emaciated and unsightly; others were
dancing naked in the sky; some there were proficient
with Chamunda;[15] others were horrifying skeletons or
Vetalas with knives and corpses in their hands; some
had the color of soot and looked inauspicious, playing
with human heads on garlands of skulls; others were
drinking blood as wine, dancing, rolling,

अण्णइँ सोणियमइर पियन्तइँ ।
णच्चन्तइँ घुम्मन्तघुलन्तइँ ॥
अण्णइँ किलकिलन्ति चउपासेँहिँ ।
अण्णइँ कहकहन्ति उवहासेँहिँ ॥
अण्णइँ भीसणइँ
दुद्दरिसणइँ
मरु मारि मारि जम्पन्तइँ ।
देसविहूसणहँ
कुलभूसणहँ
आयइँ उवसग्गु करन्तइँ ॥

१०

पुणु अण्णइँ अण्णण्णपयारेँहिँ ।
ढुक्कइँ विसहरफणफुक्कारेँहिँ ॥
अण्णइँ जम्बुवसिवफेक्कारेँहिँ ।
वसहझडक्कमुक्कढेक्कारेँहिँ ॥
अण्णइँ करिवरकरसिक्कारेँहिँ ।
सरसन्धियधणुगुणटङ्कारेँहिँ ॥
अण्णइँ गद्दहमण्डलसद्देँहिँ ।
अण्णइँ वहुविहभेसियणद्देँहिँ ॥
अण्णइँ गिरिवरतरुवरघाएँहिँ ।
पाणियपाहणपवणुप्पाएँहिँ ॥
अण्णइँ अमरिसरोसफुरन्तइँ ।

and stumbling; others were screeching on all sides; others roared with laughter;
others were terrifying and hideous, saying, "Die, kill, kill," creating a calamity for Deshavibhushana and Kulabhushana.

10

Then others approached in many different forms, some hissing from the hoods of snakes; some with howls of different kinds of jackals[16] or bellowing like charging bulls; others with shrieks from the trunks of elephants; twangs of a bow-string and bow united with an arrow; some with the sounds of a herd of donkeys; others with different kinds of horrific roars; some with blows from great mountains and trees, with dreadful phenomena of water, rocks, and wind; others were quivering with indignation and wrath, emitting

णयणेहिँ अग्गिफुलिङ्ग मुयन्तइँ ॥
अण्णइँ दहवयणइँ सयवयणइँ ।
अण्णइँ सहसमुहइँ वहुणयणइँ ॥
तहिँ तेहएँ वि कालें मइविमलहुँ ।
तो वि ण चलिउ झाणु मुणिधवलहुँ ॥
वइरु सरन्ताइँ
पहरन्ताइँ
सव्वलहुलिहलमुसलग्गेहिँ ।
कालें अप्पणउ
भीसावणउ
दरिसाविउ णं वहुभङ्गेहिँ ॥

११

उवसग्गु णिएॅवि हरिसियमणेहिँ ।
णीसङ्केहिँ वलणारायणेहिँ ॥
मम्भीसेॅवि सीय महावलेहिँ ।
मुणिचलण धराविय करयलेहिँ ॥
धणुहरइँ विहि मि अप्फालियइँ ।
णं सुरभवणइँ संचालियइँ ॥
वुण्णइँ भयभीयविसण्ठुलइँ ।
णं रसियइँ णहयलमहियलइँ ॥
तं सद्दु सुणेॅवि आसङ्कियइँ ।
रिउचित्तइँ माणकलङ्कियइँ ॥

fiery sparks with their eyes; some had ten faces, a
hundred faces, others had a thousand faces and many
eyes. Even at that very time the meditation of the
splendid sages, pure in their minds, did not waver.
Remembering their hostility and attacking with javelins,
knives, plows, and the tips of maces, it was as if Death
showed his horrifying self in many parts.

11

When the mighty, fearless Baladeva and Vasudeva beheld
the calamity, their hearts grew excited and they
reassured Sita as they made her hold the feet of the
sages with the palms of her hands. Both shot their
bows, as if shaking the palaces of the gods. Heaven
and earth seemed to resound, frightened, horror-
struck, and agitated. Hearing that sound, the enemies'
hearts were distressed and tainted in their pride.

धणुहरटङ्कारेहिँ वहिरियइँ ।
णट्टइँ खलखुद्दइँ वइरियइँ ॥
णं अट्ठ वि कम्मइँ णिज्जियइँ ।
णं पञ्चेन्दियइँ परज्जियइँ ॥
णं णासेवि गयइँ परीसहइँ ।
तिह असुरसहासइँ दूसहइँ ॥
छुडु छुडु णट्टाइँ
भयतट्टाइँ
मेल्लेप्पिणु मच्छरु माणु ।
ताव भडाराहुँ
वयधाराहुँ
उप्पण्णउ केवलणाणु ॥

१२

ताव मुणिन्दहँ णाणुप्पत्तिएँ ।
आय सुरासुर वन्दणहत्तिएँ ॥
जेहिँ कित्ति तइलोक्कें पगासिय ।
जोइस वेन्तर भवणिवासिय ॥
पहिलउ भावण सङ्घणिणद्दें ।
वेन्तर तूरयफालियसद्दें ॥

Deafened by the twangs of the bows, the wretched
    foes fled, vanquished like the eight forms of karma
    and overcome like the five senses. Thus the thousands
    of unstoppable demons vanished and went away as if
    they were the afflictions.
Abandoning their wrath and pride, they steadily
    disappeared, alarmed with fear. Then omniscience
    arose for the noble lords, bearers of the vows.

12

Then, as the knowledge of the great sages emerged,
    gods and demons[17] came to praise and revere
    them, to spread their fame in the three worlds: the
    Jyotis, Vyantara, and Bhavanavasin gods. First the
    Bhavanavasin gods came with the sound of a conch,
    then the Vyantaras with the sound of a drum being

जोइसदेव वि सीहणिणाएं ।
कप्पामर जयघण्टणिणाएं ॥
संचलिएं चउदेवणिकाएं ।
छाइउ णहु णं घणसंघाएं ॥
वहइ विमाणु विमाणें चप्पिउ ।
वाहणु वाहणणिवहझडप्पिउ ॥
तुरउ तुरङ्गमेण ओमाणिउ ।
सन्दणु सन्दणेण संदाणिउ ॥
गयवरु गयवरेण पडिक्खलियउ ।
लग्गेवि मउडें मउडु उच्छलियउ ॥
भावें पेल्लियउ
भयमेल्लियउ
सुरसाहणु लीलएँ आवइ ।
लोयहुँ मूढाहुँ
तमें छूढाहुँ
णं धम्मरिद्धि दरिसावइ ॥

१३

ताव पुरन्दरेण अइरावउ ।
साहिउ जणमणणयणसुहावउ ॥
सोह दिन्तु चउसट्ठीणयणेहिँ ।
गुलुगुलन्तु वत्तीसहिँ वयणेहिँ ॥
वयणें वयणें अट्टुट्टु विसाणइँ ।

392

struck, then the Jyotis gods with the roar of a lion,
and the Kalpa gods with the sound of a victory bell.[18]
When the fourfold congregation of gods departed,
they obscured the sky like a cluster of clouds. A
celestial chariot set out and was overrun by another
celestial chariot; a vehicle was cut off by a group of
other vehicles; a horse was disregarded by another
horse; a chariot became tied up with another chariot;
a great elephant was hindered by another great
elephant; a crown that had become stuck on another
crown flew up.

The fearless army of gods that was truly dispatched,
arrived with ease. It was as if it demonstrated the
success of the doctrine to the foolish people who were
cast in darkness.

13

Then Indra prepared Airavata, who brought happiness to
the hearts and eyes of the people, spreading brilliance
with his sixty-four eyes and roaring with his thirty-two
mouths. In every mouth there were eight tusks, like

णाइँ सुवण्णणिवद्धणिहाणइँ ॥
एक्केक्कएँ विसाणें जणमणहरु ।
एक्केक्कउ जें परिट्ठिउ सरवरु ॥
सरें सरें सरपरिमाणुप्पण्णी ।
कमलिणि एक्कएक्क णिप्पण्णी ॥
एक्केक्कहें पउमिणिहें विसालइँ ।
पङ्कयाइँ वत्तीस सणालइँ ॥
कमलें कमलें वत्तीस जि पत्तइँ ।
पत्तें पत्तें णट्टाइ मि तेत्तइँ ॥
वड्ढिउ जम्वूदीवपमाणें ।
पुणु जि परिट्ठिउ तेण जि थाणें ॥
तहिँ दुग्घोट्टें चडेॎवि सुरसुन्दरु ।
वन्दणहत्तिएँ आउ पुरन्दरु ॥
पुरउ सुरिन्दहों णयणाणन्देहिँ ।
गुरु पोमाइउ वन्दिणवन्देहिँ ॥
देवहों दाणवहों
खलमाणवहों
रिसिचलणेहिँ केव ण लग्गहों ।
जेहिँ तवन्तएॎहिँ
अचलन्तएॎहिँ
इन्दु वि अवयारिउ सग्गहों ॥

treasures of gold that were fixed to them. On every single tusk there lay exactly one great lake that took people's breaths away. In every lake one single lotus plant arose that grew to the size of the lake. On every single lotus plant there were thirty-two large lotuses with stems. On every lotus there were precisely thirty-two petals. On every petal there were as many performances. He grew to the size of Jambudvipa. Even more, he was enveloped by that place alone. Climbing onto that elephant, Indra, the Adonis of the gods, came to offer praise and reverence. Before the lord of the gods, bands of bards—a joy to the eye— praised the master:

"Gods, demons, lowly people, why do you not cling to the feet of the seers, who by performing self-mortification without moving made Indra come down from heaven?"

१४

जिणवरचलणकमलदलसेवहिँ ।
केवलणाणपुज्ज किय देवहिँ ॥
भणइ पुरन्दरु अहों अहों लोयहों ।
जइ सङ्किय जरमरणविओयहों ॥
जइ णिव्विण्णा चउगइगमणहों ।
तो किं ण ढुक्कहों जिणवरभवणहों ॥
पुत्तु कलत्तु जाव मणें चिन्तहों ।
जिणवरविम्बु ताव किं ण चिन्तहों ॥
चिन्तहों जाव मासु मयरासणु ।
किं ण चिन्तवहों ताव जिणसासणु ॥
चिन्तहों जाव रिद्धि सिय सम्पय ।
किं ण चिन्तवहों ताव जिणवरपय ॥
चिन्तहों जाव रूउ धणु जोव्वणु ।
धणु सुवण्णु अण्णु घरु परियणु ॥
चिन्तहों जाव वलिउ भुवपञ्जरु ।
किं ण चिन्तवहों ताव परमक्खरु ॥
पेक्खहु धम्मफलु
चउरङ्गवलु
पयहिण तिवार देवाविउ ।
सइं भुवणेसरहों
परमेसरहों
अत्थक्कएँ सेव कराविउ ॥

14

The gods, who served the petals of the lotus-like feet
of the great Jina, performed the ritual of worship
for omniscience. Indra said, "Ah, ah, my people, if
you fear old age, death, and separation, if you are
disgusted with going through the four destinies,[19]
then why do you not go to the temple of the great
Jina? Just as you reflect in your mind about a son or
wife, why do you not look to the icon of the great Jina?
Just as you think about meat and lust, why do you
not ponder over the teaching of the Jina? Just as you
care for success, luster, and abundance, why do you
not look to the feet of the great Jina? Just as you think
about beauty, riches, youth, grain, gold, food, a house,
and a retinue, just as you ponder over powerful cage-
like arms, why do you not reflect upon the supreme
indestructible?

Behold the fruit of the doctrine: the fourfold army is
forced to circle them thrice and to promptly perform
service itself to the supreme lord, the master of the
world."

तेत्तीसमो संधि

उप्पण्णाएँ णाणेँ
पुच्छइ रहुतणउ ।
कुलभूसणदेव
किं उवसग्गु कउ ॥

१

तं णिसुणेॅवि पभणइ परमगुरु ।
सुणु जक्खथाणु णामेण पुरु ॥
तहिँ कासवसुरव महाभविय ।
एयारहगुणथाणग्घविय ॥
एक्कोवर किंङ्कर पुरवइहेँ ।
णं तुम्वुरुणारय सुरवइहेँ ॥
हम्मन्तु विहङ्गमु लुद्धऍहिँ ।
परिरक्खिउ तेहिँ पवुद्धऍहिँ ॥
खगवइ पुणु वहुकालेण मुउ ।
विज्झाचलेँ भिल्लाहिवइ हुउ ॥
तो कासवसुरव वे वि मरेॅवि ।
थिय अमियसरहों घरेँ ओअरेॅवि ॥
उवओवादेविहेँ दोहलेँहिँ ।
उप्पण्णा वड्ढेँहिँ सोहलेँहिँ ॥

Chapter 33

When the knowledge had emerged, Rama, the descendant of Raghu, asked, "Lord Kulabhushana, what caused this calamity?"

1

At this, the supreme master said, "Listen, there is a city named Yakshasthana. Kashyapa and Surapa lived there, both of them most gracious men, endowed with the eleven stages of renunciation.[1] They were brothers, servants of the city's leader, like Tumburu and Narada of the king of the gods.[2] These wise men saved a bird as it was being struck by hunters. Then a long while later the noble bird died and became a leader of the Bhillas in the Vindhya mountains. When both Kashyapa and Surapa died, they were reborn and lived in the house of Amritasvara, born through the illustrious and blissful pregnancies of the lady Upayoga. Relatives came to celebrate the birth, and they were given the names Udita and Mudita.

वद्धावउ आयउ वन्धुजणु ।
किउ उइयमुइय णामग्गहणु ॥
णं अमरकुमार
छुडु सग्गहों पडिय ।
णाणङ्कुसहत्थ
जोव्वणगएँ चडिय ॥

२

तो पउमिणिपुरपरमेसरहों ।
दरिसाविय विजयमहीहरहों ॥
तेण वि णियसुअहों जयन्धरहों ।
किय किङ्कर वड्ढियरणभरहों ॥
अच्छन्ति जाम भुञ्जन्ति सिय ।
तो ताम जणेरहों गमणकिय ॥
पट्टविउ णरिन्देँ अमियसरु ।
अइभूमिलेहरिञ्छोलिधरु ॥
वसुभूइ सहेज्जउ तासु गउ ।
तें णवर पाणविच्छोउ कउ ॥
पल्लट्टइ पल्लट्टिउ भणेवि ।
ते उइयमुइय तिणसमु गणेवि ॥
सों उवउवाएविएँ सहुँ जियइ ।
अमिओवमु अहरपाणु पियइ ॥

Like princes of the gods who had suddenly fallen from
heaven, they climbed onto the elephant of youth,
holding the goad of knowledge in their hand.

2

"They were then introduced to Vijayamahidhara, the
supreme lord of Padminipura. He made them
servants to his son Jayandhara, who could endure ever
fiercer battles. While they were there and enjoyed
luster, their father received a travel assignment. The
king sent Amritasvara away transporting a collection
of letters to a distant land. Vasubhuti went along as
his companion. He, however, robbed Amritasvara
of his life. He returned saying that Amritasvara had
sent him away. Disregarding that Udita and Mudita
as if they were grass, he lived together with the lady
Upayoga and drank the ambrosia-like liquor of her

परियाणेॅवि जेट्टें दुच्चरिउ ।
वसुभूइहें जीविउ अवहरिउ ॥
उप्पण्णउ विज्झें
होप्पिणु पल्लिवइ ।
पुव्वक्किउ कम्मु
सव्वहों परिणवइ ॥

३

जयपव्वयपवरुज्जाणु जहिँ ।
रिसिसङ्घु पराइउ ताव तहिँ ॥
किय रुक्खें रुक्खें आवासकिय ।
णं रुक्खें रुक्खें अवइण्ण सिय ॥
संजायइँ अङ्झइँ कोमलइँ ।
अहियइँ पण्णइँ फुल्लइँ फलइँ ॥
रिसि रुक्ख व अविचल होवि थिय ।
किसलएँ परिवेढावेढि किय ॥
रिसि रुक्ख व तवणताव तविय ।
रिसि रुक्ख व मूलगुणग्घविय ॥
रिसि रुक्ख व आलवालरहिय ।
रिसि रुक्ख व मोक्खफलब्भहिय ॥
गउ णन्दणवणिउ तुरन्तु तहिँ ।
सो विजयमहीहरराउ जहिँ ॥

lips. Learning of the scandalous behavior, the eldest
took Vasubhuti's life.

He was born in the Vindhya, becoming the head of a
village. A previously done deed ripens for everyone.

3

"Then a group of seers arrived where the beautiful park
Jayaparvata lay. They settled themselves under every
tree, as if under every tree the goddess of luster had
descended. Soft limbs, abundant foliage, flowers,
and fruits sprouted. Like the trees, the seers stood
there, becoming motionless, encircled all around by a
young branch. Like the trees were heated by the sun,
the seers were scorched by ascetic practice. Like the
trees were endowed with roots as virtues, the seers
were endowed with the basic restraints. Like the trees
were without a water basin around the root, the seers
were wanting in nonsensical speech. Like the trees
were brimming with fruits, the seers were exceptional
in the result of their liberation.[3] The park warden
quickly went to where that king Vijayamahidhara was,

परमेसर केसरिविक्कमेहिँ ।
उज्जाणु लइउ जइपुङ्वेंहिँ ॥
वारन्तहों मज्झु
उम्मग्गिम करेंवि ।
रिसिसीहकिसोर [व]
थिय वणें पइसरेंवि ॥

४

तं णिसुण्णेंवि णरवइ गयउ तहिँ ।
आवासिउ महरिसिसत्थु जहिँ ॥
वोल्लाविय अहों अहों मुणिवरहों ।
अवुहहों अयाणपरमक्खरहों ॥
परमप्पउ अप्पउ होवि थिउ ।
कज्जेण केण रिसिवेसु किउ ॥
अइदुलहु लहेंवि मणुअत्तणउ ।
कें कज्जें विणडहों अप्पणउ ॥
कहों केरउ परममोक्खगमणु ।
वरि माणिउ मणहरु तरुणियणु ॥
सच्छायइँ आयइँ अङ्गाइँ ।
सोलहआहरणहँ जोग्गाइँ ॥
वित्थिण्णइँ आयइँ कडियलइँ ।
हयगयरहवाहणपञ्चलइँ ॥

'Supreme lord, eminent ascetics, courageous as lions,
    have taken over the park.
Even though I refused them, the seers, like young lions,
    have settled in the park, after entering it by taking an
    unsanctioned road.'

4

"At this, the king went to where the group of great seers
    had settled. He called them, 'Great sages, you are
    all fools: you take ignorance to be the most perfect
    thing. The self you have is the highest one there is.
    For what reason do you dress up as a sage? You have
    obtained a human existence that is difficult to get, why
    do you let yourself flounder? For whom is the course
    toward supreme liberation? It is better to enjoy a
    breathtaking flock of young women. These handsome
    bodies are suited for sixteen ornaments. These ample
    buttocks are fit for horses, elephants, chariots, and

लायण्णइँ रूवइँ जोव्वणइँ ।
णिप्फलइँ गयइँ तुम्हहँ तणइँ ॥
सुपसिद्धउ लोएँ
एक्कु वि तउ ण कउ ।
तुम्हाण किलेसु
सयलु णिरत्थु गउ ॥

५

तो मोक्खरुक्खफलवड्ढणेण ।
महिपालु वुत्तु मइवड्ढणेण ॥
पइँ अप्पउ काइँ विडम्वियउ ।
अच्छहि सुहदुक्खकरम्वियउ ॥
कहों घरु कहों पुत्तकलत्ताइँ ।
धयचिन्धइँ चामरछत्ताइँ ॥
सविमाणइँ जाणइँ जोग्गाइँ ।
रहतुरयमहग्गयदुग्गाइँ ॥
धणधण्णइँ जीवियजोव्वणइँ ।
जलकीलउ पाणइँ उववणइँ ॥
वइसणउ वसुन्धरि वज्जाइँ ।
णउ कासु वि होन्ति सहेज्जाइँ ॥
आयहिँ वहुयहिँ वेयारियइँ ।
वम्भाणहँ लक्खइँ मारियइँ ॥

406

vehicles. Your charms, good looks, and youthful forms
fruitlessly go to waste.
There is not one deed of yours that is well-known in
the world. You are putting yourself through all this
anguish for no good reason.'

5

"Then Mativardhana, who let the fruits of the tree of
liberation prosper, said to the king, 'Why have you
deceived yourself? You are enmeshed by happiness
and sorrow. To whom does a house belong? To
whom sons and wives, banners, standards, flywhisks,
umbrellas, proper vehicles along with celestial cars,
chariots, horses, great elephants, and fortresses,
riches and grain, life, youthfulness, water sports,
beverages, and parks, a throne, the earth, diamonds?
They are companions for no one. Lakhs of Brahmans
have been cheated and killed with these many things.
Thousands of kings of the gods have been hurled

सुरवइहिँ सहासइँ पाडियइँ ।
चक्कवइसयइँ णिद्धाडियइँ ॥
एय वि अवरे वि
कालें कवलु किय ।
सिय कहों वि समाणु
एक्कु वि पउ ण गय ॥

६

परमेसरु पुणु वि पुणु वि कहइ ।
जिउ तिण्णि अवत्थउ उव्वहइ ॥
उप्पत्तिजरामरणावसरु ।
पहिलउ जें णिवद्धउ देहघरु ॥
पुग्गलपरिमाणसुत्तु धरेंवि ।
करचलण चयारि खम्भ करेंवि ॥
वहुअत्थिजिअन्तहिँ ढङ्कियउ ।५
मासिट्टु चम्मछुहपङ्कियउ ॥
सिरकलसालङ्किउ संचरइ ।
माणुसु वरभवणहों अणुहरइ ॥
तरुण्णत्तणु जाम ताम वहइ ।
पुणु पच्छएँ जुण्णभाउ लहइ ॥
सिरु कम्पइ जम्पइ ण वि वयणु ।
ण सुणन्ति कण्ण ण णियइ णयणु ॥

down and hundreds of universal emperors have been driven out.
Death reduces these and others, too, to just a mouthful. Equally, someone's glory does not progress even one step.'

6

"Again and again the supreme lord spoke, 'A soul experiences three conditions: the moment of birth, old age, and death. First a body is built like a house: after taking hold of the thread—that is an outline of substance;[4] and making four pillars—the hands and feet; it is beset with many supporting beams—the bones; with bricks for flesh, it is covered with plaster—the skin; adorned with a pitcher-shaped pinnacle—the head; it comes together, a human resembles a beautiful house. He possesses youthfulness only for so long; later on he begets the state of old age: the head shakes, the mouth no longer speaks, the ears do not hear, and the eye does not see,

ण चलन्ति चलण ण करन्ति कर ।
जरजज्जरिहोइ सरीरु पर ॥
पुणु पच्छिमकालें
णिवडइ देहघरु ।
जिउ जेम विहङ्गु
उड्डुइ मुऍवि तरु ॥

तं णिसुर्णेवि णरवइ उवसमिउ ।
णियणन्दणु णियपऍं सण्णिमिउ ॥
अप्पुणु पुणु भावगाहगहिउ ।
णिक्खन्तु णराहिवसयसहिउ ॥
तहिँ उइयमुइय णिग्गन्थ थिय ।
करकमलेंहिँ केसुप्पाड किय ॥
पुणु सवणसङ्घु तहों पुरवरहों ।
गउ वन्दणहत्तिऍ जिणवरहों ॥
सम्मेयहों जन्त जन्त वलिय ।
पहु छड्डेँवि उप्पहेण चलिय ॥
ते उइयमुइय दुइ णिव्वडिय ।
वसुभूइभिल्लपल्लिहें पडिय ॥
धाइउ धाणुक्कु वद्धवइरु ।
गुज्झाहलणयणु पीयमइरु ॥

the feet do not walk, and the hands do not work. The
body is just ravaged by old age.
Then, in the final phase, the body that is like a house
collapses. Like a bird leaving a tree, the soul flies up.'

7

"When the king heard this, he grew calm and installed
his son in his position. Seized by the determination
of his state of mind, he himself then renounced the
material world together with a hundred other kings.
Among them were Udita and Mudita, who stood
there as naked ascetics and with their lotus-like hands
performed the ceremonies of pulling out the hair.
Then the community of wandering ascetics went away
from that great city to praise and revere the excellent
Jina. As they were going along toward Mount
Sammeta,[5] they took a turn and, leaving the road,
they proceeded the wrong way. Those two, Udita and
Mudita, reemerged and landed in the village of the
Bhilla Vasubhuti. Rigid in his hostility, the archer ran
at them, his eyes like crab's-eye berries, having drunk

दुप्पेच्छवच्छु थिरथोरकरु ।
अप्फालियधणुहरु गहिरसरु ॥
वइरइँ ण कुहन्ति
होन्ति ण जज्जरइँ ।
हउ हणइ णिरुत्तु
सत्तभवन्तरइँ ॥

हक्कारिय विण्णि वि दुद्धरेण ।
णियवइयरवइरविरुद्धएण ॥
अहो संचारिमणरवणयरहों ।
कहिँ गम्मइ एवहिँ महु मरहों ॥
तं सुणेवि महावयधारएण ।
धीरिउ लहुवउ वड्डारएण ॥
मं भीहि थाहि अण्णहों भवहों ।
उवसग्गसहणु भूसणु तवहों ॥
तहिँ तेहएँ विहुरें समववडिएँ ।
अधुरन्धरें गरुअभारें पडिएँ ॥
थिउ खन्धु समडेँवि एक्कु जणु ।
भिल्लाहिउ अब्भुद्धरणमणु ॥
जो पुव्वभवन्तरें पक्खिवयउ ।
पुरें जक्खथाणें परिरक्खियउ ॥

wine, his chest unsightly, his hands firm and strong,
and shot his bow with a deep sound.
Hostilities do not decay. They do not become decrepit.
It is clear: one who is killed, kills for the next seven
lifetimes.

8

"Hateful because of his own misfortune and hostility,
the unstoppable man challenged the two, 'Hey, you
men who roam the forest like spies, where do you
journey to? Now you die because of me.' At this, the
elder brother, bearer of the great vows, reassured the
younger, 'Do not fear, surrender to the next existence.
Enduring a calamity is the gem of ascetic practice.'
While this adversity transpired there and the great
burden came down on them without anyone to
help, one man stood there, having prepared an army
division, the Bhilla king, his mind set on saving them.
He was the one who in a previous existence as a bird
was rescued in the city of Yakshasthana, and he spoke,

तें वुच्चइ लोद्धा ओसरहि ।
को मारइ रिसि तुहुँ महु मरहि ॥
वोलाविय तेण
कालन्तरॆण मय ।
दय चडॆवि णिसेणि
लीलएँ सग्गु गय ॥

पावासउ पउरु पाउ करॆवि ।
वहुकालु णरयतिरियहिँ फिरॆवि ॥
वसुभूझभिल्लु धणजणपउरॆं ।
पट्टणॆं उप्पण्णु अरिट्ठउरॆं ॥
णामेण अणुद्धरु दुद्दरिसु ।
कणयप्पहजणणिजणियहरिसु ॥
दुलङ्घहॊं णियकुलपव्वयहॊं ।
णन्दण णरवइहॆं पियव्वयहॊं ॥
ते उइयमुइय तासु जि तणय ।
विण्णाणकलापरपारगय ॥
गिरिधीर महोवहिगहिरगुण ।
पयपालण रज्जकज्जणिउण ॥
णामङ्किय रयणविचित्तरह ।
पउमावइसुअ ससिसूरपह ॥

'Hunter, get away. Who kills seers? You die because of
me.'
This is what he said to them. In due course, they passed
away. Having climbed the ladder of compassion, they
went to heaven with ease.

9

"The one whose thoughts were set on evil, the Bhilla
Vasubhuti, committing plenty of sins and for a
long time passing through existences in hell and
as an animal, was born in the city of Arishtapura,
abounding in riches and people. Named Anuddhara,
he was hideous, but brought joy to his mother
Kanakaprabha. King Priyavrata, an unascendable
mountain to his family, had sons. His children were
that Udita and Mudita, thoroughly learned in the
skills and the arts, firm like mountains, their qualities
profound like the ocean, protectors of their subjects,
and conversant in the business of kingship. They
bore the names Ratna and Vichitraratha, born from
Padmavati, with a splendor like the moon and the sun.
After performing absolute abstention for six days and
passing away there, Priyavrata went to heaven. The

छद्दिवसइँ सल्लेहणु करेंवि ।
गउ सग्गु पियव्वउ तहिँ मरेंवि ॥
जगडन्तु अणुद्धरु डामरिउ ।
रणें रयणविचित्तरहें धरिउ ॥
पच्चण्डेहिँ तेहिँ
छड्डाावियडमरु ।
हुउ अवरभवेण
अग्गिकेउ अमरु ॥

१०

वहुकालें रयणविचित्तरह ।
तउ करेंवि मरेंवि परिभमेंवि पह ॥
उप्पण्ण वे वि सिद्धत्थपुरें ।
कणकञ्चणजणधणपयपउरें ॥
विमलग्गमहिसिखेमङ्कुरहुँ ।
अवरोप्परु णयणसुहङ्करहुँ ॥
कुलभूसणु पढमु पुत्तु पवरु ।
लहु देसविहूसणेक्कु अवरु ॥६
अण्णु वि उप्पण्ण एक्क दुहिय ।
कमलोच्छव रुन्दचन्दमुहिय ॥
वेण्णि मि कुमार सालहिँ णिमिय ।
आयरियहों कहों वि समुल्लविय ॥
पढमाण जुवाणभावें चडिय ।

rampaging troublemaker Anuddhara was checked by
Ratna and Vichitraratha in a fight.
Forced to give up his rioting by those fierce men, he
became the god Agniketu in a later existence.

10

"After the two, Ratna and Vichitraratha, had practiced
asceticism for a long time, they died, wandered
various paths, and were born in Siddharthapura—
abounding in grain, gold, people, riches, and
subjects—to the chief queen Vimala and
Kshemankara, who brought happiness to each other's
eyes. Kulabhushana was the first and eldest son. The
other one was young, eminent Deshavibhushana. In
addition, a daughter was born, Kamalotsava, with a
face round like the moon. The two princes were forced
to stay in the house and entrusted to a teacher. As they
were studying, they became young men. It was as if

णं दइवें वे अणङ्ग घडिय ॥
वित्थयवच्छयल पलम्बभुअ ।
णं सग्गहों इन्दपडिन्द चुअ ॥
कमलोच्छव ताम
कहिं मि समावडिय ।
णं वम्महभल्लि
हियएँ झत्ति पडिय ॥

११

कुलभूसणदेसविहूसणहुँ ।
णियवहिणिरूवपेसियमणहुँ ॥
पडिहाइ ण चन्दणलेवछवि ।
धवलामलकोमलकमलु ण वि ॥
ण वि जलु जलद्द दाहिणपवणु ।
कुसुमाउहेण ण णडिउ कवणु ॥
पेक्खेप्पिणु पयइँ सुकोमलइँ ।
ण सहन्ति रूइरत्तुप्पलइँ ॥
पेक्खेंवि थणवट्टइँ चक्कलइँ ।
उच्चिट्टइँ करिकुम्भत्थलइँ ॥
पेक्खेप्पिणु मुहु वालहें तणउ ।
पडिहाइ ण चन्दणु चन्दिणउ ॥

fate had fashioned two Kamas. With their vast chests and long arms, they were like Indra and Pratindra fallen from heaven.
Then they somehow caught sight of Kamalotsava, and it was as if Kama's arrow suddenly fell into their heart.

11

"To Kulabhushana and Deshavibhushana, whose hearts were incited by the beauty of their own sister, neither the splendor of sandalwood unguent, nor a white, spotless, soft lotus brought pleasure, nor water, a wet cloth, nor a southern breeze. Who is not cheated by flower-armed Kama? When they saw her very soft feet, they could not endure beautiful, red lotuses. When they saw her curvy, round breasts, they found the frontal globes of elephants unappealing. When they saw the girl's face, neither sandalwood nor moonlight appealed to them. Their eyes were buried

लोयणइँ रूवें पज्झत्ताइँ ।
ढोरा इव कद्दमें खुत्ताइँ ॥
पेक्खेप्पिणु केसकलाउ मणें ।
ण सुहन्ति मोर णच्चन्त वण्णें ॥
दिट्ठीविस वाल
सप्पहाँ अणुहरइ ।
जो जोअइ को वि
सो सयलु वि मरइ ॥

१२

तहिँ अवसरें पणइहिँ पहु भणिउ ।
खेमङ्कर तुहुँ जणणिएँ जणिउ ॥
तुहुँ महियलें धण्णउ एक्कु पर ।
कमलोच्छव दुहिय जासु पवर ॥
कुलदेसविहूसण जमल सुय ।
तं णिसुणेविं णाइँ कुमार मुय ॥
हयहियय काइँ चिन्तवसि तुहुँ ।
पाविज्जइ जेहिँ महन्तु दुहु ॥
खलखुद्दइँ दुक्कियगाराइँ ।
णारइय णरयपइसाराइँ ॥
गयवाहिदुक्खहक्काराइँ ।
सिवसासयगमणणिवाराइँ ॥

in her beauty, like white cows stuck in mud. When they beheld the abundance of her hair, the peacocks dancing in the forest did not cause any joy in their heart.
The girl resembled a snake, with her glance as poison. Everyone who looked, perished.

12

"At that time supporters said to the king, 'Kshemankara, you were born from a woman. On earth you alone are fortunate, to whom the beautiful daughter Kamalotsava belongs and the pair, Kulabhushana and Deshavibhushana, as sons.' When the princes heard this, it was as if they died, 'Wretched heart, what are you thinking? You do not control the five senses, because of which one begets great sorrow, those vile, low hellish things that lead to hell, that summon sickness, disease, and pain, that thwart the progress toward eternal bliss, rejected by the Tirthankaras and their foremost disciples. Because of beauty a moth,

तित्थङ्करगणहरणिन्दियइँ ।
णउ खञ्चहि पञ्च वि इन्दियइँ ॥
रूवेण पयङ्कु मीणु रसेण ।
मिगु सवणें भसलु गन्धवसेंण ॥
फरिसेण विणासु
मत्तगइन्दु गउ ।
जो सेवइ पञ्च
तहों उत्तारु कउ ॥

१३

तो किय णिवित्ति परिणेवाहों ।
सावज्जु रज्जु भुञ्जेवाहों ॥
पारद्धु पयाणउ तवपहेंण ।
णियदेहमएण महारहेंण ॥
विहिविण्णाणियउप्पाइएँण ।
दुट्ठट्ठकम्मपच्छाइएँण ॥
इन्दियतुरङ्गसंचालिएँण ।
सत्तविहधाउवन्धालिएँण ॥
चलचलणचक्कसंजोइएँण ।
मणपक्कलसारहिचोइएँण ॥
तवसंजमणियमधम्मभरेंण ।
आइय णियणियतणुरहवरेंण ॥

because of taste a fish, because of hearing a deer,
because of smell a bee,
and because of touch a rutting elephant—all go to
destruction.[6] He who serves these five, how is there
deliverance for him?'

13

"They then withdrew from marrying and ruling over a
contemptible kingdom, and commenced the journey
along the path of ascetic practice, with a large chariot
consisting of their own bodies: designed by the expert,
Fate, enveloped by the eight wicked forms of karma,
set in motion by the senses as horses, bound up by the
sevenfold constituent elements[7] as fetters, attached
to agile feet as wheels, urged on by their mind as
a capable charioteer, conveying ascetic practice,
discipline, restraint, and righteousness. With each
of their bodies as a great chariot, they arrived and

थिय पडिमाजोग्गें गिरिसिहरें ।
सो अग्गिकेउ तेहएँ ऽवसरें ॥
संचलिउ णहङ्गणें कहिँ वि जाम ।
गउ अम्हहँ उप्परि खलिउ ताम ॥
पुव्वभउ सरेंवि कोहें जलिउ ।
थिउ रुन्धेंवि णहयलें किलिकिलिउ ॥
उवसग्गु जाम पारम्भियउ ।
वहुरूवेंहिँ गयणें वियम्भियउ ॥
पडिवण्णएँ तहिँ तेहएँ ऽवसरें ।
वट्टन्तएँ गुरुउवसग्गभरें ॥
तुम्हहँ जें पहावें तट्ठाइँ ।
असुरइँ धणुरवेंण पणट्ठाइँ ॥
तो अम्हहँ वप्पु ।
कालन्तरेंण मुउ ॥
सो दीसइ एत्थु ।
गारुडु देउ हुउ ॥

१४

तो गरुडें परिओसियमणेंण ।
वे विज्जउ दिण्णउ तक्खणेंण ॥
राहवहों सीहवाहणि पवर ।
लक्खणहों गरुडवाहणि अवर ॥

424

settled on the top of the mountain in the *pratimāyoga* position. At that time Agniketu, roaming about somewhere in the sky, went and was halted above us. Remembering his previous existence, he was incensed with anger. Pausing in the sky he stood there and shrieked. As soon as the calamity commenced, he appeared in the sky in many forms. As that situation went on and the heavy burden of the calamity was unfolding, the demons fled from the sound of your bows, frightened by your power.

Then some time later, our father died. You can see him, right here: he has become a Garuda god."

14

With a delighted heart the Garuda then immediately gave two *vidyās:* to Rama, the descendant of Raghu, the exceptional *vidyā* Simhavahini and to Lakshmana another *vidyā* Garudavahini. The first

पहिलारी सत्तसऍहिँ सहिय ।
अणुपच्छिम तिहिँ सएहिँ अहिय ॥
तो कोसलसुऍण सुदुलहेंण ।
वुच्चइ वइदेहीवल्लहेंण ॥
अच्छन्तु ताव तुम्हहुँ जें घरें ।
अवसरें पडिवण्णें पसाउ करें ॥
सहुँ गरुडें संभासणु करेंवि ।
गुरु पुच्छिउ पुणु चलणेंहिँ धरेंवि ॥
अम्हहुँ हिण्डन्तहुँ धरणिवहें ।
जं जिम होसइ तं तेम कहें ॥
कुलभूसणु अक्खइ हलहरहों ।
जलु लऍँवि दाहिणसायरहों ॥
संगामसयाइँ
विहि मि जिणेवाइँ ।
महिखण्डइँ तिण्णि
सइँ भुञ्जेवाइँ ॥

was accompanied by seven hundred vehicles, the latter by three hundred more. Then Rama, the son of Kosala's daughter, the most beloved husband of the daughter of Videha, spoke to the *vidyās*, "For now, stay in your home. Please help us when an opportunity arises." After he had conversed with the Garuda, he asked the master again, while holding onto his feet, "Explain what will happen to us as we wander along the path of the earth." Kulabhushana clarified to Rama, "After you have crossed the water of the ocean in the south,

hundreds of battles will be won by the two of you. You yourself will rule three parts of the earth."

चउतीसमो संधि

केवलें केवलीहें उप्पण्णएँ
चउविहदेवणिकायपवण्णएँ ।
पुच्छइ रामु महावयधारा
धम्मपावफलु कहहि भडारा ॥

१

काइं फलु पञ्चमहव्वयहुँ ।
अणुवयगुणवयसिक्खावयहुँ ॥
काइं फलु लइएँ अणत्थमिएँ ।
उववासपोसहएँ संथविएँ ॥
फलु काइँ जीवमम्भीसियएँ ।
परहणें परदारें अहिंसियएँ ॥
काइं फलु सच्चें वोलिएँण ।
अलिअक्खरेण आमेल्लिएँण ॥
काइं फलु जिणवरअञ्चियएँ ।
वरविउलें घरासमें वञ्चियएँ ॥
काइं फलु मासें छण्डिएँण ।
रत्तिद्धिउ देहें दण्डिएँण ॥
काइं फलु जिणसंमज्जणेण ।
वलिदीवङ्गारविलेवणेण ॥

428

Chapter 34

When omniscience had manifested in the omniscient ones, accompanied by the fourfold assembly of the gods, Rama asked the bearers of the great vows, "Noble lords, explain the fruit of righteousness and of sin.

1

"What is the fruit of the five great vows, the minor vows, the restrictive vows, and vows of spiritual discipline? What is the fruit when one took the vow of not eating after sunset, or when one upheld the vow of fasting on holy days?[1] What is the fruit when one consoled a living being and when one did not harm a stranger's wealth or another man's wife? What is the fruit when one spoke truthfully and when one forsook deceitful words? What is the fruit when one honored the great Jina and when one upheld the appealing and important householder way of life? What is the fruit when one gave up meat and chastised the body night and day? What is the fruit in the bathing of the Jina, sacrificial food, lamps, incense,[2] and ointment?

किं चारित्तें णाणें वएँ दंसणें
अण्णु पसंसिएँ जिणवरसासणें ।
जं फलु होइ अणङ्गवियारा
तं विण्णासेंवि कहहि भडारा ॥

२

पुणु पुणु वि पडीवउ भणइ वलु ।
कहें सुक्कियदुक्कियकम्मफलु ॥
कम्मेण केण रिउडमरकर ।
सयरायर महि भुञ्जन्ति णर ॥
कम्मेण केण परचक्कधर ।
रहतुरयगएँहिँ वुज्झन्ति णर ॥
परियरिय सुणारिहिँ णरवरेंहिँ ।
विज्जिज्जमाण वरचामरेंहिँ ॥
सुन्दर सच्छन्द मइन्द जिह ।
जोहेहिँ जोह वुज्झन्ति किह ॥
कम्मेण केण किय पङ्गुलय ।
णर कुण्ट मुण्ट वहिरन्धलय ॥
काणीण दीणमुहकायसर ।
वाहिल्ल भिल्ल णाहल सवर ॥
दालिद्दिय परपेसणइँ कर ।
कें कम्में उप्पज्जन्ति णर ॥

430

What when one moreover praised the good conduct,
   knowledge, vow, and viewpoint of the Jina's teaching?
   Noble lord, you who have destroyed lust, tell us,
   expounding what this fruit is."

2

The Baladeva then spoke again, "Explain the fruit of
   karma from good and bad deeds. By which karma do
   men, scourges of their enemies, reign on the earth
   with all its moving and motionless elements? By
   which karma are men known to hold back a hostile
   army with chariots, horses, and elephants, surrounded
   by good women and noblemen, being fanned by great
   flywhisk bearers? How are warriors known in battles,
   handsome and uninhibited like lions? By which karma
   are men rendered lame, hunchbacked, disabled, deaf,
   or blind, born of a young girl, with a wretched face,
   body, and voice, sickly, Bhillas, Lahalas,* or Shabaras?
   By which karma are men born poor and doing service
   to others?

* A tribal community.

धीरसरीर वीर तवसूरा
सव्वहुँ जीवहुँ आसाऊरा ।
इन्दियपसवण परउवयारा
ते कहिँ णर पावन्ति भडारा ॥

३

के वि अण्ण णर दुहपरिचत्ता ।
देवलोएँ देवत्तणु पत्ता ॥
चन्दाइच्चराहुअङ्गारा ।
अण्णहॉ अण्ण होन्ति कम्मारा ॥
हंस समेसमहिसविसकुञ्जर ।
मोरतुरङ्गरिच्छमिगसम्वर ॥
जइ देवहुँ जें मज्झें संभूआ ।
तो किं कज्जें वाहण हूआ ॥
ऍहु जो दीसइ कुलिसप्पहरणु ।
सहसणयणु अइरावयवाहणु ॥
गिज्जइ किण्णरमिहुणसहासेँहिँ ।
सुरवर जय भणन्ति चउपासेँहिँ ॥
हाहाहूहूतुम्वुरुणारा ।
तेज्जातेण्णा जसु चक्कारा ॥
चित्तङ्गो वि मुरव पडिपेल्लइ ।
रम्भ तिलोत्तिम सइ उव्वेल्लइ ॥

Heroes with firm bodies, warriors in ascetic practice,
fulfilling the hope of all living beings, who subdue the
senses and sustain others, where might such men be
found, great lord?

3

"Some other men obtain an existence as a god in the realm
of the gods, free of sorrow, as a sun, a moon, Rahu, or
the planet Mars. Others become servants of someone
else, geese along with rams, buffaloes, snakes,
elephants, peacocks, horses, bears, deer, or sambars.
If they were born amid the gods, then for what
reason did they become vehicles? That thousand-
eyed Indra, who is seen brandishing a thunderbolt
as his weapon and with Airavata as his mount,
about whom thousands of Kinnara pairs sing, for
whom the great gods everywhere say hail, for whom
Haha, Huhu, Tumburu, Narada, Tejja, and Tenna
form an entourage, for whom Chitranga strikes the
tambourines, and Rambha and Tilottama themselves
perform,[3]

अप्पणु असुरसुरहुँ अब्भन्तरें
मोक्खु जेम थिउ सव्वहुँ उप्परें ।
दीसइ जसु एवड्डु पहुत्तणु
पत्तु फलेण केण इन्दत्तणु ॥

४

तं वयणु सुणेवि कुलभूसणेण ।
कन्दप्पदप्पविद्धंसणेण ॥
सुणु अक्खमि वुच्चइ तेण वलु ।
आयण्णहि धम्महों तणउ फलु ॥
महु मज्जु मंसु जो परिहरइ ।
छज्जीवणिकायहों दय करइ ॥
पुणु पच्छइ सल्लेहणें मरइ ।
सो मोक्खमहापुरें पइसरइ ॥
जो घइँ दरिसावइ पाणिवह ।
अण्णु वि महुमंसहों तणिय कह ॥
सो जोणीजोणि परिब्भमइ ।७
चउरासी लक्ख जाम कमइ ॥
ऍउ सुक्किरयदुक्किरयकम्मफलु ।
सुणु एवहिँ सच्चहों तणउ फलु ॥
तुलतोलिय महि समहीहरिय ।
ससुरासुर सघण ससायरिय ॥

he who himself stands among the gods and demons above
all, like liberation, by which fruit does one obtain an
existence as Indra, of such evident majesty?"

4

Hearing these words, Kulabhushana, destroyer of Kama's
pride, said to the Baladeva, "Listen, I will explain.
Hear the fruit of the doctrine: he who forsakes
honey, wine, and meat, who shows compassion for
the group of six sentient beings,[4] and who later dies
in absolute abstention, enters into the great city of
liberation. However, he who proves himself a killer of
living beings and whose talk is filled with honey and
meat, he roams from womb to womb until he passes
through eighty-four lakhs of them. This is the fruit
of the karma from good and bad deeds. Now listen
to the fruit of truth: even if the earth along with the
mountains, gods and demons, clouds, and oceans is
weighed,

वरुणु कुवेरु मेरु कइलासु वि
तुलतोलिउ तइलोक्कु असेसु वि ।
तो वि ण गरुवत्तणउ पगासिउ
सच्चु सउत्तरु सव्वहुँ पासिउ ॥

५

जो सच्चउ ण चवइ कापुरिसु ।
सो जीवइ जणवएँ तिणसरिसु ॥
जो णरु परदव्वु ण अहिलसइ ।
सो उत्तिमसग्गलोएँ वसइ ॥
जो घइँ रत्तिद्दिणु मूढमणु ।
चोरन्तु ण थक्कइ एक्कु खणु ॥
सो हम्मइ छिज्जइ भिज्जइ वि ।
कप्पिज्जइ सूलें भरिज्जइ वि ॥
जो दुद्दरु वम्भचेरु धरइ ।
तहों जमु आरुट्ठउ किं करइ ॥
जो घइँ तं जोणि चारु रमइ ।
सो पङ्कएँ भमरु जेम मरइ ॥
जो करइ णिवित्ति परिग्गहहों ।
सो मोक्खहों जाइ सुहावहहों ॥
जो घइँ अविअण्हु परिग्गहहों ।
सो जाइ पुरहों तमतमपहहों ॥

even if Varuna, Kubera, Mount Meru, and Mount Kailasa,* the entire threefold world, is weighed, they do not seem all that grand. The truth is superior to them all.

5

"An evil person who does not speak the truth lives among people and is worth no more than a blade of grass. The man who does not desire the wealth of others resides in the realm of the highest heavens. He, however, who whether it be day or night stupidly does not for one moment refrain from stealing, he is murdered, slashed, broken, cut, and speared. He who maintains celibacy—a difficult task—what can furious Yama do to him? He, however, who takes delight in a pleasant vagina, he dies like a bee trapped in a lotus. He who abstains from possession goes to delightful liberation. But the one who is full of desire for possessions, he goes to the city of Tamastamahprabha.†

---

* Legendary mountain in the Himalayas.
† The seventh and lowest hell.

अहवइ णिव्वण्णिज्जइ केत्तिउ
एक्केक्कहो वयहॊ फलु एत्तिउ ।
जो घइँ पञ्च वि धरइ वयाइं
तासु मोक्खु पुच्छिज्जइ काइं ॥

६

फलु एत्तिउ पञ्चमहव्वयहॊ ।
सुणु एवहिँ पञ्चाणुव्वयहॊ ॥
जो करइ णिरन्तर जीवदया ।
पविरलु असच्चु सच्चउ मि सया ॥
किस हिंस अहिंस सउत्तरिय ।
ते णरयमहाणइउत्तरिय ॥
जे णर सदारसंतुट्ठमण ।
परहणपरणारीपरिहरण ॥
अपरिग्गहदाणकरण पुरिस ।
ते होन्ति पुरन्दरसमसरिसु ॥
फलु एत्तिउ पञ्चाणुव्वयहुँ ।
सुणु एवहिँ तिहि मि गुणव्वयहुँ ॥
दिसपञ्चक्खाणु पमाणवउ ।
खलसंगहु जासु ण वड्ढियउ ॥

Or rather, how can it be described? Thus is the fruit of
each single vow. As for the one who bears all five vows,
can his liberation be questioned?

6

"Such is the fruit of the five great vows. Now listen to
that of the five minor vows. He who always acts
with compassion toward living beings, from whom
falsehood is rare and truth is persistent, from whom
violence is little and nonviolence is predominant,
these ones cross the great rivers of hell. Men whose
hearts are satisfied with their own wives, who shun
the riches and wives of others, people who are active
in nonpossession and the giving of alms, they become
just like Indra. Such is the fruit of the five minor vows.
Now listen to that of the three restrictive vows: the
curtailment of travel to distant places, the vow of
restraint,[5] and the one where wicked deeds do not
proliferate.[6]

इय तिहिँ गुणवएहिँ गुणवन्तउ
अच्छइ सग्गें सुहइँ भुञ्जन्तउ ।
जासु ण तिहि मि मज्झें एक्कु वि गुणु
तहों संसारहों छेउ कहिँ पुणु ॥

७

फलु एत्तिउ तिहि मि गुणव्वयहुँ ।
सुणु एवहिँ चउसिक्खावयहुँ ॥
जो पहिलउ सिक्खावउ धरइ ।
जिणवरें तिकालवन्दण करइ ॥
सो णरु उप्पज्जइ जहिँ जें जहिँ ।
वन्दिज्जइ लोऍहिँ तहिँ जें तहिँ ॥
जो घइँ पुणु विसयासत्तमणु ।
वरिसहों वि ण पेच्छइ जिणभवणु ॥
सो सावउ मज्झें ण सावयहुँ ।
अणुहरइ णवर वणसावयहुँ ॥
जो वीयउ सिक्खावउ धरइ ।
पोसहउववाससयइँ करइ ॥
सो णरु देवत्तणु अहिलसइ ।
सोहम्में वहुवमज्झें रमइ ॥
जो तइयउ सिक्खावउ धरइ ।
तवसिहिँ आहारदाणु करइ ॥

Because of these three restrictive vows the virtuous man
   resides in heaven enjoying pleasures. How can there
   be an end to samsara for one who does not even have
   one virtue among these three?

7

"Such is the fruit of the three restrictive vows. Now listen
   to that of the four vows of spiritual discipline. He who
   bears the first vow of spiritual discipline and worships
   the great Jina three times a day, such a man is honored
   by people wherever he may be born. But the one who
   does not even look at a Jina temple for a whole year,
   whose mind is attached to the sense objects, he is not
   a layman among laymen, and only resembles wild
   beasts in the forest. The one who bears the second
   vow of spiritual discipline and upholds hundreds
   of fasts on holy days seeks after existence as a god;
   he experiences pleasure amid the young women in
   Saudharma.* He who bears the third vow of spiritual

* The lowest Kalpa heaven.

अण्णु वि सम्मत्तभारु वहइ ।
देवत्तणु देवलोऍं लहइ ॥
जो चउथउ सिक्खावउ धरइ ।
सण्णासु करेप्पिणु पुणु मरइ ॥
सो होइ तिलोयहों वड्ढियउ ।
णउ जम्मणमरणविओअभउ ॥
सामाइउ उववासु सभोयणु
पच्छिमकालें अण्णु सल्लेहणु ।
चउ सिक्खावयाइँ जो पालइ
सो इन्दहों इन्दत्तणु टालइ ॥

८

ऍउ फलु सिक्खावऍं संथविऍं ।
सुणु एवहिँ कहमि अणत्थमिऍं ॥
वरि खद्धु मंसु वरि मज्जु महु ।
वरि अलिउ वयणु हिंसाऍं सहुँ ॥
वरि जीविउ गउ सरीरु ल्हसिउ ।
णउ रयणिहिँ भोयणु अहिलसिउ ॥
पुव्वण्हउ गणगन्धव्वयहुँ ।
मज्झण्हउ सव्वहुँ देवयहुँ ॥
अवरण्हउ पियरपियामहहुँ ।
णिसि रक्खसभूयपेयगहहुँ ॥

discipline and donates food to ascetics, who moreover
supports the weight of righteousness, he obtains
an existence as a god in the realm of the gods. He
who bears the fourth vow of spiritual discipline
and subsequently dies after abstention, he becomes
elevated above the three worlds and no longer fears
birth, death, or privation.
The man who guards the four vows of spiritual discipline,
meditation, fasting along with donating food, and also
absolute abstention in his final moments, he disrupts
Indra's existence as Indra.[7]

8

"Thus is the fruit when one has upheld the vow of spiritual
discipline. Now listen, I explain the one when the
vow of not eating after sunset is upheld. It is better
that meat is eaten, wine or honey are better, telling
a lie is better along with violence, it is better that life
has vanished or that the body has withered, than that
food be desired at night. The forenoon is for Ganas
and Gandharvas, noon for all the deities, afternoon
for the Pitris and Pitamahas, night for Rakshasas,

णिसिभोयणु जेण ण परिहरिउ ।
भणु तेण काइँ ण समायरिउ ॥
किमिकीडपयङ्गसयइँ असइ ।
कुसरीरकुजोणिहिँ सो वसइ ॥
जो घइँ णिसिभोयणु उम्महइ ।
विमलत्तणु विमलगोत्तु लहइ ॥
सुअउ ण सुणइ ण दिट्ठउ देक्खइ
केण वि वोल्लिउ कहों वि ण अक्खइ ।
भोअणे मउणु चउत्थउ पालइ
सो सिवसासयगमणु णिहालइ ॥

९

परमेसरु सुट्ठु एम कहइ ।
जो जं मग्गइ सो तं लहइ ॥
सम्मत्तइँ को वि को वि वयइँ ।
कों वि गुणगणवयणरयणसयइँ ॥
तवचरणु लइज्जइ पत्थिवेण ।
वंसत्थलणयरणराहिवेण ॥
गय वन्दणहत्ति करेवि सुर ।
जाणइएँ धरिज्जइ धम्मधुर ॥
राहवेण वि वयइँ समिच्छियइँ ।
गुरुदिण्णइँ सिरेण पडिच्छियइँ ॥

Bhutas, Pretas, and Grahas.[8] He who does not avoid
eating at night, tell me, what would he not do? He eats
hundreds of worms, insects, and moths, and resides in
vile bodies and vile wombs. He, however, who rejects
eating at night, obtains purity and an auspicious
lineage.

He who does not listen to what is heard, who does not look
at what is seen, who does not speak to anyone though
spoken to, and who fourthly guards his silence during
a meal, perceives the course toward blissful eternity."

9

Thus the supreme lord explained things well. Whatever
someone asked, they received. Someone received
righteousness, another the vows, another hundreds
of gem-like words with masses of virtues. The lord,
the king of the city of Vamshasthala, took up ascetic
practice. After they had praised and revered them,
the gods left. Janaka's daughter took up the yoke
of righteousness. Rama, the descendant of Raghu,
longed for the vows and accepted them with his head

वउ णवर ण थक्कइ लक्खणहों ।
वालुअपहणरयणिरिक्खणहों ॥
तहिँ तिण्णि वि कइ वि दिवस थियइँ ।
जिणपुज्जउ जिणण्हवणइँ कियइँ ॥
णिग्गन्थसयइँ भुञ्जावियइँ ।
दीणहँ दाणइँ देवावियइँ ॥
तिहुअणजणमणणयणाणन्दहों
वन्दणहत्ति करेवि जिणिन्दहों ।
जाणइहरिहलहरइँ पहिट्ठइँ
तिण्णि वि दण्डारण्णु पइट्ठइँ ॥

१०

दिट्ठु महाडइ णाइँ विलासिणि ।
गिरिवरथणहरसिहरपगासिणि ॥
पञ्चाणणणहणियरवियारिय ।
दीहरसरलोयणविप्फारिय ॥
कन्दरदरिमुहकुहरविहूसिय ।
तरुवररोमावलिउद्दूसिय ॥
चन्दणअगरुगन्धडिविडिक्किय ।
इन्दगोवकुङ्कुमचञ्झिक्किय ॥
अहवइ किं वहुणा वित्थारें ।
णं णच्चइ गयपयसंचारें ॥

as the master gave them. For Lakshmana, however,
who was looking at a stay in Valukaprabha hell,*
no vow endured. The three stayed there for some
days and performed rituals of worship and bathing
ceremonies for the Jina. They provided food for
hundreds of naked ascetics and arranged for gifts to be
donated to the poor.

After they had praised and revered the lord Jina, the joy to
the hearts and eyes of the people of the three worlds,
the three—Janaka's daughter, the Vasudeva, and the
Baladeva—contentedly entered the Dandaka forest.

10

They beheld the great forest as if it were a woman full
of desire: revealing peaks of great mountains—her
breasts, scratched by the plentiful nails of her lions,
spreading the wide eyes of her lakes, adorned with
caverns and caves; the cavities of her face, with grand
trees; the bristling row of body hair above her navel,
furnished with sandalwood and agarwood trees;
her perfume, beautified with lac insects, saffron. Or
rather, why elaborate? She seemed to dance with

---

* The third region of hell.

उज्झरमुरवप्फालियसद्दें ।
वरहिणथिरसुपरिट्ठियच्छन्दें ॥
महुअरितियउवगीयवमालें ।
अहिणवपल्लवकरसंचालें ॥
सीहोरालिसमुट्ठियकलयलु ।
णाइँ पढइ मुणिसुव्वयमङ्गलु ॥
तहों अब्भन्तरें अमरमणोहरु
णयणकडक्खिउ एक्कु लयाहरु ।
तहिँ रइ करेंवि थियइँ सच्छन्दइँ
जोगु लएविणु जेम मुणिन्दइँ ॥

११

तहिँ तेहएँ वर्णें रिउडमरकरु ।
परिभमइ समुद्दावत्तधरु ॥
आरण्णगइन्दें समारुहइ ।
वणगोवउ वणमहिंसिउ दुहइ ॥
तं खीरु वि चिरिडिहिल्लु महिउ ।
जाणइहें समप्पइ घियसहिउ ॥
स वि पक्कावइ घणहण्डियहिँ ।
वणधण्णन्दुलेहिँ सुकण्डिएँहिँ ॥
णाणाविहफलरसतिम्मणेहिँ ।
करवन्दकरीरेहिँ सालणेंहिँ ॥

the movement of the elephants' feet, to the sound of
waterfalls for beaten tambourines, to a calm and well-
settled tempo of the peacocks, to the droning song of
the female bees, with a shaking of the hands that were
her new sprouts. It was as if she recited a benediction
to Muni Suvrata in the clamor arising from the roaring
of her lions.

Inside that forest, they eyed an arbor that beguiled the
minds even of the gods. They stayed there enjoying
themselves at their leisure, like great sages having
taken up yoga.

11

Lakshmana, the scourge of his enemies wandered around
in that forest, bearing his bow Samudravarta. He
climbed onto an enormous forest elephant, milked
forest cows and forest buffaloes. That milk, curd,
buttermilk, along with ghee, he handed over to
Janaka's daughter. She prepared food in thick earthen
pots with properly husked grains and rice from
the forest, with manifold fruits, juices, and sauces,
with *karamardas,*[9] capers, and pickles. As they thus

इय विविहभक्ख भुञ्जन्ताहुँ ।
वणवासें तिहि मि अच्छन्ताहुँ ॥
मुणि गुत्तसुगुत्त ताव अइय ।
असुदाणिय दोडुमहव्वइय ॥
कालामुहकावालिय भगव ।
मुणि संकर तवण तवसि गुरव ॥
वन्दाइरिय भोय पव्वइया ।
हवि जिह भूइपुञ्जपच्छविया ।
ते जरजम्मणमरणवियारा ।
वणचरियएँ पइसन्ति भडारा ॥

१२

जं पइसन्त पदीसिय मुणिवर ।
सावय जिह तिह पणविय तरुवर ॥
अलिमुहलिय खरपवणायम्पिय ।
थाहु थाहु णं एम पजम्पिय ॥
के वि कुसुमपब्भारु मुअन्ति ।
पायपुज्ज णं विहि मि करन्ति ॥
तो वि ण थक्क महव्वयधारा ।
रामासमें पइसन्ति भडारा ॥
रिसि पेक्खेप्पिणु सीय विणिग्गय ।
णं पञ्चक्ख महावणदेवय ॥

enjoyed many kinds of food and all three resided in
their forest abode, then the sages Gupta and Sugupta
arrived, generous toward living beings, holding
on to their great vows with both hands, their faces
directed toward death, displeasing for the god of lust,
venerable sages, bringers of prosperity, burning with
self-mortification, ascetics, teachers,
laudable masters worthy of being served, renunciants,
covered in a heap of dust like a fire in a heap of ashes.[10]
These noble lords, vanquishers of old age, birth, and
death, embarked on ascetic practice in the forest.[11]

12

When they saw the excellent sages entering, the great
trees took a bow as if they were laymen. Resounding
with bees and stirred by a fierce breeze it was as if they
said, "Stay, stay!" Some emitted a load of flowers,
as if performing a ritual of worship for the feet of
the two. Nevertheless the bearers of the great vows
did not halt. The noble lords entered into Rama's
hermitage. When Sita beheld the seers, she went
outside, like the great forest goddess in person, "Look,
Rama, look: it is a miracle. A pair of sages has arrived
in order to practice asceticism." These words made

राहव पेक्खु पेक्खु अच्छरियउ ।
साहुजुअलु चरियएँ णीसरियउ ॥
वलु वयणेण तेण गज्जोल्लिउ ।
थाहु थाहु सिरु णर्वेवि पवोल्लिउ ॥
विणयङ्कुसेण साहुगय वालिय ।
किउ सम्मज्जणु पाय पखालिय ॥
दिण्ण तिवार धार सलिलेण वि ।
कम चम्पिय गोसीररसेण वि ॥
पुप्फक्खयवलिदीवङ्गारेहिँ ।
एम पयञ्चेवि अट्टपयारेहिँ ॥
वन्दिय गुरु गुरुभत्ति करेवि
लग्ग परीसवि सीयाएवि ।
मुहपिय अच्छ पच्छ मणभाविणि
भुत्त पेज्ज कामुऍहिँ व कामिणि ॥

१३

दिण्णु पाणु पुणु मुहहोँ पियारउ ।
चारणभोग्गु जेम हलुवारउ ॥
सिद्धउ सिद्धु जेम सिद्धीहउ ।
जिणवरआउ जेम अइदीहउ ॥
पुणु अग्गिमउ दिण्णु हियइच्छिउ ।
जिह सुकलत्तु सुणेहु सइच्छउ ॥

the Baladeva's body hair bristle. While bowing his
head, he said, "Stay, stay." The sages were convinced
to turn around by his polite conduct, like elephants
by a goad. They were cleansed and their feet washed.
Three times water was given in streams. Their feet
were smeared with sandalwood paste. Having thus
paid homage to their feet with the eight substances:
flowers, uncooked rice, morsels of food, lamps,
incense, et cetera,[12]
they praised the masters. When they had shown their
devotion to the masters, Lady Sita subsequently
began serving them fine food, pleasant to the mouth
and agreeable to the mind. They ate and drank it like
gallants enjoy a lovely lady.

13

First she gave them something to drink, even more
pleasant to the mouth. It was light like the amusement
of wandering singers, prepared like a Siddha has an
essence of Siddhi, and very long-lasting like the life of
the great Jina. Then the first dish, dear to the heart,
was served as per their desire with good oil, like a good
wife, desirous and with abundant affection,[13] then

सुद्धइँ पुणु सालणइँ विचित्तइँ ।
तिक्खइँ णाइँ विलासिणिचित्तइँ ॥
दिण्णइँ पुणु तिम्मणइँ मणिट्ठुइँ ।
अहिणवकइवयणा इव मिट्ठुइँ ॥
पच्छइ सिसिरु समच्छरु सुद्धउ ।
दुट्टकलत्तु जेम अइथद्धउ ॥
पुणु मयसलिलु दिण्णु सीयालउ ।
णं जिणवयणु पावपक्खालउ ॥
लीलएँ जिमिय भडारा जावेंहिँ ।
पञ्चच्छरिउ पदरिसिउ तावेंहिँ ॥
दुन्दुहि गन्धवाउ रयणावलि
साहुक्कारु अण्णु कुसुमञ्जलि ।
पुण्णपवित्तइँ सासयदूअइँ
पञ्च वि अच्छरियइँ सइँ भूअइँ ॥

pure and varied pickles, spicy like the thoughts of a
wanton lady. Then delicious sauces were served, tasty
like the words of a young poet. Afterward there was
curd, quickening, pure, and very thick, like a wrathful,
very arrogant bad wife.[14] Pleasant water, a receptacle
of coolness, was given to wash the feet, like the words
of the Jina wash away sin.[15] As the noble lords ate at
their leisure, five miracles manifested:

a kettledrum, a fragrant wind, a row of gems, applause,
and also a handful of flowers. The five miracles
appeared themselves, filters of virtue, messengers of
the Eternal.

पञ्चतीसमो संधि

गुत्तसुगुत्तहँ तर्णेण पहावें
रामु ससीय परमसब्भावें ।
देर्वेहिँ दाणरिद्धि खर्णे दरिसिय
वलमन्दिरें वसुहार पवरिसिय ॥

१

जाय महग्घ रयण सुपगासइँ ।
लक्खहँ तिण्णि सयइँ पञ्जासइँ ॥
वरिसेवि रयणवरिसु सइँ हत्थें ।
रामु पसंसिउ सुरवरसत्थें ॥
तिहुवणें णवर एक्कु वलु धण्णउ ।
दिव्वाहारु जेण वर्णे दिण्णउ ॥
मणें परितुट्टइँ अमरसयाइं ।
अण्णें दार्णे किज्जइ काइं ॥
अण्णें धरिउ भुवणु सयरायरु ।
अण्णें धम्मु कम्मु पुरिसायरु ॥
अण्णें रिद्धिविद्धि वंसुब्भउ ।
अण्णें पेम्मु विलासु सविब्भमु ॥
अण्णें गेउ वेउ सिद्धक्खरु ।
अण्णें जाणु झाणु परमक्खरु ॥

456

Chapter 35

Because of the power and extremely virtuous nature of Gupta and Sugupta, the gods instantly revealed to Rama, together with Sita, the supernatural effect of charity: they let a stream of treasures rain down on the Baladeva's house.

1

There appeared three hundred fifty lakhs of precious, most brilliant gems. After the band of great gods had poured the rain of gems with their own hand, they praised Rama: "In the threefold world only the Baladeva, who gave divine food in the forest, is fortunate." Hundreds of gods were delighted in their heart, "What is done with food as a gift? Because of food the world is sustained, with all its movable and motionless elements; there is righteousness, karma, and bravery; prosperity, wealth, and the rise of noble dynasties; affection and grace and charm; song, wisdom, and doctrine; knowledge, meditation, and the supreme indestructible. When someone obtains great profit, what might they have given, other than food?

अण्णु मुएवि अण्णु किं दिज्जइ ।
जेण महन्तु भोगु पाविज्जइ ॥
अण्णसुवण्णकण्णगोदाणहुँ
मेइणिमणिसिद्धन्तपुराणहुँ ।
सव्वहुँ अण्णदाणु उच्छासणु
परसासणहुँ जेम जिणसासणु ॥

२

दाणरिद्धि पेक्खेवि खगेसरु ।
णवर जडाइ जाउ जाईसरु ॥
गग्गरवयणउ मुणिअणुराएं ।
पहउ णाइँ सिरें मोग्गरघाएं ॥
जिह जिह सुमरइ णिययभवन्तरु ।
तिह तिह मेल्लइ अंसु णिरन्तरु ॥
मइँ पावेण तिलोयाणन्दहुँ ।
पञ्चसयइँ पीलियइँ मुणिन्दहुँ ॥
एम पलाउ करन्तु विहङ्गउ ।
गुरुचलणेहिँ पडिउ मुच्छंगउ ॥
पयपक्खालणजलेंणासासिउ ।
राहवचन्दें पुणु उवयासिउ ॥
सीयएँ वुत्तु पुत्तु महु एवहिँ ।
छुडु वड्ढउ छुडु धरउ सुखेवेहिँ ॥

The gift of food is of a higher status than others, whether
gifts of other things, gold, daughters, or cows, land,
gems, the doctrine, or ancient lore, just as the Jina's
teaching resides above other teachings."

2

When a lord among birds, Jatayin, beheld the
magnificence of the donation, he promptly came to
remember his previous birth, his voice stammering
from affection for the sages, as if struck on the
head with the blow from a hammer. While he was
remembering his previous existence, he shed tears
incessantly, "A sinner, I tortured five hundred
eminent sages, bringers of joy to the three worlds."
As the bird lamented thus, he fell unconscious at
the feet of the masters. He was brought to with the
water of the footbath. Then moon-like Rama, the
descendant of Raghu, embraced him. Sita said, "He is
my son now. May he soon rejoice, may he soon resort

ताव रयणउज्जोवें भिण्णा ।
जाय पक्ख चामीयरवण्णा ॥
विदुमचञ्चु णीलणिहकण्ठउ
पयवेरुलियवण्ण मणिपट्टउ ।
तक्खणें पञ्चवण्णु णिव्वडियउ
वीयउ रयणपुञ्जु णं पडियउ ॥

३

भावें विहि मि पयाहिण देन्तउ ।
णडु जिह हरिसविसाऍहिँ जन्तउ ॥
दिट्ठु पक्खि जं णयणाणन्दणु ।
भणइ णवेप्पिणु दसरहणन्दणु ॥
हे मुणिवर गयणङ्गणगामिय ।
चउगइदुक्खमहाणइणामिय ॥
कहि कज्जेण केण सच्छायउ ।
पक्खि सुवण्णवण्णु जं जायउ ॥
तं णिसुणेवि वुत्तु णीसङ्कें ।
सयलु वि उत्तिमपुरिसपसङ्कें ॥
णरु हलुवो वि होइ गरुआरउ ।
रुक्खु वि सेलसिहरें वड्ढारउ ॥
मेरुणियम्वें तिणु वि हेमुज्जलु ।
सिप्पिउडेसु जलु वि मुत्ताहलु ॥

460

to peacefulness." Then, mixed with the luster of the gems, his wings became golden colored.

With his beak of coral, his throat like sapphires, the color of cat's-eye on his feet, and his back like pearls, he instantly appeared five-colored. It was as if a second heap of gems had fallen down.

3

When he saw the bird circling the two and moving with happiness and sadness as if he were an actor, the son of Dasharatha, a joy to behold, bowed deeply and said, "Hey great sages, you who move through the sky, who turn away from the great rivers of sorrow of the four modes of existence, explain to me why the bird has become beautifully golden-colored." At this, the passionless one said, "By associating with an exceptional person, every man, however insignificant, becomes more worthy. A tree is taller on top of a mountain, on the flank of Mount Meru grass is splendid like gold, in the hollows of oysters even water becomes a pearl. In the same way the bird became

तिह विहङ्गु मणिरयणुज्जोएं ।
जाउ सुवण्णवण्णु मुणितोएं ॥
तं णिसुणेवि वयणु असगाहें
पुच्छिउ पुणु वि णाहु णरणाहें ।
विहलङ्घलु घुम्मन्तु विहङ्गउ
कवणें कारणेण मुच्छंगउ ॥

४

भणइ तिणाणपिण्डपरमेसरु ।
एहु विहङ्गु आसि रज्जेसरु ॥
पट्टणु दण्डाउरु भुञ्जन्तउ ।
दण्डउ णामु वउद्धहँ भत्तउ ॥
एक्कदिवसें पारद्धिएँ चलियउ ।
ताव तिकालजोगि मुणि मिलियउ ॥
थिउ अत्तावणें लम्वियवाहउ ।
अविचलु मेरु जेम दुग्गाहउ ॥
तं पेक्खेंवि आरुटु महव्वलु ।
अवसु अज्जु अवसवणु अमङ्गलु ॥
एम चवन्तें विसहरु घाएंवि ।
रोसें मुणिवर कण्ठें लाएंवि ॥
गउ णियणयरु णराहिउ जावेंहिँ ।
थिउ णीसङ्गु णिरोहें तावेंहिँ ॥

golden-colored with the luster of pearls and gems
because of the sages' water."
When he heard those words, the king persisted and again
asked the master, "For what reason did the bird,
moving about in confusion, fall unconscious?"

4

The supreme lord of the mass of threefold knowledge said,
"This bird was a king named Dandaka, ruling over
the city of Dandapura; he was a Buddhist devotee.
One day he set out for the hunt and then encountered
a sage, a yogi who knew the three times. He stood
engaged in self-mortification, his arms hanging down,
as immovable and unfathomable as Mount Meru.
Seeing him, the mighty man became enraged, 'Surely,
this is an inauspicious sign.' When the king, as he
spoke thus, killed a snake, angrily put it around the
great seer's neck, and went to his city, the passionless
man remained standing in control, 'When someone

एउ को वि फेडेसइ जइयहुँ ।
लम्विय हत्थुच्चायमि तइयहुँ ॥
जावण्णेक्कदिवसें पहु आवइ
तं जें भडारउ तहिं जें विहावइ ।
गलएँ भुअङ्गममडउ णिवद्धउ
कण्ठाहरणु णाइँ आइद्धउ ॥

५

जं अविचलु वि दिट्ठु मुणिकेसरि ।
फेडेवि विसहरकण्ठामञ्झरि ॥
वोल्लाविउ वोल्लहिं परमेसर ।
तवचरणेण काइँ तवणेसर ॥
खणिउ सरीरु जीउ खणमेत्तउ ।
जो झायहि सो गयउ अतीतउ ॥
तुहु मि खणिउ ण ऽज्ज वि सिद्धत्तणु ।
आयहोँ किं पमाणु किं लक्खणु ॥
सयलु णिरत्थु वुत्तु जं राएं ।
मुणिवरु चर्वेवि लग्गु णयवाएं ॥
जइ पुणु सो ज्जें पक्खु वोल्लेवउ ।
ता खणसद्दु ण उच्चारेवउ ॥
खणिउ खयारु णयारु वि होसइ ।
खणसद्दहोँ उच्चारु ण दीसइ ॥

will remove this, then will I raise my pendulous
hands.'
When, on another day, the king returned, he observed
that same noble lord in that same place, the dead
snake tied to his neck, like a neck ornament he had put
on.

5

"When he saw that the lion of a sage had not moved, he
addressed him, removing the snake-garland from his
neck, 'Explain, supreme master, lord of asceticism,
what is the use of ascetic practice? The body is
transient. A soul only exists for a moment. That
which you meditate on, that has gone and passed on.
You too are transient. There is no Siddha-hood now.
What is the evidence to this? What is the scope?'
When the king had called everything useless, the
great sage began to speak according to the doctrine of
partial truths,[1] 'If this exact argument would have to
be explained again, then the word *khaṇa*, "moment,"
could not be uttered. The syllable *kha* and the syllable
ṇa would be transient and the expression of the word
khaṇa would not manifest.

अघडिउ अघडमाणु अघडन्तउ
खणिएं खणिउ खणन्तरमेत्तउ ।
सुण्णें सुण्णवयणु सुण्णासणु
सव्वु णिरत्थु वउद्धहँ सासणु ॥

६

खणसद्देण णिरुत्तरु जायउ ।
पुणु वि पवोल्लिउ दण्डयरायउ ॥
तो घइँ सव्वु अत्थि जं दीसइ ।
पुणु तवचरणु कासु किज्जेसइ ॥
तं णिसुणेप्पिणु भणइ मुणीसरु ।
जो कइगवय वाइ वाईसरु ॥
अम्हइँ राय ण वोल्लहुँ एवं ।
णेआइएँहिँ हसिज्जहुँ जेवं ॥
अत्थि णत्थि दोण्णि वि पडिवज्जहुँ ।
तुहुँ जिह णउ खणवाएं भज्जहुँ ॥
तं णिसुणेवि भणइ दणुदारउ ।
जाणिउ परमपक्खु तुम्हारउ ॥
अत्थि ण अत्थि णिच्चसंदेहो ।
पुणु धवलउ पुणु सामलदेहो ॥
पुणु वि मत्तकरि पुणु पञ्चाणणु ।
खत्तिउ वइसु सुद्दु पुणु वम्भणु ॥

The teaching of the Buddhists is that nothing has
  been produced, is being produced, or is producing
  something; that because of transience, the transient
  only lasts for an instant; that because of emptiness,
  words are empty and space is empty, and that all is
  without purpose.'

6

"Because of the word *khaṇa,* King Dandaka had become
  speechless. He then said, 'So what can be seen is
  truly all that exists. Then why should one practice
  asceticism?' At this, the master sage, who brought
  clarity to poets, the orator, the excellent debater, said,
  'King, we do not say that: this is just how logicians
  mock us. We accept both that something exists and
  does not exist. We are not defeated because of the
  doctrine of transitoriness, as you are.' Hearing this,
  the vanquisher of demons said, 'Your final position is
  understood. Whether something exists or not is an
  eternal uncertainty: first one is white, then one has a
  black body, then one is a rutting elephant, then a lion,
  a Kshatriya, a Vaishya, a Shudra, then a Brahman.'

भणिउ भडारउ किं वित्थारें
एक्कु चोरु चिरु धरिउ तलारें ।
गीवामुहणासच्छि गविट्ठउ
सीसु लएन्तहुँ कहि मि ण दिट्ठउ ॥

७

अहवइ एण काइँ संदेहें ।
अत्थि वि णत्थि वि णीसंदेहें ॥
जेत्थु अत्थि तहिँ अत्थि भणेवउ ।
जहिँ ण अत्थि तहिँ णत्थि भणेवउ ॥
सच्छन्देण णराहिउ भाविउ ।
लइउ धम्मु पुणु मुणि पाराविउ ॥
साहुहुँ पञ्चसयइँ धरियाइं ।
णिसुअइँ तेसट्ठि वि चरियाइं ॥
तो एत्थन्तरें जणमणभाविणि ।
कुइय खणद्धें दुण्णयसामिणि ॥
पुणु मयवद्धणु वुत्तु महन्तउ ।
णरवइ जाउ जिणेसरभत्तउ ॥
तो वरि मन्तु किं पि मन्तिज्जइ
जिणहरें सव्वु दव्वु पुञ्जिज्जइ ।
जेण गवेसण पहु कारावइ
साहुहुँ पञ्चसयइँ मारावइ ॥

The noble lord said, 'Why elaborate? A thief was captured
by a policeman only after a long time. He searched
for the neck, mouth, nose, and eye, but did not see it
anywhere because they were hiding the head.

7

"'Or rather, what is the point of this uncertainty? There
is no doubt that something exists and does not exist.
When something exists, it must be said that it exists.
When something does not exist, it must be said that
it does not exist.' The king contemplated by himself.
He accepted the doctrine and then broke the sage's
fast. He supported five hundred sages and listened
to the sixty-three biographies.[2] Thereupon Queen
Durnayasvamini, who fostered the hearts of the
people, in half an instant became enraged. She said to
the minister Madavardhana, 'The king has become a
devotee of the lord Jina.
We had better come up with a plan: have all the treasure
stored up in the Jina temple, so that when the king
conducts an investigation, he will have the five
hundred sages put to death.'

एक्कदिवसें तं तेम कराविउ ।
जिणहरें सव्वु दव्वु पुज्जाविउ ॥
मयवद्धणेण णिवहों वज्जरियउ ।
तुह भण्डारु मुनिन्देहिँ हरियउ ॥
तें आलावें दण्डयराएं ।
हसियउ पुणु पुणु सीहणिणाएं ॥
पत्तिय सेलसिहरें सयवत्तइँ ।
पत्तिय महियलें गहणक्खत्तइँ ॥
पत्तिय विवरिय चन्ददिवायर ।
पत्तिय परिभमन्ति रयणायर ॥
पत्तिय णहें हवन्ति कुलपव्वय ।
पत्तिय एक्कहिँ मिलिय दिसागय ॥
पत्तिय णउ चउवीस वि जिणवर ।
पत्तिय णउ चक्कवइ ण कुलयर ॥
पत्तिय णउ तेसट्ठि पुराणइँ ।
पञ्चेन्दियइँ ण पञ्च वि णाणइँ ॥
सोलह सग्ग भग्गइँ उपत्तिय ।८
मुणि चोरन्ति मन्ति मं पत्तिय ॥
जं णरवइ वोल्लिउ कइवारें
मन्तिउ मन्तु पुणु वि परिवारें ।
लहु रिसिरूउ एक्कु दरिसावहुँ
पुणु महएविपासु वइसारहुँ ॥

8

"One day it was thus arranged and all the wealth was
  amassed in the Jina temple. Madavardhana reported
  to the king, 'The great sages have taken your treasury.'
  King Dandaka laughed ceaselessly at these words with
  the roar of a lion, 'I would sooner believe that there
  are lotuses on a mountaintop, that the planets and
  stars are on the earth's surface, that the moon and the
  sun have reversed their course, that the oceans are
  migrating, that there are mighty mountain ranges in
  the sky, that the elephants of the cardinal directions
  have assembled in one place, that there are no twenty-
  four great Jinas, that there are no universal emperors,
  no patriarchs, that there are no sixty-three ancient
  treatises, no five senses, nor five forms of knowledge,[3]
  nor that the sixteen heavens have been destroyed, or
  the births. I do not believe the counsel that the sages
  are stealing.'

When the king spoke with praise, his retinue then gave as
  advice, 'Let us quickly show him a man in the guise of
  a seer and then make him sit near the chief queen.

९

अवसें रोसें पुरपरमेसरु ।
मुणिवर घल्लेसइ रज्जेसरु ॥
एम भणेवि पुणु वि कोक्काविउ ।
तक्खणें मुणिवरवेसु धराविउ ॥
तेण समाणउ जणमणभाविणि ।
लग्ग वियारेंहिँ दुण्णयसामिणि ॥
तो एत्थन्तरें गज्जोलियतणु ।
गउ णियणिवहों पासु मयवद्धणु ॥
णरवइ पेक्खु पेक्खु मुणिकम्मइँ ।
ढुक्कु पमाणहों वोल्लिउ जं मइँ ॥
मूढा अवुह ण वुज्झहि अज्ज वि ।
हिउ भण्डारु जाव हिय भज्ज वि ॥
जाणन्तो वि तो वि मरणें मूढउ
णरवइ कोवगइन्दारूढउ ।
दिण्णाणत्ती णरवरविन्दहुँ
धरियइँ पञ्च वि सयइँ मुणिन्दहुँ ॥

472

9

"'Surely the king, the supreme lord of the city, will angrily banish the great sages.' Speaking thus, someone was then summoned and instantly made to put on the guise of a great sage. Durnayasvamini, who fostered the hearts of the people, was passionately engaged with him. Thereupon Madavardhana approached the king, his body covered in bristling body hair. 'King, behold, behold the deeds of sages. What I have said has come true.[4] You ignorant fool, even now you do not realize that, just as your treasury was stolen, your wife too has been taken.'

Even though he knew, the king felt bewildered in his heart. He mounted the enormous elephant of anger, gave an order to the troops of great men, and imprisoned the five hundred great sages.

१०

पहुआएसें धरिय भडारा ।
जे पञ्चेन्दियपसरणिवारा ॥
जे कलिकलुसकसायवियारा ।
जे संसारघोरउत्तारा ॥
जे चारित्तपुरहों पागारा ।
जे कम्मट्टदुट्टदणुदारा ॥
जे णीसङ्ग अणङ्गवियारा ।
जे भवियायणअब्भुद्धारा ॥
जे सिवसासयसुहहक्कारा ।
जे गारवपमायविणिवारा ॥
जे दालिद्ददुक्खखयकारा ।
सिद्धिवरङ्गणपाणिपियारा ॥
जे वायरणपुराणइँ जाणा ।
सिद्धन्तिय एक्केक्कपहाणा ॥
तें तेहा रिसि जन्तें छुहाविय ।
रसमसकसमसन्त पीलाविय ॥
पञ्च वि सय पीलाविय जावेंहिँ
मुणिवर वेण्णि पराविय तावेंहिँ ।
घोरवीरतवचरणु चरेप्पिणु
आतावणें तवतवणु तवेप्पिणु ॥

10

"On the king's order the noble lords were taken captive.
   They who checked the advance of the five senses, who
   annihilated discord, sin, and passion, who escaped
   the horrors of samsara, walls to the city of good
   behavior, who crushed the wicked demonic eight
   forms of karma, the passionless ones who vanquished
   lust, who uplifted the people capable of salvation,
   who summoned happiness of blissful eternity, who
   restrained pride and apathy, who destroyed poverty
   and sorrow, loving husbands of the beautiful Lady
   Siddhi, who knew grammar and the ancient lore,
   experts in the doctrine, eminent men—such seers
   as these he ordered one by one to be thrown into a
   machine and crushed as they screeched and creaked.
As the five hundred were crushed, two great sages arrived,
   practicing terrible, heroic asceticism and suffering
   penance and pain in self-mortification.

११

केण वि ताम वुत्तु मं पइसहों ।
वेण्णि वि पाण लएप्पिणु णासहों ॥
गुरु तुम्हारा आवइ पाविय ।
राएं जन्तें छुहेंवि पीलाविय ॥
तं णिसुणेवि एक्कु मुणि कुद्धउ ।
णं खयकालें कियन्तु विरुद्धउ ॥
घोरु रउद्दु झाणु आऊरिउ ।
वउ सम्मत्तु सयलु संचूरिउ ॥
अप्पाणेणप्पाणु विहत्तिउ ।
तक्खणें छारपुञ्जु परिअत्तिउ ॥
जो कोवाणलु तेण विमुक्कउ ।
गउ णयरहों सवडम्मुहु ढुक्कउ ॥
पट्टणु चाउद्दिसु संदीविउ
सधरु सराउलु जालालीविउ ।
जं जं कुम्भसहासेंहिँ घिप्पइ
विहिपरिणामें जलु वि पलिप्पइ ॥

१२

पट्टणु दड्ढु असेसु वि जावेंहिँ ।
खल जमजोह पराविय तावेंहिँ ॥
जे तइलोक्कु वि जिणेवि समत्था ।
असिघणसङ्कलणियलविहत्था ॥

11

"Then someone said, 'Do not enter! Both of you flee to
   save your life. Your masters have been brought to
   adversity. The king ordered them to be crushed by
   throwing them into a machine.' At this, one sage
   grew enraged, like furious Yama, the god of death,
   at the time of destruction. He undertook dreadful,
   perverse meditation[5] and pulverized every vow and
   righteousness. He separated his self from himself and
   instantaneously was reduced to a heap of ashes. The
   fire of anger that he discharged went toward the city
   and reached it.
On all sides the city was set ablaze. With its land and
   palace it was ignited by the flames. Even the water
   that was poured on it in thousands of pitchers caught
   fire by a reversal of natural law.

12

"While the entire city burned, the wicked soldiers of
   Yama arrived, capable of subduing the threefold
   world, skilled with swords, clubs, chains, and fetters,
   their hair coarse and red, horrifying, demonstrating

कक्कडकविलकेस भीसावण ।
कालकियन्तलीलदरिसावण ॥
कसणसरीर वीर फुरियाधर ।
पिङ्गलणयण झसरमोग्गरधर ॥
जीहललन्त दन्तउद्दन्तुर ।
उब्भडवियडदाढ भयभासुर ॥
जमदूएहिँ तेहिँ कन्दन्तउ ।
णरवइ णिउ समन्ति सकलत्तउ ॥
गम्पिणु जमरायहोँ जाणाविउ ।
एण मुणिन्दणिवहु पीलाविउ ॥
तं णिसुणेप्पिणु कुइउ पयावइ ।
तीहि मि दरिसावहोँ गरुयावइ ॥
पहुआएसें दुण्णयसामिणि
घत्तिय छट्टिहिँ पुढविहिँ पाविणि ।
जहिँ दुक्खइँ अइघोररउद्दइँ
णवराउसु वावीससमुद्दइँ ॥

१३

अण्णोण्णेण जेत्थु हक्कारिउ ।
अण्णोणेण पहरणिद्दारिउ ॥
अण्णोण्णेण दलेँवि दलवट्टिउ ।
अण्णोण्णेण हर्णेवि णिव्वट्टिउ ॥

the amusements of Kala, the time of death, and
Yama, the terminator, warriors with black bodies
and trembling lips, yellow eyes, holding daggers and
hammers, lolling their tongue, projecting their teeth,
terrifying with enormous, monstrous tusks. These
messengers of Yama took the king away as he cried,
together with his minister and wife. Going to King
Yama, they announced, 'This one ordered a group of
eminent sages to be squashed.' At this, Prajapati, lord
of creation, became furious, 'Let the three of them
experience severe adversity.'
On the order of the king, evil Durnayasvamini was cast
into the sixth level,* where there were the most
terrible, cruel forms of sorrow, and a lifetime lasted
for twenty-two *sāgaras*.[6]

13

"Where they challenged each other, tore each other apart
with blows, crushed and annihilated each other,
murdered and destroyed each other, pierced each
other with a trident, offered each other as sacrificial

---

* The hell region Tamahprabha.

अण्णोण्णेण तिसूलें भिण्णउ ।
अण्णोण्णेण दिसावलि दिण्णउ ॥
अण्णोण्णेण कडाहें पमेल्लिउ ।
अण्णोण्णेण हुआसणें पेल्लिउ ॥
अण्णोण्णेण वइतरणिहें घत्तिउ ।
अण्णोण्णेण धरेंवि णिज्जन्तिउ ॥
अण्णोण्णेण सिलहु अप्फालिउ ।
अण्णोण्णेण दुहाएँहिँ फालिउ ॥
अण्णोण्णेण धरेंवि आवीलिउ ।
अण्णोण्णेण वत्थु जिह पीलिउ ॥
अण्णोण्णेण घरट्टएँ दलियउ ।
अण्णोण्णेण पयरु जिह मिलियउ ॥
अण्णोण्णेण वि कूवें पमुक्कउ ।
अण्णोण्णेण धरेप्पिणु रुक्कउ ॥
अण्णोण्णेण पलोइउ रागें
अण्णोण्णेण वियारिउ खग्गें ।
अण्णोण्णेण गिलिज्जइ जेत्थु
दुण्णयसामिणि पत्तिय तेत्थु ॥

food in all directions, cast each other into a frying
pan, threw each other into a fire, flung each other
into the river Vaitarani, took each other captive and
tied each other up, hurled each other against rocks,
split each other into two, captured and squeezed each
other, wrung each other like a cloth, crushed each
other under a grindstone, encountered each other like
arrows, cast each other into a hole, caught and injured
each other,

beheld each other with envy, and afflicted each other
with a sword, where they devoured each other: that is
where Durnayasvamini ended up.

१४

अण्णु वि कियउ जेण मन्तित्तणु ।
घत्तिउ असिपत्तवर्णे अलक्खणु ॥
जहिँ तं तिणु मि सिलीमुहसरिसउ ।
अण्णु वि अग्गिवण्णु णिप्फरिसउ ॥
जहिँ ते लोहरुक्ख कण्टाला ।
असिपत्तल असराल विसाला ॥
दुग्गम दुण्णिरिक्ख दुल्ललिया ।
णाणाविहपहरणफलभरिया ॥
जहिँ णिवडन्ति ताहँ फलपत्तइँ ।
तहिँ छिन्दन्ति णिरन्तर गत्तइँ ॥
तं तेहउ वणु मुएँवि पणट्टउ ।
पुणु वइतरणिहेँ गम्पि पइट्टउ ॥
जहिँ तं सलिलु वहइ दुगन्धउ ।
रसवससोणियमंससमिद्धउ ॥
उण्हउ खारु तोरु अइविरसउ ।
मण्ड पियाविउ पूयविमिस्सउ ॥
इय संतावदुक्खसंतत्तउ
खणें खणें उप्पज्जन्तु मरन्तउ ।
थिउ सत्तमएँ नरएँ मयवड्ढणु
मेइणि जाम मेरु गयणङ्गणु ॥

14

"Also, the wretched one who had done the counseling
was cast into the forest of *asipattras*,* where the grass
was like arrows, moreover the color of fire, and hard;
those thorny trees of iron, with swords as foliage,
abundant and enormous, unapproachable, unsightly,
and unpleasant, bearing different kinds of weapons
for fruit. Where their fruits and leaves fell down, they
endlessly slashed bodies. He escaped, leaving behind
that forest there, and went and entered into the
Vaitarani river, where that stinking water flows, full
of chyle, fat, blood, and flesh. Hot, acrid, astringent,
most unpleasant and mixed with pus, he was forced to
drink it.
Thus being born and dying again and again, tormented
by pain and sorrows, Madavardhana stayed in the
seventh hell† for as long as the earth, Mount Meru,
and the sky existed.

* Trees with swords for leaves.
† Tamastamahprabha.

ताव विरुद्धएहिँ हक्कारिउ ।
णरवइ णारएहिँ पच्चारिउ ॥
मरु मरु संभरु दुच्चरियाइं ।
जाइँ आसि पइँ संचरियाइं ॥
पञ्चसयइँ मुणिवरहुँ हयाइं ।
लइ अणुहुञ्जहि ताइँ दुहाइं ॥
एम भणेप्पिणु खग्गेहिँ छिण्णउ ।
पुणु वाणेहिँ भल्लेहिँ भिण्णउ ॥
पुणु तिलु तिलु करवत्तेहिँ कप्पिउ ।
पुणु गिद्धहुँ सिवसाणहुँ अप्पिउ ॥
पुणु पेल्लाविउ मग्गगइन्देहिँ ।
पुणु वेढाविउ पण्णयविन्देहिँ ॥
पुणु खण्डिउ पुणु जन्तें छुहाविउ ।
अद्धु सहासु वार पीलाविउ ॥
दुक्खु दुक्खु पुणु कह वि किलेसेहिँ ।
परिभमन्तु भवजोणिसहासेहिँ ॥
एत्थु विहङ्गु जाउ णियकाणणे ।
एवहिँ अच्छइ तुम्हघरङ्गणे ॥
ताव पक्खि मरणे पच्छुत्ताविउ
किह मइँ सवणसङ्घु संताविउ ।
एत्तियमत्तें अब्भुद्धरणउ
महु मुयहों वि जिणवरु सरणउ ॥

15

"Then the hostile hellish beings summoned the king
and scolded him, 'Die, die, think of the evil deeds
that you committed! Five hundred eminent sages
were murdered. Now you experience these sorrows.'
Speaking thus, they slashed him with swords, then
pierced him with arrows and *bhallas,** then cut him
into tiny pieces with saws, then threw him to the
vultures, jackals, and dogs, then had him cast under
enormous elephants as they walked, then surrounded
him with masses of snakes, then squashed him, then
had him thrown into a machine and crushed five
hundred times. Somehow making it through these
afflictions and thousands of existences and births,
with great difficulty he then was born here as a bird in
his own forest. Now he sits in the yard of your house."
Thereupon the bird felt remorse in his heart, "How did
I torture a community of mendicants? Only now is
there salvation. Now that I remember, the great Jina is
my refuge."

* Crescent-shaped missiles or arrows.

१६

जं आयण्णिउ पक्खिभवन्तरु ।
जाणइकन्तें पभणिउ मुणिवरु ॥
तो वरि अम्हहुँ वयइँ चडावहु ।
पक्खिहें सुहयपन्थु दरिसावहु ॥
तं वलएवहों वयणु सुणेप्पिणु ।
पञ्चाणुव्वय उच्चारेप्पिणु ॥
दिण्ण पडिच्छिय तिहि मि जणेहिं ।
पुणु अहिणन्दिय एक्कमणेहिं ॥
मुणिवर गय आयासहों जावेहिँ ।
लक्खणु भवणु पराइउ तावेहिँ ॥
राहव एउ काइँ अच्छरियउ ।
जं मन्दिरु णियरयणेहिँ भरियउ ॥
तेण वि कहिउ सव्वु जं वित्तउ ।
मइँ आहारदाणफलु पत्तउ ॥
तक्खणें पञ्चच्छरिउ पदरिसिउ ।
मेहेँहिं जिह अणवरउ पवरिसिउ ॥
रामहों वयणु सुणेवि अणन्तें
गेण्हवि मणिरयणइँ वलवन्तें ।
वडपारोहसमेहिँ पचण्डेहिँ
रहवरु घडिउ सयं भुवदण्डेहिँ ॥

16

When they had listened to the previous existence of the bird, Sita's husband spoke to the great sage, "Please permit us to further our vows and demonstrate the auspicious path to the bird." Hearing the Baladeva's words, they explained and offered the five minor vows, and the three accepted them. Then they unanimously praised them. As the great sages went off to the sky, Lakshmana arrived at the house, "What is this miracle, Rama, that the house is filled with gems that have been brought?" Rama recounted all that had transpired, "I obtained the fruit of donating food. Promptly five miracles appeared, raining down incessantly as if by clouds."

Hearing Rama's words, the mighty Vasudeva himself, grabbing the pearls and gems, constructed an excellent chariot with his fierce club-like arms, resembling branches of a banyan tree.

The Death of Shambuka

छत्तीसमो संधि

रहु कोड्डावणउ
मणिरयणसहासेहिँ घडियउ ।
गयणहों उच्छलेवि
णं दिणयरसन्दणु पडियउ ॥

१

तहिँ तेहएँ सुन्दरें सुप्पवहें ।
आरण्णमहागयजुत्तरहें ॥
धुरें लक्खणु रहवरें दासरहि ।
सुरलीलएँ पुणु विहरन्ति महि ॥
तं कण्हवण्णणइ मुऍवि गय ।
वणें कहिँ मि णिहालिय मत्त गय ॥
कत्थ वि पञ्झाणण गिरिगुहेँहिँ ।
मुत्तावलि विक्खिरन्ति णहेँहिँ ॥
कत्थ वि उड्डाविय सउणसय ।
णं अडविहें उड्डेँवि पाण गय ॥
कत्थ वि कलाव णच्चन्ति वणें ।
णावइ णट्टावा जुवइजणें ॥
कत्थ इ हरिणइँ भयभीयाइँ ।
संसारहों जिह पव्वइयाइँ ॥

Chapter 36

An extraordinary chariot made of thousands of pearls and gems flying up, fell out of the sky, as if it were the sun's chariot.

1

There in that lovely chariot that moved along beautifully, yoked with enormous forest elephants, Lakshmana sat in the driver's seat, and Dasharatha's son Rama inside the great coach. With divine ease they wandered over the earth. Leaving behind the river Krishnavarna, they went on. In the forest they beheld rutting elephants in one place; in another, lions in mountain caves were spreading out a row of pearls with their claws;* in another, hundreds of vultures were stirred up into the air, as if they were the life of the forest that flew up and went away; elsewhere peacocks were dancing in the forest, like dance masters amid a group of young ladies; in another place deer stood stock-still, like renouncers of samsara; in another, there was

---

* Pearls from the heads of elephants they killed.

कत्थ वि णाणाविहरुक्खराइ ।
णं महिकुलवहुअहें रोमराइ ॥
तहों दण्डयवणहों
अग्गएँ दीसइ जलवाहिणि ।
णामें कोञ्चणइ
थिरगमण णाइँ वरकामिणि ॥

२

कोञ्चणइहें तीरेण संठियइँ ।
लयमण्डवें गम्पि परिट्ठियइँ ॥
छुडु जें छुडु जें सरयहों आगमणें ।
सच्छाय महादुम जाय वण्णें ॥
णवणलिणिहें कमलइँ विहसियइँ ।
णं कामिणिवयणइँ पहसियइँ ॥
धवलेण णिरन्तरणिग्गएँण ।
घणकलसेहिँ गयणमहग्गएँण ॥
अहिसिञ्चेंवि तक्खणें वसुहसिरि ।
णं थविय अवाहिणि कुम्भइरि ॥
तहिँ तेहएँ सरएँ सुहावणएँ ।
परिभमइ जणद्दणु काणणएँ ॥
कोवण्डसिलीमुहगहियकरु ।
गज्जन्तमत्तमायङ्गधरु ॥

a row of different types of trees, like the line of hair
above the navel of that fine lady, the Earth.
In the first part of that Dandaka forest they beheld a
stream, a river named Krauncha, with a steady flow
like the stride of a lovely woman.

2

They halted on the bank of that river, the Krauncha.
Going into an arbor of creepers, they settled there.
Gradually, with the onset of autumn, the great trees
in the forest became beautifully colored. Lotuses
bloomed on a new lotus plant, like the smiling faces of
lovely ladies. Like the work of a potter, firmly raised,
the earth seemed like an icon of the goddess Lakshmi,
being showered with pitchers—the clouds—by the
great white elephant that is the sky appearing in full
glory. There in that pleasant autumn the Vasudeva
walked around in the forest, holding bow and arrows
in the hand, warding off roaring, rutting elephants.

वण्णें ताम सुअन्धु वाउ अइउ ।
जो पारियायकुसुमब्भहिउ ॥
कड्ढिउ भमरु जिह
तें वाएं सुट्ठु सुअन्धें ।
धाइउ महुमहणु
जिह गउ गणियारिहें गन्धें ॥

३

थोवन्तरें परिओसियमणेण ।
वंसत्थलु लक्खिउ लक्खणेण ॥
णं सयणविन्दु आवासियउ ।
णं मयउलु वाहें तासियउ ॥
अण्णेक्कपासें कोड्डावणउ ।
जमजीह जेम भीसावणउ ॥
गयणङ्गणें खग्गु णिहालियउ ।
णाणाविहकुसुमोमालियउ ॥
लक्खणहों णाइँ अब्भुद्धरणु ।
णं सम्बुकुमारहों जमकरणु ॥
तं सूरहासु णामेण असि ।
जसु तेएं णिय पह मुअइ ससि ॥
जसु धारहों कालदिट्ठि वसइ ।
जसु कालु कियन्तु वि जमु तसइ ॥

494

Then a fragrant wind came into the forest, surpassing
even the flowers of the coral tree.
Drawn like a bee by that truly fragrant wind, the Vasudeva
rushed in like an elephant drawn by the smell of an
elephant cow.

3

A bit farther into the forest, Lakshmana was delighted to
see a bamboo thicket, as if it were a group of kinfolk
living closely together, or a herd of deer frightened by
a tiger. On one side he beheld an extraordinary sword
floating in the air, as terrifying as the tongue of Yama,
garlanded with different kinds of flowers. A sign of
triumph for Lakshmana, for Shambuka it was like an
act of Yama. That was the sword named Suryahasa; its
glow made the moon lose its radiance, and the glance
of Kala, the time of death, dwelled on its edge, which
terrified even Kala and Yama, the terminator, himself.
Lakshmana stretched out his hand: how did he grab

तें हत्थु पसारेंवि लइउ किह ।
परणरणिप्पसरु कलत्तु जिह ॥
पुणु कीलन्तएँण
असिवत्तें हउ वंसत्थलु ।
ताव समुच्छलेंवि
सिरु पडिउ समउड्डु सकुण्डलु ॥

४

जं दिट्ठु विवाइउ सिरकमलु ।
सिरिवच्छें विहुणिउ भुयजुअलु ॥
धिम्मइँ णिक्कारणु वहिउ णरु ।
वत्तीस वि लक्खणलक्खवधरु ॥
पुणु जाम णिहालइ वंसवणु ।
णररुण्डु दिट्ठु फन्दन्ततणु ॥
तं पेक्खेंवि चिन्तइ खग्गधरु ।
थिउ मायारूवें को वि णरु ॥
गउ एम भणेप्पिणु महुमहणु ।
णिविसेण परायउ णियभवणु ॥
राहवेंण वुत्तु भो सुहडससि ।
कहिँ लद्धु खग्गु कहिँ गयउ असि ॥
तेण वि तं सयलु वि अक्खियउ ।
वंसत्थलु जिह वण्णें लक्खियउ ॥

it? As if it were a wife who was denied to other men. And as he played with the blade of the sword, he struck the bamboo thicket. Jerking upward, a head with a crown and earrings suddenly fell down.

4

When he saw the lotus-like head that he had cut off, Lakshmana shook both his arms, "Shame on me, I killed a man for no reason, a bearer of the thirty-two auspicious marks and signs."[1] When he again looked at the bamboo grove, he saw the headless corpse of a man, the body convulsing. Seeing that, the swordsman reflected, "Some man stood here in an illusory form." With these words, the Vasudeva went and in the blink of an eye reached his home. Rama, the descendant of Raghu, said to him, "Moon-like warrior, where did you get that sword? Where did you go?" He told him everything, how he saw the bamboo thicket in the

जिह लद्धु खग्गु तं अतुलवलु ।
जिह खुंडिउ कुमारहों सिरकमलु ॥
वुच्चइ राहवेण
मं एत्तिय मुहिवएँ साडिय ।
असि सावण्णु णवि
पइँ जमहों जीह उप्पाडिय ॥

५

जं एहिय भीसण वत्त सुय ।
वेवन्ति पजम्पिय जणयसुय ॥
लयमण्डवें विउलें णिविट्ठाहुँ ।
सुहु णाहिं वणे वि पइट्ठाहुँ ॥
परिभमइ जणद्दणु जहिँ जें जहिँ ।
दिवेंदिवें कडमद्दणु तहिँ जें तहिँ ॥
करचलणदेहसिरखण्डणहुँ ।
णिव्विण्ण माएँ हउँ भण्डणहुँ ॥
हउँ ताएं दिण्णी केहाहुँ ।
कलिकालकियन्तहुँ जेहाहुँ ॥
तं वयणु सुणेप्पिणु भणइ हरि ।
जइ राजु ण पोरिसु होइ वरि ॥
जिम दाणें जेंम सुकइत्तणेंण ।
जिम आउहेण जिम कित्तणेंण ॥

498

forest, how he got that sword of unequaled power, and how he hacked off the lotus-like head of a boy.

Rama spoke, "Heaven forbid such pointless destruction! This is not an ordinary sword: it is Yama's tongue that you have drawn out."

5

When she heard that horrifying account, Janaka's daughter trembled and said, "There can be no happiness for us, whether we have settled in a vast creeper arbor or entered into the forest. Wherever the Vasudeva roams, destruction follows every time. Mother, I am disgusted with conflicts where hands, feet, bodies, and heads are cut to pieces. What kind of men did my father give me to? Men like Kali, Kala, the time of death, and Yama, the terminator." Hearing those words, the Vasudeva said, "Perhaps it is better that a king not be manly. It is either through generosity, or by being a good poet, or by a weapon,

परिभमइ कित्ति सव्वहों णरहों ।
धवलन्ति भुवणु जिह जिणवरहों ॥
आयहुँ एत्तियहुँ
जसु एक्कु वि चित्तें ण भावइ ।
सो जाउ ज्जि मुउ
परिमिसु जं जमु णेवावइ ॥

६

एत्थन्तरें सुरसंतावणहों ।
लहु वहिणि सहोयर रावणहों ॥
पायाललंकलंङ्केसरहों ।
धण पाणिपियारी तहों खरहों ॥
चन्दणहि णाम रहसुच्छलिय ।
णियपुत्तहों पासु समुच्चलिय ॥
लइ वारहवरिसइँ भरियाइँ ।
चउदिवसेंहिँ पुणु सोत्तरियाइँ ॥
अण्णहिँ तहिँ दिवसहिँ करें चडइ ।
तं खग्गु अज्जु णहें णिव्वडइ ॥
सो एव चवन्ती महुरसर ।
वलिदीवङ्कारयगहियकर ॥
सज्जणमणणयणाणन्दणहों ।
गय पासु पत्त णियणन्दणहों ॥

or by praise that a man's fame spreads, like that of the
great Jina, illuminating the world.
A man is dead the moment he is born if he does not feel
pleasure in his heart from just one of these things: he
is just a dish of food brought to Yama at his request."

6

Thereupon the young sister of Ravana, the lord of
Patalalanka and Lanka, tormentor of the Gods, the
wife of that Khara who loved her more than life,
named Chandranakhi, jumped up with excitement
and set out toward her son, "Well, twelve years and
a surplus of four days have now been completed. In a
few days that sword returns to his hand, for today it
drops down from the sky." Speaking thus with a sweet
tone, holding sacrificial food, a lamp, and incense
in her hands, she went and arrived near her son,
bringer of joy to the hearts and eyes of good people.

ताणन्तरें असिदलवट्टियउ ।
वंसत्थलु दिट्ठु णिवट्टियउ ॥
दिट्ठु कुमारसिरु
समउडु मणिकुण्डलमण्डिउ ।
जन्तेहिँ किण्णरेहिँ
वरकणयकमलु णं छण्डिउ ॥

७

सिरकमलु णिएप्पिणु गीढभय ।
रोमन्ती महियलें मुच्छगय ॥
कन्दन्ति रुवन्ति सवेयणिय ।
णिज्जीव जाय णिच्चेयणिय ॥
पुणु दुक्खु दुक्खु संवरियमण ।
मुहकायर दरमउलियणयण ॥
णं मुच्छएँ किउ सहियत्तणउ ।
जं रक्खिउ जीवु गवणमणउ ॥
पुणु उट्ठेवि विहुणइ भुअजुअलु ।
पुणु सिरु पुणु पहणइ वच्छयलु ॥
पुणु कोक्कइ पुणु धाहहिँ रडइ ।
पुणु दिसउ णिहालइ पुणु पडइ ॥
पुणु उट्ठइ पुणु कन्दइ कणइ ।
पुणुरुत्तेहिँ अप्पउ आहणइ ॥

Immediately she saw the bamboo thicket, destroyed
and hacked to pieces by the sword.
She saw the head of her son with its crown and adorned
with jeweled earrings, like a beautiful golden lotus,
plucked by Kinnaras as they passed by.

7

When she beheld the lotus-like head, she was gripped with
fear and collapsed to the ground, wailing. Moaning,
crying, and full of anguish, she became lifeless and
fell unconscious—it was only with great trouble that
her heart survived—her face perturbed and her eyes
closed with fear. It was as if the swoon did a friend's
service, that it protected a living being whose mind
was set on dying. Then, getting up, she shook both
her arms; then struck her head, then her chest; then
she called out, then screamed with sobs, then looked
around and fell again, then got up, then moaned,
howled, and beat herself again and again, then threw

पुणु सिरु अप्फालइ धरणिवहें ।
रोवन्तिहें सुर रोवन्ति णहें ॥
जे चउदिसेहिँ थिय
णिय डाल पसारेंवि तरुवर ।
मा रुव चन्दणहि
णं साहारन्ति सहोयर ॥

८

अप्पाणउ तो वि ण संथवइ ।
रोवन्ति पुणु वि पुणु उट्ठवइ ॥
हा पुत्त विउज्झहि लुहहि मुहु ।
हा विरुअएँ णिद्दएँ सुत्तु तुहुँ ॥
हा किण्णालावहि पुत्त मइँ ।
हा किं दरिसाविय माय पइँ ॥
हा उवसंहारहि रूवु लहु ।
हा पुत्त देहि पियवयणु महु ॥
हा पुत्त काइँ किउ रुहिरवडु ।
हा पुत्त एहि उच्छङ्गें चडु ॥
हा पुत्त लाइ मुहें मुहकमलु ।
हा पुत्त एहि पिउ थणजुअलु ॥
हा पुत्त देहि आलिङ्गणउ ।
जें णच्चमि वण्णें वद्धावणउ ॥

504

her head to the ground. While she was crying, the gods in heaven cried along.

The great trees that stood on her four sides, extending their branches, comforted her as if they were her siblings, "Do not cry, Chandranakhi."

8

Nevertheless she did not compose herself. As she wept, she pulled him up again and again, "Ah son, wake up, rub the sleep from your eyes! Ah, you have fallen into an evil sleep. Ah son, why do you not talk to me? Ah, what sort of trick are you playing? Ah, quickly get rid of this form! Ah son, give me loving words! Ah son, why have you bloodied these clothes? Ah son, come and climb onto my lap! Ah son, bring your lotus-like face near to mine! Ah son, come and drink from both my breasts! Ah son, embrace me, and I will dance in jubilation with you in the forest. You spent nine

णवमासु छुड्डु जें मइँ उअरें ।
तं सहल मणोरह अज्जु जणें ॥
हा हा दड्डु विहि
कहिँ णियउ पुत्तु कहों सड्ढमि ।
काइँ कियन्त किउ
हा दइव कवण दिस लड्ढमि ॥

९

हा अज्जु अमङ्गलु विहिँ पुरहँ ।
पायाललङ्कुलङ्काउरहँ ॥
हा अज्जु दुक्खु वन्धवजणहों ।
हा अज्जु पडिय भुअ रावणहों ॥
हा अज्जु खरहों रोवावणउ ।
हा अज्जु रिउहुँ वड्ढावणउ ॥
हा अज्जु फुट्टु कि ण जमहों सिरु ।
हा पुत्त णिवारिउ मइ मि चिरु ॥
तं खग्गु ण सावण्णहों णरहों ।
पर होइ अद्धचक्केसरहों ॥
किं तेण जि पाडिउ सिरकमलु ।
मणिकुण्डलमण्डियगण्डयलु ॥
पुणु पुणु दरिसावइ सुरयणहों ।
रविहुअवहवरुणपहञ्जणहों ॥

506

months inside my womb—make my wishes come true
today.
Wretched fate, where have you taken my son? Who do
I tell? Yama, why did you do it? Ah destiny, how far
must I travel?

9

"Today there is misfortune for two cities, Patalalanka
and the city of Lanka! Today there is sorrow for our
kinfolk! Today Ravana's arms have fallen! Today for
Khara there is reason to cry! Today there is elation for
the enemies! Why did Yama's head not burst today?
Ah son, I discouraged you long ago: that sword is
not for an ordinary man; it is only for a half universal
emperor. Was he the one who struck off your lotus-
like head, its cheeks adorned with jeweled earrings?"
Again and again she showed him to the gods, Surya,

अहों देवहों वालु ण रक्खियउ ।
सव्वेहिँ मिलेवि उप्पेक्खियउ ॥
तुम्हहँ दोसु णवि
महु दोसु जाहें मणु ताविउ ।
मञ्छुडु अण्णभर्वें
मइँ अण्णु को वि संताविउ ॥

१०

एत्थन्तरें सोएं परियरिय ।
णडि जिह तिह पुणु मच्छरभरिय ॥
णिट्ठुरियणयण विप्फुरियमुह ।
विकराल णाइँ खयकालछुह ॥
परिवड्ढिय रविमण्डलें मिलिय ।
जमजीह जेम णहें किलिगिलिय ॥
जें घाइउ पुत्तु महु त्तणउ ।
खरणन्दणु रावणभायणउ ॥
तहों जीविउ जइ ण अज्जु हरमि ।
तो हुयवहपुञ्जें पईसरमि ॥
इय पइज करेप्पिणु चन्दणहि ।
किर वलेवि पलोवइ जाम महि ॥
लयमण्डवें लक्खिय वे वि णर ।
णं धरणिहें उब्भिय उभय कर ॥

Agni, Varuna, and Vayu, "Oh gods, my child was not
  protected. All of you paid him no mind.
But it is not your fault. The fault is all mine, and my heart
  now is anguished. Perhaps in a previous existence I
  aggrieved someone else."

10

Thereupon she was enveloped by sadness; she became
  overwhelmed by wrath, as if she were an actress,
  her eyes grew terrifying and her face quivered, as if
  she were awesome Durga,* hungry for the time of
  destruction. She swelled and merged with the disk of
  the sun, as if she were Yama's tongue, as she screeched
  into the sky, "He who has killed my boy, the son of
  Khara, nephew of Ravana, if I do not take his life
  today, then I enter into a massive fire." Chandranakhi
  made this promise, at once spun around, and looked
  over the earth: she saw two men in a creeper arbor,
  like the two raised hands of the earth. She saw that

* A fierce goddess.

509

तहिँ एक्कु दिट्ठु करवालभुउ ।
लइ एण जि हउ महु तणउ सुउ ॥
एण जि असिवरेंण
णियमत्थहों कुलपायारहों ।
सहुँ वंसत्थलेंण
सिरु पाडिउ सम्बुकुमारहों ॥

११

जं दिट्ठु वणन्तरें वे वि णर ।
गउ पुत्तविओउ कोउ णवर ॥
आयामिय विरहमहाभडेंण ।
णच्चाविय मयरद्धयणडेंण ॥
पुलइज्जइ पासेइज्जइ वि ।
परितप्पइ जरखेइज्जइ वि ॥
मुच्छिज्जइ उम्मुच्छिज्जइ वि ।
रुणुरुणइ वियारहिँ भज्जइ वि ॥
वरि एउ रूउ उवसंघरमि ।
सुरसुन्दरु कण्णवेसु करमि ॥
पुणु जामि एत्थु उम्वरभवणु ।
परिणेसइ अवसें एक्कु जणु ॥
हियइच्छिउ तक्खणें रूउ किउ ।
णं कामहों कोड्डु जें तिं विहिउ ॥

one there was holding a sword, "That must be the one who killed my son.

With that great sword he cut off the head of Prince Shambuka along with the bamboo thicket, as he stood in penance, a bulwark for his family."

11

But when she beheld the two men in the middle of the forest, the anger and sorrow for her son immediately went away. She was seized by the great warrior of lovesickness, and made to dance by the actor Kama, the god of love. The hair on her body bristled, she broke out in a sweat, she felt pain and exhaustion from fever. She fainted, came back to consciousness, wept, and was wrecked by her feelings, "I had better do away with this appearance and assume the disguise of a young lady who even the gods would find beautiful. Then I will go to their dwelling of cluster-fig branches. One of them will marry me for sure." She instantly took on the appearance that her heart desired, as if Kama thereby accomplished some miracle. She went

गय तहिँ जहिँ तिण्णि वि जणइँ वण्णें ।
पुणु धाहहिँ रुअणहिँ लग्ग खण्णें ॥
पभणइ जणयसुय ।
वल पेक्खु कण्ण किह रोवइ ॥
जं कालन्तरिउ ।
तं दुक्खु णाइँ उक्कोवइ ॥

१२

रोवन्ती वडुँ मलहरेंण ।
हक्कारेंवि पुच्छिय हलहरेंण ॥
कहि सुन्दरि रोवहि काइँ तुहुँ ।
किं पडिउ किं पि णियसयणदुहु ॥
किं केण वि कहिँ वि परिब्भविय ।
तं वयणु सुणेवि वाल चविय ॥
हउँ पाविणि दीण दयावणिय ।
णिव्वन्धव रुवमि वराय णिय ॥
वण्णें भुल्ली णउ जाणमि दिसउ ।
णउ जाणमि कवणु देसु विसउ ॥
कहिँ गच्छमि चक्कवूहें पडिय ।
महु पुण्णेहिँ तुम्ह समावडिय ॥
जइ अम्हहुँ उप्परि अत्थि मणु ।
तो परिणउ विण्ह वि एक्कु जणु ॥

where the three of them were there in the forest and
then promptly began to sob and cry.

Janaka's daughter said, "Baladeva, look: why is that girl
crying? She seems to let out a sadness that she kept
inside for a long time."

12

Calling her, the Baladeva asked her, as she bitterly wept,
"Beautiful girl, tell me: why are you crying? Did
some trouble befall your family? Were you insulted
by someone somewhere?" Hearing these words, the
girl said, "I am a miserable, pitiable sinner. I cry as
I am without relations, wretched and vile. I got lost
in the forest. I do not know the directions. I do not
know which country or territory this is. Where do I
go? I have fallen into a circular array.[2] Because of my
good karma I met you. If you have a heart toward us,
then one of you two marry me." When he heard those

तं वयणु सुणेवि हलाउहेंण ।
किय णक्खच्छोडी राहवेंण ॥
करयलु दिण्णु मुहें
किय वङ्कु भउँह सिरु चालिउ ।
सुन्दर ण होइ वहु
सोमित्तिहें वयणु णिहालिउ ॥

१३

जो णरवइ अइसम्माणकरु ।
सो पत्तिय अत्थसमत्थहरु ॥
जो होइ उवायणें वच्छलउ ।
सो पत्तिय विसहरु केवलउ ॥
जो मित्तु अकारणें एइ घरु ।
सो पत्तिय दुट्ठु कलत्तहरु ॥
जो पन्थिउ अलियसणेहियउ ।
सो पत्तिय चोरु अणेहियउ ॥
जो णरु अत्थक्कएँ लल्लिकरु ।
सो सत्तु णिरुत्तउ जीवहरु ॥
जा कामिणि कवडचाडु कुणइ ।
सा पत्तिय सिरकमलु वि लुणइ ॥
जा कुलवहु सवहेहिँ ववहरइ ।
सा पत्तिय विरुयसयइँ करइ ॥

words, the Baladeva, the descendant of Raghu, clicked
his fingernails together.
He put his hand on his mouth, frowned, and shook
his head. He looked at the face of Sumitri's son,
"Handsome man, this is no bride!

13

"The king who gives too many compliments is known
to take away all of one's wealth. He who is fond of
making gifts is known to be nothing more than a
snake. The friend who comes to one's house for no
reason is known as a villain who will abduct one's
wife. The traveler who is disingenuously friendly
is known as an ill-disposed thief. The man who
constantly flatters, he is definitely a mortal enemy.
The lovely lady who produces deceitfully pleasing
words is known to even cut off one's lotus-like head.
The noblewoman who does her business with curses
is known to undertake hundreds of wicked things. She

जा कण्ण होवि परणरु वरइ ।
सा किं वड्ढन्ती परिहरइ ॥
आयहुँ अट्ठहु मि
जो णरु मूढउ वीसम्भइ ।
लोइउ धम्मु जिह
छुडु विप्पउ पएँ पएँ लब्भइ ॥

१४

चिन्तेप्पिणु थेरासणमुहेँण ।
सोमित्ति वुत्तु सीराउहेँण ॥
महु अत्थि भज्ज सुमणोहरिय ।
लइ लक्खण वहु लक्खणभरिय ॥
जं एव समासएँ अक्खियउ ।
कण्हेण वि मणे उवलक्खियउ ॥
हउँ लेमि कुमारि सलक्खणिय ।
जा आगमे सामुद्दएँ भणिय ॥
जङ्घोरुअहङ्घय वट्टथण ।
दीहरकरणक्खङ्गुलिणयण ॥
रत्तहि गइन्दणिरिक्खणिय ।
चामीयरवण्ण सपुज्जणिय ॥
जा उण्णय णासेँ णिलाडेँ तिय ।
सा होइ तिपुत्तहुँ मायरिय ॥

516

who woos a stranger when she is a young girl, will she
give it up as she matures?
Any man who trusts these eight is a fool. It is common
knowledge that with every step he soon runs into
trouble."

14

Thinking this over, the Baladeva turned his lotus-like
face to Sumitri's son and spoke, "I have a most
breathtaking wife. Lakshmana, you take her, full of
qualities, as a wife." While he spoke so succinctly, the
Vasudeva knew well what he meant: "I should take a
girl with good qualities, as described in books on good
omens: smooth on her shanks and thighs, with curvy
breasts, with long hands, nails, fingers, and eyes, with
reddish feet, the appearance of a great elephant,[3]
and with a golden complexion, most honorable. The
woman who is pronounced in nose and forehead, she
becomes a mother of three sons. A woman with feet
like a crow and a stammering voice, she is an ascetic.

कायद्धि सगग्गर तावसिय ।
समचलणङ्गुलि अचिराउसिय ॥
जा हंसवंस वरवीणसर ।
महुवण्ण महाघणछायधर ॥
सुहभमरणाहिसिर भमरथण ।९
सा वहुसुय वहुधण वहुसयण ॥
जहें वामएँ करयलें होन्ति सय ।
मीणारविन्दविसदामधय ॥
गोउरु घरु गिरिवरु अहव सिल ।
सुपसत्थ सलक्खण सा महिल ॥
चक्कङ्कुसकुण्डलउद्धरिह ।
रोमावलि वलिय भुयङ्ग जिह ॥
अद्धेन्दुणिडालें सुन्दरेंण ।
मुत्ताहलसमदन्तन्तरेंण ॥
आएँहिँ लक्खणेँहिँ
सामुद्देहिँ वणि<य> सुणिज्जइ ।
चक्काहिवहों तिय
चक्कवइ पुत्तु उप्पज्जइ ॥

She whose toes are all the same will not live a long life. She who has the backbone of a goose, a voice like an excellent vina, and a honey-like complexion, who bears the gracefulness of a great cloud, whose navel and head have auspicious bees near them and whose breasts are like whirlpools, she will have many sons, many riches, and many relatives. The woman on whose left hand there are hundreds of fish, lotuses, bulls, garlands, and flags, a gateway, a house, a great mountain, or a rock—she who bears such signs is very auspicious. She here, who bears a wheel, a goad, and an earring as marks, who has a line of hair appearing above the navel like a snake, with a beautiful forehead like a half moon and with a space between her pearl-like teeth,

the omens say that a woman with these characteristics is the wife of a universal emperor and that a universal emperor is born as her son.

१५

वहु राहव एह अलक्खणिय ।
हउँ भणमि ण लक्खणेण भणिय ॥
जङ्घोरुकरेहिँ समंसलिय ।
चललोयण गमणुत्तावलिय ॥
कुम्मुण्णयपय विसमञ्झुलिय ।
धुयकविलकेसि खरि पञ्झुलिय ॥
सव्वङ्गसमुट्ठियरोमरइ ।
तहें पुत्तु वि भत्तारु वि मरइ ॥
कडिलउच्छण भउँहावलिमिलिय ।
सा देव णिरुत्तउ झेन्दुलिय ॥
दालिद्दिणि तित्तिरलोयणिय ।
पारेवयच्छि जणभोजणिय ॥
विरसउहदिट्ठि विरसउहसर ।
सा दुक्खहुँ भायण होइ पर ॥
णासग्गें थोरें मन्थरेण ।
सा लज्झिय किं वहुवित्थरेण ॥
कडिचिहुर णाहि मुहमासुरिय ।१०
सा रक्खसि वहुभयभासुरिय ॥
कडुअङ्झिय मत्तगइन्दछवि ।
हउँ एहिय परिणमि कण्ण णवि ॥

15

"This girl, Rama, has inauspicious characteristics. I do not say so myself; her characteristics announce it: she is fleshy in her shanks, thighs, and hands, she has an unsteady glance, is hasty in her gait, has feet arched like a tortoise, rugged fingers and toes, ruffled red hair, is harsh and lame, and has rows of body hair bristling over her entire body. Both her son and husband will perish. With the characteristics of her hips and the coming together of her eyebrows in a continuous line, lord, she is definitely a prostitute. She is a pauper, with the glance of a partridge and the eyes of a pigeon, one who feeds on people. With her look of a crow and her voice like one too, she is nothing but a vessel of sorrows. With the tip of her nose, bulky and crooked, she is a slave. Why give more detail? With hair that does not reach to her hips and a mustache and beard on her face, she is a most horrifying demon, with a pungent body and the hue of an enormous rutting elephant. I will not marry this girl."

पभणइ चन्दणहि
किं णिययसहावें लज्जमि ।
जइ हउँ णिसियरिय
तो पइ मि अज्जु सइँ भुञ्जमि ॥

Chandranakhi replied, "Am I ashamed because of my disposition? If I am a demon, then I will eat you now myself!"

सत्ततीसमो संधि

चन्दणहि अलज्जिय
एम पगज्जिय
मरु मरु भूयहुँ देमि वलि ।
णियरूवें वड्ढिय
रणरसें अड्ढिय
रावणरामहुँ णाइँ कलि ॥

पुणु पुणु वि पवड्ढिय किलिकिलन्ति ।
जालावलिजालासय मुअन्ति ॥
भयभीसण कोवाणलसणाह ।
णं धरऍं समुब्भिय पवर वाह ॥
णहसरिरविकमलहों कारणत्थि ।
अहवइ णं अब्भुद्धारणत्थि ॥
णं घुसलइ अब्भचिरिडुहिल्लु ।
तारावुब्वुवसयविड्डुरिल्लु ॥
ससिलोणियपिण्डउ लेवि धाइ ।
गहडिम्भहों पीहउ देइ णाइँ ॥
अहवइ किं वहुणा वित्थरेण ।
णं णहयलसिल गेण्हइ सिरेण ॥

524

Chapter 37

Shamelessly Chandranakhi roared thus, "Die, die, I give you as sacrificial food to the Bhutas." Her form swelled, full of desire for battle, as if she were the hate between Ravana and Rama.

1

She expanded more and more, screeching and emitting hundreds of rows of fire and flames, horrifying and overwhelmed by the fire of anger, as if the Earth had lifted her enormous arm. She was the one who created the lotus-like sun in the river-like sky, or rather, it was as if she were the one who raised it up. It was as if she stirred the clouds like curd, studded with hundreds of stars like bubbles. She ran away, taking the moon like a lump of fresh butter, and she seemed to feed it as newborn food to her child, Rahu, the eclipser. Or rather, what is the point of going on? It was as if she caught the sky like a rock with her head, and instantly ripped apart the oyster of earth and heaven on

णं हरिवलमोत्तियकारणेण ।
महिगयणसिप्पि फोडइ खणेण ॥
वलएवं वुच्चइ वच्छ वच्छ ।
तुहुँ वहुयहें चरियइँ पेच्छ पेच्छ ॥
चन्दणहि पजम्पिय
तिणु वि ण कम्पिय
लइउ खग्गु हउ पुत्तु जिह ।
तिण्णि वि खज्जन्तइँ
मारिज्जन्तइँ
रक्खेज्जहों अप्पाणु तिह ॥

२

वयणेण तेण असुहावणेण ।
करवालु पदरिसिउ महुमहेण ॥
दढकढिणकढोरुप्पीलणेण ।
अङ्गुलिअङ्गुट्ठावीलणेण ॥
तं मण्डलग्गु थरहरइ केम ।
भत्तारभएं सुकलत्तु जेम ॥
अणवरयमउज्झरें णरणिसुम्भें ।
तहिँ दारिज्जन्तें गइन्दकुम्भें ॥
जो धारहिँ मोत्तियणियरु लग्गु ।
पासेवफुलिङ्ग वहु व वलग्गु ॥

account of its pearls, the Vasudeva and the Baladeva. The Baladeva said, "Dear, dear, you see, see the actions of the girl!"

Chandranakhi spoke, trembling like grass, "Because you took the sword and killed my son, may you three save yourselves while being devoured and murdered!"

2

At these unpleasant words, the Vasudeva took out his sword, squeezing it hard, tight, and firm and gripping it with his fingers and thumb. How did that scimitar shudder? Like a good wife out of fear for her husband. The kind of sword that when the frontal globe of an enormous elephant, with an uninterrupted flow of ichor and intent on killing people, is being slashed open by it, a mass of pearls gets stuck to its edge, like

तं तेहउ खग्गु लएवि तेण ।
विज्जाहिरि पभणिय लक्खणेण ॥
जें लइउ सीसु तुह नन्दणासु ।
करवालु एउ तं सूरहासु ॥
जइ अत्थि को वि रणभरसमत्थु ।
तहों सव्वहों उब्भिउ धम्महत्थु ॥
खरघरणिएँ वुत्तु ण होइ कज्जु ।
को वारइ मारइ मइ मि अज्जु ॥
सा एव भणेप्पिणु
गलगज्जेप्पिणु
चलणेहिँ अप्फालेवि महि ।
खरदूसणवीरहुँ
अतुलसरीरहुँ
गय कूवारें चन्दणहि ॥

३

रोवन्ति पधाइय दीणवयण ।
जलहर जिह जिह वरिसन्ति णयण ॥
लम्बन्ति लम्बकडियलसमग्ग ।
णं चन्दणलयहें भुअङ्ग लग्ग ॥
वीयामयलञ्छणसण्णिहेहिँ ।
अप्पाणु वियारिउ णियणहेहिँ ॥
रुहिरोल्लियथणघिप्पन्तरत्त ।

a spark of sweat risen up in abundance. Holding that
sword, Lakshmana said to the Vidyadhara woman,
"This is that sword Suryahasa that has taken the head
of your son. If there is someone fit for the weight of
battle, the hand of duty is raised against them all."
Khara's wife said, "It is not the case. Who could
restrain and kill me today?"

Speaking and roaring thus, Chandranakhi with a scream
went to the warriors Khara and Dushana with their
unequaled bodies, tearing up the earth with her feet.

3

She rushed forth, sad-faced and crying. Her eyes poured
down just like clouds. Everything was hanging
down to her droopy hips, like snakes attached to
a sandalwood creeper. She cut herself with her
nails that resembled the moon on the second day
of its cycle. Her breasts, wet with blood, were red
from being struck, like golden pitchers smeared

णं कणयकलस कुङ्कुमविलित्त ॥
णं दावइ लक्खणरामकित्ति ।
णं खरदूसणरावणभवित्ति ॥
णं णिसियरलोयहों दुक्खखाणि ।
णं मन्दोयरिहें सुपुरिसहाणि ॥
णं लङ्कहें पइसारन्ति सङ्क ।
णिविसेण पत्त पायाललङ्क ॥
णियमन्दिरें धाहावन्ति णारि ।
णं खरदूसणहों पइट्टु मारि ॥
कूवारु सुणेप्पिणु
धण पेक्खेप्पिणु
राएं वलेंवि पलोइयउ ।
तिहुयणु संघारेंवि
पलउ समारेंवि
णाइँ कियन्तें जोइयउ ॥

४

कूवारु सुणेंवि कुलभूसणेण ।
चन्दणहि पपुच्छिय दूसणेण ॥
कहें केणुप्पाडिउ जमहों णयणु ।
कहें केण पजोइउ कालवयणु ॥
कहि केण कियन्तहों कियउ मरणु ।
कहि केण कियउ विसकन्दचरणु ॥

with saffron. It was as if she displayed the glory of
Lakshmana and Rama, like Khara's, Dushana's, and
Ravana's doom, like a mine of sorrow for the Rakshasa
people, like Mandodari's loss of her good man, as if
she was bringing fear into Lanka. In the blink of an eye
she reached Patalalanka. The howling woman entered
her home, like the death of Khara and Dushana.

When he heard the weeping and beheld his wife, the king,
turning around, cast a glance, just like Yama, the
terminator, looked when he annihilated the threefold
world and set loose destruction.

4

When he heard the weeping, Dushana, the ornament of
his family, asked Chandranakhi, "Tell me, who tore
out Yama's eye? Who looked at the face of Kala, the
time of death? Who caused the death of Yama, the
terminator? Who allowed the grazing of poisonous

कहिं केण वड्ढु पवणेण पवणु ।
कहिं केण दड्ढु जलणेण जलणु ॥
कहिं केण भिण्णु वज्जेण वज्जु ।
कहिं केण धरिउ जलु जलेँण अज्जु ॥
कहिं केण भाणु उण्हेण तविउ ।
कहिं केण समुद्दु तिसाएँ खविउ ॥
कहिं केण खुडिउ फणिमणिणिहाउ ।
कहेँ केण सहिउ सुरकुलिसघाउ ॥
कहेँ केण हुआसणेँ झम्प दिण्ण ।
कहेँ केण दसाणणपाय छिण्ण ॥
चन्दणहि पवोल्लिय
अंसुजलोल्लिय
जणवल्लहु महु तणउ सुउ ।
ओलग्गइ पाणेँहिँ
विणयसमाणेँहिँ
णरवइ सम्बुकुमारु मुउ ॥

५

आयण्णेँवि सम्बुकुमारमरणु ।
संतावणसोयविओयकरणु ॥
पविरलमुहु वाहभरन्तणयणु ।
दुक्खाउरु दरओहुल्लवयणु ॥

roots? Who tied up wind with wind? Who burned fire with fire? Who shattered lightning with lightning? Who caught water with water today? Who warmed the sun with his heat? Who ruined the ocean with his thirst? Who broke a heap of snake-jewels? Who endured a blow from the divine thunderbolt? Who jumped into fire? Who cut off the feet of ten-faced Ravana?"

Chandranakhi answered, wet with the water of her tears, "My son, the darling of the people, has perished.[1] King, Prince Shambuka is dead."

5

When he heard about the death of Prince Shambuka, a cause of sorrow, anguish, and loss, Khara cried woefully, his mouth agape, his eyes filling with tears, afflicted with pain, his face downcast with terror:

खरु रुयइ सदुक्खउ अतुलपिण्डु ।
हा अज्जु पडिउ महु वाहुदण्डु ॥
हा अज्जु जाय मणेँ गरुअ सङ्कु ।
हा अज्जु सुण्ण पायाललङ्कु ॥
हा णन्दण सुरपज्झाणणासु ।
कवणुत्तरु देमि दसाणणासु ॥
एत्थन्तरेँ ताम तिमुण्डधारि ।
वहुवुद्धि पजम्पिउ वम्भयारि ॥
हे णरवइ मूढ रुअहि काइँ ।
संसारेँ भमन्तहुँ सुअसयाइँ ॥
आयाइँ मुआइँ गयाइँ जाइँ ।
को सक्कइ राय गणेवि ताइँ ॥
कहोँ घरु कहोँ परियणु
कहोँ सम्पयधणु
माय वप्पु कहोँ पुत्तु तिय ।
केँ कज्जेँ रोवहि
अप्पउ सोयहि
भवसंसारहोँ एह किय ॥

६

जं दुक्खु दुक्खु संथविउ राउ ।
पडिवोल्लिउ णियघरिणिएँ सहाउ ॥
कहेँ केण वहिउ महु तणउ पुत्तु ।
तं वयणु सुण्णेवि धणिआएँ वुत्तु ॥

"It knows no equal, yet today my club-like arm has
fallen. Today grave anxiety has welled up in my heart.
Ah, today Patalalanka is empty. Ah, son, what should I
tell that lion to the gods, ten-faced Ravana?" At once,
a wise man, a celibate who wore the *tripuṇḍra,* said,
"Foolish king, why do you cry? Those who wander in
samsara have hundreds of sons. The ones who have
died and passed on, king, who can count them?
To whom belongs a house? To whom a retinue? To whom
success and riches, a mother and a father? To whom a
son and a wife? Why do you cry and torment yourself?
This is the work of the cycle of rebirth."

6

It was difficult, but the king took solace in this. Then
he spoke to his wife, "Tell me, who killed my son?"
Hearing these words, his wife said, "Listen, king,

सुणु णरवइ दुग्गमें दुप्पवेसें ।
दुग्घोट्टृथट्टृघट्टृणपवेसें ॥
पञ्झाणणलक्खुक्खयकरालें ।
तहिँ तेहएँ दण्डयवण्णें विसालें ॥
वे मणुस दिट्ठु सोण्डीर वीर ।
मेहारविन्दसण्णिहसरीर ॥
कोवण्डसिलीमुहगहियहत्थ ।
परवलवलउत्थल्लणसमत्थ ॥
तहिँ एक्कु दिट्ठु तियसहुँ असज्झु ।
तें लइउ खग्गु हउ पुत्तु मज्झु ॥
अण्णु वि अवलोवहि देव देव ।
कक्खोरु वियारिउ पेक्खु केव ॥
वण्णें धरेंवि रुयन्ती
धाह मुअन्ती
कह वि ण भुत्त तेण णरेंण ।
णियपुण्णेंहिँ चुक्की
णहमुहलुक्की
णलिणि जेम सरें कुञ्जरेंण ॥

there in that impenetrable, inaccessible, vast Dandaka
forest, with passageways created by the friction of
elephant herds and dreadfully dug up by lakhs of lions,
I saw two haughty, heroic men, one dark as a cloud,
the other bright like a lotus, each clutching a bow and
arrows in hand, and each able to withstand the force
of enemy armies. I saw one there, unstoppable even by
the thirty gods. He took the sword and killed my son.
Lord, lord, look further, see how my flank was cut.
Seizing me in the forest, crying and sobbing, somehow I
was not raped by that man. I escaped due to my good
karma, cut by the tips of his nails, as an elephant
leaves a lotus in a lake."

तं वयणु सुर्णेवि वहुजाणएहिँ ।
उवलक्खिवय अण्णेहिँ राणएहिँ ॥
मालूरपवरपीवरथणाएँ ।
पर एयइँ कम्मइँ अडयणाएँ ॥
मज्छुडु ण समिच्छिय सुपुरिसेण ।
अप्पउ विड्ढंसेंवि आय तेण ॥
एत्थन्तरेँ णिवइ णिएइ जाव ।
णहणियरवियारिय दिट्ठु ताव ॥
किंसुयलय व्व आरत्तवण्ण ।
रत्तुप्पलमाल व भमरछण्ण ॥
तहिँ अहरु दिट्ठु दसणग्गभिण्णु ।
णं वालतवणु फग्गुणें उइण्णु ॥
तं णयणकडक्खेंवि खरु विरुद्धु ।
णं केसरि मयगलगन्धलुद्धु ॥
भडु भिउडिभयङ्कुरु मुहकरालु ।
णं जगहोँ समुट्ठिउ पलयकालु ॥
अमर वि आकम्पिय
एम पजम्पिय
कहोँ उप्परि आरुट्टु खरु ।
रहु खञ्झिउ अरुणें
सहुँ ससिवरुणें
मइँ वि गिलेसइ णवर णरु ॥

7

Other kings, men of great learning, heard those words,
and they carefully looked her over, "These are simply
the deeds of a prostitute with splendid, round breasts
like *mālūra* fruits. Perhaps that good man Khara did
not look at her closely. She harmed herself before she
came." The king examined her, and he saw that she
was cut by a cluster of nails, colored red like a creeper
of a *palāśa* tree, or a garland of red lotuses covered
with bees. He saw her lips there, split by the tips of
teeth, like a young sun that had come up in Phalguna.
Once Khara saw that, he grew furious, like a lion eager
from the smell of an elephant. With his terrifying
frown and his dreadful face the soldier rose up, like the
time of destruction for the world.

The gods trembled and spoke thus, "Who is Khara angry
with?" Aruna* drew back his chariot together with
Chandra† and Varuna, "The man will certainly devour
me too."

* Dawn, the charioteer of the sun.
† The moon.

८

उड्डन्तें उड्डिउ भडणिहाउ ।
अट्टाणखोहु णिविसेण जाउ ॥
चूरन्त परोप्परु सुहड ढुक्क ।
णं जलणिहि णियमज्जायचुक्क ॥
सीसेण सीसु पट्टेण पट्टु ।
चलणेण चलणु करु करणिहट्टु ॥
मउडेण मउडु तुट्टेवि लग्गु ।
मेहलु मेहलणिवहेण भग्गु ॥
उड्डन्ति के वि तिणसमु गणन्ति ।
ओहावणमाणें ण वि णमन्ति ॥
अह णमइ को वि किवणत्तणेण ।
पडिओ वि ण उट्ठइ भडु भरेण ॥
दूसण्णेण णिवारिय वड्ढकोह ।
विहडप्फड सण्णज्झन्ति जोह ॥
जइ पउ वि देहु आरूसमाण ।
तो होसइ रायहों तणिय आण ॥
मं कज्जु विणासहों
ताम वईसहों
जो असिरयणु मण्ड हरइ ।
सिरु खुडइ कुमारहों
विज्जापारहों
सो किं तुम्हहिँ ओसरइ ॥

8

As he stood, so did a group of his soldiers. All at once chaos arose in the assembly hall. Warriors swarmed in, squashing each other, like an ocean overwhelming its shore. A hand was crushed by a hand, a head by a head, a turban by a turban, a foot by a foot; a crown fell to pieces as it got stuck to a crown; a belt was broken by the mass of belts. Some stood up, considering it futile like grass. Out of contempt for the insult they did not bow: a person rather takes a bow out of wretchedness. A fallen soldier, borne down by the weight, did not get up. Consumed by anger, the soldiers rushed to put on their armor. Dushana stopped them, "If you take one more step in fury, there will be an order of the king.

There is no need for destruction. Now sit down. How could that man escape, the one who took the gem of a sword by force and cut off the head of the prince who was pursuing *vidyās*?

९

तो वरि किज्जउ महु तणिय बुद्धि।
णरवइ असहायहों णत्थि सिद्धि॥
णाव वि ण वहइ विणु तारएण।
जलणु वि ण जलइ विणु मारुएण॥
एक्कलउ गम्पिणु काइँ करहि।
रयणायरें सन्तें तिसाएँ मरहि॥
सन्ते वि महग्गएँ विसहें चडहि।
जिणें अच्चिए वि संसारें पडहि॥
जसु सारहि फुडु भुवणेक्कवीरु।
सुरवरपहरणचड्डियसरीरु॥
जगकेसरि अरिकुलपलयकालु।
परवलवगलामुहु भुअविसालु॥
दुद्दमदाणवदुग्गाहगाहु।
सुरकरिकरसमथिरथोरवाहु॥
तेलोक्कभुवग्गलभडतडक्क।
दुद्दरिसण भीसण जमझडक्क॥
तहों तिहुअणमल्लहों
सुरमणसल्लहों
तियसविन्दसंतावणहों।
गउ सम्बु सुहग्गइ
पइँ ओलग्गइ
गम्पि कहिज्जइ रावणहों॥

542

9

"It would be best that my plan be carried out. King, there is no success for one who is without allies. A ship does not sail without a star, a fire does not burn without wind. What are you doing, going on your own? You die of thirst, though you are in the ocean. You climb onto a bull, though a great elephant is present. You fall into samsara, though you honored the Jina, you whose companion is indeed a unique hero in the world, his body crushed by the attacks of the great Gods, a lion in the world, the time of destruction for the families of our enemies, an inferno for hostile armies, with his vast arms, the one who seizes unconquerable, insurmountable demons, whose firm and solid arms resemble the trunks of the divine elephant. You—thrusting like Yama—an unsightly, terrifying annihilator of soldiers in the three worlds with your bare hands.

Go with reverence to that wrestler of the three worlds, a thorn in the hearts of the Gods, the tormentor of all thirty Gods, go to Ravana and say, 'Shambuka has passed on to an auspicious mode of existence.'"

१०

आयण्णेंवि तं दूसणहों वयणु ।
खरु खरउ पवोल्लिउ गुज्झणयणु ॥
धिद्धि लज्जिज्जइ सुपुरिसाहुँ ।
पर एयइँ कम्मइँ कुपुरिसाहुँ ॥
साहीणु जीउ देहत्थु जाव ।
किह गम्मइ अण्णहों पासु ताव ॥
जाएं जीवें मरिएवउं जें ।
तो वरि पहरिउ वरवइरिपुज्झें ॥
जें लब्भइ साहुक्कारु लोएं ।
अजरामरु को वि ण मच्चुलोएं ॥
जिम भिडिउ अज्जु अरिवरसमुद्दें ।
जिम जणिय मणोरह सयणविन्दें ॥
जिम असिसव्वलकोन्तेहिँ भिण्णु ।
जिम जसपडहउ तइलोक्कें दिण्णु ॥
जिम णहें तोसाविउ सुरणिहाउ ।
जिम महु मि अज्जु खयकालु आउ ॥
जिम सत्तुसिलायलें
वहुसोणियजलें
धुउ परिहवपडु अप्पणउ ।
जिम सधउ ससाहणु
सभडु सपहरणु
गउ णियपुत्तहों पाहुणउ ॥

10

When he heard those words of Dushana, Khara, his eyes
like crab's-eye peas, spoke harshly, "Damn it, damn
it! He should feel shame before good men. These can
only be the actions of the ignoble. How can a man go
to someone else, as long as his soul yet firmly resides
in his body? A soul that is born has to die: all the better
that one is struck amid a great mass of enemies. No
one who gains renown in the world of mortals is free
from old age or death. This day, I have either waged
battle in the great ocean of enemies, or fulfilled wishes
among the group of our relations; either I am hit with
swords, javelins, and lances, or I have struck the drum
of triumph in the threefold world; either a band of
gods in the sky is satisfied, or the time of destruction
has come for me;

I myself washed the cloth of insult on the slab of my
enemies with their abundant blood for water, or
I went to my son as a guest, with my flags, army,
soldiers, and weapons."

११

तं णिसुर्णेवि णियकुलभूसणेण ।
लहु लेहु विसज्जिउ दूसणेण ॥
सण्णद्धु खरु वि वहुसमरसूरु ।
अप्फालेॅवि वलेॅ संगामतूरु ॥
विहडप्फड भड सण्णद्ध के वि ।
सम्माणदाणु रिणु संभरेवि ॥
केण वि करेण करवालु गहिउ ।
केण वि धणुहरु तोणीरसहिउ ॥
केण वि मुसण्ढि मोग्गरु पचण्डु ।
केण वि हुलि केण वि चित्तदण्डु ॥
णाणाविहपहरणगहियहत्थ ।
सण्णद्ध सुहड रणभरसमत्थ ॥
णीसरिउ सेण्णु परिहरेॅवि सङ्कु ।
णं वर्मेॅवि लग्ग पायाललङ्कु ॥
रहतुरयगइन्दणरिन्दविन्द ।
णं सुकइमुहहोॅ णिग्गन्ति सद् ॥
खरदूसणसाहणु
हरिसपसाहणु
अमरिसकुद्धउ धाइयउ ।
गयणङ्गणेॅ लीयउ
णावइ वीयउ
जोइसचक्कु पराइयउ ॥

11

At this, Dushana, an ornament to his family, quickly
   sent a letter. Khara, a champion in many battles,
   put on his armor, while amid his army the drum of
   war was struck. Some soldiers put on their armor
   hastily, thinking of it as a debt paid with their respect.
   Someone seized a sword with the hand; another a bow
   along with a quiver; another a *musuṇḍhi*-club and
   a fierce hammer; another a knife and a *citradaṇḍa*-
   club. The warriors, fit for the burden of battle, put
   on their armor, their hands grasping different kinds
   of weapons. Forsaking their doubt, the army set out.
   It was as if Patalalanka began to vomit them forth.
   Hordes of chariots, horses, enormous elephants, and
   kings poured out like words from the mouth of a good
   poet.
Decked with excitement and furious with indignation, the
   army of Khara and Dushana advanced. It stuck to the
   sky,* as if it were a second zodiac that appeared.

---

* Being Vidyadharas, they fly.

जं दिट्ठु णहङ्गणें दणुणिहाउ ।
वलएवें वुत्तु सुमित्तिजाउ ॥
ऍउ दीसइ काइँ णहग्गमग्गें ।
किं किण्णरणिवहु व चलिउ सग्गें ॥
किं पवर पक्खि किं घण विसट्टु ।
किं वन्दणहत्तिऍ सुर पयट्टु ॥
तं वयणु सुणेप्पिणु भणइ विण्हु ।
वल दीसइ वइरिहिँ तणउ चिण्हु ॥
खग्गेण विवाइउ सीसु जासु ।
कुढें लग्गउ मञ्छुडु को वि तासु ॥
अवरोप्परु ए आलाव जाव ।
हक्कारिउ लक्खणु खरेंण ताव ॥
जिह सम्बुकुमारहों लइय पाण ।
तिह पाव पडिच्छहि एन्त वाण ॥
जिह लइउ खग्गु परणारि भुत्त ।
तिह पहरु पहरु पुण्णालिपुत्त ॥
एक्केक्कपहाणहुँ
खरेंण समाणहुँ
चउदह सहस समावडिय ।
गय जेम मइन्दहों
रिउ गोविन्दहों
हक्कारेप्पिणु अब्भिडिय ॥

548

12

When the Baladeva noticed the crowd of Rakshasas in the
   sky, he said to Sumitri's son, "What is it that appears
   up high in the sky? Is it a group of Kinnaras set out
   in heaven? Is it beautiful birds? Is it clouds that have
   appeared? Is it the gods as they departed to praise
   and revere?" Hearing those words, the Vasudeva
   said, "Baladeva, the banner of our enemies appears.
   Perhaps someone has come after the man whose head
   was cut off with the sword." While they exchanged
   these words between them, Khara challenged
   Lakshmana, "For as the life of Prince Shambuka
   that was taken, wretch, you now shall receive a wave
   of arrows. Since you took up the sword and raped a
   stranger's wife, attack, attack, you son of a whore!"
Along with Khara fourteen thousand men, each one a
   leader, rushed toward him. Challenging him, the
   enemies attacked the Vasudeva, as elephants attack a
   lion.

१३

एत्थन्तरें भडकडमद्दणेण ।
जोक्कारिउ रामु जणद्दणेण ॥
तुहुँ सीय पयत्तें रक्खु देव ।
हउँ धरमि सेण्णु मिगजूहु जेम ॥
जव्वेल करेसमि सीहणाउ ।
तव्वेल एज्ज धणुहरसहाउ ॥
तं वयणु सुणेॅवि विहसियमुहेण ।
आसीस दिण्ण सीराउहेण ॥
जसवन्तु चिराउसु होहि वच्छ ।
करें लग्गउ जयसिरिवहुअ सच्छ ॥
तं लेवि णिमित्तु जणद्दणेण ।
वइदेहि णमिय रिउमद्दणेण ॥
तं णिसुणेॅवि सीयएँ वुत्तु एम ।
पञ्चिन्दिय भग्ग जिणेण जेम ॥
वावीस परीसह चउ कसाय ।
जरजम्ममरण मणकायवाय ॥
जिह भग्गु परम्मुहु
रणें कुसुमाउहु
लोहु मोहु मउ माणु खलु ।
तिह तुहुँ भञ्जेज्जहि
समरें जिणेज्जहि
सयलु वि वइरिहिँ तणउ वलु ॥

13

Thereupon the Vasudeva, destroyer of soldiers, spoke
victoriously to the Baladeva, "Lord, you guard Sita
with care. I will hold back this army like a flock of
deer. When I let loose a lion's roar, please come to me
with your bow." Hearing those words, the Baladeva
smiled and gave him his blessing, "Be glorious and
steadfast, my good man. May the bride Lady Triumph
cling to your hand." Accepting this charge, the
Vasudeva, crusher of enemies, bowed to the daughter
of Videha. At this, Sita said, "Just as the five senses,
the twenty-two afflictions, the four passions, old
age, birth, and death, mind, body, and speech were
defeated by the Jina,
just as unfavorable lust, greed, bewilderment, conceit,
and wretched pride were overthrown in battle, may
you vanquish and overcome the entire army of our
enemies."

१४

आसीसवयणु तं लेवि तेण ।
अप्फालिउ धणुहरु महुमहेण ॥
तें सद्दें वहिरिउ जगु असेसु ।
थरहरिय वसुन्धरि डरिउ सेसु ॥
खरलक्खण वे वि भिडन्ति जाव ।
हक्कारिउ हरि तिसिरेण ताव ॥
ते भिडिय परोप्पर हणु भणन्त ।
णं मत्त महागय गुलुगुलन्त ॥
णं केसरि घोरोरालि देन्त ।
वाणेहिँ वाण छिन्दन्ति एन्त ॥
मोग्गरखुरुप्पकण्णिय पडन्ति ।
जीवेहिँ जीव णं खयहोँ जन्ति ॥
एत्थन्तरें अतुलपरक्कमेण ।
अद्धेन्दु मुक्कु पुरिसोत्तमेण ॥
तहोँ तिसिरउ चुक्कु ण कह वि भिण्णु ।
धणुहरु पाडिउ धयदण्डु छिण्णु ॥
अण्णुण्ण पुणुप्पुणु
समरें वहुग्गुणु
जं जं तिसिरउ लेवि धणु ।
तं तं उक्कण्ठइ
खणु वि ण संथइ
दइवविहूणहोँ जेम धणु ॥

14

Accepting these words of blessing, Vasudeva let loose his
bow. The entire world was deafened by the sound.
The earth shook and Shesha trembled. As Khara and
Lakshmana both attacked each other, the Vasudeva
was challenged by Trishiras. They charged at each
other, saying, "Kill!" like rumbling, rutting great
elephants, like lions emitting a string of roars. They
shot down incoming arrows with arrows of their own.
Hammers, knife-shaped and *karṇika*-arrows* fell, like
beings going to destruction because of other beings.
Then that sublime man of unequaled prowess fired a
crescent-headed arrow. Somehow Trishiras evaded
it and was not hurt, but his bow was smashed and his
flagstaff broken.
Every many-strung bow Trishiras took up in the fight was
broken to pieces. It did not last for even a moment,
like riches of a man forsaken by fate.

---

* The top of this arrow resembles an ear.

धणुहरु सरु सारहि छत्तदण्डु ।
जं वाणहिँ किउ सयखण्डखण्डु ॥
तं अमरिसकुद्धेँ दुद्धरेण ।
संभरिय विज्ज विज्जाहरेण ॥
अप्पाणु पदरिसिउ वद्धमाणु ।
तिहिँ वयणेहिँ तिहिँ सीसेहिँ समाणु ॥
पहिलउ सिरु कक्कडकविलकेसु ।
पिङ्गललोयणु कियवालवेसु ॥
वीयउ सिरु वयणु वि णवजुवाणु ।
उब्भिण्णवियडमासुरिसमाणु ॥
तइयउ सिरु धवलउ धवलवयणु ।
फुरिआहरु दरणिड्डुरियणयणु ॥
दुद्दरिसणु भीसणु वियडदाढु ।
जिणभत्तउ जिणवरधम्मगाढु ॥
एत्थन्तरें परवलमद्दणेण ।
वच्छत्थलें विद्धु जणद्दणेण ॥
णाराएँहिँ भिन्देवि
सीसइँ छिन्देवि
रिउ महिमण्डलें पाडियउ ।
सुरवरेहिँ पचण्डेहिँ
सइँ भुवदण्डेहिँ
कुसुमवासु सिरें पाडियउ ॥

15

When his bow and arrow, his charioteer and umbrella staff
    had been rendered into hundreds of shattered shards
    by the arrows, the unstoppable Vidyadhara, furious
    with indignation, thought of a *vidyā*. As he grew in
    size he appeared with three faces and three heads.
    The first head had coarse, red hair, yellow eyes, and
    assumed the appearance of a child. The second head
    and face were fresh and youthful, sprouting a dreadful
    beard and mustache. The third head was white and
    had a white face, quivering lips, and horrifying eyes:
    it was terrifying, unsightly, and had monstrous tusks.
    He was a devotee of the Jina, seized by the doctrine of
    the great Jina. Then the Vasudeva, crusher of enemy
    armies, pierced him in the chest.
Slashed with arrows and his heads cut off, the enemy
    collapsed to the ground. The fierce great gods
    themselves dropped a rain of flowers onto his head
    with their club-like arms.

The Abduction of Sita

अट्ठतीसमो संधि

तिसिरउ लक्खणेण
समरङ्गणें घाइउ जार्वेहिँ ।
तिहुअणडमरकरु
दहवयणु पराइउ तार्वेहिँ ॥

लेहु विसज्जिउ जो सुरसीहहोँ ।
अग्गएँ पडिउ गम्पि दसगीवहोँ ॥
पडिउ णाइँ वहुदुक्खहँ भारु ।
णाइँ णिसायरकुलसंघारु ॥
णाइँ भयङ्करु कलहहोँ मूलु ।
णाइँ दसाणणमत्थासूलु ॥
लेहें कहिउ सव्वु अहिणाणेहिँ ।
सम्बुकुमारु उलग्गइ पाणेहिँ ॥
अण्णु वि खग्गरयणु उद्दालिउ ।
खरघरिणिहें हियवउ विद्दारिउ ॥
तं णिसुणेवि वे वि जसभूसण ।
परवलें भिडिय गम्पि खरदूसण ॥
णारिरयणु णिरुवमु सोहग्गउ ।
अच्छइ रावण तुज्झु जें जोग्गउ ॥

Chapter 38

As Lakshmana killed Trishiras on the battlefield, ten-faced Ravana, tormentor of the three worlds, arrived.

1

The letter that had been sent to ten-necked Ravana, a
lion to the Gods, fell before him once it arrived. It fell
like a load of plentiful sorrows, like the destruction
of the Rakshasa lineage, like the terrible root of the
conflict, like a spear to each of Ravana's ten heads.
The letter explained everything through subtle signs,
"Prince Shambuka is dead. Also, the gem of a sword
was taken away, and the heart of Khara's wife was
torn asunder. Hearing this, Khara and Dushana, who
made an emblem of their fame, both went and waged
war on the enemy's army. There is a gem of woman
among them, of unequaled grace. Ravana, she is
suitable for you alone." Seeing the letter, he hastened

लेहु णिएॅवि अत्थाणु विसज्जेॅवि ।
पुप्फविमाणें चडिउ गलगज्जेॅवि ॥
करें करवालु करेप्पिणु धाइउ ।
णिविसें दण्डारण्णु पराइउ ॥
ताव जणद्दॄणॅण
खरदूसणसाहणु रुद्धउ ।
थिउ चउरङ्गु वलु
णहें णिच्चलु संसएॅ छुद्धउ ॥

२

तो एत्थन्तरें दीहरणयणें ।
लक्खणु पोमाइउ दहवयणें ॥
वरि एक्कलओ वि पञ्चाणणु ।
णउ सारङ्गणिवहु वुण्णाणणु ॥
वरि एक्कलओ वि मयलच्छणु ।
ण य णक्खत्तणिवहु णिल्लच्छणु ॥
वरि एक्कलओ वि रयणायरु ।
णउ जलवाहिणिणियरु सवित्थरु ॥
वरि एक्कलओ वि वइसाणरु ।
णउ वणिणवहु सरुक्खु सगिरिवरु ॥
चउदह सहस एक्कु जो रुम्भइ ।
सो समरङ्गणें मइ मि णिसुम्भइ ॥

from the assembly, and he thundered as he mounted the celestial chariot Pushpa. Holding his sword in his hand, he set out. In the blink of an eye, he reached the Dandaka forest.

The Vasudeva meanwhile held back the army of Khara and Dushana. Their fourfold army stood motionless in the sky, thrown into doubt.

2

Wide-eyed Ravana, the ten-faced, took in Lakshmana, "Better one single lion than a flock of deer with frightened faces. Better a single moon than an ordinary throng of stars. Better a single ocean than an abundance of rivers for all their meanderings. Better a single fire than a cluster of forests with trees and great mountains. This one man, who all alone holds back fourteen thousand, could even kill me on the

पेक्खु केम पहरन्तु पईसइ ।
धणुधरु सरु संधाणु ण दीसइ ॥
णहि गय णहि तुरय
णहि रहवर णहि धयदण्डइँ ।
णवरि पडन्ताइँ
दीसन्ति महियले रुण्डइँ ॥

३

हरि पहरन्तु पसंसिउ जार्वेहिँ ।
जाणइ णयणकडक्खिय तार्वेहिँ ॥
सुकइकह व्व सुसन्धि सुसन्धिय ।
सुपय सुवयण सुसद्द सुवद्धिय ॥
थिरकलहंसगमण गइमन्थर ।
किस मज्झारें णियम्वें सुवित्थर ॥
रोमावलि मयरहरुत्तिण्णी ।
णं पिम्पिलिरिञ्छोलि विलिण्णी ॥
अहिणवहुण्डपिण्डपीणत्थण ।
णं मयगल उररखम्भणिसुम्भण ॥
रेहइ वयणकमलु अकलङ्कउ ।
णं माणससरें वियसिउ पङ्कउ ॥
सुललियलोयण ललियपसण्णहँ ।
णं वरइत्तमिलिय वरकण्णहँ ॥

battlefield. Look how he enters as he fights:
you cannot even see him fit arrow to bow-string.
There are no elephants, nor horses, nor excellent chariots,
nor flagstaffs. Only decapitated corpses can be seen,
as they fall on the ground."

3

While he praised the battling Vasudeva, he eyed Janaka's
daughter: with beautiful joints, well built, with
beautiful feet, a beautiful face, a beautiful voice, and
fully developed, like the story of a good poet has good
sandhi, is well put together, has good verses, fine
expressions, good words, and exhausts its theme.[1]
She had the steady walk of a goose, slow in her gait,
slender at her waist, and very wide at her buttocks.
The sensual trail of hair above her navel resembled a
line of ants that clung to her. Her young, full, round
breasts, without prominent nipples, could crush the
rigidity of any man's chest, like elephants destroying
pillars with their broad fronts.[2] Her spotless lotus-like
face beamed, like a lotus blooming in the Manasa lake.
Her very graceful eyes were like those of charming,

घोलइ पुट्ठिहिँ वेणि महाइणि ।
चन्दणलयहिँ ललइ णं णाइणि ॥
किं वहुजम्पिएँण
तिहिँ भुवणेहिँ जं जं चङ्गउ ।
तं तं मेलवेंवि
णं दइवें णिम्मिउ अङ्गउ ॥

४

तो एत्थन्तरें णियकुलदीवें ।
रामु पसंसिउ पुणु दहगीवें ॥
जीविउ एक्कु सहलु पर एयहों ।
जसु सुहवत्तणु गउ परिच्छेयहों ॥
जेण समाणु एह धण जम्पइ ।
मुहमुहेण तम्वोलु समप्पइ ॥
हत्थें हत्थ धरेंवि आलावइ ।
चलणजुअलु उच्छङ्गें चडावइ ॥
जं आलिङ्गइ वलयसणाहहिँ ।
मालइमालाकोमलवाहहिँ ॥
जं पेल्लावइ थणमायङ्गेंहिँ ।
मुहु परिचुम्वइ णाणाभङ्गेंहिँ ॥
जं अवलोयइ णिम्मलतारेंहिँ ।
णयणहिँ विब्भमभरियवियारेंहिँ ॥

gracious, beautiful girls meeting the eyes of their
suitor. Her thick braid rolled about on her back, like
a female snake at play on a sandalwood creeper.
Why say any more? It was as if fate had fashioned her body
out of whatever is beautiful in the three worlds.

4

Thereupon ten-necked Ravana, the light of his family,
praised Rama, "His life alone is fruitful, he enjoys the
furthest limit of conjugal bliss, whom this lovely lady
speaks to and feeds betel, mouthful after mouthful.
Holding his hands in hers, she speaks to him. She
takes his two feet up into her lap. The man she
embraces with her soft arms like jasmine garlands,
bound tight with bracelets, the one she squeezes
against with her elephant-like breasts, whose face she
covers with many kinds of kisses, whom she looks
at with her bright, shining eyes that tremble with
emotions, whom she enjoys as she loves him deep in

जं अणुहुञ्जइ इच्छेॅवि णियमणें ।
तासु मल्लु को सयलेॅ वि तिहुअणें ॥
धण्णउ एहु णरु
जसु एह णारि हियइच्छिय ।
जाव ण लइय मइँ
कउ अङ्घहोॅ ताव सुहच्छिय ॥

५

सीय णिएॅवि जाउ उम्माहउ ।
दहमुहु वम्महसरपहराहउ ॥
पहिलएॅ वयणु वियारॅहिँ भज्जइ ।
पेम्मपरव्वसु कहोॅ वि ण लज्जइ ॥
वीयएॅ मुहपासेउ वलग्गइ ।
सरहसु गाढालिङ्गणु मग्गइ ॥
तइयएॅ अइ विरहाणलु तप्पइ ।
कामगहिल्लउ पुणु पुणु जम्पइ ॥
चउथएॅ णीससन्तु णउ थक्कइ ।
सिरु संचालइ भउँहउ वङ्कइ ॥
पञ्चमें पञ्चमझुणि आलावइ ।
विहसेॅवि दन्तपन्ति दरिसावइ ॥
छट्ठएॅ अङ्घु वलइ करु मोडइ ।
पुणु दाढियउ लएॅप्पिणु तोडइ ॥
वट्टइ तल्लवेल्ल सत्तमयहोॅ ।

her heart, who in the entire threefold world can stand
against him in combat?
Blessed is this man, who cherishes this woman in his heart.
How is there comfort for my body, as long as I have
not taken her?"

5

A madness emerged as he looked at Sita. Ravana was
struck by the fall of Kama's arrow. First his face was
broken by emotions. As love overpowered him, he lost
all sense of shame. Second, sweat arose on his face.
He longed fiercely for a tight embrace. Third, the fire
of lovesickness burned him completely. Possessed by
love, he babbled on and on. Fourth, he did not stop
sighing. He shook his head and curved his eyebrows.
Fifth, he sang the fifth note. Laughing, he showed off
his teeth. Sixth, he twisted his body and worried his
hands. Then he grasped his mustache and tore at it. In
the seventh phase bewilderment rose.

मुच्छउ एन्ति जन्ति अट्टमयहों ॥
णवमउ वट्टइ मरणहों ढुक्कउ ।
दसमएँ पाणिहिँ कह वि ण मुक्कउ ॥
दहमुहु दहमुहेंहिँ
जाणइ किर मण्डएँ भुञ्जमि ।
अप्पउ संथवइ
णं णं सुरलोयहों लज्जमि ॥

६

तो एत्थन्तरें सुरसंतासें ।
चिन्तिउ एक्कु उवाउ दसासें ॥
अवलोयणिय विज्ज मणें झाइय ।
दे आएसु भणन्ति पराइय ॥
किं घोट्टेण महोवहि घोट्टमि ।
किं पायालु णहङ्गणें लोट्टमि ॥
किं सहुँ सुरेंहिँ सुरेन्दु परज्जमि ।
किं मयरद्धयपुरिगउ भञ्जमि ॥
किं जममहिससिङ्घु मुसुमूरमि ।
किं सेसहों फणिमणि संचूरमि ॥
किं तक्खयहों दाढ उप्पाडमि ।
कालकियन्तवयणु किं फाडमि ॥

In the eighth, fainting sensations came and went.
Ninth, he truly came close to death. In the tenth
phase, he was somehow not forsaken by his life's
breaths.

Ravana said, "Indeed, I will enjoy Janaka's daughter by
force with all my ten faces." He composed himself,
"No, no, I am ashamed before the gods."

6

Then Ravana, tormentor of the Gods, thought of a plan.
He called the *vidyā* Avalokani[3] to mind. She arrived
and spoke to him, "Give an order. Should I drink the
great ocean with a single gulp? Should I roll a Patala
in the sky? Should I vanquish the lord of the gods
together with the other gods? Should I crush the
elephant of the city of Kama? Should I pound the
horn of Yama's buffalo? Should I pulverize the jewel
in Shesha's forehead? Should I pull out Takshaka's[4]

किं रविरहतुरङ्ग उद्दालमि ।
किं गिरि मेरु करग्गें टालमि ॥
किं तइलोक्कचक्कु संघारमि ।
किं अत्थक्कऍ पलउ समारमि ॥
वुत्तु दसाणर्णेण
एक्केण वि ण वि महु कज्जु ।
तं सङ्केउ कहें
जें हरमि एह तिय अज्जु ॥

७

दहवयणहों वयणेण सुपुज्जऍ ।
पभणिउ पुणु अवलोयणिविज्जऍ ॥
जाव समुद्दावत्तु करेक्कहों ।
वज्जावत्तु चाउ अण्णेक्कहों ॥
जावग्गेउ वाणु करें एक्कहों ।
वायवु वारुणत्थु अण्णेक्कहों ॥
जाम सीरु गम्भीरु करेक्कहों ।
करयलें चक्काउहु अण्णेक्कहों ॥
ताव णारि को हरइ दिसेवहुँ ।
मण्डऍ वासुएववलएवहुँ ॥
इय पच्छण्ण वसन्ति वणन्तरें ।
तेसट्टीपुरिसहुँ अब्भन्तरें ॥

570

fangs? Should I slash the face of Kala, the time of death, and Yama, the terminator? Should I tear away the horses from Surya's chariot? Should I disturb Mount Meru with my finger? Should I demolish the wheel of the threefold world? Should I bring about total destruction on this very day?"

Ravana said, "I have no need for any of these. Tell me that information through which I might abduct that woman today."

7

At Ravana's words, the most honorable *vidyā* Avalokani said, "As long as the bow Samudravarta is in the hand of the one and the Vajravarta in the hand of the other, as long as there is a fire missile in the hand of one and a wind and water missile in that of the other, as long as there is a firm plow in the hand of one and the discus weapon in the hand of the other, who could abduct a woman by force from Vasudeva and Baladeva, as they wander the world? They live hidden inside the forest. They are among the sixty-three exemplary

जिण चउवीस अद्ध गोवद्धण ।
णव केसव सराम णव रावण ॥
ओए भवट्टम
इय वासुएववलएव ।
जाव ण वहिय रणें
तिय ताम लइज्जइ केव ॥

८

अहवइ एण काइँ सुणें रावण ।
एह णारि तिहुअणसंतावण ॥
लइ लइ जइ अजरामरु वट्टहि ।
लइ लइ जइ उप्पहेंण पयट्टहि ॥
लइ लइ जइ वड्डत्तणु खण्डहि ।
लइ लइ जइ जिणसासणु छण्डहि ॥
लइ लइ जइ सुरवरहुँ ण लज्जहि ।
लइ लइ जइ णरयहों गमु सज्जहि ॥
लइ लइ जइ परलोउ ण जाणहि ।
लइ लइ जइ णियआउ ण माणहि ॥
लइ लइ जइ णियरज्जु ण इच्छहि ।
लइ लइ जइ जमसासणु पेच्छहि ॥
लइ लइ जइ णिव्विण्णउ पाणहुँ ।
लइ लइ जइ उरु उड्डहि वाणहुँ ॥

572

men: the twenty-four Jinas, half as many universal emperors, nine Vasudevas and Baladevas, and nine Prativasudevas.

These two are the Vasudeva and Baladeva in their eighth manifestation. As long as they have not been killed in battle, how could I possibly take the woman?

8

"But really, what is the use of this? Listen, Ravana: this woman is a cause of affliction to the three worlds. Take her, by all means take her if you are indeed free from old age and pain, if you proceed along the wrong path, if you wish to shatter your greatness, if you forsake the teaching of the Jina, if you feel no shame toward the great gods, if you are prepared to go to hell, if you have no knowledge of the other world, if you do not value your life, if you do not desire your kingship, if you are looking for Yama's punishment, if you are fed up with life, if you jump up high from arrows!" Hearing these

तं णिसुणेवि वयणु असुहावणु ।
अइमयणाउरु पभणइ रावणु ॥
माणवि एह तिय
जं जिज्जइ एक्कु मुहुत्तउ ।
सिवसासयसुहहों
तहों पासिउ एउ वहुत्तउ ॥

९

विसयासत्तचित्तु परियाणेॅवि ।
विज्जएॅ वुत्तु णिरुत्तउ जाणेॅवि ॥
णिसुणि दसाणण पिसुणमि भेउ ।
वेण्ह वि अत्थि एक्कु सङ्केउ ॥
ऍहु जो दीसइ सुहडु रणङ्गणें ।
वावरन्तु खरदूसणसाहणें ॥
एयहों सीहणाउ आयण्णेॅवि ।
इट्टकलत्तु व तिणसमु मण्णेॅवि ॥
धावइ सीहु जेम ओरालेॅवि ।
वज्जावत्तु चाउ अप्फालेॅवि ॥
तुहुँ पुणु पच्छऍं धण उद्दालहि ।
पुप्फविमाणें छुहेॅवि संचालहि ॥
तं णिसुणेप्पिणु पभणिउ राउ ।
तो घइँ पइँ जें करेवउ णाउ ॥

574

unpleasant words, Ravana answered, suffering terribly
from lust,
"That I may spend one moment honoring that woman is
more important to me than the happiness of blissful
eternity."

9

Understanding that his mind was attached to sensory
objects, the *vidyā* spoke, making plain her meaning,
"Listen, Ravana, I will reveal something.[5] There is
an agreement between those two: that warrior who
you can see on the battlefield, as he engages the army
of Khara and Dushana: should he let out a lion's
roar and the husband hears it, he will rush off after
him, considering his beloved wife to be as worthless
as grass, growling like a lion and shooting his bow
Vajravarta. Then you can take away the lovely lady
and bring her along, once you have thrown her into
Pushpa, your celestial chariot." At this, the king said,
"Then you must quickly make the sound." On the

पहुआएसें विज्ज पधाइय ।
णिविसें तं संगामु पराइय ॥
लक्खणु गहियसरु
जं णिसुणिउ णाउ भयङ्करु ।
धाइउ दासरहि
णहें सधणु णाइँ णवजलहरु ॥

१०

भीसणु सीहणाउ णिसुणेप्पिणु ।
धणुहरु करें सज्जीउ करेप्पिणु ॥
तोणाजुवलु लएवि पधाइउ ।
मञ्छुडु लक्खणु रणें विणिवाइउ ॥
कुढें लग्गन्तें रामें सुणिमित्तइँ ।
सउणु ण देन्ति होन्ति दुणिमित्तइँ ॥
फुरइ सवाहउ वामउ लोयणु ।
पवहइ दाहिणपवणु अलक्खणु ॥
वायसु विरसु रसइ सिव कन्दइ ।
अग्गएँ कुहिणि भुअङ्गमु छिन्दइ ॥
जम्बू पङ्करन्त उद्धाइय ।
णाइँ णिवारा सयण पराइय ॥
दाहिणेण पिङ्गलय समुट्ठिय ।
णहें णव गह विवरीय परिट्ठिय ॥

576

order of the king, the *vidyā* rushed forth and in the
blink of an eye reached that battlefield.

When Rama heard Lakshmana's terrifying roar, the sound
that they had agreed upon, he set out with his bow,
like a fresh raincloud racing across the sky.

10

Hearing the terrible lion's roar, he rushed forth, taking
up his strung bow in his hand and seizing a pair of
quivers, "Perhaps Lakshmana has been struck down
in battle." As Rama went in pursuit, no good omens
gave an auspicious outcome. There were bad omens:
his left eye trembled, together with his arm; an
inauspicious wind blew from the south; a crow made
an unpleasant sound, a jackal cried; a snake crossed
the road in front of him; jackals rushed out of their
hiding places, like relatives that had come to stop
him; in the south a whispering rose up; in the sky the

तो वि वीरु अवगण्णेवि धाइउ ।
तक्खणें तं सङ्घामु पराइउ ॥
दिट्ठइँ राहवेण
लक्खणसरहंसेहिँ खुडियइँ ।
गयणमहासरहाँ
सिरकमलइँ महियलें पडियइँ ॥

११

दिट्ठु रणङ्गणु राहवचन्दें ।
रमिउ वसन्तु णाइँ गोविन्दें ॥
कुण्डलकडयमउडफल दरिसिय ।
दणुदवणामञ्झरिय पदरिसिय ॥
गिद्धावलिकियचक्कन्दोलउ ।
णरवरसिरइँ लएप्पिणु केलउ ॥
रणें खेळन्ति परोप्परु चच्चरि ।
पुणु पियन्ति सोणियकायम्वरि ॥
तेहउ समरवसन्तु रमन्तउ ।
लक्खणु पोमाइउ पहरन्तउ ॥
साहु वच्छ पर तुज्झु जि छज्जइ ।
अण्णहाँ कासु एउ पडिवज्जइ ॥
पइँ इक्खाउवंसु उज्जालिउ ।
जसपडहउ तिहुअणें अप्फालिउ ॥

nine planets stood in reversed course. Nevertheless,
disregarding it all, the hero advanced. He promptly
arrived at that battle.
Rama, the descendant of Raghu, saw heads like lotuses
torn off by geese—Lakshmana's arrows, fallen from
the great lake of the sky onto the ground.

11

Moon-like Rama, the descendant of Raghu, beheld the
battlefield. It was as if the Vasudeva celebrated spring:
he presented fruits—earrings, bracelets, and crowns;
displayed garlands of wormwood—the Rakshasas;
there was a swing—the circling of flocks of vultures;
the heads of great men played merrily together in
battle, raising their cups and then drinking the wine
that was blood. He praised fighting Lakshmana, as
he reveled in that spring-like war, "Well done, good
man. It is looking well just for you. Who else could
undertake such a thing? You have made Ikshvaku's
dynasty shine and sounded the drum of fame in the

तं णिसुणेप्पिणु भणइ महाइउ ।
विरुअउ कियउ देव जं आइउ ॥
मेल्लेवि जणयसुय
किं राहव थाणहों चलियउ ।
अक्खइ मज्झु मणु
हिय जाणइ केण वि छलियउ ॥

१२

पुणरवि वुच्चइ मरगयवण्णें ।
हउँ ण करेमि णाउ किउ अण्णें ॥
तं णिसुणेवि णियत्तइ जावेंहिँ ।
सीयाहरणु पढुक्किउ तावेंहिँ ॥
आउ दसाणणु पुप्फविमाणें ।
णाइँ पुरन्दरु सिवियाजाणें ॥
पासु पढुक्किउ राहवघरिणिहें ।
मत्तगइन्दु जेम परकरिणिहें ॥
उभयकरेंहिँ संचालिय थाणहों ।
णाइँ सरीरहाणि अप्पाणहों ॥
णाइँ कुलहों भवित्ति हक्कारिय ।
लङ्कहें सङ्क णाइँ पइसारिय ॥
णिसियरलोयहों णं वज्जासणि ।
णाइँ भयङ्कररामसरासणि ॥

threefold world." At this, the magnanimous man said,
"Lord, you have done wrong, that you have come.
Why, Rama, descendant of Raghu, did you go from your
place, leaving Janaka's daughter behind? My mind
tells me that Sita has been taken and that someone has
tricked you."

12

Emerald-hued Lakshmana spoke again, "I did not make
a sound, someone else did." Rama heard this and
rushed back, but the abduction of Sita was at hand.
Ten-faced Ravana swept in with his celestial chariot
Pushpa, like Indra with his palanquin. He came to the
side of Rama's wife, like a rutting elephant to another
elephant's cow. With both hands he pulled her away
from her abode, as if she were the destruction of his
body, the doom he summoned for his family, the
uncertainty he brought for Lanka, a lightning bolt
for the Rakshasa people, a terrifying thunderbolt-
like arrow of Rama, the demise of his fame, a mine of

णं जसहाणि खाणि वहुदुक्खहुँ ।
णं परलोयकुहिणि किय मुक्खहुँ ॥
तक्खणें रावणेण
ढोइउ विमाणु आयासहों ।
कालें कुद्धऍण
हिउ जीविउ णं वणवासहों ॥

१३

चलिउ विमाणु जं जें गयणङ्गणें ।
सीयएँ कलुणु पकन्दिउ तक्खणें ॥
तं कूवारु सुणेवि महाइउ ।
धुणेवि सरीरु जडाइ पधाइउ ॥
पहउ दसाणणु चञ्झूघाऍहिँ ।
पक्खुक्खवेवेहिँ णहरणिहाऍहिँ ॥
एक्कवार ओससइ ण जावेहिँ ।
सयसयवार झडप्पइ तावेहिँ ॥
जाउ विसण्ठुलु वइरिवियारणु ।
चन्दहासु मणें सुमरइ पहरणु ॥
सीय वि धरइ णियङ्छु वि रक्खइ ।
लज्जइ चउदिसु णयणकडक्खइ ॥
दुक्खु दुक्खु तें धीरेवि अप्पउ ।
करणिट्टुरदढकढिणतलप्पउ ॥

plentiful sorrows, a road to the other world made for
fools.
As Ravana swiftly flew the celestial chariot to the sky, it
seemed as if enraged Kala, the time of death, took
away the life of the forest abode.

13

From the very moment that the celestial chariot set
out into the sky, Sita cried woefully. Hearing her
screams, the noble Jatayin rushed in, shaking his
body. He struck at Ravana with blows from his beak,
with beatings of his wings and swipes of his claws.
Before Ravana could draw a single breath, he was hit
hundreds upon hundreds of times. The crusher of
enemies was stunned. In his mind he remembered his
weapon Chandrahasa. He used Sita to shield his body;
he felt shame at this and cast guilty glances all around.
It was very difficult, but he steeled himself and struck
the bird with harsh, firm, cruel slaps from his hands.

पहउ विहङ्गु पडिउ समरङ्गणे ।
देवेहिँ कलयलु कियउ णहङ्गणे ॥
पडिउ जडाइ रणे
खरपहरविहुरफन्दन्तउ ।
जाणइहरिवलहुँ
तिण्ह मि चित्तइँ पाडन्तउ ॥

पडिउ जडाइ जं जें फन्दन्तउ ।
सीयएँ किउ अक्कन्दु महन्तउ ॥
अहों अहों देवहों रणे दुवियड्ढहों ।
णिय परिहास ण पालिय सण्ढहों ॥
वरि सुहडत्तणु चञ्चूजीवहों ।
जो अब्भिट्टु समरें दसगीवहों ॥
णउ तुम्हेहिँ रक्खिउ वड्डुत्तणु ।
सूरहों तणउ दिट्ठु सूरत्तणु ॥
सच्चउ चन्दु वि चन्दगहिल्लउ ।
वम्भु वि सोत्तिउ हरु दुम्महिलउ ॥
वाउ वि चवलत्तणेण दमिज्जइ ।
धम्मु वि रण्डसएहिँ लइज्जइ ॥
वरुणु वि होइ सहावें सीयलु ।
तासु कहि मि किं सङ्कइ परवलु ॥

The bird fell on the battlefield. In the sky the gods
were in an uproar.
Jatayin fell in battle, convulsing helplessly from the
terrible blows, directing his thoughts toward the
three: Janaka's daughter, the Vasudeva, and the
Baladeva.

14

As Jatayin fell, convulsing, Sita let out a long cry, "Ah,
ah, gods, idiots in battle! Weaklings, you did not
keep your word. This bird, who lives by his beak,
confronted Ravana in battle: he is a far greater warrior.
You did nothing to defend your greatness: Surya's
only heroism is being the sun; truly Chandra was just
possessed by his own brilliance; Brahma is a docile
Brahman and Shiva is a henpecked husband;* Vayu is
fickle and so holds himself back; Dharma is waylaid
by hundreds of sluts; Varuna is cold by nature—does

---

* Referring to the fierce goddess Kali, his wife.

इन्दु वि इन्दवहेण रमिज्जइ ।
को सुरवरसण्ढेहिँ रक्खिज्जइ ॥
जाउ किं जम्पिॲण
जगें अण्णु ण अब्भुद्धरणउ ।
राहउ इहभवहाँ
परलोयहाँ जिणवरु सरणउ ॥

१५

पुणु वि पलाउ करन्ति ण थक्कइ ।
कुढें लग्गउ लग्गउ जो सक्कइ ॥
हउँ पावेण एण अवगण्णेवि ।
णिय तिहुअणु अमणूसउ मण्णेवि ॥
पुणु वि कलुणु कन्दन्ति पयट्टइ ।
ॲउ अवसरु सप्पुरिसहाँ वट्टइ ॥
अह मइँ कवणु णेइ कन्दन्ती ।
लक्खणराम वे वि जइ हुन्ती ॥
हा हा दसरह माम गुणोवहि ।
हा हा जणय जणय अवलोयहि ॥
हा अपराइॲं हा हा केक्कइ ।
हा सुप्पहें सुमित्तें सुन्दरमइ ॥
हा सत्तुहण भरह भरहेसर ।
हा भामण्डल भाइ सहोयर ॥

an enemy army ever fear him? Indra is only gladdened
with a festival in honor of himself. Who is protected
by these weaklings, the great gods?
What is the point of speaking? There is no other salvation
in the world. In this world it is Rama, the descendant
of Raghu; in the other world the great Jina is my only
refuge."

15

Again she did not stop lamenting, "Come after me, come,
whoever is able! I have been taken by this sinner, who
disregards me and considers the world to be lacking in
men." Once more she kept on crying woefully, "This
is an opportunity for a good man. But who could
abduct me as I cry, if both Lakshmana and Rama were
present? Ah, ah, dear Dasharatha, ocean of virtues,
ah, ah, father Janaka, see! Ah, Aparajita! Ah, ah,
Kaikeyi! Ah, Suprabha! Sumitri with your beautiful
thoughts! Ah, Shatrughna! Bharata, lord of Bharata!
Ah, brother Bhamandala, with whom I shared the

हा हा पुणु वि राम हा लक्खण ।
को सुमरमि कहों कहमि अलक्खण ॥
को संथवइ मइँ
को सुहि कहों दुक्खु महन्तउ ।
जहिँ जहिँ जामि हउँ
तं तं जि पएसु पलित्तउ ॥

१६

तहिँ अवसरें वट्टन्तें सुविउलएँ ।
दाहिणलवणसमुद्दहों कूलएँ ॥
अत्थि पचण्डु एक्कु विज्जाहरु ।
वरकरवालहत्थु रणे दुद्धरु ॥
भामण्डलहों चलिउ ओलग्गएँ ।
सुअ कन्दन्ति सीय तामग्गएँ ॥
वलिउ विमाणु तेण पडिवक्खहों ।
णं तिय का वि भणइ मइँ रक्खहों ॥
लक्खणराम वे वि हक्कारइ ।
भामण्डलहों णामु उच्चारइ ॥
मज्छुट्टु एह सीय ऍहु रावणु ।
अण्णु ण परकलत्तसंतावणु ॥
अच्छउ णिवहों पासु जाएवउ ।
एण समाणु अज्जु जुज्झेवउ ॥

588

womb! Ah, ah, Rama too! Ah, Lakshmana! Whom do I think of? Whom do I, unfortunate one, speak to? Who supports me? Who is a friend? Who knows great sorrow? Wherever it is that I am going, that region will be set alight."

16

As this event transpired, there was a fierce Vidyadhara, wielding an excellent sword, invincible in battle, standing on the broad coast of the southern salt ocean. Set out in service of Bhamandala, he then heard Sita crying before him. He turned his celestial chariot toward the enemy, "Some woman seems to cry out, 'Save me!' She summons the two, Lakshmana and Rama, and utters the name of Bhamandala. Perhaps she is Sita and he is Ravana. There is no other who torments strangers' wives. I should quickly go to the king, but now I must fight with him." Saying thus, he

एम भणेवि तेण हक्कारिउ ।
कहिँ तिय लेवि जाहि पच्चारिउ ॥
विहि मि भिडन्ताहुँ
जिह हणइ एक्कु जिह हम्मइ ।
गेण्हेवि जणयसुय
वलु वलु कहिँ रावण गम्मइ ॥

१७

वलिउ दसाणणु तिहुअणकण्टउ ।
सीहहों सीहु जेम अब्भिट्टउ ॥
जेम गइन्दु गइन्दहों धाइउ ।
मेहहों मेहु जेम उद्धाइउ ॥
भिडिय महावल विज्जापाणेँहिँ ।
वे वि परिट्ठिय सिवियाजाणेँहिँ ॥
वे वि पसाहिय णाणाहरणेँहिँ ।
वेण्णि वि वावरन्ति णियकरणेँहिँ ॥
वेण्णि वि घाय देन्ति अवरोप्परु ।
मणेँ विरुद्ध भामण्डलकिङ्करु ॥
वरकरवालु करेप्पिणु करयलें ।
पहउ दसाणणु वियडउरत्थलें ॥
पडिउ घुलेप्पिणु जण्हुवजोत्तेँहिँ ।
रुहिरु पदरिसिउ दसहि मि सोत्तेँहिँ ॥
पुणु विज्जाहरेण पच्चारिउ ।

590

challenged him, "Where are you going, taking the
woman?" He scolded,
"When two men are fighting, one either kills or is killed.
Turn around, turn around! Where, Ravana, are you
headed with Janaka's daughter?"

17

Ravana, an affliction to the three worlds, turned around.
Like a lion attacking a lion, an enormous elephant
charging an enormous elephant, a cloud rushing on
a cloud, the almighty men fought, holding *vidyās* in
their hands. Both stood in palanquins, were adorned
with various decorations, employed their own
stratagems, and gave each other blows. Bhamandala's
servant felt rage in his heart. Taking his great sword in
his hand, he struck Ravana, the ten-faced, on his wide
chest. He fell down, stumbling, onto his two knees.
Blood appeared in ten streams. Then the Vidyadhara
scolded him, "You, who were not restrained in

सुरवरसमरसऍहिँ अणिवारिउ ॥
तुहुँ सो रावणु तिहुवणकण्टउ ।
एक्कें घाएं णवर पलोट्टिउ ॥
चेयणु लहेंवि रणें
भडु उट्ठिउ कुरुडु समच्छरु ।
तहों विज्जाहरहों
थिउ रासिहिँ णाइँ सणिच्छरु ॥

१८

उट्ठिउ वीसपाणि असि लेन्तउ ।
णाइँ सविज्जु मेहु गज्जन्तउ ॥
विज्जाछेउ करेंवि विज्जाहरें ।
घत्तिउ कम्बूदीवब्भन्तरें ॥
पुणु दससिरु संचल्लु ससीयउ ।
णहयलें णाइँ दिवायरु वीयउ ॥
मज्झें समुद्दहों जयसिरिमाणणु ।
पुणु वोल्लेवऍ लग्गु दसाणणु ॥
काइँ गहिल्लिऍं मइँ ण समिच्छहि ।
किं महएविपट्टु ण समिच्छहि ॥
किं णिक्कण्टउ रज्जु ण भुञ्जहि ।
किं ण वि सुरयसोक्खु अणुहुज्जहि ॥

hundreds of battles with the great Gods, you are that
Ravana, an affliction to the three worlds. With just
one blow you were thrown down."
Regaining consciousness in the fight, the warrior stood up,
furious and full of wrath, against that Vidyadhara, like
the planet Saturn against a star sign.

18

Ravana picked himself up with all twenty of his hands, and
held his sword, like a thundering cloud accompanied
by a lightning bolt. Stripping the Vidyadhara of
his *vidyā,* he threw him onto the island of Kambu.
Ravana set out again together with Sita, like a second
sun in the sky. In the middle of the ocean, Ravana,
who worshiped the goddess of victory, again began
to talk, "Silly girl, why do you not desire me? Do you
not long for a chief queen's turban? Would you not
enjoy a kingdom free of all troubles? Do you not relish
the pleasure of lovemaking? Did someone crush my

किं महु केण वि भग्गु मडप्फरु ।
किं दूहउ किं कहि मि असुन्दरु ॥
एम भणेवि आलिङ्घइ जावेंहिँ ।
जणयसुयएँ णिब्भच्छिउ तावेंहिँ ॥
दिवसेंहिँ थोवएँहिँ
तुहुँ रावण समरें जिणेवउ ।
अम्हहुँ वारियएँ
रामसरेंहिँ आलिङ्घेवउ ॥

१९

णिठुरवयणेंहिँ दोच्छिउ जावेंहिँ ।
दहमुहु हुअउ विलक्खउ तावेंहिँ ॥
जइ मारमि तो एह ण पेच्छमि ।
वोलउ सव्वु हसेप्पिणु अच्छमि ॥
अवसें कं दिवसु इ इच्छेसइ ।
सरहसु कण्ठग्गहणु करेसइ ॥
अण्णु वि मइँ णियवउ पालेव्वउ ।
मण्डएँ परकलत्तु ण लएव्वउ ॥
एम भणेवि चलिउ सुरडामरु ।
लङ्क पराइउ लद्धमहावरु ॥
सीयएँ वुत्तु ण पइसमि पट्टणें ।
अच्छमि एत्थु विउलें णन्दणवणें ॥

594

pride? Am I repugnant? Am I somehow ugly?" When
he embraced her after these words, Janaka's daughter
threatened him,
"In a few days, Ravana, you will be vanquished in battle.
   In due course, you will be embraced by Rama's arrows
   because of me."

19

Rebuked by her harsh words, Ravana's ten faces darkened,
   "If I kill her, I will never see her again. So I will carry
   on, and laugh off all her words. No doubt some day
   she will want me and cling passionately to my neck.
   Moreover, I must guard my vow and not take another
   man's wife by force." Speaking thus, the scourge of
   the Gods, who had received great rewards, went on his
   way and reached Lanka. Sita said, "I will not enter into
   the city. I will stay here, in this vast pleasure grove.

जाव ण सुणमि वत्त भत्तारहों ।
ताव णिवित्ति मज्झु आहारहों ॥
तं णिसुणेॅवि उववणें पइसारिय ।
सीसवरुक्खमूलें वइसारिय ॥
मेलेॅवि सीय वणें
गउ रावणु घरहों तुरन्तउ ।
धवलेॅहिं मङ्गलेॅहिं
थिउ रज्जु सइं भुञ्जन्तउ ॥

As long as I do not hear news from my husband, I will refrain from eating."[6] At this, he led her into the park and settled her at the root of an *aśoka* tree.

Leaving Sita in the forest, Ravana quickly went to his house. He continued to rule over his kingdom, to the praises of heroic and benedictory songs.

एगुणचालीसमो संधि

कुढें लग्गेप्पिणु लक्खणहों
वलु जाम पडीवउ आवइ ।
तं जि लयाहरु तं जि तरु
पर सीय ण अप्पउ दावइ ॥

१

णीसीयउ वणु अवयज्जियउ ।
णं सररुहु लच्छिविसज्जियउ ॥
णं मेहविन्दु णिव्विज्जुलउ ।
णं मुणिवरवयणु अवच्छलउ ॥
णं भोयणु लवणजुत्तिरहिउ ।
अरहन्तविम्बु णं अवसहिउ ॥
णं दत्तिविवज्जिउ किविणधणु ।
तिह सीयविहूणउ दिट्ठु वणु ॥
पुणु जोअइ गुहिलेंहिँ पइसरेंवि ।
थिय जाणइ जाणइ ओसरेंवि ॥
पुणु जोवइ गिरिविवरन्तरेंहिँ ।
थिय जाणइ ल्हिक्केंवि कन्दरेंहिँ ॥
ताणन्तरें दिट्ठु जडाइ वणें ।
संसूडियगत्तउ पडिउ रणें ॥

598

Chapter 39

When the Baladeva returned after going in pursuit of Laksh-
mana, he found only that arbor and that tree, but not Sita.

1

He beheld the forest without Sita: it was like a lotus
   abandoned by Lakshmi, like a mass of clouds without
   lightning, like the words of a great sage without
   kindness, like a meal without salt, like an icon of the
   lord Jina without a home, like the property of a poor
   man deprived of gifts. Thus the forest looked without
   Sita. He searched, entering into caves, and looked
   to see if Janaka's daughter had run away there. Then
   he looked inside mountain chasms and looked to see
   if she stood there, hidden away in their fissures. As
   he searched, he found Jatayin in the forest, his body
   wasted, fallen in battle.

पहरविहुरघुम्मन्ततणु
जं दिट्ठु पक्खि णिट्ठलियउ ।
तार्वेहिँ वुज्झिउ राहवेण
हिय जाणइ केण वि छलियउ ॥

२

पुणु दिण्ण तेण सुह वसुहार ।
उच्चारेवि पञ्च णमोक्कार ॥
जे सारभूय जिणसासणहों ।
जे मरणसहाय भव्वजणहों ॥
लद्धेहिँ जेहिँ दिढ होइ मइ ।
लद्धेहिँ जेहिँ परलोयगइ ॥
लद्धेहिँ जेहिँ संभवइ सुहु ।
लद्धेहिँ जेहिँ णिज्जरइ दुहु ॥
ते दिण्ण विहङ्गहों राहवेण ।
कियणिसियरणियरपराहवेण ॥
जाएज्जहि परमसुहावहेँ ।
अणरण्णाणन्तवीरपहेँ ॥
तं वयणु सुणेवि सव्वायरेण ।
लहु पाण विसज्जिय णहयरेण ॥
जं मुउ जडाइ हिय जणयसुअ ।
धाहाविउ उब्भा करेवि भुअ ॥

When he saw the massacred bird, his body rolling about
helplessly from the blows, Rama, the descendant of
Raghu, knew, "Sita has been taken. Someone has
tricked me."

2

He gave him an incomparable treasure, reciting the five
namaskāras[1] that are the essence of the teaching of
the Jina, companions in death for people capable of
salvation; by which, once received, the mind becomes
firm, one gains a path to the other world, happiness
appears, and sorrow vanishes. Rama, wrecker of the
clan of Rakshasas, bestowed these on the bird, "May
you go along the favorable path of Anaranya and
Anantavirya." Hearing these words, the noble bird
instantly let go of life. With Jatayin dead and Janaka's
daughter taken, Rama wailed, raising his arms,

कहिँ हउँ कहिँ हरि कहिँ घरिणि
कहिँ घरु कहिँ परियणु छिण्णउ ।
भूयवलि व्व कुडुम्बु जगें
हयदइवें कह विक्खिवण्णउ ॥

३

वलु एम भणेवि पमुच्छियउ ।
पुणु चारणरिसिहिँ णियच्छियउ ॥
चारण वि होन्ति अट्टविहगुण ।
जे णाणपिण्ड सीलाहरण ॥
फलफुलपत्तणहगिरिगमण ।
जलतन्तुअजङ्घासंचरण ॥
तहिँ वीर सुधीर विसुद्धमण ।
णहचारण आइय वेण्णि जण ॥
तें अवहीणाणें जोइयउ ।
रामहों कलत्तु विच्छोइयउ ॥
आऊरेंवि गलगम्भीरझुणि ।
पुणु लग्गु चवेवएँ जेट्ठमुणि ॥
भो चरमदेह सासयगमण ।
कें कज्जें रोवहि मूढमण ॥
तिय दुक्खहुँ खाणि विओयणिहि ।
तहें कारणें रोवहि काइँ विहि ॥

602

"Where am I? Where is the Vasudeva? Where is my wife?
Where is my home? Where is my retinue? Vanished!
How did wretched fate scatter my family in the world
like food sacrificed to the Bhutas?"

3

Saying this, the Baladeva fainted. Then he was spotted by
sky-wandering seers.[2] Sky-wanderers are gifted with
eight kinds of qualities and masses of knowledge,
endowed with good conduct, traveling by fruits,
flowers, leaves, the sky, or mountains, or moving via
water, threads, and shanks. The two sky-wandering
ascetics alighted: they were heroic, very steadfast,
and possessed of pure hearts. They observed through
their *avadhi* knowledge that Rama's wife had been
abducted. Then, making a deep sound with his throat,
the eldest sage began to speak, "You are in your final
body, advancing toward the eternal: why then do you
weep as if your heart swoons? A woman is a mine
of sorrows, a treasure of loss. Fate, why do you cry
because of her?

किं पइँ ण सुइय एह कह
छज्जीवणिकायदयावरु ।
जिह गुणवइअणुअत्तर्णेण
जिणयासु जाउ वर्णे वाणरु ॥

४

जं णिसुणिउ को वि चवन्तु णहें ।
मुच्छाविहलङ्घलु धरणिवहें ॥
हा सीय भणन्तु समुट्ठियउ ।
चउदिसउ णियन्तु परिट्ठियउ ॥
णं करि करिणिहें विच्छोइयउ ।
पुणु गयणमग्गु अवलोइयउ ॥
तहिँ ताव णिहालिय विण्णि रिसि ।
संगहिय जेहिँ परलोयकिसि ॥
ते गुरु गुरुभत्ति करेवि थुय ।
हो धम्मविद्धि सिरिणमियभुय ॥
गिरिमेरुसमाणउ जेत्थु दुहु ।
तहें कारणें रोवहि काइँ तुहुँ ॥
खल तियमइ जेण ण परिहरिय ।
तहों णरयमहाणइ दुत्तरिय ॥
रोवन्ति एम पर कप्पुरिस ।
तिणसमु गणन्ति जे सप्पुरिस ॥

Have you not heard that story of how Jinadasa,
exceptional in his compassion toward all six sorts
of beings, became a monkey in the forest out of his
obedience to Gunavati?"[3]

4

Rama had collapsed in a faint onto the ground and was
perplexed as he heard someone speaking in the sky.
He stood up, saying, "Alas, Sita." As he stood there,
he looked all around, like an elephant bereft of his
elephant cow. Then he looked at the path of heaven.
There he now saw the two seers, who had reaped the
harvest of the other world. Demonstrating his deep
devotion to the masters, he praised them. They spoke
to him, "Righteousness surges within you, and your
arms are revered by Lakshmi, yet you are filled with
a sorrow as great as Mount Meru. Why do you cry
because of her? There is only the great uncrossable
river of hell for the man who does not forsake
wretched woman. Only ignoble men cry like this.
Those who consider them as grass, they are good men.

तियमइ वाहिहें अणुहरइ
खणें खणें दुक्खन्ति ण थक्कइ ।
हम्मइ जिणवयणोसहेंण
जें जम्मसए वि ण ढुक्कइ ॥

५

तं वयणु सुणेप्पिणु भणइ वलु ।
मेल्लन्तु णिरन्तरु अंसुजलु ॥
लब्भन्ति गामवरपट्टणइँ ।
सीयलविउलइँ णन्दणवणइँ ॥
लब्भन्ति तुरङ्गम मत्त गय ।
रह कणयदण्डधुव्वन्तधय ॥
लब्भन्ति भिच्चवर आणकर ।
लब्भइ अणुहुञ्ञेवि सधर धर ॥
लब्भइ घरु परियणु वन्धुजणु ।
लब्भइ सिय संपय दव्वु धणु ॥
लब्भइ तम्वोलु विलेवणउ ।
लब्भइ हियइच्छिउ भोयणउ ॥
लब्भइ भिङ्गारोलम्वियउ ।
पाणिउ कप्पूरकरम्वियउ ॥
हियइच्छिउ मणहरु पियवयणु ।
पर एहु ण लब्भइ तियरयणु ॥

Woman is like a disease: she never stops causing pain.
This can be destroyed by the medicine of the words
of the Jina, by which one does not fall headlong into a
hundred rebirths."

5

Hearing these words, the Baladeva spoke, as he wept wet
tears ceaselessly, "I had villages and beautiful cities,
and pleasure groves, cool and vast. I kept horses and
rutting elephants, and chariots and waving flags with
golden flagstaffs. I had excellent servants waiting
to obey my orders. I had the whole earth, together
with its mountains, to enjoy. A house, retinue, and
relatives: I had them all. I had luster, success, wealth,
and riches. I had betel and ointment. I had food that
was dear to my heart, and I kept water mixed with
camphor resting in a golden pitcher. But I could not
keep that breathtaking jewel of a woman, dear to my
heart, with her lovely face.

तं जोव्वणु तं मुहकमलु
तं सुरउ सवट्टणहत्थउ ।
जेण ण माणिउ एत्थु जगें
तहों जीविउ सव्वु णिरत्थउ ॥

६

परमेसरु पभणइ वलेॅवि मुहु ।
तियरयणु पसंससि काइँ तुहुँ ॥
पेक्खन्तहुँ पर वण्णुज्जलउ ।
अब्भन्तरें रुहिरचिलिव्विलउ ॥
दुगन्धदेहु चिणिविट्टलउ ।
पर चम्में हड्डुहुँ पोट्टलउ ॥
मायामें जन्तें परिभमइ ।
भिण्णउ णवणाडिहिँ परिसवइ ॥
कम्मट्टुगण्ठिसयसिक्क्रिउ ।
रसवससोणियकद्दमभरिउ ॥
वहुमंसरासि किमिकीडहरु ।
खट्टहें वइरिउ भूमीहें भरु ॥
आहारहों पिसिवउ सीवियउ ।
णिसि मडउ दिवसें संजीवियउ ॥
णीसासूसासु करन्ताहुँ ।
गउ जम्मु जियन्तमरन्ताहुँ ॥

608

Her youth, that lotus-like face, that lovemaking with her
flexible hands—if these can no longer be enjoyed here
on earth, then life is utterly pointless."

6

Turning his face, the supreme master spoke, "Why do
you praise this woman as if she were a jewel? It is nice
enough for those who look on it from the outside;
on the inside it is bloody and moist, a stinking body,
appalling and impure, merely a bundle of bones with
skin. Through some magical contraption it walks
around and, pierced by nine tubes, it moves about. It
croaks with hundreds of joints in the eight forms of
karma and is filled with chyle, fat, blood, and slime, a
heap of copious flesh, a home for worms and insects, a
hostile weight for a couch and a burden for the earth,
a stitched-up sack of food, a corpse by night and alive
by day. For those who breathe in and out, who live and
die, life has passed.

मरणकालें किमिकप्परिउ
जें पेक्खेंवि मुहु वङ्किज्जइ ।
चिणिहिणन्तु मक्खियसऍहिँ
तं तेहउ केम रमिज्जइ ॥

७

तं चलणजुअलु गइमन्थरउ ।
सउणहिँ खज्जन्तु भयङ्करउ ॥
तं सुरयणियम्बु सुहावणउ ।
किमिविलविलन्तु चिलिसावणउ ॥
तं णाहिपएसु किसोयरउ ।
खज्जन्तमाणु थिउ भासुरउ ॥
तं जोव्वणु अवरुण्डणमणउ ।
सुज्जन्तु णवर भीसावणउ ॥
तं सुन्दरु वयणु जियन्ताहुँ ।
किमिकप्पिउ णवर मरन्ताहुँ ॥
तं अहरविम्बु वण्णुज्जलउ ।
लुञ्चन्तु सिवहिँ घिणिविट्टलउ ॥
तं णयणजुअलु विब्भमभरिउ ।
विच्छायउ काऍहिँ कप्परिउ ॥
सो चिहुरभारु कोड्डावणउ ।
उड्डुन्तु णवर भीसावणउ ॥

Seeing it torn up by maggots at the time of death and
buzzing with hundreds of flies, one grimaces; how
does one find pleasure in it?

7

"That pair of feet, slow in their gait, are horrible when
they are devoured by vultures. That pleasant,
tender buttock is disgusting, wriggling with worms.
That area near the navel, the slender waist, is
absolutely terrible when its pride is being consumed.
That youthfulness, that desire to embrace, is just
horrifying when the body swells up. That beautiful
face, when they are alive, is just torn up by maggots
when they are dead. Those round lips, beautiful on
the outside, are appalling and impure, being ripped to
bits by jackals. That pair of eyes, filled with coquetry,
become lusterless when they are torn out by crows.
That marvelous load of hair is just terrifying when it
flies away.

तं माणुसु तं मुहकमलु
ते थण तं गाढालिङ्गणु ।
णवर धरेप्पिणु णासउड्डु
वोल्लेवउ धिधि चिलिसावणु ॥

८

तहिँ तेहएँ रसवसपूयभरें ।
णव मास वसेवउ देहघरें ॥
णवणाहिकमलु उत्थल्लु जहिँ ।
पहिलउ जें पिण्डसंवन्धु तहिँ ॥
दसदिवसु परिट्ठिउ रुहिरजलें ।
कणु जेम पइण्णउ धरणियलें ॥
विहिँ दसरत्तेहिँ समुट्ठियउ ।
णं जलें डिण्डीरु परिट्ठियउ ॥
तिहिँ दसरत्तेहिँ बुब्बुउ घडिउ ।
णं सिसिरविन्दु कुङ्कुमें पडिउ ॥
दसरत्तें चउत्थएँ वित्थरिउ ।
णावइ पवलङ्कुरु णीसरिउ ॥
पञ्चमें दसरत्तें जाउ वलिउ ।
णं सूरणकन्दु चउप्फलिउ ॥
दसदसरत्तेहिँ करचरणसिरु ।
वीसहिँ णिप्पण्णु सरीरु थिरु ॥

That human being, that lotus-like face, those breasts, that firm embrace, one will say while holding one's nostrils, 'Damn it, damn it, it is disgusting.'

8

"For nine months one must reside there in such a body as a home, filled with chyle, fat, and pus. Where the navel rose up like a new lotus, there was first a merging into a ball. For ten days it remained in bloody water, like a seed sown into the earth's surface. After twenty days it rose up like foam settled on water. After thirty days a bubble formed, like a dollop of curd fallen in saffron. In the fourth period of ten days it grew, like a branch of coral that came forth. In the fifth period of ten days it became strong, like an elephant-foot yam bearing four fruits. After a hundred days there were hands, feet, and a head, and after two hundred the solid body

णवमासिउ देहहों णीसरिउ ।
वड्ढन्तु पडीवउ वीसरिउ ॥
जेण दुवारें आइयउ
जो तं परिहरेंवि ण सक्कइ ।
पन्तिहिँ जुत्तु वइलु जिह
[भव]संसारें भमन्तु ण थक्कइ ॥

९

ऍउ जाणेंवि धीरहि अप्पणउ ।
करें कङ्कणु जोवहि दप्पणउ ॥
चउगइसंसारें भमन्तऍण ।
आवन्तें जन्तमरन्तऍण ॥
जगें जीवें को ण रुवावियउ ।
को गरुअ धाह ण मुआवियउ ॥
को कहि मि णाहिँ संतावियउ ।
को कहि मि ण आवइ पावियउ ॥
को कहिं ण दड्ढु को कहिँ ण मुउ ।
को कहिँ ण भमिउ को कहिँ ण गउ ॥
कहिँ ण वि भोयणु कहिँ ण वि सुरउ ।
जगें जीवहों किं पि ण वाहिरउ ॥
तइलोक्कु वि असिउ असन्तऍण ।
महि सयल दड्ढु डज्झन्तऍण ॥

was completed. After nine months it left the body.
As it grew up, it forgot all of this.

He who is unable to forsake that entryway through which
he came does not stop wandering through samsara of
existence, like an ox tied to an oil press.

9

"Realize this and take comfort. Look at the bracelet on
your wrist, and at the mirror. Who has not been
brought to tears by a being in the world, wandering
in samsara with its four modes of existence, coming,
going, and dying? Who has not been moved to emit
deep sobs? Who has never been tormented? Who has
never been brought to distress? Who has not been
scorched somewhere? Who has not died somewhere?
Who has not roamed around somewhere? Who has
not passed away somewhere? Where has there been
no meal? Where has there been no lovemaking? For a
being in the world there is nothing aside from it. The
threefold world is eaten by one who eats. The entire
earth is burned by one who burns.

सायरु पीउ पियन्तऍण
अंसुऍहिँ रुअन्तें भरियउ ।
हड्डुकलेवरसंचऍण
गिरि मेरु सो वि अन्तरियउ ॥

१०

अहवइ किं वहुचविएण राम ।
भवें भमिउ भयङ्करें तुहु मि ताम ॥
णडु जिह तिह वहुरूवन्तरेहिँ ।
जरजम्मणमरणपरम्परेहिँ ॥
सा सीय वि जोणिसएहिँ आय ।
तुहुँ कहि मि वप्पु सा कहि मि माय ॥
तुहुँ कहि मि भाउ सा कहि मि वहिणि ।
तुहुँ कहि मि दइउ सा कहि मि घरिणि ॥
तुहुँ कहि मि णरऍ सा कहि मि सग्गें ।
तुहुँ कहि मि महिहिँ सा गयणमग्गें ॥
तुहुँ कहि मि णारि सा कहि मि जोहु ।
किं सिविणारिद्धिहें करहि मोहु ॥
उम्मेट्टु विओअगइन्दएसु ।
जगडन्तु भमइ जगु णिरवसेसु ॥
जइ ण धरिउ जिणवयणङ्कुसेण ।
तो खज्जइ माणुसु माणुसेण ॥

The ocean is drunk by one who drinks and filled with tears
by one who cries. Even Mount Meru is concealed
beneath a heap of bones and corpses.

10

"Or rather, what is the use of elaborate talk, Rama: for
now you too have roamed around through terrifying
existence in many different forms, just like an actor,
through successions of old age, birth, and death.
This Sita of yours also has passed through hundreds
of wombs. You were sometimes a father and she was
sometimes a mother; you were sometimes a brother
and she a sister; you were sometimes a husband and
she a wife; you were sometimes in hell, she in heaven;
you were sometimes on earth, she on the path of
heaven; you were sometimes a woman, she a warrior.
Are you bewildered from an abundance of dreams?
This enormous driverless elephant that is separation
wanders about besieging the entire earth. If he is not
restrained by the goad of the Jina's words, then a man
gets eaten by a man."

एम भणेप्पिणु वे वि मुणि
गय कहिं मि णहङ्गणपन्थें ।
रामु परिट्ठिउ किविणु जिह
धणु एक्कु लएवि सहत्थें ॥

११

विरहाणलजालपलित्ततणु ।
चिन्तेवएँ लग्गु विसण्णमणु ॥
सच्चउ संसारें ण अत्थि सुहु ।
सच्चउ गिरिमेरुसमाणु दुहु ॥
सच्चउ जरजम्मणमरणभउ ।
सच्चउ जीविउ जलविन्दुसउ ॥
कहों घरु कहों परियणु वन्धुजणु ।
कहों मायवप्पु कहों सुहिसयणु ॥
कहों पुत्तु मित्तु कहों किर घरिणि ।
कहों भाय सहोयर कहों वहिणि ॥
फलु जाव ताव वन्धव सयण ।
आवासिय पायवें जिह सउण ॥
वलु एम भणेप्पिणु णीसरिउ ।
रोवन्तु पडीवउ वीसरिउ ॥

Speaking thus, the two sages went away elsewhere along the path of the sky. Rama stood there like a pauper who has had a single valuable thing placed in his hand.

11

His body burning with flames from the fire of lovesickness and his heart dejected, he started to think, "There truly is no happiness in samsara. There truly is sadness as vast as Mount Meru. There truly is fear of old age, birth, and death. Life truly is a hundred drops of water. To whom belongs a house? To whom a retinue and relatives? To whom a mother and father? To whom friends and kinsmen? To whom a son or a friend? To whom indeed a wife? To whom brothers with whom one shared the womb? To whom a sister? As long as there is something to be had, there are relatives and kinsmen, like vultures sitting in a tree." Speaking thus, the Baladeva set out. As he cried, he forgot again.

णिद्दुणु लक्खणवज्जियउ
अण्णु वि वहुवसणेहिँ भुत्तउ ।
राहउ भमइ भुअङ्गु जिह
वणे हा हा सीय भणन्तउ ॥

१२

हिण्डन्तें भग्गमडप्फरेंण ।
वणदेवय पुच्छिय हलहरेंण ॥
खणें खणें वेयारहि काइँ मइँ ।
कहें कहि मि दिट्टु जइ कन्त पइँ ॥
वलु एम भणेप्पिणु संचलिउ ।
तावग्गएँ वणगइन्दु मिलिउ ॥
हे कुञ्जर कामिणिगइगमण ।
कहें कहि मि दिट्टु जइ मिगणयण ॥
णियपडिरवेण वेयारियउ ।
जाणइ सीयएँ हक्कारियउ ॥
कत्थइ दिट्ठइँ इन्दीवरइँ ।
जाणइ धणणयणइँ दीहरइँ ॥
कत्थइ असोयतरु हल्लियउ ।
जाणइ धणवाहाडोल्लियउ ॥
वणु सयलु गवेसेंवि सयल महि ।
पल्हट्टु पडीवउ दासरहि ॥

Without his beloved, without Lakshmana, and moreover consumed by many misfortunes, Rama, the descendant of Raghu, wandered about in the forest, saying, "Ah, ah, Sita," like a dissolute man without money or good qualities and consumed by his many vices.[4]

12

As the Baladeva walked around, his pride shattered, he asked the goddess of the forest, "Why do you mislead me again and again? Tell me if you have seen my beloved somewhere." Speaking thus, the Baladeva roamed. Then he encountered a forest elephant before him, "Hey elephant, who walks with the gait of a lovely lady, tell me if you have seen a deer-eyed woman somewhere." Deceived by his own echo, he thought that Sita called him. In one place he saw blue water lilies—he thought they were the wide eyes of his beloved. Elsewhere an *aśoka* tree swayed—he thought it shook with the arms of his beloved. Searching the entire forest and the entire earth, Rama, the son of Dasharatha, returned.

तं जि पराइउ णियभवणु
जहिँ अच्छिउ आसि लयत्थलें।
चावसिलिम्मुहमुक्ककरु
वलु पडिउ सइं भुवमण्डलें॥

The Baladeva arrived back at that abode of his where he had resided in the arbor. His hands let go his bow and arrows, and he himself fell to the ground.

चालीसमो संधि

दसरहतवकारणु
सव्वुद्धारणु
वज्जयण्णसम्मयभरिउ ।
जिणवरगुणकित्तणु
सीयसइत्तणु
तं णिसुणहु राहवचरिउ ॥

१

तं सन्तं गयागसं धीसं संतावपावसंतासं ।१?
चारुरुचाणएण वंदे देवं संसारघोरसासं ॥
असाहणं ।
कसायसोयसाहणं ॥
अवाहणं ।
पमायमायवाहणं ॥
अवन्दणं ।
तिलोयलोयवन्दणं ॥
अपुज्जणं ।
सुरिन्दरायपुज्जणं ॥
असासणं ।
तिलोयछेयसासणं ॥

Chapter 40

Listen to this biography of Rama, the descendant of Raghu, which uplifts all: it is the reason for Dasharatha's suffering, is filled with Vajrakarna's righteousness, proclaims the virtues of the great Jina, and has the upright behavior of Sita.

1

With prudence and brilliant splendor I salute that gentle lord, whose sins have vanished, master of his mind, frightening away anguish and evil, who holds back the horrors of samsara.[1]

Lacking any means, yet suppressing the passions and sorrow; without a vehicle, yet oppressing apathy and deceit; bowing to no one, yet revered by the folk of the three worlds; not worshiping others, yet worshiped by kings and the lords of the gods; untaught, yet teaching the clever people of the three worlds; without

अवारणं ।
अपेयभेयवारणं ॥
अणिन्दियं ।
जयप्पहुं अणिन्दियं ॥
महन्तयं ।
पचण्डवम्महन्तयं ॥
रवण्णयं ।
घणालिवारवण्णयं ॥
मुणिसुव्वयसामिउ
सुहगइगामिउ
तं पणवेप्पिणु दिढमणॆण ।
पुणु कहमि महव्वलु
खरदूसणवलु
जिह आयामिउ लक्खणॆण ॥

२

हिय एत्तहें वि सीय एत्तहें वि विओउ महन्तु राहवे ।
हरि एत्तहें वि भिडिउ एत्तहें वि विराहिउ मिलिउ आहवे ॥
ताव तेत्थु भीसावणे वणे ।
एक्कमेक्कहक्कारणे रणे ॥
कुरुडदिट्ठिवयणुब्भडे भडे ।
विरइए महावित्थडे थडे ॥

hindrance, yet warding off the harm caused by that which should not be drunk; the irreproachable lord of the world who transcends the senses, the great one who causes the downfall of fierce Kama, the god of lust; the agreeable one, with the complexion of masses of clouds or bees.

Bowing with a resolute heart to that master Muni Suvrata, who leads us to an auspicious existence, I again recount how Lakshmana overpowered the mighty army of Khara and Dushana.

2

When Sita was taken, that was a great loss for Rama; the Vasudeva was fighting; Viradhita turned up in the battle.

All the while in that terrifying forest, in the war where one man challenged another, a soldier was intense in his cruel glance and face, a troop took up a widespread position, a horrifying sound raged, a chest suffered with blows and maimed limbs, a massive shield fell

वावरन्तभयभासुरे सुरे ।
जज्जरङ्घपहराउरे उरे ॥
असिसवाहुपडियप्फरे फरे ।
जम्पमाणकडुअक्खरे खरे ॥
दलियकुम्भवियलङ्घए गए ।
सिरु धुणाविए आहए हए ॥
रुहिरविन्दुचच्चिक्किए किए ।
सायरे व्व सुरमन्थिए थिए ॥
छत्तदण्डसयखण्डखण्डिए ।
हड्डुरुण्डविच्छड्डुमण्डिए ॥
तहिँ महाहवे घोरदारुणे ।
दिट्ठु वीरु पहरन्तु साहणे ॥
तिलु तिलु कप्परियइँ
उरें जज्जरियइँ
रत्तच्छइँ फुरियाणणइँ ।
दिट्ठुइँ गम्भीरइँ
सुहडसरीरइँ
सरसल्लियइँ सवाहणइँ ॥

628

together with sword and arm, as harsh and sharp-sounding words were spoken, where an elephant lay with mutilated body and slashed frontal globes, a horse was made to shake its head in battle, speckled with drops of blood, resembling the ocean churned by the gods, where umbrella sticks were shattered into hundreds of pieces, as it was bedecked with heaps of bones and headless corpses—in that dreadful, brutal great battle a warrior was seen battering the army. Dense bodies of soldiers were seen chopped into tiny pieces, torn up at the chest, with blood red eyes and quivering faces, pierced with arrows, along with their vehicles.

३

को वि सुभडु सतुरङ्गमु को वि सजाणु सल्लिओ ।
को वि पडन्तु दिट्ठु आयासहों लक्खणसरविरल्लिओ ॥
भडो को वि दिट्ठो परिच्छिन्नगत्तो ।
सदन्ती समन्ती सचिन्धो सछत्तो ॥
भडो को वि वावल्लभल्लेहिँ भिण्णो ।
भडो को वि कप्पदुमो जेम छिण्णो ॥
भडो को वि तिक्खग्गणारायविद्धो ।
महासत्थवन्तो व्व सत्थेहिँ विद्धो ॥
भडो को वि कुद्धाणणो विप्फुरन्तो ।
मरन्तो वि हक्कारडक्कार देन्तो ॥
भडो को वि भिण्णो सदेहो समत्थो ।
पमुच्छाविओ को वि कोवण्डहत्थो ॥
मुओ को वि कोवुब्भडो जीवमाणो ।
चलच्चामरच्छोहविज्जिज्जमाणो ॥
वसाकद्दमे मद्दवे को वि खुत्तो ।
खलन्तो वलन्तो णियन्तेहिँ गुत्तो ॥
भडो को वि भिण्णो खुरुप्पेहिँ एन्तो ।
णियत्तो कुसिद्धो व्व सिद्धिं ण पत्तो ॥१२

3

A warrior with a horse, and another with a vehicle was
    wounded; another could be seen falling from the sky,
    covered over by Lakshmana's arrows.
Another soldier could be seen as his body was ripped
    to bits, along with his elephant, his minister, his
    standard, and his umbrella; another was pierced by
    vāvallas and *bhallas;*[2] another was cut down like a
    wishing tree; another was shot through with sharp-
    tipped iron arrows, as wounded by weapons as a wise
    man is learned in teachings;[3] another was trembling
    with a face full of rage, emitting cries of provocation
    and defiance even though he was dying; another
    mighty soldier was shattered, along with his body;
    another was struck unconscious still holding his bow;
    another died who had been passionate with anger
    and fanned with multitudes of shaking flywhisks
    while alive; another sank into a softness of fat and
    mud, stumbling and turning, and covered in his own
    entrails; another soldier was pierced by knife-shaped
    arrows as he came near, checked like a failed Siddha
    who did not reach Siddhi.

लक्खणसरभरियउ
अद्धव्वरियउ
खरदूसणवलु दिट्ठु किह ।
साहारु ण वन्धइ
गमणु ण सन्धइ
णवलउ कामिणिपेम्मु जिह ॥

४

परधणपरकलत्तपरिसेसहुँ परवलसण्णिवायहुं ।
एक्कें लक्खणेण विणिवाइय सत्त सहास रायहुं ॥
जीवन्तएँ अद्धएँ वइरिसेण्णें ।
अद्धएँ दलवट्टिएँ महिणिसण्णें ॥
तहिँ अवसरें पवरजसाहिएण ।
जोक्कारिउ विण्हु विराहिएण ॥
पाइक्कहों वट्टइ एहु कालु ।
हउँ भिच्चु देव तुहुँ सामिसालु ॥
कहिओ ऽसि आसि जो चारणेहिँ ।
सो लक्खिओ ऽसि सइँ लोयणेहिँ ॥
तं सहल मणोरह अज्जु जाय ।
जं दिट्ठ तुहारा वे वि पाय ॥
णियजणणिहें हउँ गब्भत्थु जइउ ।
विणिवाइउ पिउ महु तणउ तइउ ॥

How did the army of Khara and Dushana seem, filled with
　　Lakshmana's arrows and only half remaining? Like
　　the naïve love of a beautiful lady: it could not draw
　　back, nor could it move forward.

4

Lakshmana alone struck down seven thousand kings, who
　　had abstained from the riches and wives of strangers,
　　and destroyed hostile armies.
As half of the enemy army survived and half lay
　　slaughtered on the ground, at that moment Viradhita,
　　abounding in excellent glory, sung the Vasudeva's
　　praise, "It is a good time to be a foot soldier. I am your
　　servant, lord, you are my master. I have observed
　　you with my own eyes: you are as the sky-wandering
　　seers have described. Today my wishes have become
　　fulfilled, that I have seen your two feet. When I was
　　in my mother's womb, my father was slain. Together
　　with my father the city of Patalalanka, renowned for

सहुँ ताएं महु पाइक्कपवरु ।
उद्दालिउ तमलङ्कारणयरु ॥
तें समरमहब्भयभीसणेहिँ ।
सहुँ पुव्ववइरु खरदूसणेहिँ ॥
जयलच्छिपसाहिउ
भणइ विराहिउ
पहु पसाउ महु पेसणहों ।
तुहुँ खरु आयामहि
रणउहें णामहि हउँ अब्भिट्टमि दूसणहों ॥

५

तं णिसुणेवि वयणु विज्जाहरु मम्भीसिउ कुमारेणं ।
वइसरु ताव जाव रिउ पाडमि एक्कें सरपहारेणं ॥
एउ सेण्णु खरदूसणकेरउ ।
वाणेहिँ करमि अज्जु विवरेरउ ॥
सधउ सवाहणु सपहु सहत्थें ।
लायमि सम्बुकुमारहों पन्थें ॥
तुज्झु वि जम्मभूमि दरिसावमि ।
तमलङ्कारणयरु भुञ्जावमि ॥
हरिवयणेहिँ हरिसिउ विज्जाहरु ।
चलणेहिँ पडिउ सीसें लाएँवि करु ॥

its foot soldiers, was taken away from me. Hence I
have an old feud with Khara and Dushana, both most
horrifying in battle."
Endowed with the glory of victory, Viradhita said, "Lord,
please, my service: you defeat Khara and bring
him into submission on the battlefront. I will fight
Dushana."

5

Hearing those words, the youth Lakshmana reassured
the Vidyadhara, "Have a seat while I strike down the
enemy with a single arrow's blow.
Now I will reduce this army of Khara and Dushana with
arrows. With its flags, vehicles, and lords, I, with
my own hand, will lead it along Prince Shambuka's
path. I will show you the land of your birth and let
you rule the city of Patalalanka." The Vidyadhara was
delighted by the Vasudeva's words. He fell at his feet,
accepting his hand on his head. Meanwhile, Khara,
accomplished in battle, mounted on his celestial
chariot, asked his minister, "Who is that courageous

ताव खरेण समरें णिव्वूढें ।
पुच्छिउ मन्ति विमाणारूढें ॥
दीसइ कवणु एहु वीसत्थउ ।
णरु पणमन्तु कियञ्जलिहत्थउ ॥
वाहुवलेण वलेण विवलियउ ।
णं खयकालु कियन्तहों मिलियउ ॥
पभणइ मन्ति विमाणें पइट्ठउ ।
किं पइँ वइरि कयावि ण दिट्ठउ ॥
णामेण विराहिउ
पवरजसाहिउ
वियडवच्छु थिरथोरभुउ ।
अणुराहाणन्दणु
सवलु ससन्दणु
ऍहु सो चन्दोअरहों सुउ ॥

६

मन्तिणिवाण विहि मि अवरोप्परु ए आलाव जार्वेहिं ।
विण्हुविराहिएहिँ आयामिउ परवलु सयलु तार्वेहिं ॥
तो खरो ऽरिमट्ठणेण ।
कोक्किओ जणट्ठणेण ॥
एत्तहे ससन्दणेण ।
सो ऽणुराहणन्दणेण ॥

636

man who I can see, bowing with hands cupped in
reverence? With an army he is turned toward the
mighty-armed one, as if the time of destruction has
come together with Yama, the terminator." The
minister, who sat in the celestial chariot, said, "Did
you not once see the enemy?

He is called Viradhita, abounding in excellent glory, with a
vast chest and firm, strong arms, Anuradha's greatest
joy, together with an army and chariots. He is the son
of Chandrodara."

6

In the time it took for these words to pass between the
minister and the king, the Vasudeva and Viradhita
overpowered the entire enemy army.

Next the Vasudeva, destroyer of foes, challenged Khara.
Then, with his chariot, Viradhita, that son of
Anuradha, skilled in war, wielding a bow and arrows,

आहवे समत्थयेण ।
चाववाणहत्थयेण ॥
गुञ्जवण्णलोयणेण ।
भीसणावलोयणेण ॥
कुम्भिकुम्भदारणेण ।
पुव्ववइरकारणेण ॥
दूसणो जसाहिवेण ।
कोक्किओ विराहिएण ॥
एहु वे हओ हयस्स ।
चोइओ गओ गयस्स ॥
वाहिओ रहो रहस्स ।
धाइओ णरो णरस्स ॥
सगुडससण्णाहइँ
कवयसणाहइँ
सप्पहरणइँ सवाहणइँ ।
णियवइरु सरेप्पिणु
हक्कारेप्पिणु
भिडियइँ वेण्णि मि साहणइँ ॥

his eyes the color of crab's-eye beans, with a terrifying glance, a crusher of elephants' frontal globes, abounding in fame, challenged Dushana on account of their former feud. At once a horse was urged toward a horse, an elephant toward an elephant, a chariot was driven toward a chariot, a man ran toward a man.

With their weapons and vehicles, harnesses for their animals and accoutrements, and protected by armor, the two armies attacked, calling out and remembering their hostility.

सेण्णहों भिडिउ सेण्णु दूसणहों विराहिउ खरहों लक्खणो ।
हय पडु पडह तूर किउ कलयलु गलगम्भीरभीसणो ॥
तहिँ रणसंगमें ।
वुण्णतुरङ्गमें ॥
रहगयगोन्दलें ।
वज्जियमन्दलें ॥
भडकडमट्टणें ।
मोडियसन्दणें ॥
णरवरदण्डिएँ ।
कियकिलिविण्डिएँ ॥
वालालुञ्छिएँ ।
रहसयखञ्छिएँ ॥
तहिँ अपरायण ।
खरणारायण ॥
भिडिय महव्वल ।
वियडउरत्थल ॥
वे वि समच्छर ।
वे वि भयङ्कर ॥
वे वि अकायर ।
वे वि जसायर ॥
वे वि महब्भड ।
वे वि अणुब्भड ॥

7

Army attacked army, Viradhita attacked Dushana,
    Lakshmana attacked Khara. Shrill drums were struck.
    A murmur rose up, terrifyingly deep from throats.
In that battle, with quivering horses, the bustle of chariots
    and elephants, beaten *mardala* drums, the crushing
    of soldiers, demolished chariots, in which great
    men were pounded, fights were fought, hair was
    torn out, and hundreds of chariots were steered, the
    insurmountable, mighty Khara and Vasudeva, with
    their vast chests, attacked each other. Both were full
    of wrath, horrifying, audacious, mines of fame, great
    soldiers, humble, archers, unrestrainable.

वे वि धणुद्धर ।
वेण्णि वि दुद्धर ॥
वेण्णि वि जसलुद्धा
अमरिसकुद्धा
तिहुयणमल्ल समावडिय ।
अमरिन्ददसाणण
विप्फुरियाणण
णाइँ परोप्परु अब्भिडिय ॥

८

ताम जणद्दणेण अद्धेन्दु विसज्जिउ रणे भयङ्करो ।
णं खयकालें कालु उद्धाइउ तिहुअणजणखयङ्करो ॥
संचल्लु वाणु ।
णहयलसमाणु ॥
रिउरहहों ढुक्कु ।
खरु कह वि चुक्कु ॥
सारहि वि भिण्णु ।
धयदण्डु छिण्णु ॥
धणुहरु वि भग्गु ।
कत्थ वि ण लग्गु ॥
पाडिउ विमाणु ।
विज्जएँ समाणु ॥

Desirous for glory and furious with indignation, these two
   prizefighters of the three worlds rushed forth, just like
   the lord of the Gods and Ravana, the ten-faced, fought
   each other with trembling faces.

8

Then the Vasudeva fired a dreadful *ardhacandra*-arrow
   in the midst of the fight. Like Death at the time of
   destruction, annihilating the people of the three
   worlds, it rushed forth.
The arrow shot up as high as the sky. It sped toward
   his enemy's chariot. Somehow Khara escaped. His
   charioteer was hit, the flagstaff shattered, the bow
   broken, but somehow it did not touch him. The
   celestial chariot was struck down together with the

खरु विरहु जाउ ।
थिउ असिसहाउ ॥
धाइउ तुरन्तु ।
मुहविप्फुरन्तु ॥
एत्तहें वि तेण ।
णारायणेण ॥
तं सूरहासु ।
किउ करें पगासु ॥
अब्भिट्ट वे वि ।
असिवरइं लेवि ॥
णाणाविहथाणेंहिँ
णियविण्णाणेंहिँ
वावरन्ति असिगहियकर ।
कसणङ्घय दीसिय
विज्जुविहूसिय
णं णवपाउसें अम्वुहर ॥

९

हत्थि व उद्धसोण्ड सीह व लङ्गूलवलग्गकन्धरा ।
णिट्ठुर महिहर व्व अइखार समुद्द व अहि व दुद्धरा ॥
अब्भिट्ट वे वि सोण्डीर वीर ।
संगामधीर ॥

vidyā. Khara had become chariotless. He stood there with his sword as his sole companion, then quickly ran forward, quivering in his face. Then that Vasudeva made Suryahasa appear in his hand. The two fought, holding their excellent swords.

As they clutched their swords in their hands, they focused on their skills in different positions. With their dark bodies they appeared like rainclouds in the new monsoon adorned with lightning.

9

Like elephants with trunks held high, like lions with necks stretched above their tails, hard like mountains, acrid like oceans, unrestrainable like snakes,

एत्थन्तरें अमरवरङ्गणाहँ ।
हरिसियमणाहँ ॥
अवरोप्परु वोल्लालाव हुय ।
कहों गुण पहूय ॥
तं णिसुणेंवि कुवलयणयणियाएँ ।
ससिवयणियाएँ ॥
णिब्भच्छिय अच्छर अच्छराएँ ।
वहुमच्छराएँ ॥
खरु मुएंवि अण्णु किं को वि सूरु ।
परसिमिरचूरु ॥
अण्णेक्कु पजम्पिय तक्खणेण ।
सहुँ लक्खणेण ॥
खरु गद्दहु किह किज्जइ समाणु ।
जो अघडमाणु ॥
एत्थन्तरें णिसियरकुलपईवें ।
खरु पहउ गीवें ॥
कोवाणलणालउ
कलिकण्टालउ
दसणसकेसरु अहरदलु ।
महुमहणसरग्गें
असिणहरग्गें
खुण्टेंवि घत्तिउ सिरकमलु ॥

the two proud heroes, skillful in combat, attacked. Words
were exchanged between the beautiful women of
the gods, their hearts delighted, "Whose qualities
are superior?" At this, an *apsaras* with eyes like blue
water lilies and a face like the moon, full of wrath,
scolded another *apsaras,* "Is there another hero apart
from Khara who can pulverize the royal camp of the
enemy?" The other replied immediately, "How can
that donkey Khara, who has never accomplished
anything, be compared to Lakshmana?" Then Khara,
the light of the Rakshasa dynasty, was struck in the
neck.

His lotus-like head, his fiery anger its stalk, his wrath its
thorns, his teeth its filaments, and his lips its petals,
was flung, struck off by the tip of the Vasudeva's arrow
and the crooked point of his sword.

एत्तहें लक्खणेण विणिवाइउ णिसियरसेण्णसारओ ।
एत्तहें दूसणेण किउ विरहु विराहिउ विण्णि वारओ ॥
छुडु छुडु समरें परज्जिउ साहणु ।
रहगयवाहणु ॥
छुडु छुडु जीवगाहि आयामिउ ।
परवलसामिउ ॥
छुडु छुडु चिहुरहँ हत्थु पसारिउ ।
कह वि ण मारिउ ॥
ताव खरहों सिरु खुडेँवि महाइउ ।
लक्खणु धाइउ ॥
णियसाहणें मम्भीस करन्तउ ।
रिउ कोक्कन्तउ ॥
दूसण पहरु पहरु जइ सक्कहि ।
अहिमुहु थक्कहि ॥
तं णिसुणेवि वयणु आरुट्ठउ ।
चित्तें दुट्ठउ ॥
वलिउ णिसिन्दु गइन्दु व सीहहों ।
रणसयलीहहों ॥

10

Here Lakshmana struck down the leader of the Rakshasa
army; there Dushana twice made Viradhita
chariotless.

Slowly but surely, his army with its chariots, elephants,
and vehicles, succumbed in the fight; bit by bit the
lord of the hostile army was being captured alive; little
by little his hand stretched out toward his hair, but
somehow he was not killed. Meanwhile, after cutting
off Khara's head, magnanimous Lakshmana rushed
forth, bringing reassurance in his army and calling out
the enemy, "Dushana, attack, attack if you can! Take
up position before me!" Hearing those words, the
Rakshasa lord, enraged and wicked at heart, turned
around like an enormous elephant to a lion, with
scratches from hundreds of fights.

दससन्दणजाएं
वरणाराएं
वियडउरत्थलें विद्धु अरि ।
रेवाजलवाहें
मयरसणाहें
णाइँ वियारिउ विज्झइरि ॥

११

उद्धुअपुच्छदण्डवेयण्डरसन्तयमत्तवाहणं ।
पाडिएँ अतुलमल्लें खरें दूसणें पडियमसेससाहणं ॥
सत्त सहास भिडन्तें मारिय ।
दूसणेण सहुँ सत्त वियारिय ॥
चउदह सहस णरिन्दहुँ घाइय ।
णं कप्पदुम व्व विणिवाइय ॥
मण्डिय मेइणि णरवरछत्तेहिँ ।
णावइ सरयलच्छि सयवत्तेहिँ ॥
कत्थइ रत्तारत्त पदीसिय ।
णाइँ विलासिणि घुसिणविहूसिय ॥
तो एत्थन्तरें रहगयवाहणें ।
कलयलु घुट्टु विराहियसाहणें ॥
दिण्णाणन्दभेरि अणुराएं ।
रणु परिअञ्झिउ दसरहजाएं ॥

Dasharatha's son struck his enemy in his vast chest with
    an excellent iron arrow, like the Vindhya mountains
    cleft by the river Narmada, inhabited by crocodiles.

11

Now that those unequaled prizefighters, Khara and
    Dushana, were annihilated, their whole army fell, with
    roaring, rutting elephants as vehicles, their club-like
    tails raised up.
Seven thousand were killed by Lakshmana as he fought;
    seven thousand torn to pieces along with Dushana.
    Fourteen thousand great men were slaughtered, felled
    like wishing trees. The earth was covered with the
    umbrellas of those great men, like the luster of a lake
    with lotuses. Elsewhere it appeared red with blood,
    like a wanton lady adorned with saffron. Thereupon
    in Viradhita's army, with its chariots, elephants, and
    vehicles, a clamor resounded. The kettledrum of
    joy was beaten with passion. Dasharatha's son went

चन्दोअरसुअ महु करें वुत्तउ ।
ताम महाहवें अच्छु मुहुत्तउ ॥
जाव गवेसमि भाइ महारउ ।
सहुँ वइदेहिएँ पाणपियारउ ॥
खरदूसण मारेंवि
जिणु जयकारेंवि
लक्खणु रामहों पासु गउ ।
णं तिहुअणु घाएँवि
जमपहें लाएँवि
कालु कियन्तहों सम्मुहउ ॥

१२

हलहरु लक्खणेण लक्खिज्जइ सीयासोयणिब्भरो ।
घत्तिय तोणवाण महिमण्डलें करपरिचत्तधणुहरो ॥
विओयसोयतत्तओ ।
करि व्व भग्गदन्तओ ॥
तरु व्व छिण्णडालओ ।
फणि व्व णिप्फणालओ ॥
गिरि व्व वज्जसूडिओ ।
ससि व्व राहुपीडिओ ॥
अपाणिउ व्व मेहओ ।
वणे विसण्णदेहओ ॥

652

around the battle, "Son of Chandrodara, do as I say: stay on the great battlefield for a moment, while I search for my brother, whom I love more than life, together with Videha's daughter."

Having killed Khara and Dushana and praised the Jina, Lakshmana went to Rama. It was as if Death, having slaughtered the three worlds and taking them along Yama's path, turned toward the god of death, the terminator.

12

Lakshmana saw the Baladeva, full of sorrow over Sita. He threw his arrows and quivers to the ground; the bow dropped from his hand.

Afflicted by the pain of the separation, he was like an elephant with broken tusks, like a tree with cut-off branches, like a hoodless snake,[4] like a mountain struck by lightning, like the moon eclipsed by Rahu,

वलो सुमित्तिपुत्तिणं ।
पपुच्छियो तुरन्तिणं ॥
ण दीसए विहङ्गओ ।
ससीयओ कहिं गओ ॥
सुणेवि तस्स जम्पियं ।
तमक्खिवयं ण जं पियं ॥
वणे विणट्ठु जाणई ।
ण को वि वत्त जाणई ॥
जो पक्खि रणे ऽज्जउ
दिण्णु सहेज्जउ
सो वि समरें संघारियउ ।
केणावि पचण्डें
दिढभुअदण्डें
णेवि तलप्पएँ मारियउ ॥

१३

ए आलाव जाव वट्टन्ति परोप्परु रामलक्खणे ।
ताव विराहिओ वि वलपरिमिउ पत्तु तहिं जि तक्खणे ॥
तो ताव कियञ्जलिहत्थएण ।
महिवीढोणामियमत्थएण ॥
वलएउ णमिउ विज्जाहरेण ।
जिणु जम्मणें जेम पुरन्दरेण ॥

like a cloud without water. Sumitri's son quickly
questioned the Baladeva with his dejected body in
the forest, "The bird is nowhere to be seen; where
did it go, together with Sita?" Hearing his words,
he explained that which was not pleasant, "Janaka's
daughter vanished in the forest. Nobody knows what
happened.

The bird, invincible in battle, the companion who was
delivered to us, was slain in battle. Some fierce man
with firm, club-like arms killed him with a blow,
taking her away."

13

At the very instant these words circulated between Rama
and Lakshmana, Viradhita arrived there, surrounded
by his army.

With his hands cupped in reverence and his head bent
toward the earth's surface, the Vidyadhara then
bowed to the Baladeva, like Indra to the Jina at his

आसीस देवि गुरुमलहरेण ।
सोमित्ति पपुच्छिउ हलहरेण ॥
सहुँ सेण्णें पणमिउ कवणु एहु ।
णं तारापरिमिउ हरिणदेहु ॥
तं वयणु सुणेप्पिणु पुरिससीहु ।
थिरथोरमहाभुअफलिहददीहु ॥
सब्भावें रामहों कहइ एम ।
चन्दोयरणन्दणु एहु देव ॥
खरदूसणारि महु परममित्तु ।
गिरि मेरु जेम थिरथोरचित्तु ॥
तो एम पसंसेंवि तक्खणेण ।
हिय जाणइ अक्खिउ लक्खणेण ॥
कहिँ कुडें लग्गेसमि
कहि मि गवेसमि
दइवें परम्मुहें किं करमि ।
वलु सीयासोएं
मरइ विओएं
एण मरन्तें हउँ मरमि ॥

birth. Expressing a blessing, the Baladeva, destroyer of grave evil, asked Sumitri's son, "Who is this who has bowed down together with his army, like the moon surrounded by the stars?" Hearing these words, the lion among men, his strong, firm, big arms like long iron clubs, sincerely said thus to Rama, "Lord, this is the son of Chandrodara, enemy of Khara and Dushana and my best friend, with a heart, firm and stable, like Mount Meru." After speaking these words of praise, Lakshmana immediately said, "Janaka's daughter has been taken.

Whom shall I pursue? I go and search somewhere. What do I do when fate is unfavorable? The Baladeva is dying from sorrow over Sita, from his separation. If he dies, I die."

तं णिसुणेवि वयणु चिन्ताविउ चन्दोयरहॊ णन्दणो ।
विमणु विसण्णदेहु गहपीडिउ णं सारङ्गलञ्छणो ॥

जं जं किं पि वत्थु आसङ्घमि ।
तं तं णिप्फलु कहिँ अवठम्भमि ॥

एय मुएवि कालु किह खेविउ ।
णिद्धणॊ वि वरि वड्ढु सेविउ ॥

होउ म होउ तो वि ओलग्गमि ।
मुणि जिह जिण दिठु चलणहिँ लग्गमि ॥

विहि केत्तडउ कालु विणडेसइ ।
अवसें कं दिवसु वि सिय होसइ ॥

एम भणेवि वुत्तु णारायणु ।
कुढें लग्गेवउ केत्तिउ कारणु ॥

ताव गवेसहुँ जाम णिहालिय ।
लहु सण्णाहभेरि अप्फालिय ॥

साहणु दसदिसेहिँ संचल्लिउ ।
आउ पडीवउ जयसिरिमेल्लिउ ॥

जोइसचक्कु णाइँ परियत्तउ ।
णं सिद्धत्तणु सिद्धि ण पत्तउ ॥

14

Hearing those words, Chandrodara's son reflected,
    heartbroken and his body dropping with dejection,
    like the moon afflicted by Rahu, the eclipser:
"Whatever thing I might resort to proves fruitless. Whom
    do I lean on? How might I spend my time if I forsake
    them? Better to serve a great man, even if he is poor.
    Be that as it may,[5] I offer my service like a sage to the
    Jinas, and firmly attach myself to their feet. For how
    long will fate waver? Surely someday there will be
    success." Speaking thus, he addressed the Vasudeva,
    "For what reason must you go in pursuit? We will
    search until she is spotted." Immediately he sounded
    the kettledrum for the call to arms. The army set out
    in the ten directions. It returned without the glory of
    victory. It was as if the zodiac had reversed its course,
    as if becoming a Siddha did not lead to Siddhi.

विज्जाहरसाहणु
सधउ सवाहणु
थिउ हेट्ठामुहु विमणमणु ।
हिमवाएं दड्ढउ
मयरन्दड्ढउ
णं कोमाणउ कमलवणु ॥

१५

वुत्तु विराहिएण सुरडामरें तिहुअणजणभयावणे ।
वण्णें णिवसहुँ ण होइ खरदूसणें मुएँ जीवन्तें रावणे ॥
सम्बुक्कु वहेॅवि असिरयणु लेवि ।
को जीवइ जममुहें पइसरेॅवि ॥
जहिँ अच्छइ इन्दइ भाणुकण्णु ।
पञ्चामुहु मउ मारिञ्चि अण्णु ॥
घणवाहणु जहिँ अक्खयकुमारु ।
सहसमइ विहीसणु दुण्णिवारु ॥
हणुवन्तु णीलु णलु जम्बवन्तु ।
सुग्गीउ समरभरउव्वहन्तु ॥
अङ्गङ्गयगवयगवक्ख जेत्थु ।
तहों वन्धु वहेॅवि को वसइ एत्थु ॥
वयणेण तेण लक्खणु विरुद्धु ।
गयगन्धें णाइँ मइन्दु कुद्धु ॥

With its flags and vehicles the Vidyadhara army stood
there with dejected hearts and all faces turned toward
the ground, like a withered lotus cluster, abounding in
filaments, scorched by a frosty wind.

15

Viradhita said, "Khara and Dushana may have been killed,
but Ravana, the scourge of the Gods, who terrifies the
people of the three worlds, remains alive. We should
not stay in the forest.
Having killed Shambuka, having taken the jewel-like
sword, who remains alive having entered into
the mouth of Yama? Where there is Indrajit,
Kumbhakarna, Panchamukha, Maya, and also
Maricha, Ghanavahana, Prince Akshata, Sahasramati,
and the unstoppable Vibhishana, Hanuman, Nila,
Nala, Jambavat, and Sugriva, elevating the weight
of battle, Anga, Angada, Gavaya, and Gavaksha.[6]
Who would stay here, after killing a relative of one of
them?" Infuriated by those words, Lakshmana was
like a lion enraged by the scent of an elephant, "Is a

सुट्ठु वि रुट्टेहिँ मयङ्कमेहिँ ।
किं रुम्भइ सीहु कुरङ्गमेहिँ ॥
रोमग्गु वि वङ्कु ण होइ जेहिँ ।
किं णिसियरसण्ढेहिँ गहणु तेहिँ ॥
जे णरवइ अक्खिवय
रावणपक्खिवय
ते वि रणङ्गणे णिट्ठवमि ।
छुड्डु दिन्तु णिरुत्तउ
जुज्झु महन्तउ
दूसणपन्थें पट्टवमि ॥

१६

भणइ पुणो वि एम विज्जाहरु अच्छेवि किं करेसहुँ ।
तमलङ्कारणयरु पइसेप्पिणु जाणइ तहिँ गवेसहुँ ॥
वलु वयणेण तेण सहुँ साहणेण संचल्लिउ ।
णाइँ महासमुद्दु जलयररउद्दु उत्थल्लिउ ॥
दिण्णाणन्दभेरि पडिवक्खखेरि खरवज्जिय ।
णं मयरहरवेल कल्लोलवोल गलगज्जिय ॥
उब्भिय कणयदण्ड धुव्वन्त धवल धुअधयवड ।
रसमसकसमसन्त तडतडयडन्त कर गयघड ॥
कत्थइ खिलिहिलन्त हय हिलिहिलन्त णीसरिया ।
चञ्चलचडुलचवल चलवलय पवल पक्खरिया ॥

lion hindered by even the most agitated elephants, or
by deer? What do those unmanly Rakshasas count for;
not even the tips of their body hair are harsh.
The kings that you mentioned, who take the side of
Ravana: I will annihilate all of them on the battlefield.
Beyond doubt, I soon send them along the path of
Dushana, giving them great battle."

16

The Vidyadhara spoke again thus, "What will we do by
staying? After entering the city of Patalalanka, we can
search for Janaka's daughter from there."
At those words the Baladeva set out together with the
army, as if the great ocean, fierce with aquatic animals,
had risen up: a joyous kettledrum, with malice for
the adversary, resounded harshly as it was beaten,
thundering like the ocean's coast with copious waves;
golden staffs were raised, shaking and beautiful, with
fluttering flags; the elephant troop was trumpeting,
creaking, and roaring with their trunks; in one place
whinnying, neighing horses set out, capricious,
restless, and skittish, unsteady, powerful, and kitted

कत्थइ पहें पयट्टु दुग्घोट्टृथट्टृ मयभरिया ।
सिरें गुमुगुमुगुमन्त चुमुचुमुचुमन्त चञ्चरिया ॥
चन्दणवहलपरिमलामोयसेयकियकद्दमें ।
रहखुप्पन्तचक्कवित्थक्कछडयभडमद्दवें ॥
एम पयट्टु सिमिरु णं वहलतिमिरु उद्धाइउ ।
तमलङ्कारणयरु णिमिसन्तरेण संपाइउ ॥
पियविरहेण रामु अइखामखामु झीणङ्गउ ।
पयमग्गेण तेण कन्तहें तणेण णं लग्गउ ॥
दहवयणु ससीयउ
पाणहँ भीयउ
मज्झुडु एत्तहें णट्टु खलु ।
मेइणि विद्दारेवि
मग्गु समारेवि
णं पायालें पइट्ठु वलु ॥

१७

ताव पचण्डु वीरु खरदूसणणन्दणु तण्णिवारणो ।
सो सण्णहेवि सुण्डु पुरवारें परिट्ठिउ गहियपहरणो ॥
जं थक्कु सुण्डु रणमुहें रउद्दु ।
उद्धाइउ राहववलसमुद्दु ॥
णवर कलयलारवो उट्ठिओ दोहिँ सेण्णेहिँ अब्भिट्टमाणेहिँ जायं
च जुज्झं महागोन्दलुद्दामघोरारुणं मुक्कहाहारवं ॥१३

664

out; in another place the elephant troops, overflowing
with ichor, with bees humming and buzzing near their
heads, proceeded along a path that was muddled with
sandalwood juice, copious fragrances and perfumes,
and sweat, leaving a mire in which soldiers in hordes
got stuck and wheels of chariots sank. Thus the army
set out, like a dense darkness rushing forth, and within
the blink of an eye it reached the city of Patalalanka.
Rama was completely and utterly wasted, his body
weakened from the separation of his beloved. He
followed that trail as if it were of the feet of his wife.
Tearing open the earth and forming a track, it was as if
the army entered into a Patala: perhaps wretched,
ten-faced Ravana fled here with Sita, fearing for his
life.

17

Then, to stop them, that fierce hero Sunda, the joy of
Khara and Dushana, putting on his armor, took up
position at the city gate, clutching his weapons.
While Sunda, dreadful at the battlefront, stood there, the
army of Rama, the descendant of Raghu, rushed forth
like the ocean. Immediately a murmur and crying
rose up—as the two armies attacked, battle erupted,
with a great bustle, cruel, terrible, and reddish; with
wails emitted; with hundreds of shrieking conches

विरसियसयसङ्खकंसालकोलाहलं काहलं टट्टरीझल्लरीमद्दलुल्लोल-
वज्जन्तभम्भीसभेरीसरुज्झाहुडुक्काउलं ॥
पसहियगयगिलकल्लोलगज्जन्तगम्भीरभीसावणोरालिमेल्ऌन्त-
रुण्टन्तघण्टाजुअं पाडियं मेट्टुपाइक्कयं भिण्णवच्छत्थलं ॥
सललियरहचक्कखोणीपखुप्पन्तधुप्पन्तचिन्धावलीहेमदण्डुज्जलं
चामरुच्छोहविज्जिज्जमाणं सजोहं महासन्दणावीढयं ॥
हिलिहिलियतुरङ्गमुव्वुणकण्णं चलं चञ्चलङ्गं महादुज्जयं
दुद्धरं दुण्णिरिक्खं महीमण्डलावत्तदेन्तं हयाणं वलं ॥
हुलिहलमुसलग्गकोन्तेहिँ अद्धेन्दुसूलेहिँ वावल्लभल्लेहिँ
णारायसल्लेहिँ भिण्णं करालं ललन्तन्तमालं असीसं
कवन्धं पणच्चावियं ॥
तहिँ सुन्दविराहिय
समरजसाहिय
अवरोप्परु वड्ढन्तकलि ।
पहरन्ति महारणे
मेइणिकारणे
णं भरहेसरवाहुवलि ॥

and the clatter of gongs; abounding in the clamor
of *kāhala, ṭaṭṭarī, jhallarī,* and *mardala* drums;
resounding *bhambhīsa* and *bherī* kettledrums, *saruñja*
and *huḍukka* drums;[7] and accompanied by buzzing
and droning bells, thundering deep and terrifyingly,
with waves of ichor from the elephants on which they
were mounted—an elephant driver was struck down,
his chest split open. The battle was glorious with
rows of standards and golden sticks that were borne
down and polished in the earth by the playful wheels
of the chariots, and fanned by waves of flywhisks,
with soldiers and seats of grand chariots; the restive
cavalry, with neighing horses, trembling ears, and
skittish bodies, was almost impossible to defeat,
unrestrainable, and unsightly, furrowing the earth; a
horrifying headless corpse with dangling garlands of
entrails was made to dance, struck by knives, plows,
the tips of maces, lances, *ardhacandra*-arrows, spears,
vāvallas, bhallas, iron arrows, and spikes.

There Sunda and Viradhita, abounding in military glory,
their mutual wrath surging, attacked in a great
battle for the sake of the land, like Lord Bharata and
Bahubali.[8]

१८

चन्दणहाएँ ताव जुज्झन्तु णिवारिउ णियणन्दणो ।
दीसइ ओहु जोहु खरदूसणसम्बुकुमारमद्दणो ॥

जुज्झेवउ सुन्द ण होइ कज्जु ।
जीवन्तहँ होसइ अण्णु रज्जु ॥

वरि गम्मिणु सुरपञ्चाणणासु ।
कूवारउ करहु दसाणणासु ॥

ओसरिउ सुण्डु वयणेण तेण ।
गउ लङ्कु पराइउ तक्खणेण ॥

एत्थु सविराहिउ पइट्ठु रामु ।
णं कामिणि जणु मोहन्तु कामु ॥

खरदूसणमन्दिरें पइसरेवि ।
चन्दोयरपुत्तहों रज्जु देवि ॥

साहारु ण वन्धइ कहिं मि रामु ।
वइदेहिविओएं खामु खामु ॥

रहितिक्कचउक्केँहिँ परिभमन्तु ।
दीहियविहारमढ परिहरन्तु ॥

गउ ताम जाम जिणभवणु दिट्ठु ।
परिअञ्चेवि अब्भन्तरें पइट्ठु ॥

18

Then Chandranakhi stopped her fighting son, "I see
   the soldier who killed Khara, Dushana, and Prince
   Shambuka.
Sunda, it is not good to fight. If we stay alive, there will
   be another kingdom. Better we go and complain to
   ten-faced Ravana, the lion to the Gods." At these
   words, Sunda fled. He went to Lanka and arrived
   there in an instant. Here Rama entered together
   with Viradhita, like Kama, the god of love, bringing
   bewilderment to the lovely ladies. Entering into the
   palace of Khara and Dushana and bestowing the
   kingship onto Chandrodara's son, Rama did not share
   excitement. He was completely wasted from the
   separation from Videha's daughter. Wandering about
   on the highway and at the junctions of three and four
   roads, leaving behind the oblong tanks, monasteries,
   and religious institutes, he went until he saw a Jina
   temple. Circling it, he went inside.

जिणवरु णिज्झाऍवि
चित्तें झाऍवि
जाइ णिरारिउ विउलमइ ।
आहुट्टेंहिँ भासेंहिँ
थोत्तसहासेंहिँ
थुअउ सयं भुवणाहिवइ ॥

Meditating on the great Jina and reflecting with his mind, he became completely broad-minded. He glorified the lord of the world himself with thousands of hymns of praise in three and a half languages.[9]

एक्कचालीसमो संधि

खरदूसण गिलेंवि
चन्दणिहिहें तित्ति ण जाइय ।
णं खयकालछुह
रावणहों पडीवी धाइय ॥

सम्वुकुमारवीरें अत्थन्तएँ ।
खरदूसणसंगामें समत्तएँ ॥
दूरोसारिएँ सुन्दमहव्वलें ।
तमलङ्कारणयरु गएँ हरिवलें ॥
एत्थ ऍ असुरमहें सुरडामरें ।
लङ्काहिवें वहुलद्धमहावरें ॥
परवलवलपवणाहिन्दोलणें ।
वइरिसमुद्दरउद्दविरोलणें ॥
मुक्कङ्कुसमयगलगलथलुणें ।
दाणरणङ्कणें हत्थुत्थलुणें ॥
विहडियभडथडकियकडमद्दणें ।
कामिणिजणमणणयणाणन्दणें ॥
सीयएँ सहु सुरवरसंतावणें ।
छुडु छुडु लङ्क पइट्ठएँ रावणें ॥

672

Chapter 41

Chandranakhi was not satisfied[1] that she had devoured Khara and Dushana. Like the hunger of the time of destruction she rushed back to Ravana.

1

Now that the heroic prince Shambuka was dead, Khara and Dushana's war was over, the formidable Sunda had been chased far away, and the Vasudeva and the Baladeva had gone to the city of Patalalanka, as that Rakshasa brawler, the scourge of the Gods, the king of Lanka, who had received many great rewards, stirred up a cyclone among several enemy armies, churned the dreadful ocean of his foes, vanquished elephants that had slipped their goads, who had dismissed with a wave of his hand the battlefield won with bribery, annihilated troops of soldiers, and brought joy to the minds and eyes of the lovely womenfolk, that tormentor of the great Gods, Ravana, had in due course entered Lanka together with Sita—

तहिँ अवसरें चन्दणहि पराइय ।
णिवडिय कमकमलेहिँ दुहघाइय ॥
सम्बुकुमारु मुउ
खरदूसण जमपहें लाइय ।
पइँ जीवन्तएँण
एही अवत्थ हउँ पाइय ॥

२

तं चन्दणहिहें वयणु दयावणु ।
णिसुणेॅवि थिउ हेट्टामुहु रावणु ॥
णं मयलञ्छणु णिप्पहु जायउ ।
गिरि व दवग्गिदड्ढु विच्छायउ ॥
णं मुणिवरु चारित्तविभट्टउ ।
भविउ व भवसंसारहों तट्टउ ॥
वाहभरन्तणयणु मुहकायरु ।
गहेॅण गहिउ णं हूउ दिवायरु ॥
दुक्खु दुक्खु दुक्खेणामेल्लिउ ।
सयणसणेहु सरन्तु पवोल्लिउ ॥
घाइउ जेण सम्बु खरु दूसणु ।
तं पट्टवमि अज्जु जमसासणु ॥
अहवइ एण काइँ माहप्पें ।
को वि ण मरइ अपूरें मप्पें ॥

at that very moment Chandranakhi arrived. Crushed
by sorrow, she fell at his lotus-like feet,
"Prince Shambuka is dead; Khara and Dushana were
taken along Yama's path. Though you still are alive, I
have been brought to this state."

2

Hearing those lamentable words of Chandranakhi, Ravana
stood there, his face turned toward the ground,
like the moon that had lost its luster, like a gloomy
mountain burned by forest fires, like a great sage
strayed from good behavior, like a man capable of
salvation yet frightened of the cycle of rebirth. His
eyes filling with tears and his face perplexed, he was
like the sun seized by Rahu the eclipser. With great
difficulty sorrow let go of him. Remembering his
affection for his relatives, he spoke, "This very day I
will send Yama's punishment to the one who killed
Shambuka, Khara, and Dushana. Or rather, why be so
high-minded? Who does not die too early?[2] Be brave,
ignore the pain. For whom is there no birth, death,
and separation?

धीरी होहि पमायहि सोओ ।
कासु ण जम्मणमरणविओओ ॥
को वि ण वज्जमउ
जाएं जीवें मरिएवउ ।
अम्हेहिँ तुम्हेहिँ मि
खरदूसणपहें जाएवउ ॥

३

धीरेंवि णियय वहिणि सियमाणणु ।
रयणिहिँ गउ सोवणएँ दसाणणु ॥
वरपलङ्कें चडिउ लङ्केसरु ।
णं गिरिसिहरें मइन्दु सकेसरु ॥
णं विसहरु णीसासु मुअन्तउ ।
णं सज्जणु खलखेइज्जन्तउ ॥
सीयामोहें मोहिउ रावणु ।
गायइ वायइ पढइ सुहावणु ॥
णच्चइ हसइ वियारेंहिँ भज्जइ ।
णियभूअहुँ जि पडीवउ लज्जइ ॥
दंसणणाणचरित्तविरोहउ ।
इहलोयहों परलोयहों दोहउ ॥
मयणपरव्वसु एउ ण जाणइ ।
जिह संघारु करेसइ जाणइ ॥

No one is made of diamonds. A being that is born must
die. We too, as will you, have to go along the path of
Khara and Dushana."

3

Comforting his sister, ten-faced Ravana, celebrating his
glory, that night went off to sleep. The lord of Lanka
climbed onto his excellent bed, like a maned lion onto
the top of a mountain, sighing like a hissing snake,
afflicted like a good person by a wretch. Ravana was
stupefied by his infatuation with Sita. He joyfully
sang, played music, and recited. He danced, laughed,
and was wrecked by his feelings. Still, he also felt
shame for what he had become.[3] It was an obstruction
to correct insight, knowledge, and behavior, a malice
against this world and the other. Overpowered by
love, he could not realize that Janaka's daughter would
be the cause of his destruction. He was pierced by

अच्छइ मयणसरेंहिँ जज्जरियउ ।
खरदूसणणाउ मि वीसरियउ ॥
चिन्तइ दहवयणु
धणु धण्णु सुवण्णु समत्थउ ।
रज्जु वि जीविउ वि
विणु सीयएँ सव्वु णिरत्थउ ॥

४

तहिँ अवसरेँ आइय मन्दोवरि ।
सीहहों पासु व सीहकिसोयरि ॥
वरगणियारि व लीलागामिणि ।
पियमाहविय व महुरालाविणि ॥
सारङ्गि व विप्फारियणयणी ।
सत्तावीसंजोयणवयणी ॥
कलहंसि व थिरमन्थरगमणी ।
लच्छि व तियरूवेँ जूरवणी ॥
अह पोमाणिहेँ अणुहरमाणी ।
जिह सा तिह एह वि पउराणी ॥
जिह सा तिह एह वि वहुजाणी ।
जिह सा तिह एह वि वहुमाणी ॥
जिह सा तिह एह वि सुमणोहर ।
जिह सा तिह एह वि पियसुन्दर ॥

the arrows of Kama, the god of love, and even forgot
Khara and Dushana's names.

Ravana thought to himself, "Riches, grain, gold,
everything, even kingship and life, it is all useless
without Sita."

4

At that instant Mandodari arrived, a slim-waisted lioness
to her lion, walking gracefully like a beautiful elephant
cow, with a sweet voice like a female cuckoo, wide
eyes like a doe's, a face like the moon, a steady, slow
gait like a goose, like the tormentress Lakshmi in her
woman-form. Moreover, she resembled Paulomi.*
Like her, she too was an older lady, possessed great
knowledge, was greatly respected, very charming,

---

* Wife of the god Indra.

जिह सा तिह एह वि जिणसासणॆ ।
जिह सा तिह एह वि ण कुसासणॆ ॥
किं वहुजम्पिऍण
उवमिज्जइ काहॆ किसोयरि ।
णियपडिछन्दऍण
थिय सइँ जें णाइँ मन्दोयरि ॥

५

तहिँ पल्हड्डॆँ चडेॆवि रज्जेसरि ।
पभणिय लङ्कापुरपरमेसरि ॥
अहॊ दहमुह दहवयण दसाणण ।
अहॊ दससिर दसास सियमाणण ॥
अहॊ तइलॊक्कचक्कचूडामणि ।
वइरिमहीहरखरवज्जासणि ॥
वीसपाणि णिसियरणरकेसरि ।
सुरमिगवारणदारणअरिकरि ॥
परणरवरपायारपलॊट्टण ।
दुद्दमदाणववलदलवट्टण ॥
जइयहुँ भिडिउ रणङ्गणॆ इन्दहॊं ।
जाउ कुलक्खउ सज्जणविन्दहॊं ॥
तहिँ वि कालें पइँ दुक्खु ण णायउ ।
जिह खरदूसणमरणें जायउ ॥

cherished and beautiful, and observed the teaching
of the Jina and not any bad doctrine.
What more can be said? To whom did slim-waisted
Mandodari compare? She stood there as herself in
her own form.

5

Climbing onto the bed, the queen, supreme mistress
of the city of Lanka, said, "Ravana, with your ten
mouths, ten countenances, ten faces, you with
your ten heads, ten orifices, who honors glory, you
crest-jewel of the wheel of the threefold world, you
fierce lightning bolt to the mountain of the enemies,
with your twenty arms, a lion of a man among the
Rakshasas, a raging elephant who scatters those other
elephants, the Gods, you who topples the ramparts
of great men who oppose you, crusher of the army of
unrestrainable demons, when you attacked Indra on
the battlefield and destruction arose for our family of
good men, even at that time you did not know sorrow
like that which has arisen with the death of Khara

भणइ पडीवउ णिसियरणाहो ।
सुन्दरि जइ ण करइ अवराहो ॥
तो हउँ कहमि तउ
णउ खरदूसणदुक्खु ऽच्छइ ।
एत्तिउ डाहु पर
जं मइँ वइदेहि ण इच्छइ ॥

६

तं णिसुणेवि वयणु ससिवयणएँ ।
पुणु वि हसेवि वुत्तु मिगणयणएँ ॥
अहॊ दहगीव जीवसंतावण ।
एउ अजुत्तु वुत्तु पइँ रावण ॥
किं जगॆ अयसपडहु अप्फालहि ।
उभय विसुद्ध वंस किं मइलहि ॥
किं णारइयहॊ णरएँ ण वीहहि ।
परधणु परकलत्तु जं ईहहि ॥
जिणवरसासणॆ पञ्च विरुद्धइँ ।
दुग्गइ जाइ णिन्ति अविसुद्धइँ ॥
पहिलउ वहु छज्जीवणिकायहुँ ।
वीयउ गम्मइ मिच्छावायहुँ ॥
तइयउ जं परदव्वु लइज्जइ ।
चउथउ परकलत्तु सेविज्जइ ॥

and Dushana." The lord of the Rakshasas then said,
"Beautiful woman, if it does not cause offense,
then I tell you: it is not sorrow for Khara and Dushana.
There is such burning pain only because the daughter
of Videha does not desire me."

6

Hearing those words, the deer-eyed woman with her
moon-like face again spoke as she laughed, "Ah,
Ravana, with your ten necks, tormentor of living
beings, what you say is improper. Do you strike the
drum of dishonor in the world? Do you defile both
of our virtuous dynasties? Do you not fear a hellish
existence in hell, that you desire another man's riches
and another man's wife? In the doctrine of the Jina
there are five forbidden inauspicious things that lead
to a bad mode of existence: first, there is the murder of
the six categories of life forms; second, that one thinks
of falsehoods; third, that one takes the possessions
of another man; fourth, that one has relations with
another man's wife; fifth, that there is no limit to one's

पञ्चमु णउ पमाणु घरवारहों ।
आयहिँ गम्मइ भवसंसारहों ॥
परलोएँ वि ण सुहु
इहलोएँ वि अयसपडाइय ।
सुन्दर होइ ण तिय
ऍयवेसें जमउरि आइय ॥

७

पुणु पुणु पिहुलणियम्व किसोयरि ।
भणइ हियत्तणेण मन्दोयरि ॥
जं सुहु कालकूडु विसु खन्तहुँ ।
जं सुहु पलयाणलु पइसन्तहुँ ॥
जं सुहु भवसंसारें भमन्तहुँ ।
जं सुहु णारइयहुँ णिवसन्तहुँ ॥
जं सुहु जमसासणु पेच्छन्तहुँ ।
जं सुहु असिपञ्झरें अच्छन्तहुँ ॥
जं सुहु पलयाणलमुहकन्दरें ।
जं सुहु पञ्झाणणदाढन्तरें ॥
जं सुहु फणिमाणिक्कु खुडन्तहुँ ।
तं सुहु एह णारि भुञ्जन्तहुँ ॥
जाणन्तो वि तो वि जइ वच्छहि ।
तो कज्जेण केण मइँ पुच्छहि ॥

684

household property. Because of these one continues
in the whirl of rebirth,
there is no happiness in the other world, and in this
world there is the flag of dishonor. The woman is not
beautiful, she is the city of Yama, the god of death,
that has arrived in disguise."

7

Again and again wide-hipped, slim-waisted Mandodari
spoke affectionately, "The happiness of those who
consume venom or poison, who enter the fire of
destruction, who wander around in the whirl of
rebirth, who live as hellish beings, who suffer Yama's
punishment, who reside within a cage of swords, the
happiness in the cave-mouth of the fire of destruction
or in the space between a lion's teeth, the happiness of
those who crush a snake's ruby, that is the happiness
of those who enjoy this woman. If you nevertheless
desire her even though you know this, then why do

तउ पासिउ किं कोइ वि वलियउ ।
जेण पुरन्दरो वि पडिक्खलियउ ॥
जं जसु आवडइ
तहों तं अणुराउ ण भज्जइ ।
जइ वि असुन्दरउ
जं पहु करेइ तं छज्जइ ॥

तं णिसुणेवि वयणु दहवयणें ।
पभणिय णारि विरिल्लियणयणें ॥
जइयहुँ गयउ आसि अचलिन्दहों ।
वन्दणहत्तिएँ परमजिणिन्दहों ॥
तइयहुँ दिट्ठु एक्कु मइँ मुणिवरु ।
णाउँ अणन्तवीरु परमेसरु ॥
तासु पासें वउ लइउ ण भञ्जमि ।
मण्डएँ परकलत्तु णउ भुञ्जमि ॥
अहवइ एण काइँ मन्दोअरि ।
जइ णन्दन्ति णियहि लङ्काउरि ॥
जइ मग्गहि धणु धण्णु सुवण्णउ ।
राउलु रिद्धिविद्धिसंपण्णउ ॥
जइ आरुहहि तुरङ्गगइन्देहिँ ।
जइ वन्दिज्जइ वन्दिणवन्देहिँ ॥
जइ मग्गहि णिक्कण्टउ रज्जु ।

you ask me? Is there anyone stronger than you, the one who checked Indra?

A man's attachment, once it has befallen him, cannot be destroyed.[4] For all that it may be improper, whatever the lord does is good."

8

Hearing these words, wide-eyed Ravana answered his wife, "I once went to Meru, the lord of mountains, to praise and revere the supreme lord Jina. There I saw a great sage, a supreme master named Anantavirya. I do not break the vow that I took with him: I do not enjoy another man's wife by force. Or rather, what is the use of this, Mandodari? If you see the city of Lanka rejoicing, if you strive for riches, grain, gold, a palace endowed with wealth and prosperity, if you climb onto horses and great elephants, if you are honored by bands of bards, if you strive for kingship without

जइ किर वि मइँ जियन्तेंण कज्जु ॥
सयलन्तेउरहों
जइ इच्छहि णउ रण्डत्तणु ।
तो वरि जाणइहें
मन्दोयरि करें दूअत्तणु ॥

९

तं णिसुणेंवि वयणु दहवयणहों ।
पभणिय मन्दोयरि पुरि मयणहों ॥
हो हो सव्वु लोउ जगें दूहउ ।
पइँ मेल्लेविणु अण्णु ण सूहउ ॥
सुरकरिअहिसिञ्झियसियसेविहें ।
जो आएसु देहि महएंविहें ॥
एव वि करमि तुहारउ वुत्तउ ।
पहुच्छन्देण अजुत्तु वि जुत्तउ ॥
ए आलाव परोप्परु जावेंहिँ ।
रयणिहें चउ पहरा हय तावेंहिँ ॥
अरुणुग्गमें अञ्चन्तकिसोयरि ।
सीयहें दूई गय मन्दोयरि ॥
सहुँ अन्तेउरेण उद्धूसिय ।
गणियारि व गणियारिविहूसिय ॥
वणु गिव्वाणरवणु संपाइय ।

enemies, if indeed there is a need for me to be alive,
if you do not wish for widowhood for the entire harem,
then you had better fulfill the office of messenger to
Janaka's daughter, Mandodari."

9

Having heard these words of ten-faced Ravana,
Mandodari, a city of lust, answered, "Alas, alas, all the
people in the world are unlucky. Except for you, no
other is blessed. I am your chief queen, a worshiper
of Lakshmi, the goddess of success, consecrated
by celestial elephants, and I will execute the order
that you have given exactly as you have uttered it.
According to my lord's desire, even the improper
becomes proper." While these words were being
exchanged between them, it struck four *praharas* of
the night. At sunrise Mandodari, with her extremely
slender waist, went as a messenger to Sita, the hair on
her body bristling, together with the harem, like an
elephant cow surrounded by other elephant cows. She
arrived at the Girvanaramana grove and beheld the

राहवघरिणि तेत्थु णिज्झाइय ॥
वे वि मणोहरिउ
रावणरामहुँ पियणारिउ ।
दाहिणउत्तरेण
णं दिसगइन्दगणियारिउ ॥

१०

रामघरिणि जं दिट्टु किसोयरि ।
हरिसिय णियमणेण मन्दोयरि ॥
अहिणवणारिरयणु अवइण्णउ ।
एउ ण जाणहुँ कहिँ उप्पण्णउ ॥
सुरहुँ मि कामुक्कोयणगारउ ।
मुणिमणमोहणु णयणपियारउ ॥
साहु साहु णिउणो ऽसि पयावइ ।
तुह विण्णाणसत्ति को पावइ ॥
अह किं वित्थरेण वहुवोल्लएँ ।
सइँ कामो वि पडइ कामिल्लएँ ॥
कवणु गहणु तो लङ्काराएं ।
एम पसंसेंवि मणें अणुराएं ॥
पियवयणेहिँ दसाणणपत्तिएँ ।
वुच्चइ रामघरिणि विहसन्तिएँ ॥

690

wife of Rama, the descendant of Raghu, there.
The two breathtaking, beloved wives of Ravana and Rama
were like the cows of the great cardinal elephants in
the south and the north.

10

When slim-waisted Mandodari saw Rama's wife, she felt
joy in her heart, "A gem of a young woman has come
into our midst. Where was she born? We do not know.
She excites the desire of even the gods, she bewilders
the hearts of sages, she is most dear to the eye. Bravo,
bravo, Prajapati, lord of creation, you are clever. Who
can match your skill and capability? Or rather, what
is the point of speaking more? Even Kama himself
falls for a lovely woman. How much more so the
king of Lanka!" Uttering such words of praise, the
wife of ten-faced Ravana, with passion in her heart,
spoke these loving words smilingly to Rama's wife,

किं वहुजम्पिएण परमेसरि ।
जीविउ एक्कु सहलु तउ सुन्दरि ॥
सुरवरडमरकरु ।
तइलोक्कचक्कसंतावणु ॥
काइँ ण अत्थि तउ ।
जहें आणवडिच्छउ रावणु ॥

११

इन्दइभाणुकण्णघणवाहण ।
अक्खयमयमारिच्चविहीसण ॥
जं चलणेहिँ घिवहि आरूसेवि ।
तं सीसेण लयन्ति असेस वि ॥
अण्णु वि सयलु एउ अन्तेउरु ।
सालङ्कारु सदोरु सणेउरु ॥
अट्ठारह सहास वरविलयहुँ ।
णिच्चुपसाहियसोहियतिलयहुँ ॥
आयहुँ सव्वहुँ तुहुँ परमेसरि ।
णीसावण्णु रज्जु करि सुन्दरि ॥
रावणु मुऍवि अण्णु को चङ्गउ ।
रावणु मुऍवि कवणु तणुअङ्गउ ॥
रावणु मुऍवि अण्णु को सूरउ ।
परवलमहणु कुलासापूरउ ॥

"Supreme mistress, what is the point of copious talk?
Your life alone is fruitful, beautiful woman.
Why is Ravana, tormentor of the Gods and harasser of the
wheel of the threefold world, not with you, when he
obeys your every command?

11

"Indrajit, Kumbhakarna, Ghanavahana, Akshata, Maya,
Maricha, and Vibhishana, if you angrily throw them
at your feet, they all accept it with their head. And
also this entire harem with all its baubles, ropes,
and anklets, eighteen thousand beautiful women,
each decorated with splendid forehead marks, you
are the supreme mistress of all of them. Beautiful
lady, you alone reign over us. Who else but Ravana is
handsome, has a slender body, is a warrior, destroyer
of enemy armies and fulfilling the hope of his family,

रावणु मुऍवि अण्णु को वलियउ ।
सुरवरणियरु जेण पडिक्खलियउ ॥
रावणु मुऍवि अण्णु को भल्लउ ।
जो तिहुयणहों मल्लु एक्कल्लउ ॥
रावणु मुऍवि अण्णु को सूहउ ।
जं आपेक्खेॅवि मयणु वि दूहउ ॥
तहों लङ्केसरहों
कुवलयदलदीहरणयणहों ।
भुञ्जहि सयल महि
महएॅवि होहि दहवयणहों ॥

१२

तं तहें कडुअवयणु आयण्णेॅवि ।
रावणु जीविउ तिणसमु मण्णेॅवि ॥
सीलवलेण वलिय णउ कम्पिय ।
रूसेॅवि णिट्ठुर वयण पजम्पिय ॥
हलें हलें काइँ काइँ पइँ वुत्तउ ।
उत्तिमणारिहें एउ ण जुत्तउ ॥
किह दइयहों दूअत्तणु किज्जइ ।
एण णाइँ महु हासउ दिज्जइ ॥
मज्छुड्डु तुहुँ परपुरिसपइद्धी ।
तें कज्जें महु देहि दुवुद्धी ॥

mighty, he who checked the crowd of great Gods, auspicious, he who is a unique fighter of the threefold world, blessed? Beholding him, even Kama, the god of love, is wretched.

Rule the entire earth, become chief queen of ten-faced Ravana, that lord of Lanka, whose eyes are wide like the petals of blue water lilies."

12

Hearing her caustic words and reckoning both Ravana and her life to be as worthless as grass, through the power of her chastity she neither turned away from her nor did she tremble. Becoming enraged, she spoke harsh words, "My dear, dear friend, what is it you said? This is not proper for a superior woman. How do you fulfill the office of messenger for your husband? It is as if you are mocking me with it.[5] Perhaps you are involved with another man and you give me bad advice because of that. May a lightning bolt fall on the head of your lover! I am only devoted to my husband." Hearing

मत्थएँ पडउ वज्जु तहों जारहों ।
हउँ पुणु भत्तिवन्त भत्तारहों ॥
सीयएँ वयणु सुणेवि मणे डोल्लिय ।
णिसियरणाहणारि पडिवोल्लिय ॥
जइ महएविपट्टु ण पडिच्छहि ।
जइ लङ्काहिउ कह वि ण इच्छहि ॥
तो कन्दन्ति पइँ
तिलु तिलु करवत्तेहिँ कप्पइ ।
अण्णु मुहुत्तऍण
णिसियरहँ विहडूवेवि अप्पइ ॥

१३

पुणुपुणुरुत्तेहिँ जणयहों धीयएँ ।
णिब्भच्छिय मन्दोयरि सीयएँ ॥
केत्तिउ वारवार वोल्लिज्जइ ।
जं चिन्तिउ मणेण तं किज्जइ ॥
जइ वि अज्जु करवत्तेहिँ कप्पहों ।
जइ वि धरेवि सिवसाणहों अप्पहों ॥
जइ वि वलन्तें हुआसणें मेल्लहों ।
जइ वि महग्गयदन्तेहिँ पेल्लहों ॥
तो वि खलहों तहों दुक्कियकम्महों ।
परपुरिसहों णिविति इह जम्महों ॥

Sita's words, the wife of the Rakshasa lord felt shaken in her heart and answered, "If you do not want the turban of chief queen, if for some reason you do not desire the king of Lanka,
then he will take a saw to you as you weep and cut you into little pieces. Once he has torn you apart, he will not hesitate to throw you to the demons."

13

Janaka's daughter Sita rebuked Mandodari again and again, "How many times must it be said? Do what you feel in your heart.[6] Even if you cut me with saws today, if you lay hands on me and toss me to a jackal or a dog, throw me into a blazing fire, or hurl me onto the tusks of a great elephant, then at least there is an escape from that sinful, wretched stranger, and from this birth here. Only my husband is welcome, who at no point is forsaken by the luster of triumph, dear to the

एक्कु जि णियभत्तारु पहुच्चइ ।
जो जयलच्छिएँ खणु वि ण मुच्चइ ॥
जो असुरासुरजणमणवल्लहु ।
तुम्हारिसहुँ कुणारिहिँ दुल्लहु ॥
जो णरवरमइन्दु भीसावणु ।
धणुलङ्कूललीलदरिसावणु ॥
सरणहरारुण्णेण
धणुवेयललाविययजीहें ।
दहमुहमत्तगउ
फाडेवउ राहवसीहें ॥

१४

रामणरामचन्दरमणीयहुँ ।
जाम वोळ्ळ मन्दोवरिसीयहुँ ॥
ताव दसाणणु सयमेवाइउ ।
हत्थि व गञ्झावेणि पराइउ ॥
भसलु व गन्धलुद्धु विहडप्फडु ।
जाणइवयणकमलरसलम्पडु ॥
करयल धुणइ झुणइ वुक्कारइ ।
खेड्डु करेवि देवि पच्चारइ ॥
विण्णत्तिएँ पसाउ परमेसरि ।
हउँ कवणेण हीणु सुरसुन्दरि ॥

698

hearts of demons and gods, impossible to get for bad
women like you, a terrifying lion among great men,
who flourishes his tail-like bow.
Reddish-brown with his claws—his arrows, and with his
lolling tongue—his knowledge of archery, the lion
Rama, descendant of Raghu, will tear apart that
rutting ten-faced elephant, Ravana."

14

While this conversation took place between Mandodari
and Sita, the wives of Ravana and moon-like Rama,
ten-faced Ravana himself approached, like an
elephant arriving at the Ganga's confluence,[7] like an
impetuous bee bewildered by perfumes, longing for
the nectar of the lotus-like face of Janaka's daughter.
He shook his hands, made a sound, chattered,
and playfully scolded the noble lady, "Supreme
mistress, some information, please. Am I deficient in
something, beautiful goddess? Am I lacking in charm

किं सोहग्गें भोग्गें ऊणउ ।
किं विरुयउ किं अत्थविहूणउ ॥
किं लावण्णें वण्णें हीणउ ।
किं संमाणें दाणें रणें दीणउ ॥
कहें कज्जेण केण ण समिच्छहि ।
जें महएविपट्टु ण पडिच्छहि ॥
राहवगेहिणिएँ
णिब्भच्छिउ णिसियरराणउ ।
ओसरु दहवयण
तुहुँ अम्हहुँ जणयसमाणउ ॥

१५

जाणन्तो वि तो वि मं मुज्झहि ।
गेण्हेवि परकलत्तु कहिँ सुज्झहि ॥
जाम ण अयस पडहु उब्भासइ ।
जाम ण लङ्घाणयरि विणासइ ॥
जाम ण लक्खणसीहु विरुज्झइ ।
जाम ण रामकियन्तु विवुज्झइ ॥
जाम ण सरवरधोरणि सन्धइ ।
जाम ण तोणाजुअलु णिवन्धइ ॥
जाव ण वियडउरत्थलु भिन्दइ ।
जाव ण वाहुदण्ड तउ छिन्दइ ॥

700

or pleasure? Am I ugly? Am I a pauper? Am I flawed
in beauty or luster? Do I fall short in honor, charity, or
war? Tell me, why do you not desire me, that you do
not accept the turban of chief queen?"
The wife of Rama, the descendant of Raghu, rebuked the
king of the Rakshasas, "Go away, ten-faced Ravana,
you are like a father to us.[8]

15

"Now you know this, do not delude yourself. How are
you cleared from blame, seizing another man's wife?
Before the drum of dishonor sounds, before the city
of Lanka is destroyed, the lion Lakshmana becomes
enraged, and the terminator Rama becomes aware,
before he fixes a series of excellent arrows to his bow,
ties on his two quivers, cleaves your vast chest, cuts
off your club-like arms, and tears out each of your
ten heads like a goose in a beautiful lake pulling out
lotuses with spotless petals, before a kettle of vultures

सरवरें हंसु जेम दलविमलइँ ।
जाव ण तोडइ दससिरकमलइँ ॥
जाम ण गिद्धपन्ति णिव्वट्टइ ।
जाम ण णिसियरवलु आवट्टइ ॥
जाम ण दरिसावइ धयचिन्धइँ ।
जाम ण रणें णच्चन्ति कवन्धइँ ॥
जाम ण आहयणें
कप्पिज्जहि वरणारायहिँ ।
ताव णराहिवइ
पडु राहवचन्दहों पायहिँ ॥

१६

तं णिसुणेंवि आरुट्टु दसाणणु ।
णं घणें गज्जमाणें पञ्चाणणु ॥
कोवाणलपलित्तु लङ्केसरु ।
चिन्तइ विज्जाहरपरमेसरु ॥
किं जमसासणपन्थें लायमि ।
किं उवसग्गु किं पि दरिसावमि ॥
अवसें भयवसेण इच्छेसइ ।
महु मयणग्गि समुल्हावेसइ ॥
तहिँ अवसरें सतुरङ्कु सरहवरु ।
गउ अत्थवणहों ताम दिवायरु ॥

702

appears and the Rakshasa army is wiped out, before he
shows his flags with his insignia and headless corpses
dance in battle,
before you are torn apart by excellent iron arrows in
war, king, fall at the feet of moon-like Rama, the
descendant of Raghu."

16

At this, Ravana, the ten-faced, grew furious, like a lion
when a cloud is thundering. Incensed by the fire of
anger, the lord of Lanka, the supreme Vidyadhara
master, thought, "Do I take her along the path of
Yama's punishment? Do I show her some calamity? By
the power of fear she will surely want me and quench
my fiery lust." At that time the sun, along with his
horses and great chariot, set. Night arrived in many

आय रत्ति णाणाविहरूवेहिँ ।
अट्टहास मेल्लन्तेहिँ भूएँहिँ ॥
खरसाणउलविरालसियालेहिँ ।
वहुचामुण्डरुण्डवेयालेहिँ ॥
रक्खवससीहवग्घगयगण्डेहिँ ।
मेसमहिसवसतुरयणिसण्डेहिँ ॥
तं उवसग्गु णिएवि भयावणु ।
तो वि ण सीयहें सरणु दसाणणु ॥
घोरु रउद्दु झाणु संचूरेवि ।
थिय मणें धम्मझाणु आऊरेवि ॥
जाव ण णीसरिय
उवसग्गभयहों गम्भीरहों ।
ताव णिवित्ति महु
चउविहआहारसरीरहों ॥

१७

पहय पओस पणासेंवि णिग्गय ।
हत्थिहड व्व सूरपहराहय ॥
णिसियरि व्व गय घोणावङ्किय ।
भग्गमडप्फर माणकलङ्किय ॥
सूरभएण णाइँ रणु मेल्लेंवि ।
पइसइ णयरु कवाडइँ पेल्लेंवि ॥

704

different forms, with Bhutas emitting loud laughter,
along with donkeys, flocks of dogs, cats, jackals, many
Chamundas, headless corpses, Vetalas, Rakshasas,
lions, tigers, elephants, rhinoceroses, rams, buffaloes,
bulls, horses, and herds of people. Even as she saw
that horrifying calamity, ten-faced Ravana was no
refuge for Sita. She crushed down all thoughts of
the terrible and the perverse, and she achieved the
virtuous meditation in her heart,[9]
"Until I have escaped the deep fear of this calamity, I will
cease eating all four categories of food."[10]

17

The night had struck, fled, and vanished, hit by the
prahara of the sun, like a troop of elephants struck by
the beatings of warriors.[11] Like a female demon with
a crooked nose she went, her pride shattered and her
honor sullied. It was as if she entered the city, fleeing
a battle out of fear that that warrior, the sun, would

दीवा पज्जलन्ति जे सयणेहिँ ।
णं णिसि वलेवि णिहालइ णयणेहिँ ॥
उट्ठिउ रवि अरविन्दाणन्दउ ।
णं महिकामिणिकेरउ अन्दउ ॥
णं सज्झाएँ तिलउ दरिसाविउ ।
णं सुकइहें जसपुञ्जु पहाविउ ॥
णं मम्मीस देन्तु वलपत्तिहें ।
पच्छलें णाइँ पधाइउ रत्तिहें ॥
णं जगभवणहों वोहिउ दीवउ ।
णाइँ पुणु वि पुणु सो ज्जें पडीवउ ॥
तिहुअणरक्खसहों
दारेवि दिसिवहुमुहकन्दरु ।
उवरें पईसरेवि
णं सीय गवेसइ दिणयरु ॥

१८

रयणिहें तिमिरणियररएँ भग्गएँ ।
णिव रावणहों आय ओलग्गएँ ॥
मयमारिच्चविहीसणराणा ।
अवरें वि भुवणेक्केक्कपहाणा ॥
खरदूसणसोएण णयाणण ।
णं णिक्केसर वर पञ्चाणण ॥
णियणियआसणेहिँ थिय अविचल ।

706

push the panel doors open. The lamps that burned in
the houses seemed as if night, turning around, looked
out with her eyes. The sun, the joy of the lotuses, rose
up, like the mirror for the lovely Lady Earth. It was
as if twilight showed its forehead mark, like a great
poet's mass of glory had appeared. It seemed to give
reassurances to the Baladeva's wife; as if it chased
away the night. It was like the lamp of the house of the
world that had been lit. It seemed to return again and
again.

It was as if the sun, tearing open the cavity of the mouth
of Space, the bride of the Rakshasa of the threefold
world, and entering into her belly, was searching for
Sita.

18

When the massive mist of the night's darkness had been
broken, kings came to serve Ravana. The kings Maya,
Maricha, and Vibhishana as well as others, each of
them eminent men in the world, their heads bent
from sorrow over Khara and Dushana, like great
maneless lions, sat motionless in their seats, like

भग्गविसाण णाइँ वर मयगल ॥
मन्तिमहल्लएहिँ एत्थन्तरें ।
णिसुणिय सीय रुअन्ति पडन्तरें ॥
भणइ विहीसणु ऍहु को रोवइ ।
वारवार अप्पाणउ सोअइ ॥
णावइ परकलत्तु विच्छोइउ ।
पुणु दहवयणहों वयणु पजोइउ ॥
मज्छुडु एउ कम्मु तुह केरउ ।
अण्णहों कासु चित्तु विवरेरउ ॥
तं णिसुणेवि सीय आसासिय ।
कलयण्ठि व पियवयणेहिँ भासिय ॥
ऍहु दुज्जणहों मज्झें को सज्जणु ।
णिम्ववणहों अब्भन्तरें चन्दणु ॥
विहुरें समावडिऍ
ऍहु को साहम्मियवच्छलु ।
जो मइँ धीरवइ
एवडु कासु सई भुववलु ॥

grand elephants with broken tusks. Thereupon the councilors and ministers heard Sita crying behind a curtain. Vibhishana said, "Who is that, crying and bewailing herself again and again? It is as if it were the abandoned wife of a stranger." Then he looked at the face of Ravana, the ten-faced: "Maybe this is your doing. Who else has such a perverse mind?" At this, Sita felt reassured. Like a cuckoo she spoke with loving words, "Who is this good person amid a mean crowd, like a sandalwood tree among neem trees? Who is this, full of affection toward a person of the same faith, who comforts me now that adversity has struck? Who has such power in his arms?"

बायालीसमो संधि

पुणु वि विहहीसण्णेण
दुव्वयणेहिँ रावणु दोच्छइ ।
तेत्थु पडन्तरेण
आसण्णउ होएँवि पुच्छइ ॥

अक्खहि सुन्दरि वत्त णिभन्ती ।
कहिँ आणिय तुहुँ एत्थु रुवन्ती ॥
कासु धीय कहि को तुम्हहँ पइ ।
अवरव वहन्तु विहीसणु जम्पइ ॥
कवणु ससुरु कहि को तुह देवरु ।
अत्थि पसिद्धउ को तुह भायरु ॥
सप्परियण कहि तुहुँ एक्कली ।
अक्खहि केम वणन्तरें भुल्ली ॥
कें कज्जेण वणवासु पइट्ठी ।
चक्केसरेण केम तुहुँ दिट्ठी ॥
किं माणुसि किं खेयरणन्दिणि ।
किं कुसील किं सीलहों भायणि ॥
अण्णु वि कवणु तुम्ह देसन्तरु ।
कहहि वियारेंवि णिययकहन्तरु ॥

710

Chapter 42

With harsh words Vibhishana rebuked Ravana again. Then sitting down behind the curtain, he asked,

1

"Beautiful lady who is crying here, tell me your story
without erring, where were you taken? Whose
daughter are you? Tell me, who is your husband?"
Weighing his thoughts, Vibhishana spoke, "Who is
your father-in-law? Tell me, who is your brother-in-
law? Who is your celebrated brother? Tell me, do you
have a retinue or are you alone? Explain to me: how
were you lost inside the forest? For what reason did
you embark on a stay in the forest? How did Ravana,
the universal emperor, see you? Are you a human or
a Vidyadhara's daughter? Do you have bad morals or
are you a paragon of good conduct? And also, what
is your foreign land? After reflecting over it, tell
me the course of your story." Hearing those words

एम विहीसणवयणु सुणेविणु ।
लग्ग कहेव्वएँ जिम णिसुणइ जणु ॥
अह किं वहुएण
लहुअ वहिणि भामण्डलहों ।
हउँ सीयाएवि
जणयहों सुअ गेहिणि वलहों ॥

२

वन्धेँवि रायपट्टु भरहेसहों ।
तिण्णि वि संचल्लिय वणवासहों ॥
सीहोयरहों मडप्फरु भञ्जेँवि ।
दसउरणाहहों णियमणु रञ्जेँवि ॥
पुणु कल्लाणमाल मम्भीसेँवि ।
णम्मय मेल्लेँवि विज्झु पईसेँवि ॥
रुद्दभुत्ति णियचलण्णेहिँ पाडेँवि ।
वालिखिल्लु णियणयरहों धाडेँवि ॥
रामउरिहिँ चउ मास वसेप्पिणु ।
धरणीधरहों धीय परिणेप्पिणु ॥
फेडेँवि अइवीरहों वीरत्तणु ।
पइसरेवि खेमञ्जलिपट्टणु ॥
तेत्थु वि पञ्च पडिच्छेँवि सत्तिउ ।
सत्तुदवणु मसिवण्णु पवित्तिउ ॥

of Vibhishana, she started to explain as the people
listened,
"Well, why be elaborate: I am the younger sister of
Bhamandala, Lady Sita, the daughter of Janaka and
wife of the Baladeva.

2

"When the royal turban was tied to King Bharata, we
three set out to live in the forest. After we crushed the
pride of Simhodara, gratified the heart of the king
of Dashapura, then reassured Kalyanamala, left the
Narmada behind, entered the Vindhya mountains,
made Rudrabhuti fall at our feet, liberated Valikhilya
from his city, stayed in Ramapuri for four months,
arranged a marriage with the daughter of Mahidhara,
destroyed the heroism of Anantavirya, entered the
city of Kshemanjali, and received five *saktis* there, we
brought satisfaction to Aridamana, with his soot-like

पुणु तहों तणिय धीय परिणेप्पिणु ।
मुणिजुअलहों उवसग्गु हरेप्पिणु ॥
हरिसीयवलाइँ
आयइं सज्जइँ आइयइं ।
णं मत्तगयाइँ
दण्डारण्णु पराइयइँ ॥

३

तहिं मि कालें मुणिगुत्तसुगुत्तहँ ।
संजमणियमधम्मसंजुत्तहँ ॥
वणें आहारदाणु दरिसावेंवि ।
सुरवररयणवरिसु वरिसावेंवि ॥
पक्खिहें पक्ख सुवण्ण समारेंवि ।
सम्बुकुमारु वीरु संघारेंवि ॥
अच्छहुँ जाव तेत्थु वणकीलएँ ।
एक्क कुमारि आय णियलीलएँ ॥
पासु पढुक्किय करिणि व करिणहों ।
पुणु णिल्लज्ज भणइ मइँ परिणहों ॥
वलणारायणेहिँ उवलक्खिय ।
पुणु थोवन्तरें जाय विलक्खिय ॥
गय खरदूसणाहुँ कूवारेंहिँ ।

complexion. Arranging a marriage with his daughter
and removing the calamity of a pair of sages,
the Vasudeva, I, and Baladeva arrived in a fit state, and like
rutting elephants came to the Dandaka forest.

3

"At that time, after we demonstrated in the forest the
gift of food to the sages Gupta and Sugupta, who are
devoted to discipline, restraint, and righteousness,
caused a rain of gems from the great gods to shower
down, rendered the wings of a bird gold, and killed
the heroic Prince Shambuka, as we passed our time
in the forest there,[1] a girl arrived with a game of her
own. She came in close like an elephant cow to an
elephant bull and then shamelessly said, 'Marry me.'
The Baladeva and Vasudeva noted her characteristics,
but soon she became embarrassed. She went to Khara

भिडिय ते वि सहुँ समरें कुमारेंहिँ
किं मुक्कु ण मुक्कु
सीहणाउ रणें लक्खणेणं ।
तं सद्दु सुणेवि
रामु पधाइउ तक्खणेणं ॥

४

गउ लक्खणहों गवेसउ जावेंहिँ ।
हउँ अवहरिय णिसिन्दें तावेंहिँ ॥
अज्जु वि जणमणणयणाणन्दहों ।
पासु णेहु मइँ राहवचन्दहों ॥
लइउ णाउँ जं दसरहजणयहुँ ।
हरिहलहरभामण्डलतणयहुँ ॥
चित्तु विहीसणरायहों डोल्लिउ ।
तुम्हेंहिँ सुयउ सुयउ जं वोल्लिउ ॥
ते हउँ आउ आसि विणिवाएँवि ।
णवर जियन्ति भन्ति उप्पाएँवि ॥
ढुक्कु पमाणहों मुणिवरभासिउ ।
जिह खउ लक्खणरामहों पासिउ ॥
एव वि करहि महारउ वुत्तउ ।
उत्तिमपुरिसहुँ एउ ण जुत्तउ ॥
एक्कु विणासु अण्णु लज्जिज्जइ ।
धिद्धिक्कारु लोएँ पाविज्जइ ॥

716

and Dushana with cries for help. They fought together
with Prince Lakshmana in a battle.
In the fight, Lakshmana supposedly uttered a lion's roar.[2]
When Rama heard that sound, he instantly rushed off.

4

"While he went searching for Lakshmana, I was abducted
by the Rakshasa lord. Take me to moon-like Rama
today, the descendant of Raghu, who brings joy to
the hearts and eyes of the people." When the names
of Dasharatha, Janaka, the Vasudeva, the Baladeva,
and Bhamandala were raised, King Vibhishana's heart
shook, "Did you hear it? Did you hear what was said?
I had returned after I had massacred them, but they
stayed alive through the practice of deception. What
was said by the great sage has come true, 'There will
be destruction because of Lakshmana and Rama.'
Do exactly as I say. This is not proper for men of
excellence. Firstly there is the destruction; and also,
one feels shame and endures cursing from the people.

णियकित्तिहें राय
सायररसणखलन्तियहें ।
मं भज्झहि पाय
तिहुयणें परिसक्कन्तियहें ॥

५

रावण जे रमन्ति परदारइँ ।
दुक्खइँ ते पावन्ति अपारइँ ॥
जहिँ ते सत्त णरय भयभीसण ।
हसहसहसहसन्त सहुवासण ॥
हुहुहुहुहुहुहन्त सउपद्दव ।
सिमिसिमिसिमिसिमिसिमन्तकिमिकद्दम ॥
रयणिसकरवालुयपङ्कप्पह ।
धूमप्पहतमपहतमतमपह ॥
तहिँ असरालु कालु अच्छेवउ ।
पहिलएँ उवहिपमाणु जिवेवउ ॥
तिण्णि सत्त वीसद्ध रउद्दइँ ।
सत्तारह वावीस समुद्दइँ ॥
पुणु तेतीसजलहिपरिमाणइँ ।
जहिँ दुक्खइँ गिरिमेरुसमाणइँ ॥
जो पुणु णरउ णिगोउ सुणिज्जइ ।
मेइणि जाव ताव तहिँ छिज्जइ ॥
तें कज्जें परदारु ण रम्मइ ।

King, do not destroy the foundations of your glory,
fluctuating like the roaring of the ocean and moving
around in the threefold world.

5

"Ravana, those who enjoy other men's wives incur
boundless sorrows. They must reside for a long
time in those horrifying seven hells, hissing, fiery,
roaring, full of calamities, filth, and wriggling worms:
Ratnaprabha, Sharkaraprabha, Valukaprabha,
Pankaprabha, Dhumaprabha, Tamahprabha, and
Tamastamahprabha. In the first they must live for the
length of a *sāgara,* then three, seven, ten, seventeen,
and twenty-two terrible *sāgaras,* and finally the
lengths of thirty-three *sāgaras,* where sorrows are the
size of Mount Meru. Then in the hell that is known
as *nigoda,* one is cut until one reaches the ground. For
that reason, one does not enjoy the wife of another

तं किज्जइ जं सुगइहिँ गम्मइ ॥
आरुट्टु दसासु
किं परदारहों एह किय ।
तिहुँ खण्डहुँ मज्झें
अक्खु पराइय कवण तिय ॥

६

तो अवहेरि करेवि विहीसणें ।
चडिउ महग्गएं तिजगविहूसणें ॥
सीय वि पुष्फविमाणें चडाविय ।
पट्टणें हट्टसोह दरिसाविय ॥
संचल्लउ णियमणपरिओसें ।
झल्लरिपडहहतूरणिग्घोसें ॥
सुन्दरि पेक्खु महारउ पट्टणु ।
वरुणकुवेरवीरदलवट्टणु ॥
सुन्दरि पेक्खु पेक्खु चउवारइँ ।
णं कामिणिवयणइँ सवियारइँ ॥
सुन्दरि पेक्खु पेक्खु धयछत्तइँ ।
पप्फुलियइँ णाइँ सयवत्तइँ ॥
सुन्दरि पेक्खु महारउ राउलु ।
हीरगहणु मणिखम्भरमाउलु ॥

720

man. One acts in such a way so that one proceeds
   along good modes of existence."
Ten-faced Ravana grew enraged, "Is this the doing of
   another man's wife? Tell me, what woman has come
   here in the midst of the three parts of Bharata?"[3]

6

After he had thus disrespected Vibhishana, he climbed
   onto his grand elephant Trijagadvibhushana. He
   forced Sita into the celestial chariot Pushpa and
   showed her the splendid fair in the city. With delight
   in his heart he set out to the sound of *jhallarīs* and
   other drums, "Beautiful lady, behold my city that
   crushed the heroism of Varuna and Kubera, see its
   four gates like the willing faces of lovely women,
   the banners and umbrellas like blooming lotuses,
   my palace, dense with diamonds and abounding in

सुन्दरि करहि महारउ वुत्तउ ।
लइ चूडउ कण्ठउ कडिसुत्तउ ॥
सुन्दरि करि पसाउ लइ चेलिउ ।
चीणउ लाडु घोडु हरिकेलिउ ॥
महु जीविउ देहि
वोल्लहि वयणु सुहावणउ ।
चडु गयवरखन्धें
लइ महएविपसाहणउ ॥

७

सम्पइ दक्खवन्तु इय सेज्जएँ ।
दोच्छिउ रावणु राहवभज्जएँ ॥
केत्तिउ णिययरिद्धि महु दावहि ।
अप्पउ जणहों मज्झें दरिसावहि ॥
ऍउ जं रावण रज्जु तुहारउ ।
तं महु तिणसमाणु हलुआरउ ॥
ऍउ जं पट्टणु सोमु सुदंसणु ।
तं महु मणहों णाइँ जमसासणु ॥
ऍउ जं राउलु णयणसुहङ्करु ।
तं महु णाइँ मसाणु भयङ्करु ॥
ऍउ जं दावहि खणें खणें जोव्वणु ।
तं महु मणहों णाइँ विसभोयणु ॥

jeweled pillars. Beautiful lady, do as I say: accept a
bracelet, a pendant, a girdle. Do me a favor: accept a
garment from China, one from Lata, and a horse from
Harikeliya.[4]
Give me back my life, speak pleasant words, climb
onto the shoulder of my great elephant, accept the
raiments of my chief queen.

7

As Ravana showed her this abundance in his home,
Rama's wife rebuked him, "Why do you display your
wealth to me and parade yourself before your people?
This kingdom of yours, Ravana, means no more to
me than grass. This pretty, attractive city of yours
is like Yama's punishment to my mind. This palace
that brings joy to the eye is like a terrifying cremation
ground to me. This youthfulness that you show me
time and again, it is like consuming venom to my
mind. This pendant, this bracelet, and this belt: they
are all just the filth of those who are without morals.

ऍउ जं कण्ठउ कडउ समेहलु ।
सीलविहूणहँ तं मलु केवलु ॥
रहवरतुरयगइन्दसयाइ मि ।
आयहिँ महु पुणु गण्णु ण काइ मि ॥
सग्गेण वि काइँ
जहिँ चारित्तहों खण्डणउ ।
किं समलहणेण
महु पुणु सीलु जें मण्डणउ ॥

८

जिह जिह चिन्तिय आस ण पूरइ ।
तिह तिह रावणु हियएँ विसूरइ ॥
विहि तेत्तडउ देइ जं विहियउ ।
किं वढ जाइ णिलाडएँ लिहियउ ॥
हउँ कम्मेण केण संखोहिउ ।
जाणन्तो वि तो वि जं मोहिउ ॥
धिधि अहिलसिय कुणारि विलीणी ।
वुण्णकुरङ्गि जेम मुहदीणी ॥
आयहें पासिउ जाउ सुवेसउ ।
महु घरें अत्थि अणेयउ वेसउ ॥
एव विचित्तु चित्तु साहारेवि ।
दुक्खु दुक्खु मणपसरु णिवारेवि ॥
सीयएँ समउ खेड्डु आमेल्लेवि ।

724

The hundreds of great chariots, horses, and grand
elephants, I have no esteem whatsoever for these.
What is the use of heavenly bliss, when correct conduct is
destroyed? What is the use of unguent? Good conduct
is my only ornament."

8

The more the hope that he had fostered remained
unfulfilled, the more Ravana felt distress in his
heart, "Fate gives as much as is prescribed. Fool,
does the writing on your forehead ever go away?[5]
By what karma am I afflicted, that I am bewildered,
even though I am aware of it? Damn it, damn it, I
have longed for a bad woman who has crept inside
my heart, like a frightened doe with a dejected face.
Clearly she is beautiful, but in my house there are
many courtesans." Thus comforting his capricious
heart, with great difficulty blocking the course of his
thoughts, forsaking his flirtation with Sita, and leaving

तं गिव्वाणरमणु वणु मेल्लेविं ॥
णरवरविन्देहिँ परिमिउ दहमुहु ।
संचल्लिउ णियणयरिहेँ अहिमुहु ॥
गिरि दिट्ठु तिकूडु
जणमणणयणसुहावणउ ।
रविडिम्भहो दिण्णु
णं महिकुलवहुअएँ थणउ ॥

९

णं धरु धरहेँ गब्भु णीसरियउ ।
सत्तहिँ उववणेहिँ परियरियउ ॥
पहिलउ वणु णामेण पइण्णउ ।
सज्जणहियउ जेम वित्थिण्णउ ॥
वीयउ जणमणणयणाणन्दणु ।
णावइ जिणवरविम्बु सचन्दणु ॥
तइयउ वणु सुहसेउ सुहावउ ।
जिणवरसासणु णाइँ ससावउ ॥
चउथउ वणु णामेण समुच्छउ ।
वगवलायकारण्डसकोञ्चउ ॥
चारणवणु पञ्चमउ रवण्णउ ।
चम्पयतिलयवउलसंछण्णउ ॥

that Girvanaramana grove, Ravana returned to his
city, accompanied by troops of excellent men.
He beheld Mount Trikuta, bringing joy to the hearts
and eyes of the people, as if it were the breast of the
noblewoman Earth given to her infant, the Sun.

9

The mountain was like the baby of the earth, just as it
was born. It was surrounded by seven parks: the first
grove, called Prakirna, was vast like the heart of a
good person; the second, Janamanananayananandana,
was full of sandalwood trees, like an icon of the great
Jina;[6] the third grove, delightful Sukhaseka, was full
of wild animals, just as the teaching of the great Jina
is accompanied by laymen;[7] the fourth grove, named
Samucchaya, teemed with storks, cranes, *kāraṇḍa*-
ducks, and curlews; the fifth, pleasant Charana grove,
was covered in champacs, *tilakas,* and medlars; the
sixth splendid grove, named Nibodha, buzzed with

छड्डुउ वणु णामेण णिवोहउ ।
महुअररुणुरुण्टन्तु सुसोहउ ॥
सत्तमु वणु सीयलु सच्छायउ ।
पमउज्जाणु णामविक्वायउ ॥
तहिँ गिरिवरपट्टेँ
सोहइ लङ्काणयरि किह ।
थिय गयवरखन्धेँ
गहियपसाहण वहुअ जिह ॥

१०

ताव तेत्थु णिज्झाइय वावि असोयमालिणी ।
हेमवण्ण सपयोहर मणहर णाइँ कामिणी ॥
चउदुवारचउगोउरचउतोरणरवण्णिया ।
चम्पयतिलयवउलणारङ्गलवङ्गछण्णिया ॥
तहिँ पएसेँ वइदेहि ठवेप्पिनु गउ दसाणणो ।
झिज्जमाणु विरहेण विसंथुलु विमणु दुम्मणो ॥
मयणवाणजज्जरियउ जरिउ दुवारवारओ ।
दूइआउ आवन्ति जन्ति सयवारवारओ ॥
वयणएहिँ खरमहुरेहिँ मुहु सूसइ विसूरए ।
छोहेँ छोहेँ णिवडन्तएँ जूआरो व्व जूरए ॥
सिरु धुणेइ कर मोडइ अङ्गु वलेइ कम्पए ।
अहरु लेवि णिज्झायइ कामसरेण जम्पए ॥

bees; the seventh grove, cool and shady, was known by
the name of Padmodyana.

How did the city of Lanka shine on top of that great
mountain? Like a bride who had put on her ornaments
and sat on the shoulders of a great elephant.

10

A pond could clearly be seen there, garlanded by *aśokas,*
like a busty, breathtaking lovely lady with a golden
hue. It had four doors, four gateways, and four arches,
and all of them made it delightful, and it was covered
with champacs, *tilakas,* medlars, orange trees, and
clove trees. Settling Sita there, ten-faced Ravana left
her, ravaged by lovesickness, confused, downcast, and
depressed. Torn to pieces by the arrows of Kama, the
god of love, he was like an old gatekeeper. Confidantes
came and went hundreds of times. His mouth became
dry from their words, harsh and sweet, and he felt
distress. He cursed like a gambler at the toss of the
dice. He shook his head, squeezed his hands, twisted
his body, and shivered. Biting his lip,[8] he lost himself
in thought and spoke with a voice afflicted by love.
He sang, played music, danced around, and displayed

गाइ वाइ उव्वेल्लेइ हरिसविसाय दावऍ ।
वारवार मुच्छिज्जइ मरणावत्थ पावए ॥
चन्दणेण सिंच्छिज्जइ चन्दणलेउ दिज्जए ।
चामरेहिँ विज्जिज्जइ तो वि मणेण झिज्जए ॥
किं रावणु एक्कु
जो जो गरुअइँ गज्जियउ ।
जिणधवलु मुएव्वि
कामें को ण परज्जियउ ॥

११

थिऍ दसाणणे विरहभिम्भले ।
जाय चिन्त वरमन्तिमण्डले ॥
एत्थु मल्लु को कुइऍ लक्खणे ।
सिद्धु जासु असिरयणु तक्खणे ॥
णिहउ सम्वु जें दूसणो खरो ।
होइ कुइ ण सावण्णु सो णरो ॥
भणइ मन्ति सहसमइणामेणं ।
कवणु गहणु एक्केण रामेणं ॥
लक्खणेण सह साहणेण वा ।
रहतुरङ्गगयवाहणेण वा ॥
दुत्तरे दुसञ्झारसायरे ।
कहिँ पएसु विच्छीभयङ्करे ॥

excitement and lethargy. Time and again he fainted
and came close to the state of death. He was sprinkled
and anointed with sandalwood oil and fanned with
flywhisks, but nevertheless he felt torment in his
heart.

Is Ravana the only one to have roared so profoundly?
Who has not been overpowered by lust when he has
forsaken the pure Jina?

11

As Ravana stood afflicted by lovesickness, worry arose
in the circle of his chief ministers: "Who here can
stand against Lakshmana when he is enraged, he who
got the illustrious gem of a sword in an instant, and
who struck down Shambuka, Dushana, and Khara?
This is not some ordinary man." A minister named
Sahasramati said, "What can be gained by Rama
alone, along with Lakshmana, or with an army, or
a chariot, horse, or elephant as a vehicle? Where in
the uncrossable, impassable ocean, terrible in its
waves, is there a place? Ravana's army is powerful and

रावणस्स पवलं वलं महा ।
अत्थि वीर एक्केक्क दूसहा ॥
किं मुएण दूसर्णेण सम्वुणा ।
सायरो किम् ओहट्टु विन्दुणा ॥
तं वयणु सुणेवि
विहसेवि पञ्चामुहु भणइ ।
किं वुच्चइ एक्कु
जो एक्कु जें सहसइँ हणइ ॥

१२

अण्णुएँ णिसुअ वत्त मइँ एहिय ।
रावणमन्दिरें णीसन्देहिय ॥
जे जे णरवइ केइ कइद्धय ।
जम्ववणलसुग्गीवङ्गङ्गय ॥
समउ विराहिएण वणसेवहुँ ।
मिलिया वासुएववलएवहुँ ॥
तं णिसुणेवि दसाणणभिच्चें ।
वुच्चइ पञ्चामुहु मारिच्चें ॥
एह अजुत्त वत्त पइँ अक्खिवय ।
रावणु मुएँवि ण अण्णहों पक्खिवय ॥
का वि अणङ्कुसुम वलवन्तहों ।
दिण्णि खरेण धीय हणुवन्तहों ॥
तं किं मामवइरु वीसरियउ ।

enormous. Each one of his warriors is invincible. So what that Dushana and Shambuka are dead; did the ocean shrink from a drop of water?"

Hearing those words, Panchamukha laughed out loud and spoke, "Is one man named who massacres thousands on his own?

12

"Moreover, I have heard news in no uncertain terms in Ravana's palace: some monkey-bannered kings,* Jambavat, Nala, Sugriva, Anga, and Angada, together with Viradhita, are at the disposal of the Vasudeva and the Baladeva, as they stay in the forest." At this, Maricha, ten-faced Ravana's servant, said to Panchamukha, "This news that you have reported is incorrect. They have not forsaken Ravana and sided with another. Khara gave his daughter, Anangakusuma, to mighty Hanuman. Has he forgotten that enmity of his dear friend, that he is

* Vanaras

जें पडिवक्ख मिलइ भयडरियउ ॥
तो एत्थन्तरें भणइ विहीसणु ।
केत्तिउ चवहु वयणु सुण्णासणु ॥
एवहिँ सो उवाउ चिन्तिज्जइ ।
लङ्काणाहु जेण रक्खिज्जइ ॥
एम भणेवि चउद्दिसु ताडिय ।
पुरें आसालिय विज्ज भमाडिय ॥
तियसहु मि दुलङ्घु
दिढु मायापायारु किउ ।
णीसङ्कु णिसिन्दु
रज्जु सयं भुञ्जन्तु थिउ ॥

अउज्झाकण्ड समत्तं
आइच्चुएविपडिमोवमाएँ आइच्चम्विमाए ।
वीअमउज्झाकण्डं
सयम्भूघरिणीएँ लेहवियं ॥

meeting his opponents, trembling with fear?" Then Vibhishana said, "How many senseless words can you utter? I am now conceiving a plan, whereby the lord of Lanka may be protected." Speaking thus, he sent out the *vidyā* Ashali to all corners of the city and made her go around.

She constructed a firm, illusory wall, impossible to cross even for the gods. The Rakshasa lord himself stood ruling his kingdom, free of risk.

The *Book of Ayodhya* is completed.
The second book, *Book of Ayodhya,* was written,
as inspired by Svayambhu's wife Adityambima,
an icon of Surya's wife.

NOTES TO THE TEXT

१ ससरासण] A; ससरासणु CE, P

२ समुल्लसन्ति] A; समुल्हसन्ति CE, P

३ तुम्हेँहि] P; तुम्हेँहिँ CE, A

४ जिणभवणु] A; जिणभवण CE, P

५ वहुअत्थिजिअन्तहिँ] वहुअत्थि जि अन्तहिँ CE

६ देसविहूसणेकु] A; देसविहूसणु एकु CE, P

७ जोणीजोणि] A and P; जोणिएँ जोणि CE

८ उपत्तिय] A; उप्पत्तिय CE, P

९ CE queries the text here for the obscurity of its meaning. I take the second भमर as meaning "whirlpool" (See *bhramara* 9650 in Turner 1966–1985: vol. 1, 550)

१० कडिचिहुर णाहि] कडिचिहुरणाहि CE

११ गयागसं धीसं] गयागसंधीसं CE

१२ णियत्तो] A; णियन्तो CE, P

१३ कलयलारवो उट्ठिओ दोहिँ] A; कलयलारावु उट्ठिउ दोहिं मि CE, P

NOTES TO THE TRANSLATION

Chapter 21

1   The name Sagarabuddhi, "he who possesses the knowledge of predictions," implies he is a soothsayer.

2   The Rakshasa dynasty is part of the larger Vidyadhara dynasty.

3   The sunstones and moonstones are legendary gems. The sunstone is said to come ablaze when touched by the rays of the sun; the moonstone streams with water when exposed to the moon's rays.

4   The so-called "self-choice" (*svayaṃvara*) is a typical wedding ceremony for princesses, where the bride choses her husband from a pool of suitors selected by her father by throwing a garland around his neck.

5   This reference to the four oceans, one for each cardinal direction, stems from traditional South Asian lore, different from and older than later Jain cosmology. Indra's elephant Airavata is often depicted with four tusks. Note that his description in chapter 32 differs.

6   This means that he is on the verge of death.

7   A *vidyā* is a supernatural female being, bestowing particular superhuman powers to her owner, especially the power of flight. They are the distinguishing property of the dynasty called Vidyadhara, literally, "*vidyā* bearers."

Chapter 22

1   The Gods are a clan of humans, a branch of the Vidyadhara dynasty. Their story is described in the first book. They are distinct from the gods, deities that reside in the heavens.

2   The PC gives some more information about these characters. Pingala was the teacher of a Brahman named Kubera (*kuverākhya-brāhmaṇopādhyāyaḥ*). The girl whom he abducted was named Chitrotsava (*candradhvaja-rājñaḥ putrī citrotsavā nāmnā*). The parallel versions of Vimalasuri (30.20) and Ravishena (30.43) do not mention these names, though they are explicit that

Kundalamandita committed the grave sin of abducting the wife of a Brahman.

3   Useless, "filling out a verse." The Sanskrit *padapūraṇa* is a term used to refer to meaningless particles supplied in verses for metrical reasons.

4   Aside from food, a mendicant may accept medicine as a gift. The practice of religious giving has been described as reciprocal: the ascetic too gives a donation, namely, instruction in the teachings and comfort to living beings (*abhaya*), which is considered the highest of all gifts (see Dundas 2002: 176).

Chapter 23

1   Vyasa is the legendary author of the *Mahābhārata,* including its Rama narrative, the *Rāmopākhyāna*. The collation of the Vedas and authorship of the Hindu Puranas are also attributed to him.

2   These are all names of Prakrit and Apabhramsha meters. In his treatise on prosody, *Svayambhūcchandas,* Svayambhudeva himself describes the *cakkalaka* (8.23), *kulaka* (8.23), *skandhaka* (P 1.3), *mañjarī* (3.13), and *narkuṭa(ka)* (P 3.6). Hemachandra's *Chando'nuśāsana* discusses the *pavanoddhuta* (4.75). The *khaḍahaḍa(ka)* (4.73–75) and *vilāsinī* (3.29 and 4.15) are described in Virahanka's *Vṛttajātisamuccaya*. Though not mentioned in these prosody treatises, Sheth 1986: 711 attests *rāsālubdhaka* as the meter of the tenth verse of a popular Jain hymn, the *Ajita-śāntistava*.

3   The reference to the mustache implies maturity and martial power. The story referred to is the proverbially popular story of King Vasu, who told a lie by saying that it was auspicious to sacrifice animals. He went to hell for his sins (Varni 1997–2000: vol. 3, 530). The story is known in non-Jain sources as well. See Brodbeck 2009: 164.

4   Saturn (*śaṇi*) is traditionally considered malevolent and not to be angered.

5   Snake gems, or pearls, thought to glow in the dark, are said to grow in the hood of certain snakes.

6   In this and the previous verse, the poet employs wordplay in which a word is repeated with a different meaning: the first *sāhammiya* (Skt. *śākhāmita*) means "unequal in parentage" (PC: *sākhāmitau vibhinna-jananī-jātau*), the second (Skt. *sādharmika*) means

"people from the same faith"; the first *ṇivvāhaṇa* (Skt. *nirvāhaṇa-*) means "bearing," the second "without vehicle"; *ṇīsāhaṇa* (Skt. *niḥsādhana*) is both "without ornaments" (PC: *sādhanaṃ maṇḍanaṃ prasādhanaṃ tena rahitau*) and "without an army."

7 "The Sun, Ranna's beloved;" Ranna is a goddess identified as the consort of Surya, the sun god. She is attested since medieval times in western India and is worshiped there to this day. See Pandey 1971: 109.

8 Seven fears (*bhaya*) are described in Jain doctrine: fear of this world (*ihaloka*), of the other world (*paraloka*), of being unprotected (*arakṣā*), of being without fortification (*agupti*), of death (*maraṇa*), of pain (*vedanā*), and of fear without cause (*ākasmika*). See Varni 1997–2000: vol. 1, 206.

9 The four modes of existence (*gati*) are: as a god (*deva*), as a human (*manuṣya*), as a hell being (*nāraki*), and as an animal or plant (*tiryañc*). See Jaini 1998: 108–111.

10 The word *sara* means "sounds" (Skt. *svara*) in the description of the couples, and "arrows" (Skt. *śara*) in the simile of the army.

11 Mythical elephants were thought to live at each of the cardinal directions.

12 The exact meaning and Sanskrit variant of *ohara* is unclear, but it is certainly an aquatic animal.

13 In Jainism, when someone undergoes the ceremony of renunciation to join the ascetic community, the person must manually pull out her/his hair. See Dundas 2002: 156–157.

14 A sectarian mark of three horizontal lines, especially associated with Shaiva ascetics.

Chapter 24

1 In these verses the poet plays with the double meaning of *lakkhaṇa* (from Skt. *lakṣmaṇa* and *lakṣaṇa*), suggesting the meaning of "signs," "good characteristics," "auspicious sign" (*lakṣaṇa*) in the context of music, canonical literature, etc., and at the same time thereby echoing Lakshmana's name. Whenever anyone says anything is "auspicious" or "with good characteristics," the people are reminded of Lakshmana.

2 This "good quality" again echoes the name Lakshmana.

3 It is unclear what kind of instrument a *tiriḍikkiya* is exactly. Given the context, it is most likely a percussion instrument.

4   A *mardala* is a barrel-shaped two-headed drum. A *ḍamaru* is a small hourglass-shaped drum. A *jhallarī* drum consists of two truncated cones, joined together at their smaller ends.

5   *Nigoda* is the absolute lowest form of life, below all hellish life. See Jaini 1998: 109.

6   This simile is somewhat obscure, and seems to refer to a proverb of a camel being blinded by his fondness for sweets.

7   The twenty-two afflictions (Skt. *parīṣaha*) of ascetic life form a list of hardships on which a Jain mendicant should meditate. See Jaini 1998: 249–250.

8   The four passions are anger, pride, deceit, and greed.

9   These are the five vows of a Jain monk: (1) not killing any living creature, (2) not lying, (3) not stealing, (4) no sexual activity, and (5) not getting attached to material goods.

10   The word *visahara* signifies both "supporting the doctrine" (Skt. *vṛṣa-dhara*) in the description of the man and "holding poison" (Skt. *viṣadhara*) in the simile of the snakes (PC: *viṣadharāḥ sarpāḥ; anyatra vṛṣo dharmaḥ, taṃ dharantīti viṣadharāḥ*, "poison-bearing snakes; elsewhere it is *vṛṣa*, the doctrine; thus *viṣadhara*s bear that").

11   The word *samaya* (Skt. *samaya*) signifies both "the teaching" in the description of the men, and "the weather," "the season" in the simile (PC: *samayavāla varṣākālaḥ* [sic], *āgamaś ca*). Note that this second *visahara* stands for *vṛṣa-dhara*, "rain-bearing," "cloud."

12   The compound *gayamāsāhāriya* signifies both "eating when a month has passed" (Skt. *gata + māsa + āhārin*) in the description of the men, and "eating the meat of an elephant" (Skt. *gaja + māṃsa + āhārin*) in the simile of the lions (PC: *hastimāṃsaṃ, māsopavāsāś ca yatayaḥ*).

13   The compound *paradāragamaṇa* (Skt. *para + dāra + gamana*) signifies both "going to the woman that is the other (world)" in the description of the men, as well as "going to the wife of another" in the simile (PC: *parastrī = muktī-gamana; paradāragamanaṃ ca*). JC suggests another possibility for the description of the renunciants, namely, "going to the doors of other people" (Skt. *para + dvāra + gamana*): *parastrīgamana; bhikṣārthaṃ paragṛhadvāragamanaś ca*, "going to another man's wife; and going to the door of the house of another for the sake of alms."

14   The word *tilaya* (Skt. *tilaka*) signifies "forehead mark" in the

description of Kaikeyi, and "*tilaka* tree" in the simile of the row of trees.

15 The word *paohara* (Skt. *payodhara*) signifies "breast" in the description of Kaikeyi and "cloud" in the simile of the sky.

16 "Eloquent," literally "grammatical;" *paya* (Skt. *pada*) signifies "feet" in the description of Kaikeyi, and "verse-feet" in the simile of the tale. The word *sandhi* (Skt. *sandhi*) signifies both "joints" in the description of Kaikeyi, and "sandhi" in the simile of the tale. In the description of Kaikeyi, *nāma* (Skt. *nāman*) signifies "name," and "substantive, noun" in the simile of the tale. The word *vayana* signifies both "face" (Skt. *vadana*) in the description of Kaikeyi, and "number" (Skt. *vacana*) in the simile of the tale. The word *vihatti* (Skt. *vibhakti*) signifies both "embellishment" in the description of Kaikeyi, and "case" in the simile of the tale.

17 What are described here are mendicants from other, non-Jain, traditions.

18 The first *jaḍahāriya* stands for "wearing matted locks" (Skt. *jaṭā-dhārin*) and refers in particular to Shaiva ascetics, whereas the second, in the simile of the low communities and villages, stands for "containing stupidity" (*jaḍa-dhārin*).

19 *Tridaṇḍin* ascetics bear a threefold staff. The identity of these *dhāḍīsara* ascetics is not clear. The PC and JC read: *tīrthayātrāgāminaḥ*, "going on pilgrimages."

20 The second meaning of *dhāḍīsara* (Skt. *dhāṭī-sara*) is "with a course of assault" in the simile with the kings.

21 The compound *ruddaṅkusa* (Skt. *rudra* + *aṅkuśa*) refers to "Rudra's trident" in the description of the ascetics, and to "terrible goad" in the simile of the elephant keeper.

22 The lunar month consists of a bright (*śukla*) and a dark (*kṛṣṇa*) half, referring respectively to Rama, who as a Baladeva has a light skin color, and to Lakshmana, the Vasudeva, who has a dark skin color.

23 The compound *suvesaī* signifies "good inhabitants" (Skt. *su-veśa*) in the description of the cow stations, and "good concubines" (Skt. *su-veśyā*) in the simile of the king's palaces.

24 The first *ṇisaṅgaī* (Skt. *niḥśṛṅga*) means "hornless" in the description of the calves, and has been translated as "passionless" in the simile of the renunciants. The PC offers a second suggestion for the description of the calves, namely, "without ropes" (Skt. *niḥsaṅga*): *saṅgo rajju-bandhanaṃ*.

25 The word *sāvaya* is translated as "beasts of prey" (Skt. *śvāpada*) in the description of the forest, and as "laymen" (Skt. *śrāvaka*) in the simile of the Jain order.

26 The compound *savāsaṇaṃ* means "with cries" (Skt. *sa + vāśana*) in the description of the forest, and "a seat of corpses" (Skt. *śava + āsana*) in the simile of the battlefield.

27 The compound *sakesaraṃ* (Skt. *sa + kesara*) means "with pollen" in the description of the forest, and "with a mane" in the simile of the lion.

28 The word *māuyaṃ* is translated as a kind of plant in the description of the forest and means "with anklets" in the simile of the palace. For both cases the etymology is unclear, and I take the PC as a guide: *mañjīrā vṛkṣāś ca*, "anklets and trees."

29 The word *tālayaṃ* (Skt. *tāla + ka*) here signifies "palmyras" in the description of the forest, as well as "tala" in the simile of the dance.

30 The compound *mahāsaraṃ* signifies "with great lakes" (Skt. *mahā + saras*) in the description of the forest, as well as "with great noises" (Skt. *mahā-svara*) in the simile of the bathing ceremony.

31 The compound *mayāsavaṃ* (Skt. *mada + āsrava*) signifies "the flowing of ichor" in the description of the forest, as well as "the flowing of alcohol" in the simile of the inferior ascetic.

32 The word *mokkhayaṃ* (Skt. *mokṣa + ka*) signifies "weaver's beam tree" in the description of the forest, as well as "liberation" in the simile of the sage.

33 The word *somayaṃ* signifies "soma plant" in the description of the forest, as well as "moon" in the simile of the sky.

34 This refers to the South Asian trope that the stains on the moon are thought to resemble a deer or a hare.

35 The compound *mahārasaṃ* (Skt. *mahā + rasa*) signifies "with great fluids" in the description of the forest, as well as "with great charm" in the simile of the women.

36 The compound *supattaī* (Skt. *su + pattra*) signifies "beautiful leaves" in the description of the gardens, and (Skt. *su + pātra*) "a good begging bowl" in the simile of the sages. The compound *suhalāī* (Skt. *su + phala*) signifies "with good fruits" in the description of the gardens, as well as "with good karmic fruits" in the simile of the sage.

37 The compound *ṇiyavaïlaṅghaṇaī* signifies "going beyond their

own enclosed field" (Skt. *nija* + *vṛti* + *laṅghana*) in the description of the sugarcane, as well as "insulting their own husband" (Skt. *nija* + *pati* + *laṅghana*) in the simile of bad wives.

ENCOUNTERS ON THE ROAD
Chapter 25

1   Here and elsewhere, Rama is described as a killer of "demons" (Skt. *dānava*), a general epithet for heroic characters. The word "demon" here should not be understood as a reference to the Rakshasas, who are, moreover, not demons in these Jain tellings. Nevertheless, to an audience well aware of the broader Ramayana tradition, the "demon" in this epithet for Rama carries the connotation of Rakshasa.

2   The parallel versions of Vimalasuri (33.25–60) and Ravishena (33.73–135) elaborate on this incident. Vajrakarna is converted to Jainism by a sage. After his conversion he refuses to bow to anyone except the Jina. To avoid offending his superior, Simhodara, he has a golden ring made containing the image of the Jina Muni Suvrata. With this ring on his hand, he creates the illusion of bowing to Simhodara, when in reality he is bowing to the Jina. An enemy informs Simhodara of this.

3   The chest of a Jina and a Vasudeva is marked with a stylized lock of hair or a symbol representing an endless knot, called the *śrīvatsa*. In Hindu traditions it marks the chest of Vishnu.

4   Literally, "what reflection is placed."

5   All Vasudevas are half universal emperors (*ardhacakravartin*).

6   With these words, Lakshmana, who identifies with the traveler, gives expression to the inappropriateness of Vajrakarna's offer of royal paraphernalia such as elephants, horses, etc., however generous: just as a sage has no use for happiness in samsara, sins will never correlate to liberation, Prakrit has no use for gibberish, neither lotuses for the sky ('the lotus in the sky' is a stock example of an impossible entity), a camel for a bell, nor an elephant for a plow. Associated with a camel, he, the hungry traveler, has no use for these symbols of royalty.

7   The words *sacchāu saloṇu saviñjaṇu* (Skt. *sacchāya-, sa-lavaṇa-,* and *sa-vyañjana-*) have a double meaning in this verse, translated respectively as "colorful," "tasty," and "well-seasoned" in the

745

description of the meal, and as "lovely," "charming," and "full of clever ways" in the simile.

8 The poet here alludes to the myth of the churning of the ocean, in which Mount Mandara is used as a churning stick. Note that, whereas in Hindu cosmology Meru and Mandara are distinct mountains—the first being the world axis, the second the divine mountain used to churn the ocean—Svayambhudeva uses the names interchangeably. For clarity's sake, I translate them all as Meru.

9 In Hindu mythology the Ganas are the attendants of Shiva. They do not appear to figure in any form in Jain mythology. Brahma, a prominent god in Hindu mythology, in Jainism is the Yaksha attendant of the Jina Pushpadanta. The Indra of the Brahma and Brahmottara heavens is also called Brahma. See Varni 1997–2000: vol. 3, 188; vol. 4, 510.

Chapter 26

1 A *yojana* is a distance equal to about nine miles.

2 The Apabhramsha text suggests that the gender of the ruler of Kubara is male until the tenth section.

3 Literally, "went on waves."

4 Literally, "when life was standing in the throat of the child."

5 This implies Lakshmana's status, being a Vasudeva, as a half universal emperor. Full universal emperors rule the six parts of Bharata.

6 The word *saüṇa* means "his own merits" (Skt. *sva + guṇa*) with the description of Lakshmana (cf. PC: *svaguṇaiḥ*), and "bird" (Skt. *śakuna*) in the simile of the lake.

7 Many words in this verse have double meanings: *gula* signifies "molasses" (Skt. *guḍa*) with the description of the meal, and "kiss" (*gula = cumbana* according to *Deśīnāmamālā* 2.91) in the simile of a good wife; *loṇa* (Skt. *lavaṇa*), "salt," also means "charm" in the simile; *rasa* (Skt. *rasa*), "juice," also means "affection" in the simile; *saïccha* signifies "according to one's own desire" (Skt. *sva + icchā*) with the description of the meal and "desirous" (Skt. *sa + icchā*) in the simile; *mahura* (Skt. *madhura*), "sweet," is to be taken literally with the description of the meal, as well as figuratively in the simile; for *suandha* (Skt. *sugandha*), "fragrant," the meaning is identical for the meal and the simile; *ṇeha* (Skt. *sneha*) signifies "oil" in the

description of the meal, as well as "affection" in the simile; *paccha* signifies "wholesome" (Skt. *pathya*) in the description of the meal, as well as "buttocks" (Skt. *paśca*) in the simile.

8   The identities of the musical instruments *tuṇava* and *daḍi* are not clear. The *tuṇava* appears to have originally been a flute that later evolved into a type of vina (Zin 2004). Here it appears, rather, to be a percussion instrument, as is the *daḍi*. The rest are well-known types of drums.

9   The words *mīṇa, mayara,* and *kakkaḍa* (Skt. *mīna, makara,* and *karkaṭa*) are translated as "fish, crocodiles, and crabs" in the description of the lake, and as the signs of the zodiac Pisces, Capricorn, and Cancer in the simile of the sky.

10 This is a type of small fish said to glisten when it darts in shallow water.

11 The word *paṭṭa* means "dish" (Skt. *pātra*) in the description of the meal, and "turban" (Skt. *paṭṭa*) in the simile of the kingship.

12 The words *sarasa* and *satimmaṇa* mean "with juices and sauces" (Skt. *sa + rasa* and *sa + temana*) in the description of the meal, and "passionate and with the mind directed toward the woman" (Skt. *sa + rasa* and *sa + strī + manas*) in the simile of lovemaking. JC reads *vyañjanāni strīmanaś ca* in another attestation of *timmaṇa* in this double meaning, in 71.10.

13 The word *viñjaṇa* (Skt. *vyañjana*) signifies "seasoning" in the description of the meal, and "consonant" in the simile of grammar.

14 The word *sālaṅkāra* (Skt. *sa + alaṃkāra*) signifies "with embellishments" in the description of the garments, and "with figures of speech" in the simile of the treatise.

15 The word *taraṅga* (Skt. *taraṅga*) signifies "cloth" in the description of the garments, as well as "waves" in the simile of the ocean.

16 The word *paṭṭa* here means "strip of cloth" (Skt. *paṭṭa*) in the description of the garments, and "leaf" (Skt. *pattra*) in the simile of the sugarcane.

17 The word *chea* (Skt. *cheda*) is translated as "slit" in the description of the garments, and as "interruption" in the simile of the assembly.

18 The word *ḍāla* (= *śākhā* according to *Deśīnāmamālā* 4.442) is translated as "border" with the description of the garments, following the JC: *añcalāni vastrapakṣe,* "borders in the meaning of the garments," and "branch" in the simile of the gardens.

19 The word *ṇicchidda* (Skt. *nis + chidra*) means "without tears" in the

description of the garments, and "without faults" in the simile of the poem.

20 The word *samasutta* is translated as "of smooth yarn" (Skt. *sama* + *sūtra*) in the description of the garments, and as "fallen asleep together" (Skt. *sama* + *supta*) in the simile of the Kinnaras.

21 The word *ahasammatta* means "finished at the bottom" (Skt. *adhas* + *samāpta*) in the description of the garments, and "completed with *atha*" (Skt. *atha* + *samāpta*) in the simile of the grammars. The PC explains *sammatta* as *paripūrṇāni*.

22 PC and JC elucidate: *nidrābalam*, "the army of sleep."

Chapter 27

1 Note the sound embellishment: the last word of a line is repeated as the first word of the next line, sometimes with different meanings. This pattern is repeated in this chapter in sections 2 and 5.

2 This king addressed here is Shrenika, the interlocutor of the main narrative frame, who was introduced in the first book.

3 The word *tāla* (Skt. *tāla*) is translated as "palmyra" in the description of the Vindhya, and as "tala" in the simile of the tambourine; *vamsahara* signifies "place of bamboo" (Skt. *vaṃśa* + *gṛha*) in the description of the Vindhya, as well as "support for the bamboo flute" (Skt. *vaṃśa* + *dhara*) in the simile of the tambourine.

4 The word *singa* (Skt. *śṛṅga*) signifies "peak" in the description of the Vindhya, as well as "horn" in the simile of the bulls; *ḍara* means "fear" (Hemachandra's Prakrit grammar 1.217) in the description of the Vindhya, and is also the name of a type of bull, in the simile, following JC: *vṛṣabha-viśeṣa*.

5 The word *taṇu* signifies "grass" (Skt. *tṛṇa*) in the description of the Vindhya, as well as "body" (Skt. *tanu*) in the simile of Kama, whose body was reduced to ashes by Shiva.

6 The word *vaṇa* is translated as "forest" (Skt. *vana*) in the description of the Vindhya, and means "injury" (Skt. *vraṇa*) in the simile of the soldier.

7 *Unmādana, madana, mohana, saṃdīpana,* and *śoṣana* are the names of the five arrows of Kama.

8 In the middle of the saline ocean, surrounding Jambudvipa, are several reservoirs called Patalas. They are of varying size, are shaped like a pitcher, and consist of three parts. In the top

part they contain water, in the bottom part wind, and in the middle alternately water and wind.

9   Nami and Vinami were the cousins of the Jina Rishabha. Their story is told in chapter 2 of the first book, in Volume 1.

10   The word *vayavandha* signifies both "arrangement of enclosures" (Skt. *vṛta* = *vṛti* + *bandha*) in the description of the village, and "surrounding leather straps" (Skt. *vṛta* + *vardhra*) in the simile of the tambourine. The PC reads: *vāṭī carmavardhrī ca*, "enclosure and leather."

11   The word *suhala* (Skt. *suphala*) means "successful" in the description of the village, and "bearing good fruits" in the simile of the wishing tree.

12   The word *ṇāḍaya* here means "rope for tying a yoke to a vehicle" (Skt. *nāḍī*, also Gujarati *nāṛa*) in the description of the village, and "dance, place" (Skt. *nāṭaka*) in the simile of the dance master.

13   Aside from the meanings given in these verses describing the house of the Brahman, all these words imply a second meaning with regard to the simile of the ultimate abode of the Jina: *ṇiravekkha* (Skt. *nirapekṣa*) thus signifies "without needs" in the description of the house, but also "desireless" in the simile; *ṇirakkhara* (Skt. *nirakṣara*), "without sounds," can be taken for both; *kevala* (Skt. *kevala*) signifies "isolated," but also implies "omniscience" in the simile; *ṇimmāṇa* (Skt. *nir* + *māna*) signifies "without pride" in the description of the house, as well as "without measurement, immeasurable" in the simile; *ṇirañjaṇa* (Skt. *nirañjana*) signifies "unpainted, colorless" in the description of the house, as well as "unsoiled" in the simile; *ṇimmala* (Skt. *nirmala*) signifies "without dirt" in the description of the house, and "pure" in the simile; *ṇivvatthu* (Skt. *nirvastu*) signifies "without valuable objects" in the description of the house, and "without material substance" in the simile; the meanings of *ṇirattha* (Skt. *nirartha*) "without property," *ṇirāharaṇa* (Skt. *nirābharaṇa*) "without decorations," *ṇiddhaṇa* (Skt. *nirdhana*) "without wealth," and *ṇibbhatta* (Skt. *nirbhakta*) "without food" apply for both the description of the house and the simile; *ṇimmahaṇa* (Skt. *nir* + *mathana*) signifies "without churning" in the description of the house, as well as "without agitation" in the simile.

14   The word *phala* (Skt. *phala*) signifies literally "fruit" in the

description of the tree, and "karmic fruit" in the simile of the Jina; *patta* signifies "foliage" (Skt. *pattra*) in the description of the tree, and "begging bowl" (Skt. *pātra*) in the simile.

Chapter 28

1 The words in this line have double meanings: *ghaṇa* (Skt. *ghana*) signifies "plain people" in the description of the city, and "cloud" in the simile of the sky; *kumbha* (Skt. *kumbha*) signifies "water pot" in the description of the city, and "the zodiac sign Aquarius" in the simile of the sky; *savaṇa* signifies "wandering mendicant" (Skt. *śramaṇa*) in the description of the city, and "the lunar mansion Shravana" (Skt. *śravaṇa*) in the simile of the sky; *saṅkaya* signifies "hesitation," "doubt," (Skt. *śaṅkā*) in the description of the city, and "the passage of the sun or planets through a sign of the zodiac" (Skt. *saṃkrama*) in the simile of the sky; *vuha* (Skt. *budha*) signifies "learned man" in the description of the city, and "the planet Mercury" in the simile of the sky; *tāraya* signifies "ferryman" (Skt. *tāraka*) in the description of the city, and "star" (Skt. *tārā*) in the simile of the sky; *guru* (Skt. *guru*) signifies "teacher" in the description of the city, and "the planet Jupiter" in the simile of the sky; *sasaṅkaya* signifies "with bridges" (Skt. *sa* + *saṃkrama*) in the description of the city, and "moon" (Skt. *śaśāṅka*) in the simile of the sky.

2 The word *payaïttiu* signifies "with subjects" (Skt. *prajā* + *vat*) in the description of the city, and "with proper verse portions" (Skt. *pada* + *vat*) in the simile.

3 The word *cittaya* signifies "colored" (Skt. *citra*) in the description of the city, and "thought" (Skt. *citta*) in the simile.

4 The word *caükka* (Skt. *catuṣka*) signifies "four-road junction" in the description of the city, and "courtyard" in the simile.

5 The word *chuha* signifies "plaster" (Skt. *sudhā*) in the description of the city, and "hunger" (Skt. *kṣudhā*) in the simile.

6 The word *dāṇa* (Skt. *dāna*) signifies "donation" in the description of Rāma, and "ichor" in the simile.

7 The five minor vows (*aṇuvrata*) are the principal vows for laity.

8 Literally, "laughed with the sound *kahakaha*."

9 On the position of wealth for the Jain lay community, see Dundas 2002: 195–198.

Chapter 29

1 The word *dosa* (Skt. *doṣa*) signifies "fault" in the description of the city, as well as "darkness" in the simile.

2 Literally, "moons."

3 In this passage the first word of each part of the verse has a double meaning (sometimes based on different etymologies), one in a general negative connotation of something undesirable, and a second, more positive one specific to the city: hence *haü* is both "killing" (Skt. *hata*) and "horse" (Skt. *haya*); *bhangu* (Skt. *bhanga*) is "decay" and "wave," "fold"; *jaḍaü* is "idiocy" (Skt. *jaḍa*) and "matted locks" (Skt. *jaṭā*); *khalu* (Skt. *khala*) is "villain" and "threshing floor"; *karu* (Skt. *kara*) is "tax" and "hand"; *paharu* (Skt. *prahara*) is "strike" and the time unit of a *prahara;* *dhaṇu* is "bow" (Skt. *dhanus*) and "riches" (Skt. *dhana*); *sura* is "alcohol" (Skt. *surā*, cf. PC: *surā maghaḥ [madyam]*) and "god" (Skt. *sura*); *kalahu* is "strife" (Skt. *kalaha*) and "young elephant" (Skt. *kalabha*); *anku* (Skt. *anka*) is "crime" and "act"; *ḍaru* is "fear" (Hemachandra's Prakrit grammar 1.217) and the name of a type of bull (JC: *deśībhāṣā[yāṃ] vṛṣabhaḥ śabdo vā, anyatra bhayam*); *velu* is "thief" (*Deśīnāmamālā* 7.94) and "frontier" (Skt. *velā*); *vaṇu* signifies "wound" (Skt. *vraṇa*) and "forest" (Skt. *vana*); *jhāṇu* (Skt. *dhyāna*) is "dullness" and "meditation."

4 Literally, "announcing the *aśoka* grove."

5 The PC elucidates: *kiṃ lakṣmaṇena saha āliṅganaṃ kiṃ mṛtyunā saha*, "is it an embrace with Lakshmana or with death?"

6 Apart from being various types of demonic beings in Hindu mythology, Rakshasas, Bhutas, and Pishachas are categories of Vyantara gods in Jainism. Grahas, considered as planets as well as evil spirits, are reckoned among the Jyotis gods (as planets) of the Jains. The demonic classes of Vetalas and Daityas do not appear to have been integrated into the standard Jain categories of deities.

Chapter 30

1 Literally, "bound."

2 The word *patta* signifies "leaf" (Skt. *pattra*) in the description of the letter, and "begging bowl" (Skt. *pātra*) in the simile.

3 The word *ṇāva* signifies "name" (Skt. *nāman*) in the description of the letter, and "boat" (Skt. *nāva*) in the simile.

4 The word *vellahala* signifies "agreeable" (*Deśīnāmamālā* 7.96)

in the description of the assembly hall, and "wood apple" (Skt. *bilva* + *phala*) in the simile.

5 The words *vala* and *lakkhaṇa* signify "the Baladeva" (Skt. *bala*) and "Lakshmana" (Skt. *lakṣmaṇa*) in the description of the spectacle, as well as "strength" (Skt. *bala*) and "auspicious characteristic" (Skt. *lakṣaṇa*) in the simile.

6 The word *vandhakaraṇa* (Skt. *bandha* + *karaṇa*) refers to a type of song in the description of the spectacle, and signifies "positions" and "postures" in the simile. *Bandhakaraṇa* is described as a kind of song distinguished by a combination of tone and drum syllables. See *Saṅgītaśiromaṇi* 13.213 and 218–219.

7 The words *chanda* and *sadda* signify "pleasing" (Skt. *chanda*) and "sound" (Skt. *śabda*) in the description of the spectacle, and "meter" (Skt. *chandas*) and "language," "words" (Skt. *śabda*) in the simile.

8 The words *vaṃsa* (Skt. *vaṃśa*) and *tāla* (Skt. *tāla*) signify "flute" and "cymbal" in the description of the spectacle, as well as "bamboo" and "palmyra" in the simile.

9 The words *rāya* and *seya* signify "passion" (Skt. *rāga*) and "sweat" (Skt. *sveda*) in the description of the spectacle, as well as "king" (Skt. *rājan*) and "sweat" (Skt. *sveda*) in the simile.

10 Literally, "while he took and did not take the great sword in the hand."

MEETINGS WITH SAGES AND A BIRD

Chapter 31

1 The PC explains this image: *mārgānu<y>āyināṃ madhye 'gra<y>āyī*, "going at the head in the midst of those who follow a road."

2 Several words in this verse have double meanings: *ṇaha* signifies "sky" (Skt. *nabhas*) in the description of the king, and "claw" (Skt. *nakha*) in the simile of the lion; *laṅgūla* (Skt. *lāṅgūla*) is a kind of weapon in the description of the king (PC: *praharaṇa-viśeṣaḥ;* possibly a plow, for Skt. *lāṅgala*), and signifies "tail" in the simile of the lion; *māyaṅga* signifies "the limbs of Lady Glory" (Skt. *mā* + *aṅga*) in the description of the king (PC: *mā lakṣmīḥ, aṅgaiḥ gṛhītaḥ*), and "elephant" (Skt. *mātaṅga*) in the simile of the lion.

3 Durnama, literally, "of ill name," in South Asian lore is a demon that causes disease.

4 Note how, in this and the preceding line, the same words are used with two different meanings.

5 Literally, "a favor with information."

6 The PC identifies this Shesha with Dharanendra, the Jain king of the serpent gods, though the name Shesha is typically not used for him. This Shesha may therefore refer rather to the Hindu lord of the Nagas, on whose coils Vishnu rests during his cosmic sleep.

7 Bhima is a character from the Mahabharata, known for his strength.

8 Literally, "tusks."

9 Literally, "when he took, did not take the bow in the hand."

Chapter 32

1 The word *singa* (Skt. *śṛṅga*) signifies both "peak" in the description of the mountain, and "horn" in the simile of the bull.

2 The precise identity of this tree is not clear. "Indra's tree" (*indradru, indradruma, indrataru*) has been identified as the *arjuna* tree (Monier-Williams 1995: 166; Apte 1890: 278) or the deodar (Apte 1890: 386). Other sources, however, commonly mention the silk cotton tree (*śālmalī*) or the *śāla* tree as the tree associated with Jina Sambhava (Varni 1997–2000: vol. 2, 383; Shah 1987: 132).

3 The *ghoṇasa* is identified as the Russell's viper (Slouber 2012: 65).

4 It is unclear what exactly is meant by the two sins (*doṣa*).

5 Four types of meditation (*dhyāna*) are distinguished, two negative forms (*ārta*, "unpleasant," and *raudra*, "cruel") and two positive (*dharma*, "virtuous," and *śukla*, "pure"). See Jaini 1998: 251–258. In this verse the two positive forms are meant.

6 Aside from some other classification of "auspiciousness" (*maṅgala*), the *Dhavalā* commentary on the authoritative *Ṣaṭkhaṇḍāgama* (Book 1, 1.1.1, p. 39) gives a fourfold classification as *dharma, siddha, sādhu,* and *arhat,* "the doctrine, the Siddha, the sage, and the venerable" without further specifications. How this should be interpreted in this verse is not entirely clear. Possibly it involves performing salutations to these four elements.

7 The Four Refuges (*catuḥ-śaraṇa*) is a popular mantra in which the supremacy of the doctrine is saluted. See Jaini 1998: 164

8   These are the thirty-six virtues (*guṇa*) of a master (*ācārya*). For a
     discussion, see Varni 1997–2000: vol. 1, 242.

9   These six categories are earth (*pṛthivī*), water (*ap*), fire (*tejas*),
     wind (*vāyu*), plant (*vanaspati*), and movable (*trasa*). See Varni
     1997–2000: vol. 2, 44 and 333.

10   According to Jain cosmology, the netherworld is divided into seven
     regions, each containing a number of hells. See Glasenapp 1999:
     258–262.

11   This possibly refers to the *sapta-bhaṅgi-naya,* the sevenfold
     application of *syāt,* "it may be." It represents the Jain system of
     making statements without violating the basic principles of the
     Jain view of reality, *anekāntavāda,* the doctrine of multifacetedness
     (Jaini 1998: 94–97).

12   Jains divide karma, seen as a substance that adheres to a soul,
     causing its rebirth in samsara, into eight main categories. The
     first four categories, the vitiating karmas, have a direct negative
     effect on a soul. The last four, the nonvitiating karmas, bring about
     particular conditions of embodiment. Different sources provide
     different lists of arrogances (*mada*). They include things such as
     power, family, caste, and physical beauty. For an overview, see
     Varni 1997–2000: vol. 3, 259.

13   Near the peak of Mount Meru lies a platform with four pedestals
     on which Jinas are consecrated by the gods. See Varni 1997–2000:
     vol. 3, 450–452, and Cort 2010: 91–92.

14   *Bharatanāṭyaśāstra* (Treatise on Drama) is the standard classical
     treatise on performance theory.

15   Chamunda is known from Hindu mythology as a fearsome
     manifestation of the goddess Durga. It is not entirely clear what
     the expression "proficient with Chamunda" means. Moreover, in
     41.16.7 Chamundas appear to be a category of fearsome beings,
     parallel to Vetalas, Rakshasas, etc.

16   Literally, "jackals and jackals."

17   Here the Bhavanavasin and Vyantara gods are meant, who
     reside in the netherworld and are therefore termed "demons"
     (*asura*).

18   Kalpa gods are born in a Kalpa heaven. Three lower categories of
     gods live outside the celestial realm: the Bhavanavasin gods reside in
     mansions between earth and hell or earth and heaven; the Vyantara
     gods dwell on earth on continents beyond human habitation;

and the Jyotis gods reside in the sun, moon, constellations, and stars. See Jaini 1998: 129–130.

19 The four destinies (*gati*) are human, hellish, heavenly, and animal/plant.

Chapter 33

1 Note that *guṇathāṇa* here does not refer to the *guṇasthānas,* the stages of purification of the monk, as later it becomes clear that Kashyapa and Surapa are laymen, to whom only the first five of the *guṇasthānas* apply. I follow the suggestion of the PC (*ekādaśa-pratimā-yuktāḥ*) in taking the word *guṇasthāna* here to actually refer to *pratimā,* the eleven stages of renunciation for the layman. See Jaini 1998: 186 and 272–273.

2 Tumburu and Narada are Gandharvas, celestial musicians in the service of Indra.

3 In the preceding lines, the second part of each verse-foot has a double meaning, one for the description of the seers, and one in the simile of the trees: *tavaṇatāva taviya* (Skt. *tapana-tāpās taptāḥ*) is both "scorched, with the heat of ascetic practice," and "scorched, with the heat of the sun." The term *mūlaguṇa* (Skt. *mūla + guṇa*) signifies both "the basic restraints" and "roots as virtues." These basic restraints concern foods that a Jain is not allowed to consume, namely, meat, alcohol, honey, and five types of figs. See Jaini 1998: 166–167. The word *ālavāla* signifies "nonsensical speech" (Skt. echo word *āda + vāda*) in the description of the seers, as well as "water basin around the root" (Skt. *ālavāla*) in the description of the trees. The compound *phalabbhahiya* (Skt. *phala-abhyadhika*) is both figuratively "exceptional in the fruits, i.e., success (toward liberation)" and literally "exceptional in fruits."

4 The Sanskrit expression *sūtraṃ dhṛ,* "to hold the thread," signifies the activity of an architect or carpenter.

5 This is a sacred mountain in modern Bihar where twenty out of twenty-four Tirthankaras are thought to have passed away.

6 A moth is attracted by the form of the flame and dies by flying into the fire. Sound is used to lure and catch deer. A bee is attracted by the smell of a lotus. When the lotus closes at sunset, the bee is stuck inside the flower and dies. Elephant cows are used to lure and catch a male elephant. It is thought that the touch of a female alone is enough to calm him and thereby make his capture possible.

7   Lymph, blood, muscle, fat, bone, marrow, and semen.

Chapter 34

1   The five minor vows (*aṇuvrata*) are the principal vows for laity. They resemble the great vows (*mahāvrata*) of the ascetics, but are less strict. The three restrictive vows (*guṇavrata*) expand the minor vows. The four vows of spiritual discipline (*śikṣāvrata*) are (temporary) restraints for ritual purposes. *Poṣadhopavāsa* entails fasting on the eighth and fourteenth day of every two-week period of the waning or waxing of the moon. It corresponds to the third vow of spiritual discipline and the fourth stage of renunciation of the layman (*pratimā*). Jaini 1998: 180 and 182.

2   The word *aṅgāra* generally means "charcoal" but in this context seems to refer to incense.

3   Haha, Huhu, Tumburu, Narada, and Chitranga (for Chitrangada) are well known as Gandharvas. Tejja and Tenna do not occur in other sources. For a discussion, see Bhayani 1993–1998: vol. 1, 98–99. Rambha and Tilottama are well-known celestial nymphs.

4   All sentient beings (*jīva*) belong to one of six groups, depending on the level of karmic stains they have. This corresponds to a particular shade (*leśyā*) that souls possess. See Jaini 1998: 114–115.

5   The second restrictive vow entails the restraint against certain professions and certain foods (*bhogopabhogaparimāṇa*). See Jaini 1998: 179.

6   The third restrictive vow restricts five types of evil activities. See Jaini 1998: 179–180.

7   This list of vows of spiritual discipline does not correspond completely to the most frequently cited list (in e.g. Jaini 1998: 180–181) but is enumerated by some Digambara authors. See Williams 1991: 56–57.

8   In Hindu lore Pitris (literally, "fathers;" either Manes, departed forefathers, or a class of gods considered the progenitors of humankind), Pitamahas (literally, "grandfathers," also referring to the Manes), and Pretas (ghosts, spirits possessing a dead body) are well-known as underworldly creatures. They do not appear to have been integrated into the categories of Jain deities.

9   A plant whose berries are said to resemble cranberries or cherries in texture and taste. It is regularly used in condiments like chutney and jam.

10   The word *bhūi* (Skt. *bhūti*) signifies "ashes" in the simile of the fire, but in the description of the two sages it is rather "dust" or "earth," since Jain monks are not typically covered with ashes.

11   Several of the words in the final two verses describing the sages Gupta and Sugupta clearly echo the names of other ascetic traditions, particularly Shaivite. The words *kālāmuha* and *kāvāliya*, which mean "faces directed toward death" (Skt. *kāla* + *mukha;* PC: *kālasya maraṇasyāpy abhimukhā, vā trikālayoginaḥ*) and "displeasing for the god of lust" (Skt. *kāma* + *alīka*), echo the well-known historical Shaiva ascetic communities called the Kalamukhas and Kapalikas. Also the word *saṃkara,* here taken literally as "causing prosperity" (Skt. *śaṅkara;* PC: *saṃ* [*sic*] *sukhaṃ kurvantīti sukhakāriṇaḥ*) is a standard epithet of Shiva, and the possible interpretation of the sages' bodies as being covered with ashes is also a reference to a common practice among Shaiva ascetics.

12   The traditional list of eight substances in a homage ritual (*arcana*) includes water, sandalwood paste, uncooked rice, flowers, sweets, a lamp, incense, and fruits. See Jaini 1998: 201.

13   The words *suṇeha* and *saïcchaya* signify "with good oil" (Skt. *su* + *sneha*) and "according to one's desire" (Skt. *sva* + *icchā*) in the description of the meal, as well as "with good affection" (Skt. *su* + *sneha*) and "desirous" (Skt. *sa* + *icchā*) in the simile of the good wife.

14   The words *samaccharu* (Skt. *sa* + *matsara*) and *aïthaddhaya* (Skt. *ati* + *stabdha*) signify "exhilarating" and "very thick" in the description of the curd, and "wrathful" and "very arrogant" in the simile of the bad wife.

15   The word *pāva* signifies both "feet" (Skt. *pāda*) in the description of the meal, and "sin" (Skt. *pāpa*) in the simile.

Chapter 35

1   The doctrine of partial truths (*nayavāda*) is central to the Jain relativist view of reality. Jain philosophers propound seven viewpoints, the partial truths (*naya*), each of which need to be applied if one wishes to make a valid judgment. See Jaini 1998: 93–97.

2   These are the biographies of the sixty-three "great men" (*mahāpuruṣas* or *śalākāpuruṣas*).

3   In Jainism five forms of knowledge are distinguished. Whereas the lower two forms are more or less present in all humans, the third, clairvoyance (*avadhi*), is standard for gods and hell beings, and the fourth, the awareness of the thoughts of others (*manaḥparyaya*), is only available for humans who have completed a high level of ascetic practice. The fifth (*kevala*) is omniscience.
4   Literally, "come to evidence."
5   The Jains distinguish four different forms of meditation, two positive and two negative. *Raudra-dhyāna*, "perverse meditation," is a negative form whereby the person focuses on the pleasure that causes injury to other people. See Jaini 1998: 252.
6   A *sāgara* is a unit of time, equivalent to ten crores of *palyas*. A *palya* equals the time needed to completely empty a container one *yojana* high and one *yojana* in diameter filled with soft hairs, if one were to take one hair out every one hundred years.

THE DEATH OF SHAMBUKA
Chapter 36

1   In South Asian lore, thirty-two birth marks are described as indicating an exceptional man.
2   The *cakravyūha* is proverbial for something that is very difficult to escape from.
3   A woman's beauty is often compared to certain characteristics of elephants: her breasts resemble the frontal globes, her arms the trunk, and her gait is said to be similar to that of an elephant.

Chapter 37

1   Literally, "served with his vital spirits."

THE ABDUCTION OF SITA
Chapter 38

1   The words in this line have double meanings, one for the description of Sita and one in the simile of the story: *sandhi* (Skt. *sandhi*) is translated as "joints" and "sandhi," *susandhiya* (Skt. *su* + *saṃdhita*) as "well built" and "well put together," *paya* (Skt. *pada*) as "feet" and "verse-feet," *vayana* as "face" (Skt. *vadana*) and "expressions" (Skt. *vacana*), *sadda* (Skt. *śabda*) as "voice" and "words."

2   The word *khambha* (Skt. *stambha*) signifies "rigidity" in the description of Sita, and "pole" in the simile of the elephants.

3   Avalokani, literally "looking," "consulting," is Ravana's main *vidyā*. She provides him with information about adversaries.

4   Takshaka is a prince of the Nagas, or serpent demons.

5   Literally, "I tell the divulging (of a secret)."

6   Literally, "there is the cessation of eating for me."

Chapter 39

1   The fivefold sacred Jain *namaskāra* mantra.

2   *Cāraṇa* is the supernatural power attained by ascetics to move about through the air. There are various subtypes and objects used to support this travel, such as water, leaves, fruits, etc. One sub-type mentioned frequently is the so-called shank-wandering ascetic, variably described as moving through the air by using his legs, moving through the sky four fingers above the ground, and moving for hundreds of *yojanas* without harming earth-bodied beings. For a discussion, see Wiley 2012: 176–180. See also chapter 15, section 9, in Volume 1.

3   According to JC, Jinadasa became a monkey after using a *vidyā*, which he was only allowed to use once a day, twice in one day to please his wife Gunavati.

4   The words *ṇiddhaṇa, lakkhaṇa,* and *vasaṇa* signify "without his beloved" (Skt. *nis + dhanyā*), "Lakshmana" (Skt. *lakṣmaṇa*), and "misfortune" (Skt. *vyasana*) in the description of Rama, and "without wealth" (Skt. *nis + dhana*), "good characteristics" (Skt. *lakṣaṇa*), and "vices" (Skt. *vyasana*) in the simile.

Chapter 40

1   Notice in this section, a praise poem to the Jina Muni Suvrata, the intricate sound play, with syllable inversions in the opening verse, and in the main body of the section a word denoting a negative or a want (beginning with *a-*), rhymed with the corresponding positive, evoking the all-embracing nature of the Jina: he is at the same time negative and positive.

2   A *vāvalla* is a kind of arrow or a steel weapon, a kind of crowbar; a *bhalla* a crescent-shaped missile or arrow.

3   The words *satthehī viddho* mean "wounded by weapons" (Skt. *śastrair viddhaḥ*) in the description of the soldier and

"learned in the teachings" (Skt. *śāstrair vṛddhaḥ*) in the simile.

4 Literally, "an abode without a hood."

5 Literally, "be it, be it not."

6 These are all Rakshasas and Vanaras, allies of Ravana.

7 A *ṭaṭṭarī* is a kind of kettledrum. It is unclear what kind of instrument a *saruñja* is exactly. Given the context, it is most likely a percussion instrument. A *huḍukka* is a two-headed drum shaped like an hourglass.

8 This is a reference to the fight between the first universal emperor, Bharata, and his younger but stronger brother Bahubali. The story is narrated in Volume 1, chapter 4.

9 This appears to be a reference to the standard set of four literary languages, Sanskrit, Prakrit, Apabhramsha, and Paishachi. For a discussion, see Ollett 2014 and Khadabadi 1997: 419–427.

Chapter 41

1 Literally, "satisfaction did not arise for Chandranakhi."

2 Literally, "with incomplete measurement."

3 Literally, "for his own occurrences."

4 Literally, "is not broken."

5 Literally, "derision of me is given."

6 Literally, "what is thought in the heart, that is being done."

7 The most significant confluence of the river Ganga is that with the Yamuna and the celestial river Sarasvati in Prayaga (Allahabad).

8 This may very well be a reference to a motif commonly found in later Rama stories, in which Ravana is in fact Sita's biological father, who abandoned her at birth. This motif is found first in some minor Jain narratives. Interestingly, it is not present in the main Jain narrative of Vimalasuri, Ravishena, and Svayambhudeva, but Svayambhudeva seems to be aware of it. See De Clercq 2011.

9 *Raudradhyāna,* "perverse meditation," and *dharmadhyāna,* "virtuous meditation," are two of four forms of meditation described by the Jains. See Jaini 1998: 252. The first is a negative form of meditation, the second a positive form.

10 Literally, "for me there is the cessation of the body of fourfold food." In Jainism all food is divided into four categories. See Varni 1997–2000: vol. 1, 285.

11 The words *pahara* (Skt. *prahara*) and *sūra* signify *"prahara"* and

"sun" (Skt. *sūra*) in the description of the night, as well as "beating" and "warrior" (Skt. *śūra*) in the simile.

Chapter 42

1   Literally, "we were with forest-pastime."
2   Literally, "was a lion's roar uttered or not uttered by Lakshmana in the fight."
3   As a half universal emperor Ravana rules over half the territory of the universal emperor, i.e., three parts of Bharata (of the total six).
4   Lata (*Lāṭa*) is a region in southern Gujarat; Harikeliya (*Harikelīya*) corresponds to Bengal.
5   This is a reference to the popular belief that a person's fate is written on her or his forehead.
6   This simile refers to the sandalwood juice with which a sacred icon is anointed.
7   The word *sāvaya* signifies "wild animal" (Skt. *śvāpada*) in the description of the park, as well as "layman" (Skt. *śrāvaka*) in the simile.
8   Literally, "taking his lip."

GLOSSARY

AIRAVATA (*airāvata; airāvaṇa*)
The celestial elephant of Indra,
who has multiple heads, trunks,
and tusks

ANANTAVIRYA (*anantavīrya*)
"Of boundless heroism" (1)
Brother of Dasharatha and son
of Anaranya, a notable ascetic;
(2) King of Nandavarta who
becomes an ally of Bharata and
renounces the world

ANARANYA (*anaraṇya*) King of
Ayodhya, father of Dasharatha,
notably renounces the world

APARAJITA (*aparājitā*)
"Unsurpassed," mother of Rama

ARIDAMANA "Destroyer of foes,"
king of Kshemanjali, father of
Jitapadma

AYODHYA (*ayodhyā*) "Inviolable,"
city where Rama was born

BALADEVA Category of heroes
from Jain universal history,
there are nine in every time
period; the pious half-brother
of a Vasudeva

BARBARA "Barbarian," name of
a tribal community depicted as
primitive and violent

BHAMANDALA (*bhāmaṇḍala*)
"Haloed," son of Janaka, twin
brother of Sita

BHARATA (1) Son of Dasharatha
and Kaikeyi, half-brother
of Rama; (2) First universal

emperor, son of Rishabha;
(3) Region corresponding to
the Indian subcontinent, the
civilized world; (4) Legendary
author of the *Nāṭyaśāstra,* a
treatise on drama theory

CHANDRAHASA (*candrahāsa*)
"Mocker of the moon,"
supernatural sword of Ravana

CHANDRANAKHI (*candraṇakhī*)
"With nails like the moon," sister
of Ravana, wife of Khara

CHANDRODARA (*candrodara*)
Vidyadhara king, ally of the God
Vidyadharas, father of Viradhita

DASHARATHA (*daśaratha*) "Having
ten chariots," father of Rama,
king of Ayodhya

DRONA (*droṇa*) Brother of Kaikeyi,
father of Lakshmana's wife
Vishalya

DUSHANA (*dūṣaṇa*) "Corrupting,"
brother of Khara, ally of the
Rakshasas

GANDHARVA A celestial musician,
especially in the retinue of Indra;
in Jainism categorized as
a Vyantara god

GANGA (*gaṅgā*) A sacred
river originating in heaven,
descending to the earth in the
Himalayas; the Ganges

INDRA King of the gods; in Jain
cosmology thirty-two Indras
are differentiated

JANAKA "Generating," king of
Mithila, father of Sita

JATAYIN (*jaṭāyin*) A bird
companion of Rama, Sita,
and Lakshmana during
their exile

JINA "Victor, conqueror" spiritual
leader of the Jain religion; there
are twenty-four Jinas in every era

JITAPADMA (*jitapadmā*) Daughter
of Aridamana, wife of
Lakshmana

KAIKEYI (*kaikeyī*) Wife of
Dasharatha, mother of Bharata

KALYANAMALA "Garlanded
with auspiciousness," (1)
(*kalyāṇamālā*) Princess of
Kubara; (2) (*kalyāṇamāla*) Son of
Mahidhara

KAMA (*kāma*) "Love," the god of
love

KHARA "Harsh," husband of
Ravana's sister Chandranakhi,
brother of Dushana, ruler of
Patalalanka

KINNARA (*kiṃnara*) A hybrid
celestial being associated with
Indra; in Jainism, categorized as
a Vyantara god

KOSALA Father of Aparajita,
maternal grandfather of Rama

KUBERA (1) A deity, lord of the
Yakshas; (2) King of the God
Vidyadhara dynasty who was
defeated by Ravana; (3) Name of
a Brahman

LAKSHMI (*lakṣmī*) "Fortune,"
goddess of fortune, wife of
Vishnu, typically depicted

as seated on a lotus flower
and sprinkled with water by
elephants

LANKA (*laṅkā*) Island and city of
the Rakshasa dynasty, ruled by
Ravana

MAHIDHARA (*mahīdhara*) "Bearer
of the earth," king of Jivanta, ally
of Rama and Bharata

MAHORAGA "Great serpent,"
serpent deity belonging to the
Vyantara category of gods

MANDODARI (*mandodarī*) Chief
wife of Ravana

MITHILA (*mithilā*) City ruled by
Janaka

MUNI SUVRATA "Sage
characterized by good vows,"
name of the fourteenth Jina
during whose lifetime the story
takes place

NAGA (*nāga*) Serpent gods, a class
of Bhavanavasin gods; Naga
kings, including Dharanendra,
are ardent worshipers and
protectors of the Jinas

NARADA (*nārada*) A celestial
musician and seer from
the retinue of Indra with
the reputation of being a
troublemaker

PATALALANKA (*pātālalaṅkā*)
Underground city of the
Rakshasa dynasty, later of
Viradhita, its entrance is in the
Dandaka forest

PULINDA Name of a lowly tribal
community depicted as primitive
and violent

PUTANA (*pūtana*) King of the Yakshas

RAGHU Illustrious forefather of Rama and his relatives

RAHU (*rāhu*) "Seizer," the eclipse planet; a demon who roams the sky seizing the sun and the moon and thereby causing eclipses

RAKSHASA (*rākṣasa*) (1) Branch of the Vidyadhara dynasty to which Ravana belongs; Lanka is their ancestral home; (2) Type of Vyantara deity

RAMAYANA (*rāmāyaṇa*) "Ways of Rama," the story of Rama, especially the classical Sanskrit epic

RATI "Sexual enjoyment," wife of Kama

RAVANA (*rāvaṇa*) "Causing to cry," A Rakshasa, king of Lanka

RISHABHA (*ṛṣabha*) "Bull," name of the first Jina

RUDRABHUTI (*rudrabhūti*) "Whose power is Rudra," ruler in the Vindhya mountains

SAMUDRAVARTA (*samudrāvarta*) "Whirlpool in the ocean," name of Lakshmana's bow

SHABARA (*śabara*) name of a lowly tribal community depicted as primitive and violent

SHAMBUKA (*śambūka,* also *śambu* and *śambukumāra*) A Rakshasa prince, son of Chandranakhi and Khara, nephew of Ravana

SHATRUGHNA (*śatrughna*) "Enemy-killing," half brother of Rama

SHREYAMSA (*śreyāṃsa*) (1) Name of the eleventh Jina; (2) A king who broke Rishabha's fast

SIMHODARA (*siṃhodara*) "Lion-belly," king of Ujjayini, becomes an ally of Bharata

SUKHAMATI (*sukhamati*) "Of agreeable mind," father of Kaikeyi

SUMITRI (*sumitrī*) "Good friend," mother of Lakshmana

SUPRABHA (*suprabhā*) "Having a good appearance," mother of Shatrughna

SURYAHASA (*sūryahāsa*) "Mocker of the sun," supernatural sword of Lakshmana

TIRTHANKARA (*tīrthaṃkara*) "Ford maker," see JINA

VAITADHYA (*vaitāḍhya*) Mountain range parallel to the Himalaya consisting of a northern and a southern range, divides Bharata in half, inhabited by Vidyadharas

VAJRAKARNA (*vajrakarṇa*) "Whose ears are adamantine," king of Dashapura, friend and ally of Rama and Bharata

VAJRAVARTA (*vajrāvarta*) "Bent like lightning," name of Rama's bow

VALIKHILYA (*vālikhilya*) King of Kubara, father of Kalyanamala

VARUNA (*varuṇa*) (1) God associated with water and the ocean; (2) King of the God Vidyadhara dynasty who was defeated by Ravana; (3) Guardian deity of the west

VASUDEVA (*vāsudeva*) Category of heroes from the Jain universal history, there are nine Vasudevas in every time period; quick-tempered half brother of a Baladeva

VAYU (*vāyu*) (1) God of wind; (2) Guardian of the northwest

VETALA (*vetāla*) A kind of demonic being thought to occupy a dead body, sometimes likened to a vampire

VIBHISHANA (*vibhīṣaṇa*) "Terrifying," a Rakshasa, brother of Ravana

VIDEHA (*videhā*) "Bodiless," Sita's mother, wife of Janaka

VIDYADHARA (*vidyādhara*) "Bearer of supernatural powers," dynasty of the descendants of the grandsons of the first Jina Rishabha, all of whom possess one or more supernatural powers (*vidyā*), in particular the ability to fly; they especially inhabit the Vaitadhya mountain range; the Rakshasas and Vanaras are separate branches within this dynasty

VIDYUDANGA (*vidyudaṅga*) "Whose limbs are lightning," friend of Vajrakarna

VINDHYA Mountain range north of the Deccan

VIRADHITA (*virādhita*) Vidyadhara, son of Chandrodara, ally of Rama

VISHALYA "Thorn-less," (1) (*viśalyā*) Lakshmana's wife; (2) (*viśalya*) Name of a king

VYANTARA "In the intermediate," a class of gods inhabiting the space between the hells and the middle world

YAKSHA (*yakṣa*) A semidivine being, in Jainism often a guardian spirit, categorized as a Vyantara god

YAMUNA (*yamunā*) River originating in the Himalaya, tributary of the Ganges

BIBLIOGRAPHY

Editions and Translations

Svayambhudeva. 1953–1960. *Paumacariu of Kavirāja Svayambhūdeva.* Edited by Harivallabh Chunilal Bhayani. 3 vols. Bombay: Singhi Jain Shastra Shikshapith / © Bharatiya Vidya Bhavan.

———. 1957–1970. *Kavirāja Svayambhūdeva viracita Paümacariu.* Edited and translated by Devendra Kumar Jain. 5 vols. Kāśī: Bharatīya Jñānapīṭha.

———. 2002. *Jain Rāmāyaṇa-Paumacaryu.* Translated by Shantilal Nagar. Delhi: BR Publishing Corporation.

Other Sources

Apte, Vaman Shivram. 1890. *The Practical Sanskrit-English Dictionary.* Poona: Shiralkar and Company.

Bharata. 1956–1967. *The Nāṭyaśāstra Ascribed to Bharata-Muni.* Edited and translated by Manomohan Ghosh. 2 vols. Calcutta: Asiatic Society / Manisha Granthalaya.

Bhayani, Harivallabh Chunilal. 1993–1998. *Indological Studies.* 2 vols. Ahmedabad: Parshva Prakashan.

Brockington, John L. 1997. "The Name Rāmacandra." In *Lex et Litterae: Studies in Honour of Professor Oscar Botto,* ed. S. Lienhard and I. Piovano. Alessandria: Edizioni dell' Orso, pp. 83–93.

Brockington, John, and Mary Brockington. 2016. *The Other Ramayana Women: Regional Rejection and Response.* London: Routledge.

Brodbeck, Simon. 2009. *The Mahābhārata Patriline.* Farnham: Ashgate.

Bulcke, Kamil. 1950. *Rām-kathā (utpatti aur vikās).* Prayag: Hindu Parishad, Vishvavidyalay.

Chandra, K. Rishabh. 1970. *A Critical Study of Paumacariyaṃ.* Muzaffarpur: Research Institute of Prakrit, Jainology and Ahimsa Vaishali.

Cort, John E. 2010. *Framing the Jina: Narratives of Icons and Idols in Jain History.* Oxford: Oxford University Press.

De Clercq, Eva. 2008. "The Jaina *Harivaṃśa* and *Mahābhārata* Tradition: A Preliminary Survey." In *Parallels and Comparisons in the Sanskrit Epics and Purāṇas,* ed. P. Koskikallio et al. Zagreb: Croatian Academy of Sciences and Arts, pp. 399–421.

———. 2010. "Jaina Jatayus or the Story of King Dandaka." In *Svasti*, ed. Nalini Balbir, 75:168–175. Bengaluru, Karnataka, India.

———. 2011. "A Note on Rāvaṇa as Sītā's Father." *Journal of Vaishnava Studies* 20.1: 197–207.

———. 2016. "Śūrpaṇakhā in the Jain Rāmāyaṇas." In *The Other Ramayana Women: Regional Rejection and Response*, ed. Mary Brockington and John Brockington. London: Routledge, pp. 18–30.

———. 2022. "From Ayodhyā to the Daṇḍaka: Rāma's Journey in Exile According to the Jain Rāmāyaṇas." In *Visions and Revisions of Sanskrit Narrative: Studies in the Indian Epics and Purāṇas*, ed. R. Balkaran, and M. Taylor. Canberra: Australia National University Press.

———. Forthcoming. "Elements of Jain Doctrine in Svayambhūdeva's Paümacariu." In *Jain Art and Architecture*, ed. P. Flügel et al. Mumbai: Hindi Granth Karyalay.

Dundas, Paul. 2002 (1992). *The Jains*. Library of Religious Beliefs and Practices. London: Routledge.

Glasenapp, Helmut von. 1999. *Jainism: An Indian Religion of Salvation*. Translated by Shridhar B. Shrotri. Delhi: Motilal Banarsidass Publishers Private Limited.

Grafe, Jörg. 2001. *Vidyādharas*. Frankfurt am Main: Peter Lang.

Hemachandra. 1877. *Hemacandra's Grammatik der Prākritsprachen (Siddhahemacandram Adhyāya VIII)*. Edited and translated by Richard Pischel. Halle: Verlag der Buchhandlung des Waisenhauses.

———. 1931. *The Deśīnāmamālā of Hemacandra*. Edited and translated by Muraly Dhar Banerjee. Calcutta: University of Calcutta.

———. 1943. "Chandonuśāsana of Hemacandra." *Journal of the Bombay Branch of the Royal Asiatic Society*, ed. H. D. Velankar. Vol. 19: 27–74.

———. 1944. "Chandonuśāsana of Hemacandra." *Journal of the Bombay Branch of the Royal Asiatic Society*, ed. H. D. Velankar. Vol. 20: 1–46.

Jaini, Padmanabh S. 1991. *Gender and Salvation*. Berkeley: University of California Press.

———. 1993. "A Purāṇic Counter Tradition." In *Purāṇa Perennis: Reciprocity and Transformation in Hindi and Jaina Texts*, ed. W. Doniger. New York: State University of New York Press, pp. 207–249.

———. 1998. *The Jaina Path to Purification*. 1st paperback ed. Delhi: Motilal Banarsidass. Original edition, 1979.

Khadabadi, B. K. 1997. *Studies in Jainology: Prakrit Literature and Languages*. Jaipur: Prakrit Bharati Academy.

Kulkarni, Vaman Mahadeo. 1990. *The Story of Rāma in Jain Literature.* Ahmedabad: Saraswati Pustak Bhandar.

Lutgendorf, P. 2004. "Hanumān's Adventures Underground: The Narrative Logic of a *Rāmāyaṇa* 'Interpolation.'" In *The* Rāmāyaṇa *Revisited,* ed. M. Bose. Oxford: Oxford University Press, pp. 149–163.

Mahābhārata. 1933–1966. 19 vols. General editor, Vishnu Sitaram Sukhtankar. Poona: Bhandarkar Oriental Institute.

Monier-Williams, Monier. 1995. *A Sanskrit-English Dictionary.* Oxford: Clarendon Press. Original edition, 1899.

Murthy, A. V. Narasimha. 1971. *The Sevunas of Devagiri.* Mysore: Rao and Raghavan.

Ollett, Andrew. 2014. "Ghosts from the Past: India's Undead Languages." *The Indian Economic and Social History Review* 51(4): 405–456.

Pandey, Lalta Prasad. 1971. *Sun-Worship in Ancient India.* Delhi: Motilal Banarsidass.

Premi, Nathuram. 1942. *Jain Sāhitya aur Itihās.* Bambai: Hindi Granth Ratnakar.

Pushpadanta. 1936. *Harivaṃśapurāṇa.* Edited and translated by Ludwig Alsdorf. Hamburg: De Gruyter.

———. 1937–1941. *The Mahāpurāṇa or Tisaṭṭhimahāpurisaguṇālaṃkāra,* ed. Parashurama Lakshmana Vaidya. 3 vols. Bombay: Manikchand Digambara Jaina Granthamala.

———. 1999–2001. *Mahākavi Puṣpadanta's Mahāpurāṇa.* Edited and translated by Devendra Kumar Jain. 5 vols. New Delhi: Bharatiya Jnanpith. Original edition, 1979–1999.

Rāmāyaṇa. 1960–1975. *The Vālmīki-Rāmāyaṇa.* General editors, Govindlal Hargovind Bhatt and Umakant Premanand Shah. 7 vols. Baroda: Oriental Institute.

Ravishena. 1958–1959. *Padmapurāṇa of Raviṣeṇācārya with Hindi Translation.* Edited and translated by Pannalal Jain. 3 vols. Kāshī: Bhāratīya Jñānapītha.

Richman, Paula, ed. 1991. *Many Rāmāyaṇas: The Diversity of a Narrative Tradition in South Asia.* Berkeley: University of California Press.

———., ed. 2000. *Questioning Rāmāyaṇas: A South Asian Tradition.* New Delhi: Oxford University Press.

Saṅgītaśiromaṇi: A Medieval Handbook of Indian Music. 1992. Edited and translated by Emmie te Nijenhuis. Leiden: E. J. Brill.

Shadkhandāgama of Āchārya Pushpadanta and Bhootabali with the Commentary of Dhavalā. 2003. Edited by V. Satpraroopanā et al. Bangalore: National Institute of Prakrit Studies and Research Institute.

Shah, Umakant Premanand. 1987. *Jaina-Rūpa-Maṇḍana 1: Jaina Iconography*. New Delhi: Abhinav Publications.

Sheth, Hargovind Das. 1986. *Pāia-sadda-mahaṇṇavo*. Delhi: Motilal Banarsidass. Original edition, 1928.

Slouber, Michael. 2012. "Gāruḍa Medicine: A History of Snakebite and Religious Healing in South Asia." Ph.D. dissertation, University of California, Berkeley.

Svayambhudeva. 1962. *Svayambhūcchanda*. Edited by Hari Damodar Velankar. Jodhpur: Rajasthana Prachyavidya Pratishthana.

———.1985. *Kaviraja Svayambhudeva's Riṭṭhaṇemi-cariu (Arishtanemi-charita): Yadavakanda*. Edited and translated by Devendra Kumar Jain. New Delhi: Bharatiya Jnanpith.

———. 1993–2000. *Svayambhūdeva's Riṭṭhaṇemicariya*. Edited by Ram Sinh Tomar. 5 vols. Ahmedabad: Prakrit Text Society.

———. 2018. *The Life of Padma, Volume 1*. Edited and translated by Eva De Clercq. Murty Classical Library of India. Cambridge, Mass.: Harvard University Press.

Tagare, Ganesh Vasudeo. 1948. *Historical Grammar of Apabhraṃśa*. Poona: Deccan College Post-Graduate and Research Institute.

Turner, Ralph Lilley. 1966–1985. *A Comparative Dictionary of the Indo-Aryan Languages*. 4 vols. London: Oxford University Press.

Upadhye, Adinath Neminath. 1983. "More Light on the Yāpanīya Sangha: A Jaina Sect." In *Upadhye: Papers*, ed. A. N. Upadhye. Mysore: Prasaranga, University of Mysore, pp. 192–201.

Varni, Jinendra. 1997–2000. *Jainendra Siddhānta Kośa*. 5 vols. Varying editions. New Delhi: Bharatiya Jnanpith. Original edition, 1921–1983.

Vimalasuri. 1962–1968. *Ācārya Vimalasūri's Paumacariyaṃ*. Edited and translated by Hermann Jacobi, Muni Shri Punyavijayaji, and Shantilal M. Vora. Varanasi-Ahmedabad: Prakrit Text Society.

Virahanka. 1930. "The Vṛttajātisamucchaya of Virahāṅka: A Treatise on Prakrit Metres." *Journal of the Bombay Branch of the Royal Asiatic Society*, ed. H. D. Velankar. Vol. 5: 34–94.

———. 1932. "The Vṛttajātisamucchaya of Virahāṅka: A Treatise on Prakrit Metres." *Journal of the Bombay Branch of the Royal Asiatic Society*, ed. H. D. Velankar. Vol. 8: 1–28.

Wiley, Kristi. 2012. "Supernatural Powers and Their Attainment in Jainism." In *Yoga Powers: Extraordinary Capacities Attained through*

Meditation and Concentration, ed. K. A. Jacobson. Leiden: Brill, pp. 145–194.

Williams, Robert. 1991. *Jaina Yoga: A Survey of the Mediaeval Śrāvakācāras.* Delhi: Motilal Banarsidass. Original edition, 1963.

Zin, Monika. 2004. "Die Altindische *Vīṇās.*" In *Muzikarchäologie,* vol. 4. ed. E. Hickmann and R. Eichmann. Bonn: Orient-Archäologie, pp. 321–362.

INDEX

king of, 23, 25; comparisons
to, 189; flying, 133, 547n; Gods
as, 739n1; Jinas worshiped by,
143; at Kaikeyi's *svayaṃvara*, 9;
Rakshasas as, x, 7, 739n2; Ravana
attacked by, 589, 591, 593;
mortals compared to, 25,
27; Vanaras as, x; *vidyās* of,
739n7; women, 43, 529. *See also*
Khara; Dushana; Viradhita
Vidyudanga, 131, 133, 137, 175, 177,
179
Vijaya (1), 93
Vijaya (2), 303, 321
Vijayamahidhara, 401, 403
Vimala, 145, 375, 417
Vimalasuri, xi, xxviin6, xxviiin23,
xxviiin28, 739n2, 745n2, 760n8
Vimardana, 93
Vinami, 239, 748n9
Vindhyas, 651, 713, 748nn3–6;
Bharata goes to, 301; elephants
of, 241; people of, 15, 399, 403;
Rama et al. go to, 219, 221; peaks
of, 221; Putana comes from, 257;
ruler of (*see* Rudrabhuti)
Vipula, 93, 305, 321
Viradhita, xxiv, 627, 661, 669,
733; army of, 651; Dushana
challenged by, 639, 641, 649;
Lakshmana and, 633, 635, 637;
Rama meets, 655, 657; Sunda
fights, 667; Vidyadhara, 635, 655,
663

Virahanka, 740n2
Vishala, 93
Vishalya, 31, 303
Vishnu, ix, xviii, 77n, 745n3, 753n6
Vishvagati, 177
Viyoga, 93
Vṛttajātisamuccaya, 740n2
Vyantara gods, 289, 377, 391, 751n6,
754nn17–18
Vyasa, vii, 61, 740n1

Yakshas, 83, 257, 289; guards, 27,
29; lady, 265, 287; master of, 263;
Pushpadanta's attendant, 746n9;
trees of, 287. *See also* Gajamukha;
Putana
Yakshasthana, 399, 413
Yama, 105, 289, 345, 347, 437, 507;
buffalo of, 273, 569; comparisons
to, 129, 155, 159, 161, 167, 315,
477, 495, 499, 509, 531, 543,
637, 653, 685, 723; Kala or Kali
and, 77, 229, 231, 235, 245, 479,
495, 499, 571; men as food for,
501; messengers of, 479; mouth
of, 245, 315, 661; path of, 653,
675; punishment of, 573, 675,
685, 703, 723; soldiers of, 477;
vanquished, 75
Yamaghanta, 305
Yamuna, 175, 289, 760n7
Yapaniyas, vii, xxvi–xxviin3

ABOUT THE BOOK

Murty Classical Library of India volumes are designed by Rathna Ramanathan and Guglielmo Rossi. Informed by the history of the Indic book and drawing inspiration from polyphonic classical music, the series design is based on the idea of "unity in diversity," celebrating the individuality of each language while bringing them together within a cohesive visual identity.

The Sanskrit text of this book is set in the Murty Sanskrit typeface, commissioned by Harvard University Press and designed by John Hudson and Fiona Ross. The proportions and styling of the characters are in keeping with the typographic tradition established by the renowned Nirnaya Sagar Press, with a deliberate reduction of the typically high degree of stroke modulation. The result is a robust, modern typeface that includes Sanskrit-specific type forms and conjuncts.

The English text is set in Antwerp, designed by Henrik Kubel from A2-TYPE and chosen for its versatility and balance with the Indic typography. The design is a free-spirited amalgamation and interpretation of the archives of type at the Museum Plantin-Moretus in Antwerp.

All the fonts commissioned for the Murty Classical Library of India will be made available, free of charge, for non-commercial use. For more information about the typography and design of the series, please visit *http://www.hup.harvard.edu/mcli.*

Printed on acid-free paper by Maple Press, York, Pennsylvania.